Between the Conquests:

Readings in the Early Chicano Historical Experience, Third Edition

Michael R. Ornelas
Chicano Studies Department
San Diego Mesa College

KENDALL/HUNT PUBLISHING COMPANY
4050 Westmark Drive   Dubuque, Iowa 52002

CREDITS

"Aztlan, Cibola and Frontier New Spain", pp.7-22 and notes from John R. Chavez, *The Lost Land: The Chicano Image of the Southwest*, pp.7-22 and 158-60. Copyright © 1984. Reprinted by permission of the University of New Mexico Press.

"Settlement Patterns and Village Plans in Colonial New Mexico" from *Journal of the West*, Vol. 8, No.1, January 1969. Copyright © 1969 by Journal of the West. Reprinted by permission of Journal of the West and the author.

"The Arrival of the Europeans", pp.21-39 from *Arizona: A History* by Thomas E. Sheridan. Copyright © 1995 The Arizona Board of Regents. Reprinted by permission of the University of Arizona Press.

"Colonizers of the Frontier", pp.29-35 from *California: A History*, Fifth Edition, by Andrew Rolle. Copyright © 1998 by Harlan Davidson, Inc. Reprinted by permission.

"Sexual Violence in the Politics and Policies of Conquest: Amerindian Women and the Spanish Conquest of Alta California" from *Building With Our Hands: New Directions in Chicana Scholarship* by Adela de la Torre ad Beatriz M. Pesquera. Copyright © 1993 The Regents of the University of California. Reprinted by permission of the University of California Press.

"The Origins of Anti-Mexican Sentiment in the United States" from *The New Scholar*, 6, 1977. Copyright © 1977. Reprinted by permission of The New Scholar.

"Texas, This Most Precious...Territory", pp. 57-73 from Gene M. Brack, *Mexico Views Manifest Destiny, 1821-1848, Essays on the Origins of the Mexican War*. Copyright © 1975. Reprinted by permission of the University of New Mexico Press.

"Initial Contacts: Redeeming Texas from Mexicans, 1821-1836, pp.1-13 reprinted from *They Called Them Greasers: Anglo Attitudes Toward Mexicans in Texas 1821-1900* by Arnoldo de Leon, Copyright © 1983. By permission of the author and the University of Texas Press.

"Texas Declaration of Independence" and "Treaty of Velasco" reprinted from *U.S.-Mexico Borderlands, Historical and Contemporary Perspectives*, Oscar J. Martinez, ed.

"The Texas Game Again? Peopling California and New Mexico", pp.179-206 and notes pp. 400-402 from *The Mexican Frontier, 1821-1846: The American Southwest Under Mexico* by David Weber. Copyright © 1982. Reprinted by permission of the University of New Mexico Press.

"The Diplomacy of Racism" from *The Diplomacy of Racism: Manifest Destiny and Mexico, 1821-1848* by Gene Brack. Reprinted by permission of Harlan Davidson, Inc.

Articles from "The Treaty of Guadalupe Hidalgo" and "Protocol of Queretaro" reprinted from *The Treaty of Guadalupe Hidalgo: A Legacy of Conflict* by Richard Griswold Castillo, University of Oklahoma Press, 1990.

"Citizenship and Property Rights: U.S. Interpretations of the Treaty" pp.62-86 from The Treaty of Guadalupe Hidalgo: A Legacy of Conflict by Richard Griswold del Castillo. Copyright © 1990. Reprinted by permission of the University of Oklahoma Press.

For Jeff Garcilazo
student, Professor

Between the Conquests, Third Edition

Contents

Contents, Cont.

Preface

Chicanos, Americans of Mexican descent, are a fundamental component of the reshaping of the American Southwest and the nation. Demographers predict that Latinos will become the largest ethnic segment of the population of the United States around 2020. Certain regions of the Southwest have already shown signs of a similar transformation. Some political commentators have characterized this phenomenon in ominous terms. Our future will not resemble the past, they warn. But to the surprise of many, we have already been there. Long before the "browning of America," there was a brown America, and a brown Southwest before there was a Southwest. From the sixteenth through the nineteenth centuries, this region of the world had already undergone its first transformation into a multi-ethnic and multi-cultural society.

Therefore, California, and the rest of the Southwest, had already been "Latinized" by the generations of northward-bound immigrants from southern New Spain beginning in the sixteenth century. In fact, the earliest origins of this process can be traced to the efforts by Spanish explorers to locate the mythical fantastic cities and later to build the foundation for community. In the process, these settlers became the original majority. The region is simply revisiting an old pattern.

But the political upheavals of the middle nineteenth century including the Texas and Mexican wars sent us on a completely different trajectory toward the remaking of the American southwest and beyond. Both of these events were fueled by an anxiety not unlike that which is currently underway. One response to the significant presence of people of Mexican descent, and the most extreme one, to the generations of the nineteenth century, was the invention of a political imperative using pseudo-scientific rationale to invert the political order. What was also evident in these early encounters were the imported European and American based sensitivities over racial, cultural, linguistic and religious questions. Most of these early visitors and adventurers who entered the region documented their impressions of the Mexicans' "otherness." Everything about the Mexicans reminded them of something other than that with which they were familiar. Almost from the start of the earliest contacts in the early nineteenth century Mexicans became "the other," even though they had been part of the landscape for many generations. This book is an attempt to understand how we got there.

The third edition of **Between the Conquests** is divided into two major sections. Section one includes an introduction to the earliest historical roots of Chicanos in the Southwest. New this time is a brief introduction into the major developments of the major Mesoamerican civilizations and some of the factors under consideration in the first major collision of the European and American civilizations: the Spanish Conquest of the Aztec empire centered at Tenochtitlán. Section one also includes interpretive essays of this early experience beginning around the sixteenth century until the early nineteenth century. It includes the search for *El Dorado* in North America and the earliest settlement patterns which brought these regions under Spanish rule. These early examples of multi-ethnic collaborations functioned to reintroduce the various strands of Mesoamerican and southwestern peoples to one another. Spanish colonial practices, which tended to integrate indigenous peoples into the colonization projects, were unique in North America in this regard.

Section two includes an introduction into the major events taking place during the first five decades of the nineteenth century. It also includes interpretive essays which introduce students to the complex historical circumstances leading to the Texas Revolt, the Mexican American War and the Treaty of Guadalupe Hidalgo. These three events are also discussed quite extensively throughout this section. This section also includes an exploration of the complex and evolving relationship between Anglos and Mexicans in this frontier zone. Following section two is a section of **Key Terms** and **Discussion Questions** which students and instructors will find useful for study and research purposes. These can also be integrated as part of the classroom and course assignments. And finally, I would like to thank my wife, Eva, for all her help and all she does for me and our wonderful family.

Michael Raúl Ornelas
San Diego, California
mornelas@sdccd.net

Chronology of Significant Events
in Early Chicano History

1519-21
: The fall of the Aztec capital center, Tenochtitlán to Spanish conquerors. The colonial period begins.

1520-1560
: Exploration of the northern frontier, central Mexicans re-introduced to the cultures and region. Culture of central Mexico comes north. Spaniards search for Cíbola, Quivira, the mythical island of California, Aztlán, Chicomoztoc and el Nuevo Mexico.

1520-1620
: Known as the "Century of Depression" due to dramatic declines in Indian population caused by the consequences of war, forced labor conditions and imported diseases.

1528-1536
: Alvar Núñez Cabeza de Vaca, Estevan and two other Spaniards survive among the Southwestern indigenous peoples following a ship wreck in 1528 along the Texas coast. They became the first Europeans to reach the Texas, Arizona, New Mexico and northern Mexico regions. They were reunited with the Spaniards near Culiacan, Mexico in 1536. Their observations were highly regarded by Spanish officials and contributed to the formulation of the mythical image of the Southwest and more formal explorations.

1538-1539
: Fray Marcos de Niza and Esteban lead an expedition into the southwest in search of the Seven Cities of Cíbola. This expedition contributed to the early mythical image of the Southwest.

1540-1542
: In response to the reports by de Niza, Francisco Vázquez de Coronado retraces de Niza's steps to find the "new" Mexico and mythical lands of great wealth and civilization.

1542	New Laws of the Indies passed to ban slavery of indigenous Americans. "El Requierimiento" permits slavery if Indians refuse Hispanization and Catholic conversion.
1598	Permanent occupation of the northern frontier begins. Juan de Oñate establishes the first settlement in northern New Mexico. The process of cultural synthesis as well as racial miscegenation begins. Also marks the introduction of Aztec and Tlascalan Indians into the region.
1610	Santa Fe, New Mexico founded.
1680	Pueblo Revolt. Pueblo Indians, along with scores of mestizos, successfully revolt against colonial authority. Revolt unseats Spanish colonial rule for 13 years.
1692	Diego de Vargas reestablishes Spanish colonial rule in New Mexico.
1700	Colonial occupation of Pimería Alta begins. Southern Arizona, Sinaloa and Sonora are incorporated within the province. Eusebio Francesco Kino heads the colonizing expedition which transplants central Mexican culture and populations to the region.
1713	French incursions induce Spanish colonial occupation of Texas and central Mexican culture is transplanted to the frontier.
1763	Treaty of Paris is signed and ends French and Spanish rivalry in the Southwest. Spain acquires Louisiana.
1769	Russian and English threats prompt permanent occupation of California. Populations from New Spain move north.
1800	Spain cedes the Louisiana Territory to France.

1803   Louisiana Purchase by the United States. Confusion over Spain's northern boundary and the western extent of United States possessions is not resolved until the 1819 Adams-Onís Treaty (also known as the Transcontinental Treaty).

1808-1810   New Spain's Committee of Correspondence meets secretly and plans for Mexican Independence. The committee smuggles copies of the United States Declaration of Independence and documents from the French Revolution of 1789. The general uprising is slated for December 8, 1810.

1810   Spanish authorities uncover the plot for Mexican independence and Miguel Hidalgo begins the movement on September 16.

1810-1811   Miguel Hidalgo y Costilla leads the Mexican Independence Movement and calls for significant social and political reform following independence.

1811-1815   José María Morelos y Pavón assumes leadership of Mexican Independence and calls for systematic social and political reform in post-Independence Mexico.

1815-1820   Guadalupe Victoria and Vicente Guerrero continue the independence movement but represent little challenge to Spanish colonial authority.

1819   Spain and the United States negotiate the Adams-Onís Treaty (also known as the Transcontinental Treaty). The United States relinquishes claims to Texas and acquires Florida. The treaty clarifies boundary lines between Spanish and United States possessions in North America but is not ratified by Mexico until 1831.

1821	Mexico gains its independence from Spain in a conservative counter-revolution led by Agustín de Iturbide in El Plan de Iguala.
1824	Mexico's first constitution creates the federal republic and formally incorporates Alta California, Baja California and New Mexico as territories. Passage of the Immigration Act of 1824 permits foreign immigration into the northern provinces and results in significant American immigration, principally into the region known as Texas (the northeastern portion of the state of Coahuila).
1826	Haden Edwards revolts in Texas and calls for the establishment of the Republic of Fredonia.
1827	General Manuel Mier y Terán is sent on a mission of inspection to the Texas frontier. Recommends the repeal of the 1824 Immigration act and other restrictive legislation.
1829	Aimed primarily at Texas slave owners, Mexico abolishes slavery.
1830	Mexico passes the 1830 decree, curtailing further foreign immigration into Texas. Mexico also authorizes the establishment of the cities of Anáhuac, Lipantitlan and Tenoxtitlán as buffers against foreign designs on the Texas frontier. Mexico intends to encourage mestizos and indios to immigrate to the north but sees limited success.
1831	Mexico and the United States ratify the original Adams-Onís Treaty (at this time known as the Treaty of Limits) which recognized Mexican sovereignty over Texas, cedes Florida to the United States and results in the creation of an international boundary separating Mexican and United States territories in North America.

1835	Antonio López de Santa Anna comes to power and declares the Texas conference illegal. Vows to eradicate rebellion against Mexico.
1836	Rebellious Texans organize an insurrectionist convention at Washington-on-the-Brazos and ultimately declare their Texas Declaration of Independence from Mexico.
1836	After several battles on Texas soil, including the decisive battle at San Jacinto, Santa Anna is taken prisoner and signs the Treaty of Velasco. The treaty, under a secret agreement with Santa Anna, makes the Rio Grande the southern boundary of Texas. Mexico refuses to ratify the Treaty.
1836-1845	Texas boundary lines under dispute. Mexico claims the Nueces River as the southern boundary while the Lone Star Republic claims territories to the Rio Grande.
	Texas becomes the Lone Star Republic in 1836. United States statehood is delayed due its status as a slave state and Mexico's opposition under the threat of war.
1836-1848	The southern Texas boundary remains disputed. Mexico claims the Nueces River while the Lone Star Republic and later the United States claim the Rio Grande. The region remains disputed territory until Article V of the Treaty of Guadalupe Hidalgo establishes the Rio Grande as the southern boundary.
1842	In an effort to reestablish its sovereignty over Texas, Mexico invades and temporarily occupies Texas.
	Thomas Catesby Jones acting on false information that Mexico and the United States were at war occupies Monterey, capital of Mexican California.

1844   James K. Polk is elected president of the United States on an
                expansionist ticket. Vows to incorporate Texas and pursue
                the acquisition of Mexico's northern frontier.

                John L. O'Sullivan coins the phrase "Manifest Destiny" to
                embody American expansionistic ideology during the
                nineteenth century.

1845   Texas is admitted to the United States as a slave state.
                Mexico severs diplomatic relations with the United States.

1846   John Slidell is sent to Mexico to negotiate for the Rio Grande
                as the Texas border and for the sale of Mexico's northern
                provinces, including California and New Mexico. Mexico
                rejects the Slidell proposals.

1846   American and Mexican troops exchange fire near the Rio
                Grande and war against Mexico is declared by the United
                States on May 11. President James K. Polk declares that
                "American blood had been shed on American soil..." and
                Abraham Lincoln, new member of the House of
                Representatives, introduces the "Spot Resolutions,"
                demanding the identification of the precise spot where
                American blood had been spilled.

1846   In June, before news of war between Mexico and the United
                States reaches California, the region is occupied by the "Bear
                Flaggers" who attempt to "liberate" California and assert
                United States sovereignty over the region. The movement
                later merges with the larger invasion during the Mexican
                American War.

1846-48   The Mexican American War.

1848   On February 2, the United States and Mexico conclude negotiations and sign the Treaty of Guadalupe Hidalgo. The United States Congress ratifies the Treaty on March 16, Mexico on May 30.

1848   On May 26, the United States and Mexico agree to the Protocol of Querétaro which clarifies omissions and amendments in the Treaty of Guadalupe Hidalgo by the United States Senate.

1849   The California Gold Rush begins and results in the influx of hundreds of thousands of people from the United States and various nations, including Mexicans from Sonora. Mexicans in California are quickly outnumbered.

1850   The Compromise of 1850 makes New Mexico a territory and grants statehood to California.

1850   In response to pressures to eradicate the "foreigners" the California legislature passes the Foreign Miners' Tax Law, taxing "foreign" miners. It virtually eliminates Chicanos from the gold mines.

1851   The California Supreme Court upholds the constitutionality of the Foreign Miners' Tax Law in *People v. Naglee*. The Court accepts the argument that the law did not violate provisions of the Treaty of Guadalupe Hidalgo, the U. S. Constitution or the California State Constitution. This begins the erosion of rights guaranteed by the Treaty of Guadalupe Hidalgo through legal and extra-legal means.

1851   The United States Congress authorizes the California Land Act. Landowners are required to provide proof of ownership of Spanish and Mexican land grants through the California

Land Commission. Ultimately results in the loss of millions of acres.

1853   Mexico, under extreme pressure from the United States, agrees to sell "La Mesilla." This twenty-nine-million-acre triangle of territory in southern Arizona and New Mexico is also known as the Gadsden Purchase. The purchase was ratified by the United States Senate in 1854 for $10 million.

1856   The U. S. Supreme Court, in *McKinney v. Saviego*, rules that the Treaty of Guadalupe Hidalgo did not apply to Texas due to its prior separate and independent status as a nation. This ruling appears to violate the meaning of the Protocol of Querétaro and specific references to Texas in the Treaty.

I

1500-1800

I

Early Mesoamerican Civilization. Olmecs. Teotihuacan. Toltecs. Aztecs. Spanish Conquest

Modern Chicanos, products of racial miscegenation between indigenous Americans and Europeans, have inherited a legacy which extends many centuries into the past. The American Southwest, at various times called Aztlán, New Spain's frontier, Mexico's northern frontier and the modern Southwest is the homeland for modern Chicanos. Today it is the American Southwest.

As far back as the first pre-Columbian trading patterns were established, the imprint of countless cultures has shaped this part of the world. The modern Chicano is the most recent example which links this ancient pattern of migrations and settlements to the modern Southwest. But what distinguishes the Chicano from all other Americans is not only this fact but their unique racial, biological and cultural mixture with conquering Europeans for more than four centuries. This synthesis distinguishes Chicanos from all other peoples of the Southwest. They are a unique blend of European, indigenous and Southwestern cultural and biological influences. In this region of the world they helped to construct its fundamental shape through their pre-Columbian ancestors. They experienced a reintroduction to the region as reluctant participants for European adventurers, those more inclined toward conquest and plunder. They have played a pivotal role in its exploration, settlement and development for the past four centuries.

Chicano roots on the Western Hemisphere are as ancient as the presence of the first migratory hunters who crossed land bridges at the Bering Strait in search of food. Although there is no universal agreement on when this occurred, the weight of archaeological evidence conclusively asserts that the entire Western Hemisphere was fully inhabited by 20,000 B.C. Other evidence has indicated that the Valley of Mexico, the cradle of Mesoamerican civilization, has been continuously occupied since at least 12,000 B.C., a highly conservative estimate in light of evidence of human occupation of South America for thousands of years prior to this. Significant archaeological discoveries at Tepexpan and Tehuacan in Mexico's central valley indicate the presence of semi-nomadic groups, pioneering migratory colonists, who settled in the fertile central core and built the original root for Mesoamerican civilization. Within Mesoamerica, the region of Mexico inhabited by its ancient cultures, they planted the seeds for the coming waves of early agriculturalists.

Long before the arrival of Europeans in the 16th century, the Valley of Mexico and its surrounding regions were the stage for the emergence and decline of numerous advanced civilizations. The Olmec, Teotihuacan, Maya, Aztec and countless other diverse civilizations constructed vast urban centers in diverse ecological zones. At the centers they erected sacred religious districts. From this center emerged larger and more complex urban religious complexes of later eras. From the central plateaus of Mexico through Central America, civilizations emerged which were governed by strict adherence to their complex and unique cosmo visions. They exhibit a thoughtfully integrated religious, political and cultural expression in their artistic, architectural and urban planning. Their urban and religious centers testify to this complex and integrative pattern in the construction of early civilization.

The Olmecs, the first of many Mesoamerican civilizations to come, erected the first Mesoamerican urban centers as early as 1,800 B.C. in the swamp lands of southern Mexico. Emerging from jungle and swamp conditions in Tabasco and Vera Cruz, the Olmecs constructed La Venta, the jewel of the earliest civilizations. At other sacred sites such as Tres Zapotes, El Manati and Cerro de las Mesas they left their characteristic cultural stamp on artifacts of astonishing variety and complexity. They made the so-called colossal heads, carved from materials carried from as far away as sixty miles and weighing up to twenty tons. These provide clues to the degree of social cohesiveness and their dedication and talent as sculptors. They also reveal a certain ancient veneration, a sort of artistic and religious duality, placing God and man on an equal plane. Their dynastic rulers portrayed themselves in these monolithic sculptures in order to deify themselves and unite the heavens with mortals, probably deriving their powers from this divine association. Their altars, carved on an equally impressive scale, reiterated the Olmec mythic origin of man's emergence from caves in a sort of chthonic birth event uniquely their own. Also uncovered as Olmec cultural products were portable jade and stone items, all exhibiting the Olmec anthropomorphic tendency toward "were-jaguarism." Uniting all elements of the Olmec ideology was this common and universal tendency that displayed their interpretation of the human and jaguar mystique, an origin myth of unknown origin which sought to unite the human and natural worlds artistically and spiritually.

The Olmec, the "people of rubber," formed the base of all civilizations to come. They originated the notion of the planned and astronomically aligned religious site, centered on sacred religious ground. They have now been credited with the invention of the bar and dot mathematical notation system and the zero, the earliest use of the long-count date in the pre-Columbian calender system and some of the earliest hieroglyphic texts in Mesoamerica. If the Aztec of the fifteenth and sixteenth centuries A.D. were the tree of Mesoamerican cultural evolution, the Olmec formed its root. They carry the distinction as the mother culture of the Americas.

The Olmec influenced their contemporaries over a wide region of Mesoamerica. For their contemporaries and neighbors they were a sort of cultural paradigm. Cultures as far south as Central America, the Oaxacan cultures and the cultures of the Valley of Mexico, emulated certain Olmec artistic tendencies. Traces of the characteristic "were jaguarism," Olmec facial features, artistic stylizations and other innovations surfaced on artistic renderings across wide regions It is possible the Olmecs only passed through and influenced artistic expression. Maybe these regions had been visited by Olmec missionaries or were satellite states conducting trade with the Olmec heartland hundreds of miles away. Perhaps these artistic and religious expressions were imposed on subordinate cultures. Another possibility is that the Olmec were a cultural model emulated by their contemporaries. Despite its stature and pan-Mesoamerican influence, Olmec civilization appears to have been deliberately destroyed in a sequence of internal uprisings. As early as 1,200 B.C. San Lorenzo was witness to the first destruction. Another important Olmec site, La Venta, remained a viable religious center for centuries beyond this point and lasted until around 400-300 B.C..

Teotihuacan, the city of the Gods, emerged near the Valley of Mexico around 150 A.D. Hovering above the entire complex were the twin pyramids of the Sun and Moon. Teotihuacan planners had consciously built the city according to a master plan which integrated heaven and earth into a gigantic terrestrial grid pattern. Its sheer size testifies to the dedication of its leaders and the piety of its builders. Its enormity, now estimated at up to twenty-four square miles, is unprecedented in all of Mesoamerican city building. Its twin pyramids anchored Teotihuacan to its central axis, the "avenue of the dead." On either side were countless temples, various elite neighborhoods and sacred burial zones still being unearthed today. Some early Americans believed Teotihuacan to be the most sacred place of all. Aztec lords often led pilgrimages to the most sacred spot of all, a primordial sacred chamber buried beneath the Temple of the Sun. They thought of it as the place where the Gods met to make the universe.

Besides its unparalleled religious significance Teotihuacan was also the first city of the Americas. Its distinctive cosmopolitan atmosphere, including ethnic urban districts and specialized work areas, attest to Teotihuacan's stature as an urban and cultural model of the Classic ages. At its peak around 600 A.D., Teotihuacanos may have numbered around 150,000. This vast urban religious complex epitomized the sophistication and complexity of Mexico's golden ages. It was here where the archaeological evidence attests to the vast array of activities and specialized groups during Mesoamerica's Classic ages. The Teotihuacanos left behind bits and pieces of their work and ruins on a massive scale. Obsidian workers, sculptors, craftsmen, artists and religious elite all collaborated in building a powerful cultural and religious center which lasted nearly 700 years. Here they constructed a vast urban representation of the cosmos and honored their deities through mural paintings and special ceremonies. Its central religious district, like those of the Olmec civilization, centered Teotihuacan's cultural, spiritual and religious life into the sacred district. Despite its enduring allure and power the city was invaded by unknown intruders who burned and sacked the city around 700 A.D.. The city disintegrated and was left abandoned for over a thousand years.

Arriving to fill the void were northern barbaric tribesmen collectively referred to as the Chichimeca. One group, the Tolteca-Chichimeca constructed the next great city at Tula, Hidalgo. Here they constructed pyramids and temples dedicated to militarists, agriculturalists and astronomers. Tula lasted nearly two hundred years but fell victim to disastrous crop shortages and internal strife. Its end appears to have come around the middle 12th century. Later, the Aztecs fondly remembered the city as a place of powerful militarists and expert craftsmen. For them this was a place of great agriculturalists, expert builders and a people who successfully merged religious and military objectives to build a mighty empire worth emulating. They came to symbolize the successful integration of religious and military objectives geared toward the construction of a vast empire.

After the disintegration of the early post-Classic states the Aztecs arrived in the Valley of Mexico. Driven by their own messianic vision and ancient myths which predicted their greatness, they arrived at their new homeland around 1250 A.D. These nomads from some vague area to the north, which they referred to as Aztlán, were known as the people "whose face nobody knows." They were outsiders, newcomers, but a people who would mold and direct the course of civilized life in central Mexico.

By the middle of the 15th century A.D. the Aztecs, (or Mexica as they were named by their supreme deity Huitzilopochtli) through a blend of military might, timing and guidance under the watchful eye of the great military strategist Tlacaelel, had forged an empire of unparalleled political and military power. But they were also convinced of their own vulnerability to the forces of nature and the need to placate their Gods through wars of conquest. Their world was a dangerous and precarious one, susceptible to the whims of their Gods, vulnerable to predictable cataclysms. Their supreme deities had insatiable appetites. At this time the theologian, militarists and executioner were united in a common purpose. They viewed themselves as the suppliers of sustenance for their God's nearly insatiable appetites for blood. Their role was vital in the struggle against the forces of darkness and destruction. The Aztec kingdom, built upon decades of wars and conquest had, by the late fifteenth century, expanded across a wide region of Mesoamerica. Tenochtitlán was the capital center and axis of an empire stretching as far north as today's American Southwest and south to the remotest regions of Central America,

The Aztecs established extensive trade networks with the distant southwestern cultures. Through the "turquoise road" they traded with distant Southwestern nations and transmitted their culture to these regions. In the meantime they romanticized their ancient links to the people and cultures of the region. It was a bountiful land, green and lush. This would later become the source of the earliest Spanish vision of the region.

Around 1510 the Aztec world was shaken by a series of rumors and strange events. In a history now believed to be partially contrived by European conquerors, rumors abounded about mysterious beings with powerful weapons who rode on top of "two headed deer." These strange beings traveled aboard "butterflies on the sea" and had weapons that exhaled fire. There were mysterious fires, human monstrosities and weeping women could be heard crying in the night. And according to post-Conquest Spanish sources, Moctezuma Ihuilcamina, the Aztec's tragic leader, was frozen in fear. He consulted his wise men for answers and they offered an explanation. It could mean the end of their world, the return of their ancient God Quetzalcoatl, the final cataclysm. By 1519, the Aztec year ce-acatl, or one reed, the ancient prophesies were confirmed. The mysterious beings had come to restore an ancient kingdom and restore Quetzalcoatl to his rightful place. The Spanish, led by Hernan Cortez, had arrived at a fortuitous moment.

Due to a number of factors including Aztec religious prophecy, Indian alliances and superior European technology the Spanish victory over Tenochtitlán was virtually completed by 1521. Allied with tens of thousands of Tlaxcalan and Tarascan warriors, traditional enemies of the Aztec state, Hernan Cortez pulled off the most stunning military victory of the early European conquest. But the greatest weapon of all was not military weapons but European diseases. No one, not even the Aztec king Cuitlahuac, could escape the ravages of this silent but potent weapon. Not even

Cuauhtemoc, the Aztec's greatest leader, could prevent the final outcome. The scourges ravaged Mexico and began the great collapse of the Aztec world. By August, 1521, the end had come.

II

The Century of Depression. Popolucas. Antonio de Montesinos. Bartolome de La Casas. The Black Legend. Mestizaje. Ladinoization. The Millenial Kingdom. Aztlán. Cabeza de Vaca. Coronado.

The Spanish Conquest of Mexico beginning in 1519 brought Mesoamerican cultural and historical evolution to an abrupt and violent end. It also began what has been referred to as the Mesoamerican 'century of depression.' For the next five generations Mexicans would witness various calamities on a scale unprecedented in all of human history. This was the first holocaust, an American version. It was one hundred years of unprecedented cruelty and violence. For the indigenous they experienced mass food shortages, starvation and human death never seen before or since. Antonia I. Castañeda, in an article in this section, has uncovered similar patterns of physical and sexual violence taking place on the California frontier during the eighteenth century. Thomas E. Sheridan also discusses the impact of imported diseases on the indigenous of Pimeria Alta. For this the Indians called the Spanish *popolucas*, barbarians. It has been estimated that up to ninety percent of the people of the Americas met their death as a result of disease, starvation, slavery and slaughter through war. The carnage surrounding them made America's first inhabitants look back for a time "before there was starvation, death and human misery."

To their credit, some Spanish were the first to condemn this human carnage. Even before the Spanish army arrived in Mexico Antonio de Montesinos, a Dominican friar, spoke first. In 1511, almost a decade before the arrival of the Spanish army in Mexico, de Montesinos preached a revolutionary sermon of compassion for the indigenous and directed shame toward Spanish atrocities in the Caribbean. Speaking as a sort of party of humanity, men such de Montesinos, Bartolome de las Casas and others emerged as outspoken critics of the destruction by Spanish adventurers and spoke eloquently for the human rights of indigenous peoples. Through their widely circulated published accounts of Spanish adventurism in the New World they also inadvertently added to the already anti-Spanish and anti-Catholic attitudes held by their European competitors and rivals in the New World. For their European competitors, the British in particular and later the Americans, the atrocities contributed to and confirmed the image of Spanish cruelties embodied in the Black Legend. Raymund Paredes, in an article in this section, examines the historical context of anti-Spanish attitudes and the origins dating to the earliest manifestations of the Black Legend. Some Spanish accepted full responsibility for what was happening. They spoke of a need to reformulate a relationship based on humanity, kindness and Christian empathy. They may have won the moral debate but the dying continued for generations. For the indigenous it was too little too late. And their appeals were met by vigorous opposition in military and political circles. The denunciations of Spanish atrocities had little impact on the lives of the early Americans.

But military conquest did not eliminate the vast array of Mesoamerican cultures or people. It successfully eroded the visible trappings of an elite order but a new and complex cultural synthesis emerged out of the amalgamation of the old and new world societies. Modern Mexicans, and by extension modern Chicanos, are products of the fusion of imported Spanish tradition and Mesoamerican cultural survivals. To this day the indigenous people of Mexico continue to tend to their own secret world rooted in ancient religion and culture.

One of the most unexpected but notable outcomes of the three hundred year Spanish presence in the New World was widespread racial miscegenation. Although officially condemned, but pervasive nonetheless, *mestizaje* (racial mixture between Indians and Spaniards) was a common feature of the this new Mexican society after 1521. The scarcity of Spanish women, the integrative tendencies of Catholic colonial policy and the quick decline of the native populations contributed to the rapid pace of miscegenation and the emergence of the mestizo as a major element in early Mexican society. By 1800, after nearly 300 years of Spanish presence, mestizos constituted the majority of Mexican society. This development is also referred to as the ladinoization of Mexico; the gradual cultural and biological integration of the mestizo into the newly emerging Mexican society and culture. Today the vast majority of Mexican people, whether in Michigan or Michoacán, are mestizos. Chicanos are a modern example of this aspect of the racial mixture of the indigenous and the European and its cultural by-product, ladinoization.

The Spanish conquest of the Aztec Empire centered at Tenochtitlán initiated a chain of events of enormous impact not only for the Aztec Empire but also for the unexplored areas to the north. Fueled by an almost insatiable appetite for gold and silver Spanish conquerors and explorers headed in countless directions to find real and imaginary sources of quick wealth. In the process they expanded the boundaries of

Spanish dominion with the same treachery, violence and subordination. This was combined with the religious mission to pacify the natives under the sphere of European Christianity. And an additional factor also motivated explorations.

Ever since the publication of Thomas More's *Utopia* the search for lands to rejuvenate European society was in motion. Maybe European society could find its renewal in the New World. Perhaps the Spanish military triumph over the Aztec capital marked the beginning of the realization of the dream of rejuvenation. To some it meant the discovery of the "millennial kingdom," a biblically-based interval of a thousand years of earthly bliss. These new lands, filled with willing converts, would form the new earthly paradise, a potent and attractive notion driving Catholic missionaries. With the discovery of new continents, new civilizations and previously unknown territories Europeans searched vigorously for this elusive earthly paradise, a place where their dual objectives of wealth and conversion could be realized. The new American continents seemed ripe for the realization of these dreams. For the Aztecs their paradise was Aztlán, the land of their origins "*mas alla.*" The Spanish searched.

Aztec descriptions of their original homeland, frequently idealized, were met with enthusiastic notice by the early Spanish arrivals. Their descriptions of this wondrous place of abundance and advanced civilization seemed to confirm the discovery of this earthly paradise. The Aztecs were fascinated and mystified by the Spanish obsession with gold. They "danced like monkeys" at the very mention of the word. And the Spanish insisted they had diseases which could only be cured by gold. For the Spanish it was nearly impossible to resist Aztec descriptions of their mythical homeland, a land the Aztecs described as filled with abundance and great wealth. Perhaps this was the earthly paradise.

The Spanish conquistadors were almost certainly disappointed by the lack of readily available precious metals in southern Mexico. But the possibilities for the European rejuvenation were only limited by the imagination itself. Perhaps incalculable wealth, which the Aztecs referred to in descriptions of their homeland, could be found in regions "*al norte.*" So virtually every expedition to the region, from the extraordinary Cabeza de Vaca odyssey through the Southwest, to the ambitious Coronado Expedition of 1540-1542, sought the elusive lure of Aztec exaggeration. These tales assumed a special allure when merged with the Spanish imagination. From the legend of the Seven Cities of Silver to the search for the great Quivira the Spaniards searched in countless directions for the mythological place which could rejuvenate their world and bring untold wealth. John Chávez, in an article in this section, vividly describes the Spanish quest for mythical lands of unknown promise during their first fifty years in the New World. The Spanish mind was preoccupied with this promise for decades.

III

Frontier New Spain. Juan de Oñate. New Mexico. Pimeria Alta. Texas. California.

Frontier New Spain, the American Southwest under Spanish rule, underwent three distinct periods of development. First, the early 16th century explorations into the region sought various versions of a fused European and American image of the fantastic paradise. This was followed by a second and distinct period of colonizations and a series of mini-conquests begun by Juan de Oñate's expedition into northern New Mexico in the late 16th century. For the first time the objective was colonial occupation. And it was a decidedly heterogenous group, a mixture of the indigenous and European. By the late sixteenth century the occupation of New Mexico had begun. Threatened by European competitors in two regions, Texas and California, the Spanish colonial administration expanded the range of its frontier colonial circle and maneuvered to construct its "buffer zone," the third phase. The purpose was to occupy the region while maintaining European rivals at a distance, to protect and guard against intrusions into the potentially more prosperous interior regions. This was the aim of occupation for nearly 150 years following the Oñate expedition.

By 1800, Spain not only extended its sovereignty into most areas of the northern frontier they also carried instructions governing virtually every aspect of settlement. The Spanish proclivity for order and formal regulations was clearly evident during the entire Spanish occupation. Marc Simmons explores this aspect of Spanish colonial administration in his article in this section. The Spaniards also transplanted indigenous people from the south into virtually every major region of the Southwest.

By almost all indications, the southwestern indigenous populations differed in significant ways from those of their southern cousins from the heart of Mesoamerica, particularly in terms of their vast cultural and racial diversity. On account of resource shortages and desert conditions they were accomplished survivalist. Some agricultural semi-urban groups existed in the more temperate zones of Arizona, New Mexico and California. But these were the exception, not the rule. Their nomadic and communal ways were in direct response to these conditions.

The northern frontier had been inhabited for centuries by a distinctly heterogenous population. The original explorers unknowingly added to this diversity when Aztec and Tlazcalan Indians were brought into the region during the early 16th century. For John Chávez this was not a novel experience for the Indians of central and southern Mexico. It was the continuation of an ancient pattern of migrations from north to south and back again countless times. Even Juan de Oñate's original colonizing expedition was guided by Indians from southern Mexico, newly transplanted into lands of their ancient memory. Indigenous Mexican Indians also distinguished themselves by their pivotal role in the agricultural success of the first colonizing expeditions. The original settlers were also instructed by the southern Indians in the rudiments of survival in this largely arid region. The early Spanish settlers quickly became dependant upon the Pueblo tribes of northern New Mexico. And by most accounts the full-blooded Spaniards never accounted for more than a fraction of the total population in regions such as New Mexico.

Arizona's inclusion into the Spanish colonial administration was undertaken during the late 17th century. The province of Pimería Alta (upper Pima lands) incorporated what is now Baja California, Sonora and southern Arizona. In 1692 Eusebio Kino established Mission Nuestra Señora de los Dolores. It functioned as a base for future conversion and expansion into neighboring regions. By 1700, Mission San Xavier del Bac in southern Arizona extended colonial sovereignty and launched the effort to convert the native population to the Catholic faith. Southern Arizona's population, however, numbered no more than 1,000 people by 1800, mostly concentrated around Tucson to the south. Thomas E. Sheridan, in an article in this section, summarizes the two centuries of Spanish, Indian and Mexican interactions after the original colonization.

Not long after the settlement of Arizona, Texas came under the jurisdiction of Spanish colonial administration. On account of the threat posed by French explorers in East Texas, Spain spent more than $3 million in the defense and settlement of the region beginning in 1716. Like Pimería Alta, the Texas settlements were hampered by harsh environmental conditions, hostile indigenous nomadics, lack of mineral wealth and distance from the more comfortable confines of central Mexico. Beset by these unattractive conditions, the Texas region grew slowly and survived on the fringe of the colonial world. Yet despite these circumstances attempts to attract sufficient colonists were made with the establishment of Rio Grande City in 1757, Dolores in 1761 and Roma in 1767. All were located in southern Texas, the traditional area of settlement for countless generations of Texas Mexicans.

The occupation of the California region was provoked in 1769 by the arrival of Russian and English adventurers. Andrew Rolle, in an article in this section, discusses this original impulse to colonize as well as the experiences of the first generation of colonizers in Alta California. Like all other regions of the north, California's population was characterized by its cultural and racial heterogeneity. The various mixed-bloods, including the so-called *gente de razón* (people of reason), and others played vital roles in the settlement of *el rincon del mundo*, as California came to be known by its largely reluctant settlers. Most experts agree that the full-blooded Spaniards never amounted to more than ten percent of the entire population of the region. Mestizos not only comprised the vast majority of the region's population but also filled virtually every conceivable occupation, from artisan to vaquero, to pobladores and ranch bosses.

California differed in a number of respects from other regions of the Southwest. Its geographical location provided access from both land and sea. Consequently the California province became relatively prosperous, received considerable more colonial attention, and enjoyed more financial support than other regions of the frontier. And despite its image as a land on the edge of the known world, California's missions became relatively prosperous due to favorable agricultural conditions and the relatively successful hispanization and exploitation of Indian labor. By 1810, the Catholic Church, through its mission properties, was unsurpassed in its wealth and influence.

California's population also differed in another important respect. A small number of American and European immigrants had successfully assimilated into the fabric of California's predominantly Latin culture. These *hijos de país*, as they came to be known, ventured into the province and struck an accommodation with the dominant society. They frequently formed business alliances, married Mexican women became Mexican citizens and merged into California's land owning class during Mexico's privatization of church lands and secularization beginning in the 1820s. Typical of this experience was William Henry Dana who converted to Catholicism and married into the prominent de la Guerra family of Santa Barbara during the early 19th century. Some also became the front line for American expansionism decades later.

IV

Upper Sonoran Zone. Racial Miscegenation. The Buffer Zone. The Black Legend.

In general the environment of the northern frontier was distinct from the southern region in a number of respects. Its environment, a large desert and plains region, dictated the extent and amount of settlement from the south. With the exception of northern New Mexico and Arizona as well as the California coast the strongest adversary for immigrant settlers was the harsh environment. Even in places such as the "upper Sonoran zone," in the New Mexico region, scarce resources forced immigrants to become dependant on the expertise of the highly urbanized agricultural Pueblo tribes of the region. In almost all other places the real master was the environment. A tenuous and uneasy accommodation with the indigenous populations was necessary for survival. Strict resource management, sometimes in the form of communal properties, evolved in New Mexico in response to these conditions.

Unlike central Mexico where the racial caste system required marked distinctions between classes and races, the northern frontier appeared to be characterized by its relative freedom from the stigma of the caste system and the rapid pace of racial miscegenation. According to Thomas E. Sheridan, a sort of "ethnic melting pot" evolved in most of the major frontier communities. These unique features of the Spanish colonial world were due to a number of factors including the relative scarcity of Spanish women, the need for common defense against hostile Indians, distance from the paternalism of the colonial institutions, the integrative tendencies of the Catholic conversion policy and the erosion of Spanish constraints against intermarriage. All of these factors contributed to the accelerated tempo of racial miscegenation.

To a larger degree than other regions of Mexico the northern frontier was characterized by its great linguistic and cultural diversity among its indigenous groups. As a result the hispanization and exploitation of the indigenous populations presented new and vexing challenges. Some indigenous populations remained nomadic and presented unique problems for Spanish colonial officials. Never fully able to subdue the nomads such as the Apache and Comanche, the settlers reached a distant and uncomfortable accommodation. Presidios, pueblos and missions were uniquely adapted and functioned as multi-purpose institutions designed to meet the needs of the circumstances found in the region. Marc Simmons, in his article in this section, discusses the attempts to adapt to these regional conditions in urban and rural living arrangements. Thomas E. Sheridan discusses the uneasy Spanish-Indian relations during the late eighteenth century in Arizona.

Yet despite Spanish efforts to adapt to local conditions, indigenous populations such as the Pueblos of New Mexico in 1680 and the Pima and Papago of Arizona in 1751, revolted against oppressive colonial conditions. Both revolts exemplified violent resistance to Spanish rule. But nonviolent passive resistance was almost certainly far more frequent and symptomatic of tensions between the Spanish and the indigenous populations.

The northern frontier promised but never revealed its sources of mineral wealth. Visions of quick profits to satisfy Spanish greed were as elusive as the original Seven Cities of Silver. Consequently northern settlements in general remained small, isolated, and to a large extent devoid of the material possessions ordinarily utilized to distinguish among classes. It remained a region which was relatively underdeveloped. The most densely populated region of the north was New Mexico with slightly more than 45,000 inhabitants during the early 19th century, nearly half of the entire population of the northern frontier. Decades later the Mexican government faced this dilemma and launched several strategies to encourage colonization.

By 1800 the Spanish came to perceive of the northern frontier as a buffer zone. Because of the scarcity of mineral wealth, its relatively small population, resistant nomadic Indians and harsh environmental conditions the colonial administration frequently minimized its importance in the context of the colonial empire. As a result the northern frontier endured the consequences of long term neglect. Underdevelopment and vulnerability to competing European rivals were the results.

But the buffer zone had outlived its usefulness to the new Mexican government beginning in the 1820s. Mexico considered the region essential to the national progress and undertook measures, some of which backfired, to strengthen and maintain its sovereignty over the northern territories. It was José María Tornel who called Texas, "Mexico's most precious territory." For the Spanish administration of centuries past, Texas was merely a distant province which helped to keep foreigners away from the vital natural resources in the interior. The Mexicans significantly elevated the region's importance in their national planning.

Mexico inherited another old challenge from centuries before. Anti-Spanish views, which the Spanish had labeled the "Black Legend," became evident in relations between Anglo-Americans and Mexicans on the frontier during the early 19th century. In an article in this section Raymund Paredes traces these centuries-old religious and

15

racial rivalries to European anti-Catholicism exacerbated by territorial competitions in the Americas. Centuries of European anti-Catholicism, now fueled by the tales of Spanish cruelty in the Americas, helped to shape the earliest experiences between the Chicanos in the Southwest and American immigrants.

SELECTED READING LIST

Anaya, Rudolfo, A. and Lomeli, Francisco, eds. *Aztlán: Essays on the Chicano Homeland*. Albuquerque: Academia/El Norte Publications, 1989.

Bannon, John F. *The Spanish Borderlands Frontier: 1513-1821*. Albuquerque: University of New Mexico Press, 1974.

Chávez, John, R. *The Lost Land: The Chicano Image of the Southwest*. Albuquerque: University of New Mexico Press, 1984.

Coe, Michael, D. *Mexico: From the Olmecs to the Aztecs*. Fourth Edition. New York: Thames and Hudson, 1995.

Del Castillo, Adelaida R. ed., *Between Borders: Essays on Mexicana/Chicana History*. Encino: Floricanto Press, 1990.

Forbes, Jack D. *Aztecas del Norte: The Chicanos of Aztlán*. Greenwich, Conn.: Fawcett Publications, Premier Books, 1973.

Gibson, Charles. *Spain in America*. The New American Nation Series. New York: Harper & Row, Harper Torchbooks, University Library, 1966.

Jones, Oakah L., Jr. *Los Paisanos: Spanish Settlers on the Northern Frontier of New Spain*. Norman: University of Oklahoma Press, 1979.

McWilliams, Carey. *North From Mexico: The Spanish Speaking People of the United States*. New York: Greenwood Press, 1968.

Monroy, Douglas. *Thrown Among Strangers: The Making of Mexican Culture in Frontier California*. Berkeley: University of California Press, 1990.

Vigil, James Diego. *From Indians to Chicanos: The Dynamics of Mexican American Culture*, Second Edition. Prospect Heights, Illinois: Waveland Press, 1998.

Weber, David J. ed. *New Spain's Far Northern Frontier: Essays on Spain in the American West, 1540-1821*. Dallas: Southern Methodist University Press, 1979.

--*Foreigners in their Native Land: Historical Roots of the Mexican Americans*. Albuquerque: University of New Mexico Press, 1973.

Aztlán, the ancient and modern home of Chicanos, remained vivid within the historical memory of the ancient Aztecs. Spanish led explorations marked a reintroduction of the indigenous into the region and unknowingly continued ancient migration patterns across old trade networks. Beginning in the early sixteenth century Spanish explorers sought various versions of the edenic paradise. In their pursuit they wandered through most of the present-day Southwest and inadvertently delayed formal settlement for decades. John Chávez traces the image of this region through the eyes of the Aztecs, the imagination of the Spanish explorers and the earliest settlers.

Aztlán, Cíbola, and Frontier New Spain

John R. Chávez

The distant ancestors of Chicanos and other indigenous American peoples arrived in the Western Hemisphere in small groups beginning from forty to seventy thousand years ago. Since by that time human beings had existed in the Old World for millions of years already, the discovery of the Americas was clearly the finding of a "New World," and the discoverers would certainly have been justified in viewing it as a "Virgin Land." Over the millennia the descendants of the first arrivals spread south from the point of entry, at what we now call the Bering Strait, to the tip of South America, where they arrived about 11,000 B.C.[1] During this migration, of course, countless groups broke off from the general movement south to establish themselves in local areas, which in time became their homelands. Despite the occurrence of these events in prehistoric times, this migration through and occupation of the Americas would later form an important part of the Chicanos' image of themselves as a native people of the Southwest, their ancient, as well as modern homeland. Because Chicanos would know their Native American ancestry by the color of their own skin, they could be sure that their forefathers had in the distant past crossed over from Siberia and moved south. And on their way south generations of these ancestors would necessarily have entered the Southwest, inhabited it permanently, or occupied it temporarily before moving on to Mexico proper.

These early ancestors probably had no conception of the Southwest on the scale visualized by their descendants. Southwestern cultures from earliest times until after the coming of the Europeans undoubtedly regarded their particular territories as sacred lands that provided sustenance as well as space,[2] but these homelands were always local areas corresponding to specific tribes. Since the Indian tribes of the Southwest were never united,[3] they most likely perceived the region as a whole about as much as modern man would perceive the world as a whole. The conception of the region as such began from a distant perspective, from central Mexico after the arrival

Between the Conquests

of Cortés in 1519. Even though the history of Chicanos already lay deep in the Southwest itself, their modern image of the region would develop from the perspective of Mexico City.

After taking Tenochtitlan (Mexico City) in 1521, the Spanish looked to the north for new lands to conquer and projected their own myths onto the unknown region that was to become the Southwest. They imagined that to the north there was a rich land of warrior women, that in that direction there were silver cities, or that at the very least the unexplored region touched on a waterway that would link Europe to the wealth of the Orient. All these myths manifested[Edenic]aspects which when viewed together formed the first general myth of the Southwest as a whole--the myth of the region as a land of golden promise. While this image was the invention of the foreign Spaniards, it soon influenced and was influenced by Indians both in the North and in central Mexico. The Indians on the northern frontier, probably to encourage the Spanish to move on to other areas, sometimes agreed with the invaders' conceptions of the region and elaborated on them. In this way the European legend of the Seven Cities of Silver, which led to Spain's exploration of the Southwest, became the native legends of the Seven Cities of Cíbola and the riches of Quivira.

In central Mexico the Spanish myth of the golden northern land aroused interest in the legend of Aztlán, the Edenic place of origin of the Mexica (the Aztecs). Aztlán, meaning either "land of the herons" or "land of whiteness," was an old name by Cortés' arrival. According to their own histories, the Aztecs had left that homeland, located somewhere in the north, in 1168 and journeyed to the lakes where in 1325 they founded Tenochtitlan.[4] After the Spanish conquest Indian, mestizo, and Spanish chroniclers, relying on native informants, recorded the legend of Aztlán along with the rest of the history of the Aztecs. However, in their histories the chroniclers, influenced by the myth of the golden north, placed Aztlán in the southwest; in fact it was probably in Nayarit, only four hundred miles northwest of Mexico City. This error would later lead Chicanos to refer to the southwest as Aztlán, an application of the name that would, nevertheless, be paradoxically appropriate.

By the middle of the seventeenth century the Edenic picture of the north had disappeared at least from the minds of the authorities in Mexico City. By then the region was seen as a series of frontier outposts established to defend central New Spain from northern intruders. On the other hand, Spanish missionaries still viewed the borderlands as golden areas of opportunity for spiritual conquest and agricultural development. But most significant for the future Chicano image of the Southwest was the increasingly popular belief among the settlers that the region was their

18

homeland. To be more exact, the descendants of the first settlers apparently came to perceive the land in that way--especially by the late eighteenth century. Since most of the settlers from the very beginning had been Indians and mestizos from central New Spain and had intermarried with the northern natives, it was not surprising that they eventually pictured the borderlands as home, much as their indigenous ancestors had perceived their own northern tribal lands.

The oldest evidence of these ancestors in the Southwest has been found in Texas and dates back to about 35,000 B.C. Some of the earliest evidence of a clearly distinguishable culture has been found in southern Arizona and dates back to about 8,000 B.C.[5] Significantly, according to the anthropological studies of Indian languages, social organization, material culture, and origin myths, the Cochise culture of southern Arizona was the parent culture of peoples as far apart as the Ute of Colorado and the Aztec of the Valley of Mexico.[6] The ancestral Cochise people apparently spoke the language from which the Uto-Aztecan linguistic family derives. In addition to the Ute, the Gabrielino of California, the Pima of Arizona, some of the Pueblo peoples of New Mexico, the Comanche of Texas, and many other southwestern tribes have spoken Uto-Aztecan languages and probably descend from the Cochise people. In Mexico, besides the Aztec, Uto-Aztecan tribes include the Opata of Sonora, the Tarahumara of Sinaloa and Durángo, the Huichol of Jalisco, and many others, forming an almost unbroken line from the southwest to Mexico City. This together with other cultural evidence indicates that at about 1,000 B.C. descendants of the original Cochise people migrated south and became the direct ancestors of many of the Mexican people.[7] Thus, while Aztlán, the Aztecs' homeland of 1168, was relatively close to Mexico City, their more distant homeland in both time and space was in the Southwest.

Contact between the Southwest and the Valley of Mexico increased after 1,000 B.C. because just as Uto-Aztecan speakers were moving south, the technology of maize cultivation was moving north. The introduction of maize to the Southwest from Mexico led to the replacement of the hunting-and-gathering Cochise culture by the sedentary cultures of the Mogollon, Hohokam, Anasazi, and Pueblos. These cultures, which overlapped a great deal in time and space from about 300 B.C., existed largely in Arizona and New Mexico but also across the present border in Sonora and Chihuahua. As time passed, communication in the form of indirect trade became common throughout the Southwest and Mexico, and the cultural influence of the civilizations of central Mexico became dominant. After introducing squash, beans, and irrigation methods to the Southwest, the peoples of central Mexico-especially the Teotihuacanos, Toltecs, and Aztecs, from A.D. 200 to 1520-had an important impact on cloth making, pottery, architecture, and government in the region to the north.[8] Interestingly, the Indians of both the Southwest and Mexico reached their cultural high points at roughly the same time, between A.D. 900 and 1520. Clearly even in ancient times the southwest was an extension of Mexico.

This interconnection became more pronounced with the capture of Tenochtitlan by the Spanish under Hernán Cortés in 1521. Though the Southwest had felt the effects of the rise and fall of Mexican cultures for two thousand years, the founding of New Spain would lead to closer ties than ever before between that northern region and the Valley of Mexico. While many of these new ties would be provided by a foreign European power, many others would be renewals of ties that had already existed for thousands of years. The most important of the renewed bonds would be racial, for as the Spanish expanded toward the north, they would be accompanied by central Mexican Indians more numerous than the conquerors themselves.

The importance of Spain's Indian allies for the expansion and unification of New Spain can hardly be exaggerated since it was as much they as the Spaniards who toppled the Aztecs. Anthropologist Eric Wolf has convincingly argued the importance of these allies to the capture of Tenochtitlan:

> [Cortés] enlisted on his side rulers and peoples who had suffered grievously at the hands of their Mexica enemies...Spanish firepower and cavalry would have been impotent against the Mexica armies without the Tlaxcaltec, Texcocans and others who joined the Spanish cause. They furnished the bulk of the infantry and manned the canoes that covered the advance of the brigantines across the lagoon of Tenochtitlan. They provided, transported, and prepared the food supplies needed to sustain an army in the field. They maintained lines of communication between coast and highland, and they policed occupied and pacified areas. They supplied the raw materials and muscular energy for the construction of the ships that decided the siege of the Mexica capital. Spanish military equipment and tactics carried the day, but Indian assistance determined the outcome of the war.[9]

Just as the demolition of the Aztec state had been accomplished by an alliance of Spaniards and Indians, the creation of New Spain, racially and culturally, would be the accomplishment of these two groups and their descendants, the mestizos. This would be as true in the northern borderlands as in the center of the viceroyalty. Later this fact would lead to much uncertainty in the Chicanos' image of themselves in both Mexico and the Southwest, for being descendants of both conquered Indians and conquering Spaniards and Indians, Chicanos would vacillate between a self-identity as foreigners and self-identity as natives.

The fall of Tenochtitlan was only the beginning of a series of explorations and conquests that was to expand New Spain. From the ruins of the Aztec capital, expeditions moved out in all directions, and interest in the distant north was soon aroused. Although the coast of present Texas had been sighted by Spaniards as early as 1519,[10] some of the more exciting news concerning territory that was probably within today's Southwest was heard in 1524. In *De Orbe Novo*, one of the earliest European histories of the New World, Peter Martyr wrote that when a group of Spanish explorers was

> wandering through the region that separates the great Panuco River from the Rio de las Palmas [along the Gulf Coast, two hundred miles south of Texas], they enquired of the natives what existed beyond the lofty mountains [the Sierra Madre Oriental] which bounded the horizon...They answered that beyond those mountains existed vast plains and great cities ruled by warlike caciques [chiefs].[11]

To look beyond the mountains, the Spaniards had to look west or northwest; in both directions there were plains and deserts were the Pueblo villages of New Mexico, a thousand miles to the northwest. While the coastal Indians may actually have heard of the Pueblos, it is possible they were giving the Spaniards a golden picture of distant lands just to get them to leave.

During the sixteenth century, especially after the conquest of the fabulously wealthy empire of the Aztecs, Spaniards were quite willing to believe any tale of golden lands, whether they heard these tales from Indians or read them in books. Consequently, in their minds the unknown north was filled with mythical peoples and cities surrounded by riches. A few years after his capture of Tenochtitlan, Cortés wrote, regarding the Mexican coast across from present Baja California,

> I am told that down the coast [meaning "to the north," since his expeditions went in that direction]...are many provinces...where, it is believed, are great riches and that in these parts of it there is one which is inhabited by women, without a single man, who have children in the way the ancient histories ascribe to the Amazons.[12]

Between the Conquests

In a letter to Charles V, Cortés remarked that he was given this report by the Indian "lords of province of Ciguatán [country of women]."[13] Since no such place existed, clearly the Spanish were projecting images derived from Greek Mythology onto a real landscape, and most likely these images were simply being reflected by the Indians.

Interestingly, a novel involving Amazons, entitled *Las sergas de Esplandián* by Garcí Ordóñez de Montalvo, had been popular in Spain since 1510. This romance spoke of an island of gold called California ruled by an Amazon queen named Calafia, and located "on the right hand of the Indies...very near the Earthly Paradise..." That the Spaniards took their reading literally is evident since one expedition after another went into the northwest seeking the realization of this fantasy. At first the explorers went by land up the western coast of the Mexican mainland, and then they went by sea. By 1535, Cortés himself had landed on the shore of present Baja California, and the peninsula received the name of Montalvo's imaginary island. Juan Rodríguez Cabrillo carried the name north when he led the first Spanish expedition to the coast of the present California in 1542. Although Cabrillo encountered no Amazons in the northwest, the impact of those mythical women on the Spanish mind was such that in South America during the same decade, one Spaniard actually claimed to have seen a tribe of female warriors along what he named the Amazon River.[14]

Ever seeking golden lands, the Spaniards chased more than one dream into the distant north. They had barely entered Tenochtitlan in 1519 when they first heard mention of the Aztecs' wondrous land of origin, Aztlán. The description and legend of this place were preserved in the oral tradition and pictorial manuscripts of the Mexica during their rule; after the conquest Spanish chroniclers relied on these sources when they wrote histories of the Indians for the information of the king and church. In one such history, entitled *Historia de las Indias de Nueva España* (1579-81), Fray Diego Durán provided a vivid picture, derived from native informants, of this place called Aztlán:

> Our forebears dwelt in that blissful, happy place called Aztlán, which means "Whiteness." In that place there is a great hill in the midst of the waters, and it is called Colhuacan because its Summit is twisted; this is the Twisted Hill. On its slopes were caves or grottos where our fathers and grandfathers lived for many years. There they lived in leisure, when they were called Mexitin and Azteca. There they had at their disposal great flocks of ducks of different kinds, herons, water fowl, and cranes.... They also possessed many kinds of large beautiful fish. They had the freshness of groves trees along the edge of the

waters. They had springs surrounded by willows, evergreens and alders, all of them tall and comely. Our ancestors went about canoes and made floating gardens upon which they sowed maize, chili, tomatoes, amaranth, beans and all kinds of seeds which we now eat and which were brought here from there.[15]

Such an Edenic description must certainly have excited the imaginations of the Spaniards, and after seeing the gold of Tenochtitlan, they must certainly have assumed the wealth of Aztlán to be in precious metals as well as in flora and fauna. The water imagery of this description indicates that Aztlán was in a semitropical location, and early sixteenth-century pictorial manuscripts place the Aztec homeland on an island.[16] Equipped with such descriptive details and having been told that Aztlán lay to the northwest, the Spanish sought that place where they sought the Amazons--along the Pacific coast of the Mexican mainland. In 1530, about four hundred miles northwest of Mexico City, the conquistador Nuño de Guzmán encountered a place called Aztatlán, whose name and environment resembled those of the legendary Aztlán. Though the evidence indicated (and still indicates) that Aztatlán and Aztlán were one and the same place, it must have seemed too mundane a location for a land that had been idealized to the point of a paradise on earth. Furthermore, storytellers had recounted that in Aztlán there were caves, specifically the Seven Caves, the totemic shrines of the Aztec clans. Since these caves had not been found in Aztatlán, the Spanish decided Aztlán must be farther to the north.[17]

As a consequence, in 1538 Juan de la Asuncíon and Pedro Nadal, two Franciscan friars, set out in search of Chicomoztoc, another name for Aztlán meaning "place of the seven caves." Together with their Indian porters, these explorers marched west from Mexico City to the coast, then to the distant north, possibly as far as the Colorado River, which today forms the boundary between Arizona and California. If they actually went that far, they may have been the first formal expedition to reach the Southwest by land. In any case they were the first to seek Aztlán in that vicinity, and their search would lead to the centuries-old myth that Aztlán was in the Southwest. More than anything else, their expedition caused the image of the Aztec homeland to become the first known Native American image to be applied to the region as a whole. While the friars found no signs of the Seven Caves, on their return they reported hearing word from the Indians of great cities farther north--thus keeping alive the myth of the Southwest as a land of golden promise.[18]

Asuncíon and Nadal had not been the first to hear of cities in the distant north. As we have seen, such news had been heard by Spaniards as early as 1524 on the coast south of Texas. Moreover, in 1536 Alvar Núñez Cabeza de Vaca had made similar reports from the same area the friars visited in 1538 (in fact his reports were partially responsible for their journey). In an almost unbelievable adventure, Cabeza de Vaca had set sail in 1528, had been marooned on the Florida shore, had sailed by raft along the Gulf of Mexico, and had landed on the Texas coast. From there he and a few companions had wandered across the width of what is now Texas, traveled along the present border between Mexico and New Mexico, and then turned south for six hundred miles before reaching a Spanish outpost on the Gulf of California. There they finally came back into contact with other Europeans. As a result of this journey, Cabeza de Vaca became the first European to explore extensively the territory of the Southwest, and his observations were eagerly noted in Mexico City.[19]

Somewhere near modern El Paso, Indians had presented Cabeza de Vaca with arrowheads and other gifts, some made of turquoise, a stone common in the present Santa Fe area of New Mexico. "These [arrowheads] looked quite valuable," Cabeza de Vaca later reported. "I asked where they came from. They said from lofty mountains to the north, where there were towns of great population and great houses." He had received the first definite information to reach the Spanish concerning the Pueblo Indians. Interestingly, Cabeza de Vaca's report was simple; he gave a straightforward account of what the Indians had said. Having seen a great deal of the Southwest and having encountered little that resembled civilization, Cabeza de Vaca was less likely than other Spaniards to cherish a fantasy of golden cities in the region. And having lived among the Indians for years, he was also less likely to misunderstand or be misled by the stories they told. Cabeza de Vaca did indeed understand that the new land had potential for wealth, but that wealth would be in mines, rather than treasure rooms:

> The people who made it [a copper material] lived in fixed dwellings. We conceived the country they spoke of to be on the South Sea [the Pacific was thought to be quite close], which we had always understood was richer in mineral resources than that of the North [Atlantic].[20]

Naturally, Cabeza de Vaca's return from the wilderness caused excitement in Mexico City, and the less he said about the north, the more exaggerated became its image. People linked all sorts of fables with the north, the most common of which was the legend of the Seven Cities. According to the legend, sometime in the Middle Ages seven Portuguese bishops had fled the advancing Moors and founded the Seven

Cities of Antilia or Silver in a land across the Atlantic. When the Spaniards arrived in the New World, they brought the legend, as can be seen in the name they gave the West Indian islands--the Antilles. As the West Indies failed to produce any cities, the locale of the tale was naturally assumed to be elsewhere, though still in the Americas. This locale was situated in northwest New Spain when the Spaniards began to associate the Seven Cities with the Seven Caves of the Aztecs. In fact when Nuño de Guzmán entered Aztatlán in 1530 he had probably been seeking both the caves and the cities. Since neither was found there, the location was shifted farther north. When Asuncíon and Nadal sought the caves in the distant northwest and returned with news of cities matching Cabeza de Vaca's report, the myths of the seven Caves and the Seven Cities merged.[21]

These superimposed images formed the guiding myth of the Spanish exploration of the Southwest. As fairness would have it, that myth was a combination of legends pertaining to the two peoples that would participate in the exploration and conquest-- the Spanish and their central Mexican auxiliaries. The Indians of the north, not to be left out, would make their own distinct contribution to the myth during the 1539 expedition of Fray Marcos de Niza. Having taken Cabeza de Vaca's account seriously, the Spanish viceroy selected a friar to verify the report because friars, such as Asuncíon and Nadal, had shown themselves to be good explorers and diplomats. Fray Marcos, moreover, had already served in Peru with Pizarro. Esteban, an African slave who had accompanied Cabeza de Vaca on his journey, was to guide the friar.[22]

Esteban moved ahead of the main expedition and sent reports and directions back to Fray Marcos. At one point Esteban reported that he had news from the Indians of "the greatest thing in the world." He reported that ahead of him was a city called "Cíbola" (bison)--the first of seven cities. Thus, a southwestern Indian conception of a local homeland was joined to the Spanish and Aztec image of the Seven Cities to form the broader regional myth of the Seven Cities of Cíbola. The nomadic and seminomadic Indians south of the Pueblo villages were probably being truthful when they described such towns to Esteban, but these nomads did not conceive of cities as did the Europeanized mind. In the process of translation, exaggeration was almost inevitable. The description of the Pueblo villages was fairly accurate; their houses were of stone and mortar and of multiple stories. Yet it was a general description that gave rise to fantastic pictures in the minds of the explorers.[23]

All along the march north Fray Marcos continued to receive news from Esteban that further excited his imagination. Then, while in southern Arizona, Fray Marcos learned to his dismay that Esteban had been killed on reaching the first of the Seven

Cities. Although his own life was now in danger, Fray Marcos claimed that he went ahead anyway until he came within sight of the first city itself, a city

> Which is seated on a plain at the bottom of a round hill. It has the appearance of a beautiful town, the best that I've seen in these parts; the houses are just as the Indians described them to me, all of stone with storeys and flat roofs, so it appeared to me from the height where I had placed myself to see. The population is greater than that of Mexico City; . . . in my opinion [Cíbola] is the largest and the best of all [the lands] discovered.

For one who had seen both Mexico and Peru to claim that a Pueblo village was larger and better than Mexico City is surprising. Probably Fray Marcos, frightened by the news of Esteban's death, turned around and fled toward home without seeing Cíbola at all. Too ashamed to admit his failure, he most likely wrote a description of the town based on Esteban's reports and his own memories of Mexico and Peru. In any case the authorities in Mexico City soon pictured the northwest as a "new" Mexico, and before long the famous Coronado expedition of 1540-42 was on its way.[24]

This expedition, which explored much of present-day Arizona, New Mexico, Texas, Oklahoma, and Kansas, did a good deal to make the Spanish conception of the distant north more realistic, at least for a time. With one of the largest expeditions in the history of Spanish exploration, Francisco Vasquez de Coronado marched north only to be disappointed. When the "Seven Cities" were seen to be small villages, Fray Marcos was severely criticized by everyone concerned. In a letter to the viceroy, Coronado put the matter bluntly: "To make a long story short, I can assure you he [Fray Marcos] has not the truth in a single thing he has said, . . . except the name of the cities and the large stone houses."[25] Later, in a letter to the king, Coronado added,

> there wasn't a thing of those which Fray Marcos had mentioned, . . . the best that I have found is this river of Tiguex where I am and its settlements, which cannot be colonized because besides being four hundred leagues from the Sea of the North, and two hundred from the South Sea . . . the land is so cold, . . . that it seems impossible to be able to pass a winter in it.[26]

To his further embarrassment, after Coronado discovered the mundane reality of Cíbola, the local Indians convinced him that a far richer land called Quivira existed beyond the Pueblo villages in the plains to the northeast. Led on another futile search, Coronado trekked through vast sections of what we now know as Texas, Oklahoma, and Kansas, only to realize the Pueblo Indians had lied to him. A fabulously rich Quivira had probably never been part of the local Indian conception of the plains areas, but had been invented purely for the imaginations of the Spaniards. Since the Spanish had conquered and brutally occupied the Pueblo villages, the Indians most likely fabricated the urban wealth of Quivira in order to lure Coronado into a wilderness from which they hoped he would never return. They must have realized he would believe the tale because they doubtlessly understood only too well that the Spanish image of the region was of a land of great cities and valuable metals, a land the Spaniards expected to conquer and exploit. Following Coronado's disappointing experiences, Spain heeded his reports and left the region unsettled for another fifty years. The golden image of the north had tarnished.[27]

Even though the myth of the Seven Cities disappeared before the reality of the Pueblo villages, the accompanying myth of the Seven Caves of Aztlán lived on, at least in the collective mind of the Aztecs and their descendants in central Mexico. In fact, for some Aztecs and mestizos the Spanish discovery of the Pueblos confirmed the existence and location of Aztlán because, unlike the Spaniards, the Indians had seen Aztlán more as an Édenic land of the past than a golden land of the present. The Pueblo villages were, therefore, present evidence of past Aztec civilization in the distant north, evidence which was incorporated into the sixteenth-and early seventeenth-century chronicles of the Aztecs. The anonymous *Códice Ramirez* (1583-87), for example, recounted that the Aztecs had come "from another land toward the north, where recently has been discovered a kingdom which is called New Mexico." Furthermore, the ancestral Aztecs had been "a very civil people as can be readily seen from the ways of those [the Pueblos] of New Mexico from where they [the Aztecs] came." We can infer from this that if the contemporary Pueblos were civilized, the ancestral Aztecs must have been even more so. According to the *Códice Ramirez*, the Aztecs in their ancient homeland had houses and farmland, an orderly government, a complex religion, and an elaborate social organization.[28] Such descriptions caused the myth of Aztlán to take on utopian qualities, in addition to its traditional Edenic features. It was such qualities that Chicanos would later see when they chose Aztlán to symbolize their own ideal society in the Southwest.

While the Pueblos came to be seen--with some justification according to modern anthropology--as distant relatives of the Aztecs, the utopian features that had been included in the myth of Aztlán made it difficult for the chroniclers and their informants to view the Pueblo villages and Aztlán as the same place. The villages indicated that Aztlán had been in the region, but they could not be the ancestral homeland. Just as Nuño de Guzmán's Aztatlán had earlier seemed too mundane to be the mythical homeland, the Pueblo villages now also seemed too ordinary. Since the north, even after the Coronado expedition, was largely unknown terrain, there were still, many other possible locations in that region for the mysterious Aztec homeland.

Because accurate information about California, New Mexico, and Florida was poorly disseminated, the chroniclers and their informants frequently confused those places with one another; with the result that Aztlán, even after being linked to the Pueblo villages, could be placed anywhere as long as it was to the north. In his *Historia de las Indias* (1579-81) Durán's informants actually located Aztlán "toward the north and near the region of La Florida."[29] More often in the chronicles, Aztlán would appear in New Mexico, but the site would only be indirectly associated with the Pueblo villages. In the *Crónica Mexicáyotl* (1610), for instance, the mestizo chronicler Alvarado Tezozómoc said the homeland ancestors "was out there, where, today perhaps it lies very close to the extensive coasts, the extensive shores, which today the Spaniards call New Mexico."[30]

In 1652, after the Pueblo areas of New Mexico had been colonized by Spain, another chronicler took up the issue of Aztlán. In his *Crónica miscelánea* Fray Antonio Tello placed the original Aztec homeland "between the north and the west," but he meant territory beyond what we now call the Southwest, for the frontiers of the unknown had moved farther north by the mid-seventeenth century. Tello stated that the Aztecs on their journey to central Mexico had "passed the straight of Anián, and that the province of Aztatlán [Aztlán] lies on the other side of the strait." The Spaniards had long believed in the existence of a strait cutting across North America, a strait that could, if found, link Europe directly to the riches of the Orient. Given the constant interchange between Spanish and Indian myths, it is no surprise that Tello placed Aztlán beyond the mythical waterway, the last important image of the golden north to interest the Spanish. Ultimately, however, Tello admitted that he was merely speculating concerning the Aztec homeland; "even now," he wrote, "no one knows exactly where the province of Aztatlán is, nor have any of our Spaniards seen it; we only know we have heard of it and that it lies *toward* the north."[31]

While the Indians of central Mexico during and after the late sixteenth century conceived of the north as an old land to which they were somehow indigenous, by the 1580s the Spaniards once more viewed the region as a new land of riches, as a "new" Mexico. By then the disappointment of the Coronado expedition had abated. The

Spanish still remembered that New Mexico had been found "poor in provisions and minerals; but beyond, it was said, was a great salt river, and lakes where the people used gold and silver." Once again a major expedition moved north. The expedition of Juan de Oñate, which began in 1596, was especially significant because it established the first permanent colony in what is now the Southwest.[32] Moreover, the first literary work concerning this frontier region of New Spain resulted from the colonization; in 1610 Gaspar Pérez de Villagrá, a Spanish officer under Oñate, published an epic poem entitled *Historia de la Nueva México* in Spain.

This work dealt with the first stages of the conquest and colonization and discussed the preparations for the expedition at length. Emphasizing that the purpose of the expedition was settlement and not the acquisition of quick riches, the poet chastised those in the Coronado venture (1540-42) who he believed had earlier forced the abandonment of New Mexico "because they did not stumble over bars of gold and silver immediately upon commencing their march into these regions, and because the streams and lakes and springs they met flowed crystalline waters instead of liquid golden victuals."[33] Nevertheless, Oñate did search for riches beyond the Pueblo villages, but again to no avail. When the colonists realized that the chance of their leading the life of landed gentry was small, many fled, almost causing the colony to fail. Finally, the settlement was solidly established, and a new, much less glamorous image of the northern borderlands began to form in the Spanish mind.

Although explorers such as Juan Rodríguez Cabrillo had followed fables into other parts of the north, New Mexico was first conquered and settled because there was some truth to the myth of the Seven Cities. In California there were no Amazons and there was no strait of Anián, but in New Mexico there was sedentary Indians who, while not rich in precious metals, could provide an agricultural base for a colony. Above all they could provide the disciplined labor unobtainable from nomadic peoples in other areas. Once the Spanish colony became established in New Mexico, it settled into a frontier life based on subsistence farming, and the north gradually lost its glossy image. Life in the borderlands was by no means luxurious, for difficulties between the Indians and colonists were continual, and starvation and disease were always a threat. Nevertheless, except for a brief period in the late seventeenth century, the colony survived and finally prospered. Reflecting these changed conditions, later descriptions of the northern frontier spoke of the land and its produce, rather than the silver cities.

In 1773 a number of settlements on both sides of today's international boundary formed the environs of El Paso, which at the time was much more closely linked to

New Mexico than Texas. In that year a resident in the area described the vicinity in words that embodied the later Spanish picture of the borderlands:

> This settlement includes five Indian missions...The Mansos were its first inhabitants, but they are totally extinguished, and on their lands our citizens are living with their farms and homesteads, some by purchase, and some by gift from their chiefs. In these places Indians and Spaniards live commingled.

By the late eighteenth century the authorities in Mexico City perceived the borderland as a series of outposts designed to keep intruders far from the core of New Spain. Missions were part of this defensive system because they helped pacify uncivilized Indians on the frontier. In this respect El Paso fit Mexico City's picture of the north, even as it fit the missionaries' conception of the borderlands as a territory ripe for spiritual conquest. Of course, the Spanish authorities also saw the north as a colonial acquisition, and the sad facts concerning El Paso's Mansos justified that view. The lands of those Indians had been turned over to settlers for agriculture which, as the Spaniards now realized, would produce much of the real wealth of the distant north. But the most interesting aspect of the description of El Paso was the intermingling of Indians and Spaniards.[34]

"The number of its [El Paso's] inhabitants," continued the anonymous author of the town's description, "reached 9,363 [sic] adult persons and a little over 500 children, including all classes of people, Indians and whites. In the last group are included the few Spaniards that are there and about eight or nine Europeans." this comment revealed that while the Mansos may have been extinguished as an identifiable tribal group, many of them most likely intermarried with the Indians and mestizos who always accompanied the Spaniards north on their marches from central Mexico. Furthermore, the existence of five missions meant that a significant number of local Indians were still a part of El Paso's population in 1773. Since few of the people were identified as Spaniards, hispanicized Indians and mestizos made up the majority of the population.[34] Thus, despite the "extinction" of the Mansos, the population could still claim to be indigenous to El Paso, in much the way Chicanos would later claim to be native to the Southwest. Since so many of the townspeople were Indians and related to local Indians, it could not have been much of a conceptual transformation for them to see the area as home. Indeed by the late eighteenth century the "Spanish settlers" of El Paso and other localities throughout the borderlands undoubtedly saw the region as their homeland and were more at home than most people have since realized.

Although New Mexico and El Paso were colonized in the late sixteenth and early seventeenth centuries, efforts in other areas were delayed. Once the Spanish authorities realized that the riches of the north would take great effort to develop, their enthusiasm for the region waned. While missionaries had been anxious to push the frontier northward, only in the late seventeenth century did the secular authorities permit missions in eastern Texas and Arizona, and not until the late eighteenth century in California. The Spanish missionaries had a sincere interest in the conversion of the Indians and were willing to undertake the tremendous effort necessary to gather nomads into civilized, Christian communities. Since farming was a necessary base for such communities, the missionaries realized that they would need to grow crops and were therefore always grateful for any good soil they found in the borderlands.

Father Eusebio Kino, who founded the first missions in what is now Arizona, raved about the bountiful land his converts worked:

> The greater the means the greater our obligation to seek the salvation of so many souls in the very fertile and pleasant lands and valleys of these new conquests and conversions. There are already very rich and abundant fields, plantings and crops of wheat, maize, frijoles, chick-peas, beans, lentiles....

Father Kino went on to list the fruit, stock, and climate that made the region a golden land for economic as well as spiritual conquest.[36] Father Junipero Serra, the first missionary to Upper California, also saw the intrinsic economic and social value of the borderlands. The Spanish secular authorities, however, were reluctant to invest much of their treasury in the region, an attitude that contributed to the later loss of the borderlands to the United States.

Ironically, California and Texas were ultimately colonized as defensive measures to ward off foreign threats against Spain's empire from the north: Texas was established as a buffer against the French in Louisiana, California as a barrier against the English and Russians on the northwest coast. California and Texas, therefore, were perceived by the secular authorities as outposts, as frontiers rather that as colonies having intrinsic value. During the late eighteenth century, for instance, Spain abandoned all its outposts northeast of San Antonio because they were seen as unnecessary after Louisiana had come under Spanish control. Despite this official view, the people of the northeastern settlements themselves were incensed at being forced to move south, and eventually many returned north--the residents had come to perceive this region as home.[37] Nevertheless, the indifferent attitude of Spanish officials had important consequences for the future of Chicanos. Seen as less valuable than areas farther south, the borderlands received less money, fewer colonists, and in general less attention from Mexico City. Consequently, their development as integral parts of New Spain and Mexico was retarded, a situation which eventually worked to the advantage of the United States.

Yet Spain's advance into the region left an indelible mark on the Southwest, a mark that, paradoxically, was as much Mexican Indian as Spanish. While Anglo-Americans would later imagine the period of Spanish rule in terms of conquistadores and Franciscans, Chicanos would revive the facts of Indian and mestizo participation in the settlement of the region. They would note that for every conquistador and missionary who went north, ten or twenty Indians and mestizos, carrying their own customs and languages, went along as porters, soldiers, servants, and small farmers. The important expedition of Marcos de Niza, for example, was led by that friar but was composed almost entirely of central Mexican Indians. And Juan de Oñate, conqueror and colonizer of New Mexico, was himself married to a mestiza, the great-granddaughter of Moctezuma (she was also the granddaughter of Cortés).[38]

Chicanos would also point out the bonds that were felt between the Indians from central Mexico and those of the borderlands. For instance, when Vasquez de Coronado left New Mexico, he left behind several Mexican Indians who apparently felt sufficient affinity for the Pueblos to choose voluntarily to live among them. In 1680 when the Pueblos carried out a temporarily successful revolt, they were joined by many central Mexican Indians who were also disenchanted with Spanish rule. And, of course, throughout the colonial period there was a constant intermarrying between the Indians of the north and south, as well as between Indians and Spaniards. All these facts would link modern Chicanos to southwestern Native Americans and would lend credibility to the Chicanos' image of themselves as indigenous to the Southwest, their homeland, both ancient and modern.[39]

NOTES

1. Victor Barnouw, *An Introduction to Anthropology, vol. 1: Anthropology and Archaeology,* The Dorsey Series in Anthropology, 3rd ed. (Homewood, Ill.: Dorsey Press, 1978), pp. 128, 139, 186.

2. Edward H. Spicer, *Cycles of Conquest: The Impact of Spain, Mexico, and the United States on the Indians of the Southwest, 1533-1960* (Tucson: University of Arizona Press, 1962), pp. 576-77.

3. Robert F. Berkhofer, Jr., *The White Man's Indian: Images of the American Indian from*

Columbus to the Present (New York: Alfred A. Knopf, 1978), p. 3.

4. Lowell Dunham, trans., Introduction to *The Aztecs: People of the Sun,* by Alfonso Caso, The Civilization of the American Indian Series (Norman: University of Oklahoma Press, 1958), p. 1.

5. Barnouw, p. 186; and Lynn I. Perrigo, *Our Spanish Southwest* (Dallas: Banks Upshaw & Co., 1960), p. 1.

6. Florence Hawley Ellis, "What Utaztekan Ethnology Suggest of Utaztekan Prehistory," in *Utaztekan Prehistory,* ed. Earl H. Swanson, Jr., Occasional Papers of the Idaho State University Museum, no. 22 (Pocatello: Idaho State University, 1968), p. 96.

7. James A. Goss, "Culture-Historical Inference from Utaztekan Linguistic Evidence," in Swanson, pp. 3, 5 14; see also Eric R. Wolf, *Sons of the Shaking Earth* (Chicago: University of Chicago Press, Phoenix Books, 1959), pp. 34-41.

8. C.W. Ceram [Kurt W. Marek], *The First American: A Story of North American Archaeology,* trans. Richard Winston and Clara Winston (New York: Harcourt Brace Jovanovich, 1971), p. 165; Carroll L. Riley, "Early Spanish-Indian Communication in the Greater Southwest," *New Mexico Historical Review 46* (October 1971): 286-87; and Matt S. Meier and Feliciano Rivera, *The Chicanos: A History of Mexican Americans,* American Century Series (New York: Farrar, Straus & Giroux, Hill & Wang, 1972), pp. 4-5; see also William C. Sturdevant, gen. ed., *Handbook of North American Indians,* 20 vols. (Washington, D.C.: Smithsonian Institution, 1978-), Vol. 9: *Southwest,* ed. Alfonso Ortiz, pp. 26-30, 48-49, 174.

9. Wolf, pp. 154-55.

10. Perrigo, p. 15.

11. Peter Martyr D'Anghera, *De Orbe Novo: The Eight Decade of Peter Martyr D'Anghera,* trans. Francis Augustus Macnutt, Burt Franklin: Research & Source Works Series 642, Philosophy Monograph Series 44, 2 vols. (1912; reprint ed., New York: Lenox Hill, Burt Franklin, 1970), 2:350.

12. Hernándo Cortés, "Instrucciones dadas...a Francisco Cortés...," in *Colección de documentos inéditos...de Indias,* ed. Joaquin F. Pacheco, Francisco de Cárdenas, and Luis Torres de Mendoza, 42 vols. (1864-84; reprint ed., Vaduz, Liechenstein: Kraus Reprint, 1964-66), 26:153, my translation.

13. Hernán Cortés, *"Hernán Cortés: Letters from Mexico,* trans. and ed. A[nthony] R. Pagden, with an Introduction by J. H. Elliott (New York: Grossman Publishers, Orion Press, 1971), p. 298.

14. Garcí [Rodríguez] Ordóñez de Montalvo,"Las sergas de...Esplandián," in *Libros de caballerías,* ed. with a Foreword by Pascual de Gayangos, Biblioteca de autores españoles desde la formacion del lenguaje hasta nuestros días, vol. 40 (Madrid: Ediciones Atlas, 1963), p. 539, my translation; and Carl Ortwin Sauer, *Sixteenth Century North America: The Land and the People as seen by the Europeans* (Berkeley and Los Angeles: University of California Press, 1971), pp. 152-56.

15. Fray Diego Durán, *The Aztecs: The History of the Indies of New Spain,* trans. with Notes by Doris Heyden and Fernando Horcasitas, with an Introduction by Ignacio Bernal (New York: Orion Press, 1964), p. 134.

16. See *Códice Boturini* and *Mapa Siguenza,* best located through Robert Wauchope, gen. ed., *Handbook of Middle American Indians, 16 vols.* (Austin: University of Texas Press, 1964-76), vol. 14: *Guide to Ethnohistorical Sources: Part III,* ed. Howard F. Cline, pp. 100-101, 197-98.

17. Heyden and Horcasitas, Notes to Durán, p. 330, n. 5; and Durán, p. 134.

18. Perrigo, p. 18.

19. Sauer, *Sixteenth Century North America,* pp. 36-46, 108-25.

20. Alvar Nuñez Cabeza de Vaca, *Adventures in the Unknown Interior of America*, trans. Cyclone Covey (New York: Crowell-Collier Publishing Co., Collier Books, 1961), pp. 119, 110.

21. Herbert E. Bolton, *Coronado: Knight of Pueblos and Plains* (New York: Mg-Graw-Hill Book Co., Whittlesey House, 1949; Albuquerque: University of New Mexico Press, 1949), p. 6; T. H. Watkins, *California: An Illustrated History,* The Great West Series (New York: Imprint Society, Weathervane Books, 1973), p. 20; and Carl {Ortwin} Sauer and Donald Brand, *Aztatlán: Prehistoric Mexican Frontier on the Pacific Coast,* Ibero-Americana, no.1 (Berkeley: University of California Press, 1932), p. 42.

22. Bolton, *Coronado,* pp. 18-19.

23. Fray Marcos de Niza, "Relación," in Pacheco, Cárdenas, and Torres de Mendoza, 3:333, my translation.

24. Ibid., pp. 347-48; see also Fray Marcos de Niza, "Report," in *Narrations of the Coronado Expedition, 1540-1542,* ed. George P. Hammond and Agapito Rey (Albuquerque: University of New Mexico Press, 1940; reprint ed., New York: AMS Press, 1977), pp. 66, 77-79; and Sauer, *Sixteenth Century North America,* pp. 127-29.

25. Quoted in Bolton, *Coronado,* p. 128.

26. Francisco Vázquez de Coronado, " Carta...al Emperado...," in Pacheco, Cárdenas, and Tores de Mendoza, 3:368, my translation.

27. Ibid., pp. 363-69; see also Francisco Vázquez de Coronado, "Letter...to the King...," in Hammond and Rey, pp. 185-90.

28. *Códice Ramírez, manuscrito del siglo XVI intitulado; Relación del origen de los indios que habitaban esta Nueva España, según sus historias,* ed. Manuel Orozco y Berna (Mexico City: Editorial Leyenda, 1944), pp. 17-18, my translation.

29. Heyden and Horcasitas, p. 330, n. 5; and Durán, p. 6.

30. Fernando Alvarado Tezozómoc, *Crónica Mexicáyotl,* trans. from Nahuatl to Spanish by Adrián León, Publicaciones del Instituto de Historia, 1st ser., no.10 (Mexico City: Imprenta Universitaria for the Universidad Nacional Autónoma de México with the Instituto Nacional de Antropología e Historia, 1949), p. 22, my translation from Spanish to English.

31. Fray Antonio Tello, *Crónica miscelánea de la santa provincia de Xalisco: Libro segundo,* Instituto Jaliscience de Antropología e Historia, Serie de Historia, no. 9, vol. 1 (Guadalajara: Gobierno del Estado de Jalisco for the Universidad de Guadalajara, {1968}), pp. 31, 22, my translation.

32. Herbert E. Bolton, ed., *Spanish Exploration in the Southwest:1542-1706,* Original Narratives in the Early American History({New York}: Charles Scribner's Sons, 1908; reprint ed., New York: Barnes & Noble, 1969), pp. 199-200, 202.

33. Gaspar Pérez de Villagrá, *A History of New Mexico,* trans. Gilberto Espinosa, Rio Grande Classics ({Los Angeles: Quivira Society}, 1933; reprint ed., Chicago Rio Grande Press, 1962), pp. 58-59.

34. "Description of ... El Paso ...," in *Historical Documents Relating to New Mexico ..., "* ed. with an introduction by Charles Wilson Hackett, 3 vols., Papers of the Division of Historical Research (Washington, 1923-37), 3:506-8.

35. Ibid.; cf. Oakah L. Jones, Jr., *Los Paisanos: Spanish Settlers on the Northern Frontier of New Spain* (Norman: University of Oklahoma Press, 1979), pp. 119-22.

36. Eusebio Francisco Kino, "Report and Relation of the New Conversion ...," in *Spanish*

Exploration, Bolton, p. 457.

37. C{ecil} Alan Hutchinson, *Frontier Settlement in Mexican California: The Hijar Padrés Colony, and Its Origins, 1769-1835,* Yale Western American Series, 21 (New Haven: Yale University; Press, 1969), pp. 1-3; and Herbert E. Bolton, *Texas in the Middle Eighteenth Century: Studies in Spanish Colonial History and Administration,* University of California Publications in History, vol. 3 (Berkeley: University of California Press, 1915), pp. 1-2, 375-446.

38. Jack D. Forbes, *Aztecas del Norte: The Chicanos of Aztlán* (Greenwich, Conn.: Fawcett Publications, Premier Books, 1973), pp. 23-29; and Boston, *Spanish Exploration,* p. 201.

39. Pedro de Castañeda de Nájera, "Narrative of the Expedition to Cíbola, Undertaken in 1540, in Which Are Described All Those Settlements, Ceremonies, and Customs," in Hammond and Rey, p. 272: and Forbes, pp. 70-76.

In sharp contrast to early American frontier settlement patterns, Spanish and M(
order and urban planning traditions and laws as they settled in regions lik(
early 17th century. The Spanish administration regulated virtually every asp(
urban and rural settlements and the resettlement of Indians. However, conc(
forced settlers to break the urban planning tradition and invent new patterns that v
into the future.

Settlement Patterns and Village Plans . Colonial New Mexico

Marc Simmons

Patterns of settlement in New Mexico fluctuated during the two and one-quarter centuries of Spanish rule. Expansion and contraction of the European population was determined by availability of arable land, territorial requirements of the Pueblo Indians, and pressures of hostile nomadic tribes. Study of the influences which shaped settlement patterns in New Mexico and review of attempts by government officials and others to regulate the settling of new lands and towns offer insights into some of the economic and social problems of colonial times.

When the Spaniards reached the Southwest in 1540, they found the largest concentration of Pueblo Indians along the upper Río Grande and its tributaries with outlying nuclei of settlement to the west at Acoma, Zuñi and Hopi and to the east at Pecos Pueblo and the villages beyond the Manzano Mountains. The Río Grande drainage offered suitable home sites for the Pueblo people with sufficient land to meet their agricultural needs. The Spanish colonists as well, found the environment attractive, so they fixed their earliest farms, ranches, and towns on lands adjacent to the Pueblos. To the present day heavy population clusters occur in this same area.

Extensive exploration in the early colonial period quickly dashed hopes that New Mexico would yield treasure in gold, silver, or other profitable minerals. The fading of prospects for a mining boom meant that population growth and economic development would lack the spectacular quality which attended the colonization of some of the other frontier provinces. New Mexico, in fact, to the end of the colonial era remained thinly populated and dependent upon royal subsidies to meet her expenses. Land served as the principal source of what little wealth she possessed.

The Legal Basis of Settlement

The ultimate proprietorship of all lands in New Mexico belonged to the Spanish sovereign. By royal concession, private individuals or groups of persons might apply for lands, and after fulfilling certain legal requirements, receive a grant called a *gracia* or *merced real*.[1] All properties not conveyed in an official grant remained in the possession of the crown and were known as *tierras realengas y baldías* (royal and vacant lands). These served as a kind of reservoir from which new grants were made and to which lands whose grantees could not acquire final title were returned.[2]

Land grants in New Mexico were generally of three categories: (1) municipal concessions made by the crown to an individual *(poblador principal)* or to a group of settlers who wished to found a new community;[3] (2) private grants to farmers, stock raisers and others who agreed to develop rural property; and (3) Pueblo Indian grants, which awarded title and guaranteed full possession to the Indians of all lands they occupied or used.[4]

The laws regarding the laying out of new towns throughout the Spanish realm were extensive and precise. Municipal planning was to follow the grid-system, which required straight parallel streets with rectangular blocks and one or more rectangular plazas, the principal one to be designated as the *plaza mayor*.[5] Lots were distributed to the citizens *(vecinos)* or were reserved for government and church buildings. Lands on the fringe of the municipality were set aside as commons *(ejidos)*, pasture lands *(dehesas)* and municipal lands *(propios)*, revenues from which helped defray community expenses.[6] Carefully composed ordinances provided that town sites be selected after consideration had been given to matters of health, climate and defense. With regard to the last of these, settlers were instructed to erect jointly and with the greatest possible haste some kind of palisade or dig a ditch around the main plaza so that Indians could not harm them. In addition, they were encouraged to fortify their own houses.[7]

The royal regulations regarding conditions for the fulfillment of terms for private grants were somewhat less specific, since local conditions often determined particular requirements. A concession of land, however, was sure to include a demand that the recipient place it under cultivation and reside on it for a specified number of years. Restrictions ordinarily included the following: no grant could be made which was prejudicial to the rights of the Indians or which caused injury to a third party; a grant of land conveyed no judicial powers; and mineral rights were retained by the crown.[8]

New Mexico Land and Settlement Procedures

The colonial governors possessed broad powers with regard to the founding of new towns and the assignment of lands and water rights. The contract awarded to New Mexico's founder, Juan de Oñate, set forth in explicit terms his prerogatives in this area. It is apparent that the Ordinances of 1573 concerning the laying out of towns and other laws of the time served as the basis for the authority assigned to him. In addition to determining the location and boundaries of new communities, Oñate was empowered to decide whether the settlement should be designated a *ciudad, villa,* or *pueblo* and to organize the municipal government.[9]

Instructions to Don Pedro de Peralta, who assumed the governorship of New Mexico in 1609, provided for the establishment of the villa of Santa Fé, and the terms contained therein also seem to be in conformity with the current legislation.[10] The conduct of succeeding governors furnishes evidence that they were fully cognizant of the laws of the Indies that pertained to the establishment of towns and the distribution of lands.[11] Upon founding the villa of Albuquerque, Governor Francisco Cuervo y Váldez certified that he acted in accordance with royal regulations contained in title seven, book four of the *Recopilación.*[12]

Unfortunately in practically all instances the official records of the actual founding of New Mexico colonial towns are missing. The *instrumentos de la fundación,* which conveyed legal status to a new community, often contained the petition of the person or persons seeking to establish a settlement, the authorization of the governor, and an account of the formal proceedings whereby the petitioners were placed in possession.[13] Were these instruments available today, doubtless they would shed much light on the motives of Spaniards who participated in expanding New Mexico's frontier and would also aid in solving certain legal problems of modern towns whose foundations date back to Spanish colonial times.[14]

In viewing Spain's land grant policy and the influence it had on settlement patterns, it is important to keep in mind that ultimate title to all lands was retained by the king. Grants were made for occupation and use, the subject taking the rents and profits.[15] If an individual failed to meet the requirements of his grant, or if a grant was abandoned because of the Indian menace, as was often the case, the lands reverted to the crown. Even lands designated as belonging to municipalities remained subject to close royal supervision. This may be noted particularly for town lots or outlying lands which the town corporation failed to assign to citizens.[16] Occasionally after lots had been assigned, the government found it necessary to reclaim them for official use.

Such a case occurred in the villa of Santa Fé in 1788 when construction work and expansion of the presidio necessitated the retaking of the lots and houses of three citizens, who were compensated for their loss out of the *tierras realengas y baldías.*[17]

The Seventeenth-Century Pattern

The statements above provide necessary background for an understanding of the introduction and spread of settlement in colonial New Mexico. The initial attempt to found a Spanish community was made by Oñate at San Gabriel near San Juan Pueblo. By the spring of 1610, however, the effort at this site had been given up, and under viceregal orders the colonists moved southward to establish the villa of Santa Fé.[18] Governor Pedro de Peralta, who was entrusted with carrying out the transfer to the new location, received instructions on the creation of a municipal government and the manner in which lands were to be distributed to citizens. Settlers who received lots in the new villa were required to live upon them for ten years, and if they should absent themselves for three months continuously without permission of the municipal authorities, they were to forfeit all property and rights of citizenship.[19]

Down to the Pueblo revolt of 1680, Santa Fé remained the only formally organized community in the province, as the old San Gabriel settlement was totally abandoned.[20] During this period a trend was established which was carried over and reinforced in the following century: the tendency for the majority of the population to become dispersed throughout the rural areas in isolated farms, ranches and hamlets.

By tradition the Spaniard was a town dweller, accustomed to residing in communities welded into a unit by the practical necessity of defense and the common need to produce an adequate food supply. In New Mexico, as in other remote districts of northern New Spain, the municipal tradition or "sense of community" was greatly weakened and in some cases broke down altogether. This occurred, paradoxically, when the needs of defense and economic cooperation appeared the greatest.

During the seventeenth century, the small European population labored to sustain and defend the missionary friars and to extract what meager rewards it could from the province's limited resources. Land grants were made to a number of Spanish families, the more affluent of which founded fairly prosperous haciendas. In other cases simple farmsteads strung along river or stream courses were developed by the rural folk. The principal areas of occupation were the valleys north of Santa Fé and the middle Río Grande flood-plain from the Santo Domingo plains southward through the

Albuquerque and Belen valleys. The Spaniards favored these regions because the best agricultural lands were situated here as were the heaviest concentrations of the Pueblo Indian population.

The native towns were distributed in *encomienda* to the leading colonists, who received from them an annual tribute, principally in maize and cotton mantas. Of greater economic significance to the majority of the settlers was Indian labor required on farms and ranches. The going wage was half a *real* a day until 1659, at which time it was increased to a full *real* a day by Governor López de Mendizábal.[21] There is abundant evidence, however, that even this nominal sum was not always maintained, the colonists preferring to squeeze labor out of the Indians while neglecting to compensate them.

The Spaniards sought to locate themselves close to exploitable labor and within easy range of their *encomienda* grants. During the first two-thirds of the seventeenth century, the ratio of Spaniard to Indian was such that the number of potential workers probably exceeded the labor demands of the colonists. After 1665, however, famine, pestilence, and raids by nomadic tribes on the Pueblo people so depleted their numbers that the village Indians were hard-pressed to meet the labor requirements of the colonists. In fact, one of their chief complaints at the time of the Pueblo revolt was that the Spaniards so burdened them with tasks, that they had little time left to care for their own fields.

The more prosperous ranches might have developed in New Mexico a settlement pattern similar to that which soon appeared in the neighboring province of Nueva Vizcaya, with widely-scattered large properties supported by the labor of dependent Indians or poor mestizos. The Pueblo revolt of 1680, however, extinguished the Spanish settlement clusters in the upper Río Grande Valley and forced a withdrawal of surviving colonists to the El Paso district down-river. When colonization was resumed some twelve years later, new patterns emerged.[22]

New Trends of the Eighteenth Century

In the years following the Pueblo revolt and the reconquest of New Mexico by the Spaniards, the character of settlement underwent a significant change. From 1700 to the end of the Spanish period, loose agglomerations of small farmsteads termed *ranchos* became the typical unit of colonization, in marked contrast to the seventeenth century during which the *hacienda* had predominated. In considerable measure, this shift from large land holdings to farms of more modest size may be attributed to the decrease in Pueblo Indian population, which greatly reduced the labor supply, and to the increase in the numbers of Spanish colonists, whose arrival created a heavy demand for farmlands in the old core area of the Río Grande Valley.[23]

By 1695 Diego de Vargas had reclaimed New Mexico for the Spanish crown, missions had been reestablished, the villa of Santa Fé had been put in some order and a large number of colonists concentrated there in anticipation of the reoccupation of outlying areas. A survey shortly was made of abandoned farms and ranches, and lands were distributed to both new and old settlers. In some cases it was discovered that Indians had built pueblos on the foundations of former Spanish settlements. Tano people, for example, had moved into such a location in the valley of the Santa Cruz River. As recolonization proceeded they were evicted and the new villa of Santa Cruz de la Cañada was created on the site.[24]

Governor Vargas was eager to found new towns, although orders from the superior government instructed him to keep the settlers together for better defense.[25] Within a brief time, new communities appeared and advances were begun into regions which had not previously known European settlement. Since the population expanded far beyond previous limits, it becomes possible to place in sharper focus the distribution patterns for the later colonial years.

Description of Life

New Mexico was essentially a rural province dominated by a rural population living in dozens of small communities. Even in the several villas there is little evidence of true urbanism since the people did not group their houses compactly but scattered them over the neighboring countryside to be near their fields. An examination of the several categories of "village types" which can be defined for the late colonial period will serve to illustrate the direction and character which the pattern of settlement assumed. New Mexican communities may be categorized as *villas* and *poblaciones* or *plazas* for the European population, and for the Indians, *pueblos* and *reducciones*.

The Villas

No New Mexican municipality ever attained the rank of *ciudad*. The formal villas, however, numbered four and included Santa Fé, Albuquerque, Santa Cruz de la Cañada, and El Paso del Norte. All were poorly organized and had populations of probably under 2,500, conditions which elicited the following terse comment from

Fray Francisco Dominguez in 1776. Regarding Santa Fé, he declared, "Its appearance, design, arrangement, and plan do not correspond to its status as a *villa*." And he observed that in New Spain there were *pueblos* (a less pretentious title than *villa)* which had far more to recommend them than Santa Fé, a town that "in the final analysis lacked everything."[26]

According to George Kubler, the original plan of Santa Fé had embodied the royal regulations of 1573 for the laying out of new towns, so that this *villa* "of all Hispanic cities in the New World is a paradigm of these ordinances."[27] This statement, however, represents something of an exaggeration. There may have been more regularity to the *villa* in the seventeenth century than in the period after the Pueblo revolt, but at no time did it conform in more than a rudimentary way to the grid-system or to the requirement that adequate fortifications be provided. True, there was a *plaza mayor* fronting on the governor's residence and offices, and perhaps a secondary plaza existed to the west of San Miguel Church, but as to carefully marked streets required by the grid-pattern there were none.[28] Dominguez reported only the semblance of a single street for the entire *villa* in 1776.[29]

This lack of order in the municipal plan developed, not because of the negligence of local government officials, but through the willful determination of Santa Fé citizens to place their residences close to their fields, which were spread along the narrow valley of the Santa Fé River. They desired not only convenient access to farm plots, but wished to keep a constant surveillance over them to prevent the loss of crops to thieves and wild animals. As a result of this scattering, the limits of the *villa* measured about three leagues in circumference by the third quarter of the eighteenth century.[30]

Apparently the formlessness of the community of Santa Fé was repeated in the remaining *villas*. Bishop Tamarón in 1760 reported that at Santa Cruz de la Cañada there was no true town, the settlers being distributed over a wide area.[31] The people of El Paso preferred to live near their vineyards located several leagues above and below the *villa*,[32] while at Albuquerque only twenty-four houses were situated in the vicinity of the church, the rest being scattered for a league up-stream.[33] Each *villa* did possess a plaza adjacent to the main church with "town houses" of prominent families and perhaps a government building or two on the square or nearby. Otherwise, homes and small businesses were randomly placed according to the needs of their owners, and in defiance of colonial legislation which demanded adherence to an orderly plan of municipal development.

Poblaciones and Plazas

In New Mexico the loosely-grouped Spanish *ranchos* were generally referred to as *poblaciones,* or if the population consolidated for mutual defense, as *plazas.* The term "plaza," and its derivative "placita," thus were employed in this province to mean a town or village. A very small place was sometimes called merely a *lugar.*[34]

A *rancho* consisted of one or more Spanish households located adjacent to farm and orchard lands. The agricultural plots were small and generally long and narrow as a result of the Spanish custom of subdividing among all the heirs.[35] Land grants were usually apportioned along ditch or stream frontage—those made to Ojo Caliente settlers in 1793 were 150 *varas* wide—with the strip extending sometimes as much as one mile back from the water.[36]

In frontier zones *ranchos* were often established informally, that is, without government sanction, by poor family heads who owned no lands in the more settled central regions and who simply did not wish to abide by the proper legal forms. In 1772, Governor Mendinueta suggested that perhaps the majority of those living on *ranchos* were "intrusive owners of their lands or voluntary holdings."[37] If the farms prospered and survived Indian attack, the original settler or his descendants later might apply for a formal grant.

Scattered *ranchos* or "houses of the field," as they were occasionally termed, were the most characteristic units of rural New Mexico.[38] Even when the farmsteads were dispersed over several leagues, however, a church built by the settlers served as a focal point for community activity. Under pressure of severe Indian raids in the late eighteenth century, rural people increasingly forsook their isolated *ranchos* and congregated in small fortified towns or *plazas.* In such instances, permission was usually sought from the governor through a formal petition, and regulations regarding construction of fortifications were received and executed.

Walled towns were no novelty to the Spaniard. Fortified villages were a common feature on the Moorish frontier in Spain, and at least one authority asserts that the fortifications for the military camp of Santa Fé de Granada constructed by Ferdinand and Isabella served as the forerunner of defensive establishments in the New World.[39] Cities protected by walls arose in the Antilles and in those districts of New Spain subject to enemy attack. The villa of Santa Fé had an eight-foot wall with parapets, portions of which survived well into the nineteenth century. And as a defensive measure, the lieutenant-governor at El Paso in 1780 proposed that a wall be constructed around that town, though it seems nothing was done.[40]

On the New Mexico frontier, the settlers usually preferred not to construct a separate wall to shield communities from Indian assault; rather, the common practice was to place houses contiguously about a central plaza. The outer walls were left devoid of windows, livestock could be corralled in the square during attack, and the single gate barred. Often there were towers or *torreones* constructed in a circular or polygonal fashion. Defensive *plazas* of this kind were known at Chimayó, Truchas, Las Trampas, Taos, Ojo Caliente, Cebolleta and elsewhere.[41]

The type of *plaza* just described was comparatively large, was composed of a number of families, and possessed the aspect of a true town. Similar to it was the "restricted plaza" or fortified dwelling of a single extended family. Such residential clusters of kin were often known by the lineage surname, and those of more imposing nature were designated haciendas.[42] The hacienda or *casa grande* frequently had extensive walls, towers, parapets, and other defensive features similar to those found on the wealthy estates of northern New Spain.[43]

Fortified *plazas* and haciendas in varying degrees conformed to the royal ordinances which laid down measures to be taken for defense. As indicated, the same could not be said for the individual *ranchos* which were located haphazardly according to no particular plan. In certain instances, however, it seems the owners of these humble farmsteads did give some attention to the protection of their families and property. The result was a unique arrangement known as the *casa-corral* unit. As described by Conway it consisted of

> a dwelling—usually the conventional one-story adobe structure—with a corral or yard for holding livestock adjoining it in the rear. The walls of the corral were frequently as high as the walls of the house and of one piece with them. A door led directly from the dwelling into the corral . . . and the general impression was of a small fortress with stout, high walls, few openings and a compact, economical design.[44]

This kind of family unit clearly derived from the Ordinances of 1573 which required "houses to be constructed so that horses and household animals can be kept therein, the courtyards and stockyards being as large as possible to insure health and cleanliness . . . and to be planned so they can serve as . . . a fortress. . ."[45] Admittedly however, as a defensive structure, the New Mexican *casa-corral* unit was far less ambitious than the original laws intended.

Settlers on the edges of the province in the late eighteenth and early nineteenth centuries frequently petitioned the superior authorities for license to desert their homes and retreat to relative safety in the Río Grande Valley. In almost every case, their petitions were denied. Many left the frontier anyway, unmindful of threats of dire penalties. Cases of this kind were common in the Ojo Caliente-Chama district and at other points.[46] In 1805, for example, settlers at Cebolleta beyond the Río Puerco abandoned their community because of Navajo incursions, but they soon were ordered to return by Commandant General Nemesio Salcedo, who promised to send troops to punish the Indians.[47]

Indian Towns

These were of three kinds: (1) those of the Pueblo Indians; (2) the settlements of *genízaros;* and (3) the *reducciones* for members of nomadic tribes. As suggested, the colonial era saw a general reduction in the area occupied by the Pueblo peoples. This trend, which had begun as early as A. D. 1300, was greatly accelerated after the Spanish conquest, so that the Pueblo population and number of villages steadily declined. Remaining Indians concentrated into ever larger communities which were closely integrated and carefully organized for defense.[48]

The strategic value and secure shelter afforded by the pueblos was obvious, even to the Spaniard. Governor Mendinueta in 1772 urged a law with teeth in it which would require settlers to live in compact towns like the Indians.[49] The colonists, however, appear to have been less perturbed by enemy raids than were the Pueblo people; at least, they could be induced to take defensive measures only under the most severe pressure.

Many settlers in the Taos Valley, one of the areas most vulnerable to Comanche and Ute attack, spent a great deal of time in the eighteenth century living inside Taos Pueblo.[50] A *plaza* and fortified houses of their own had proven inadequate, so they took up more secure homes with the Indians. Father Domínguez in 1776 said of the pueblo, "Its plan resembles that of those walled cities with bastions and towers that are described to us in the Bible."[51] And he mentions heavy gates, fortified towers, a very high wall and solid blocks of houses. While all the pueblos were not as well-defended as this one, nevertheless, they served as a far more effective refuge for their people than did the loose communities of the Spaniards.

The settlements of *genízaros* represent a special case, and as a village type they may be classed as a variant of the Indian pueblo. Originally the *genízaros* were Indian captives or slaves of nomadic tribes who were ransomed by the Spanish government. Parceled out among the colonists, they became domestic servants or laborers. As neophytes they were given Christian names and religious instruction.

Unfortunately many were mistreated by their Spanish masters and became apostates. Others, however, with the support of Franciscan missionaries petitioned for permission to found their own settlements on the frontier. Believing in the justice of the *genízaro* complaints, the Governor of New Mexico ordered that all who were abused might apply to him for relief and receive assignment to a new town. One of the earliest of such communities was created at the Cerro de Tomé south of Albuquerque.[52] Other *genízaros* later were placed at Abiquiú and the Pecos River towns of San José and San Miguel del Bado.

Since most of these people were of nomadic ancestry, they proved useful to the Spaniards as scouts, spies, and auxiliary soldiers. More significant for the discussion here, their towns, located on the fringes of European settlement, constituted an important barrier between the Spanish farmers and the hostile tribes on the frontier.

During colonial times repeated efforts were made to reduce the nomadic native people to community life under supervision of proper religious and civil authority. The *reducción,* an instrument of Spain's Indian policy from the days of earliest settlement in the New World, aimed at nothing short of full social and cultural reorientation of native ways. In many parts of Spanish America, congregation of wandering Indians into a community had been achieved through the use of force. But in New Mexico the several tribes of nomads remained unsubjugated, so that establishment of *reducciones* or formal settlements for them depended upon their voluntary submission. At various times in the eighteenth century, the Spaniards responded to pleas from Navajos, Apaches, and Comanches for aid in establishing their own towns, but in the end the Indians returned to a roving life. Since the experimental *reducciones* were situated on the far frontiers, had they succeeded, the jurisdiction of the New Mexican government would have been appreciably expanded and new areas might have been made safe for Spanish colonization.

Attempts to Regulate Settlement Patterns

A recurrent theme in official reports of the colonial years centered upon the problems raised by dispersal of the New Mexican population and the need to consolidate for defense. As early as 1609, the people of New Mexico were described as being "scattered over [that country] so that they are destitute of administration because very few reside in each place. . . ." As a result, orders were issued to gather the colonists together so they could stand united against the Indian menace.[53] No significant action was taken, however, and consequently the Spaniards suffered heavy casualties in the 1680 revolt—the isolation of individual families or small settlement clusters permitting the Indian forces to sweep the countryside.

In spite of this tragic experience, the same patterns of dispersal appeared on an even grander scale in the eighteenth century. The case was clearly put by Antonio de Bonilla, who, in 1776, remarked that in New Mexico

> The settlements of the Spaniards are scattered and badly defended . . . and quite exposed to entire ruin. Because the greater number of them are scattered ranches, among which the force of the settlers is divided, they can neither protect themselves nor contribute to the general defense of the country. This, in consequence, results in the abandonment of their weak homes and the terror of seeing themselves incessantly beset by the enemy.[54]

Of course, the government was concerned at the loss of life and the extra expense entailed in trying to protect an area in which patterns of settlement lacked regularity. But from a long view, of even more fundamental importance was the fact that erratic colonizing practices resulted in loss of entire blocks of territory to enemy raiders and a shrinking rather than an expansion of the frontier at various places. At least one historian has called attention to the Miera y Pacheco map of 1779, which shows there were more abandoned towns in New Mexico than there were occupied towns.[55]

The scattering of *ranchos* and settlements was, in part, an out-growth of the region's peculiar agricultural requirements—in a country where plowland was scarce, farms, as pointed out, were ribboned along stream valleys, and the people insisted on living near their fields, considerations of defense aside. Critics of the dispersal pattern claimed that the obstinacy and inertia of the colonists were the principal barriers to fulfillment of numerous government orders regarding establishment of organized communities. The issue was stated most forcefully by Father Juan de Morfi, writing sometime in the 1780s, who declared that the settlers like to live apart so that, far from the prying eyes of neighbors and the restraining influence of the authorities, they could commit with impunity all manner of immoral and criminal acts. He reported that some isolated colonists "were not ashamed to go about nude so that lewdness was seen here more than in the brutes, and the peaceful Indians were scandalized."[56] While moral looseness does seem to have been common in colonial society—decrees were issued with frequency condemning concubinage, indecent dances and excessive gambling—other causes, as already noted, were chiefly responsible for population dispersal.

This problem, which Bonilla and others regarded as of considerable magnitude, was finally met head-on by the Spanish government. Action came, nevertheless, only when it was realized that consolidation of the settlers was essential to the defense of the province, and that it was less costly to issue orders to that effect than to accede to repeated requests for additional presidios to supply protection.

Governor Mendinueta in a report of 1772 to Viceroy Bucareli advocated compelling "settlers of each region who live . . . dispersed, to join and form their pueblos in plazas or streets so that a few men could be able to defend themselves."[57] The viceroy was in full agreement, but some delay arose before orders could be issued and the task of concentrating the New Mexican settlers begun.[58]

On July 4, 1778, a council was held in Chihuahua which recommended prompt measures for the unification of the New Mexico population. Commandant General Teodoro de Croix then issued orders to Governor Juan Bautista de Anza calling upon him to "regularize" the settlements of his province by collecting scattered families and obliging them to dwell in compact units.[59] By 1779 the villas, except Santa Fé, were reduced to some order, and in the following year considerable success was achieved in concentrating the rural folk.[60] It was in this period of activity that many of the fortified or walled towns on the frontier had their beginnings.

The problem of concentrating the residents of the provincial capital remained unresolved for some time. The authorities, aware of "the churlish nature of Santa Fé's inhabitants" and of "the perfect freedom in which they always lived," decided to tread slowly and to seek alternative ways to strengthen defenses of the villa.[61] A formal presidio was begun adjacent to the governor's residence on the *plaza mayor* and was brought to completion in the early 1790s. Its purpose was to provide quarters near the center of town for officers and men of the garrison. Heretofore, some of the soldiers had lived as much as a league away from the plaza, and often it required several hours merely to assemble the troops. It is not certain what other measures may have been employed at this time to pull in the limits of the capital and congregate the residents, but in the long view it is doubtful if any fundamental change in the established pattern was achieved.

Conclusion

As may be seen from the foregoing, informality and a general lack of planning characterized New Mexican settlements through much of the colonial period. Economic necessity, a strong spirit of frontier individualism, a sense of fatalism about the Indian danger, and perhaps a wish to escape the paternal eye of civil government and the Church—these all influenced the settler and nourished in him the desire to build and farm on land of his own choosing, disregarding laws which were aimed at maintaining the collective welfare of the populace.

Of all causes contributing to the dispersal pattern, that which required the small farmer to live near his fields to give them proper care and protection was of uppermost importance. In this regard, it is interesting to note that the closely integrated villages of the Pueblo Indians began to break up as soon as the hostile nomads were subdued by the United States Government in the second half of the nineteenth century. With that event, it became safe for individual farmers and their families to reside permanently near more distant fields, returning to the main pueblo only on ceremonial occasions.[62] Thus, it appears that only the threat of enemy raiders had prevented the Pueblo people from scattering as the colonial New Mexicans had always done.

Overall, then, it may be said that settlement patterns in this province during the period of Spanish rule were shaped primarily by economic needs of the rural folk and only secondarily by considerations of defense. The strong tendency toward dispersion of the population was probably characteristic of most of northern New Spain, but may well have been more pronounced in New Mexico owing to greater isolation and looser enforcement of governmental decrees.

NOTES

1. J. M. Ots Capdequi, *El estado Español en las Indias* (4th ed.; Mexico, 1965), p. 34.

2. Ibid.. p. 36; and Julio Jiménez Rueda, *Historia de la cultura en México*, El virreinato (Mexico, 1951), p.42.

3. Professor Clark S. Knowlton sharply distinguishes the "proprietary grant" (that of a poblador principal) from a community grant (one extended to a petitioning group of at least ten families seeking to establish a community). "Land Grant

Problems Among the State's Spanish Americans," *New Mexico Business*, Vol. XX (1967), p. 2.

4. The existence of actual grants for the Pueblos must be inferred, since no original title papers are known today. The "Cruzate Grants" for the Pueblos have been proven to be largely fraudulent. See Myra Ellen Jenkins, "The Baltasar Baca 'Grant': History of an Encroachment," reprinted from *El Palacio*, Vol. LXVIII (1961), pp. 51-52.

5. See Dan Stanislawski, "The Origin and Spread of the Grid-Pattern Town," *The Geographic Review*, Vol. XXXVI (1946), pp. 105-120, and by the same author, "Early Spanish Town Planning in the New World," *ibid.*, Vol. XXXVII (1947), pp. 94-105.

6. O. Garfield Jones, "Local Government in the Spanish Colonies as Provided by the Recopilacion de Leyes de los Reynos de las Indias," *The Southwestern Historical Quarterly*, Vol. XIX (1916), p. 68. Municipal plans which might show the *ejidos, propios and dehesas* for New Mexico communities are generally lacking. A colonial plan of the villa of San Fernando de Béxar in Texas, however, clearly manifests these features. Reproduced in Herbert Eugene Bolton, *Texas in the Middle Eighteenth Century* (new ed.: New York, 1962), p. 6.

7. Zelia Nuttall (trans.), "Royal Ordinances Concerning the Laying Out of New Towns." *Hispanic American Historical Review*, Vol. V (1922), p. 252.

8. Ots Capdequí, *El estado Español en las Indias*, p. 35; and Agustín Cue Cánovas, *Historia social y económica de México*, 1521-1854 (Mexico, 1963), pp. 114-16.

9. George P. Hammond and Agapito Rey. *Don Juan de Oñate, Colonizer of New Mexico*, 1595-1628 (2 vols.; Albuquerque, 1953), Vol. 11, p. 599. The classification of a municipality as *ciudad, villa or pueblo* (city, town or village) was more than a mere formality since these terms implied definite ranking according to prestige and importance. Also the number of municipal magistrates and councilmen allowed by law depended upon the status of the community. See especially Ralph Emerson Twitchell, "Spanish Colonization and the Founding of *Ciudades* and *Villas* in the Time of Oñate," New Mexico Bar Association Minutes, 32nd Annual Session, Albuquerque, August, 1918, pp. 27-43.

10. "Ynstrucción a Peralta por vi-rey," *New Mexico Historical Review*, Vol. IV (1929), pp. 178-80.

11. See, for example, the remarks of Pedro Fermín de Mendinueta in Alfred B. Thomas, "Governor Mendinueta's Proposals for the Defense of New Mexico, 1772-1778," *New Mexico Historical Review.* Vol. VI (1931), p .33.

12. Charles Wilson Hackett, *Historical Document Relating to New Mexico, Nueva Vizcaya, and Approaches Thereto, to 1773* (3 vols.; Washington, 1937), Vol. III, p. 379.

13. Lansing B. Bloom (ed.), "Albuquerque and Galisteo, Certificate of Their Founding, 1706," *New Mexico Historical Review,* Vol. X (1935), pp. 49-50.

14. Richard E. Greenleaf, "The Foundation of Albuquerque, 1706: An Historical Legal Problem," *New Mexico Historical Review,* Vol. XXXIX (1964), pp. 1-15.

15. Frank W. Blackmar, *Spanish Institutions of the Southwest* (Baltimore, 1891), p. 319.

16. The general theory of Castilian law on the subject indicates that citizens received allotments for their use and enjoyment, "but the domain itself remained in the person of the sovereign," Ralph E. Twitchell, "Spanish Colonization in New Mexico in the Oñate and De Vargas Periods," Historical Society of New Mexico, *Publications,* No. 22, p. 9.

17. Jacobo Ugarte y Loyola to Fernando de la Concha, Chihuahua, July 22, 1788, Archivo General de la Nación, México, Provincias Internas, Vol. 161, pt. 4. (From a photocopy in the Coronado Room, University of New Mexico Library, Albuquerque. Archivo General de la Nación hereinafter cited as AGN.)

18. Lansing B. Bloom, "When Was Santa Fé Founded?" *New Mexico Historical Review,* Vol. IV (1920), p. 194.

19. "Ynstrucción a Peralta," *New Mexico Historical Review,* Vol. IV (1929), p. 180.

20. France V. Scholes, "Civil Government and Society in New Mexico in the Seventeenth Century," *New Mexico Historical Review,* Vol. X (1935), p. 94.

21. France V. Scholes, *Troublous Times in New Mexico. 1659-1670,* Historical Society of New Mexico, *Publications in History, Vol. XI* (1942), p. 25.

22. Wilfred D. Kelley, "Settlement of the Middle Rio Grande Valley," *The Journal of Geography,* Vol. LIV (1955), p. 393.

23. Pueblo population in 1600 has been estimated at 35,000. According to Hubert Howe Bancroft, by 1600 it had dropped to about 20,000 and in 1760 it was down to some 9,000. *History of Arizona and New Mexico* (new ed.; Albuquerque, 1962), pp. 172, 279.

24. J. Manuel Espinosa, *Crusaders of the Rio Grande* (Chicago, 1942), pp. 221-25.

25. Ibid., p. 227.

26. Fr. Francisco Atanasio Domínguez, *The Missions of New Mexico*, trans. by Eleanor B. Adams and Fr. Angélico Chávez (Albuquerque, 1956), p. 39.

27. *The Religious Architecture of New Mexico* (Colorado Springs, 1940), p. 18.

28. Vargas mentions two *plazas* for Santa Fé in 1695 (Espinosa, *Crusaders of the Rio Grande*, p. 225), and the Urrutía map of ca. 1766-68 shows an open space in front of San Miguel Church in the Indian *barrio* of Analco. Mr. Bruce Ellis of the Museum of New Mexico suggests that the present plaza was the *plaza mayor* or *plaza de armas* of the colonial documents, and that the secondary plaza may have existed immediately to the east in front of the parish church.

29. Domínguez, *The Missions of New Mexico*, p. 40.

30. Fernando de la Concha to Jacobo Ugarte y Loyola, Santa Fe, November 10, 1787, AGN, Prov. Int., 161.

31. Eleanor B. Adams (ed.), *Bishop Tamarón's Visitation of New Mexico, 1760,* Historical Society of New Mexico, *Publications in History, Vol. XV* (1954), p. 63.

32. Petition of Residents of El Paso, April 13, 1780, Spanish Archives of New Mexico, State Records Center and Archives, Santa Fé. (Spanish Archives of New Mexico hereinafter cited as SANM).

33. Domínguez, *The Missions of New Mexico*, p. 151.

34. The designation of "pueblo" for a Spanish community was usually avoided in New Mexico since the village Indians from a very early time were called Pueblos. The term "rancho" should be translated as small farm rather than ranch. For a definition of this word as it was used in colonial New Spain see Roberto Mac-Lean y Estenós, Indios de América (Mexico, 1962), pp. 79-80.

35. Kelley, "Settlement of the Middle Rio Grande Valley," *The Journal of Geography*, Vol. LIV (1955), p. 394.

36. E. Boyd, "Troubles at Ojo Caliente, A Frontier Post," *El Palacio*, Vol. LXIV (1957), pp. 349, 359.

37. Thomas, "Governor Mendinueta's Proposals," New Mexico Historical Review, Vol. VI (1931), p. 33.

38. *Ibid,* p. 27.

39. Robert C. Smith, "Colonial Towns of Spanish and Portuguese America," *Journal of the Society of Architectural Historians*, Vol. XIV (1955), p. 4. It is

curious to note that early documents and maps occasionally designate the capital of New Mexico as "Santa Fé de la Granada."

40. Petition, April 13, 1780, SANM

41. Bainbridge Bunting and John P. Conron, "The Architecture of Northern New Mexico," *New Mexico Architecture*, Vol. VIII (1966), p. 16. There existed abundant precedent in New Spain for this type of community. For example, an early plan called for a casa-muro, or wall of houses, to be built in Mexico City soon after the conquest. George Kubler, *Mexican Architecture of the Sixteenth Century* (2 vols., New Haven, 1948), Vol. I, p. 78. Also, fortified towns had been common on the Chichimec frontier. Philip Wayne Powell, *Soldiers, Indians and Silver* (Berkeley, 1952), pp. 153-55.

42. Hugh and Evelyn Burnet, "Madrid Plaza," *Colorado Magazine*, Vol. XLII (1965), p. 224. This article includes the sketch of a "restricted plaza" of the nineteenth century.

43. For a description of the casa grande of Pablo de Villapando near Taos, see the legend on the Miera y Pacheco map, translated by Adams and Chávez in Domínguez, *Missions of New Mexico*, p. 4.

44. A. W. Conway, "Southwestern Colonial Farms," *Landscape, Human Geography of the Southwest*, Vol. I (1961), p. 6. According to the author, the casa corral unit was distributed throughout the Southwest and the north Mexican provinces.

45. Nuttall, "Royal Ordinances Concerning the Laying Out of New Towns, *Hispanic American Historical Review*, Vol. V (1922), p. 252.

46. Boyd, "Troubles at Ojo Caliente,"' *El Palacio*, Vol. LXIV (1957), passim. Regarding a petition of Chamita settlers to leave their residences, and a refusal of permission by Governor Vélez Cachupín see Ralph Emerson Twitchell, *The Leading Facts of New Mexican History* (2 vols.; Albuquerque, 1963), Vol. II, p. 317n.

47. Salcedo to Chacón, Chihuahua, January 11, 1805, SANM.

48. Fred Wendorf, "Some Distributions of Settlement Patterns in the Pueblo Southwest," in Gordon R. Willey (ed.), *Pre-historic Settlement Patterns in the New World*, Viking Fund Publications in Anthropology, No. 23 (New York, 1956), pp. 21-22.

49. Bancroft, *History of Arizona and New Mexico*, p. 259.

50. Myra Ellen Jenkins, "Taos Pueblo and Its Neighbors, 1540-1847," New Mexico Historical Review, Vol. XLI (1966), pp. 98-99.

51. Domínguez, *The Missions of New Mexico*, p. 110.

52. Declaration of Fr. Miguel de Menchero, Santa Bárbara, May 10, 1744, in Hackett, *Historical Documents*, Vol.III, pp. 401-2.

53. "Ynstrucción a Peralta," *New Mexico Historical Review*, Vol. IV (1929), p. 184.

54. Alfred B. Thomas (ed. and trans.), "Antonio de Bonilla and Spanish Plans for the Defense of New Mexico, 1777-1778," in *New Spain and the West* (2 vols.; Lancaster, Pa., 1932), Vol. I, p. 196.

55. Cleve Hallenbeck, *Land of the Conquistadores* (Caldwell, Idaho, 1950), p. 243.

56. Fr. Juan Agustín de Morfi, Desórdenes que se advierten en el Nuevo México, AGN. Historia, 25.

57. Thomas, "Governor Mendinueta's Proposals," *New Mexico Historical Review*, Vol. VI (1931), p. 29.

58. Luis Navarro Garcia, *Don José Gálvez y la comandancia general de las Provincias Internas del Norte de Nueva España* (Seville, 1964), p. 244; and Thomas, "Bonilla and Spanish Plans for the Defense of New Mexico," *New Spain and the West*, Vol. I, p. 201.

59. Concha to Ugarte, Santa Fe, June 20, 1788, AGN, Prov. Int., 161.

60. Ibid.; and Alfred B. Thomas, *Forgotten Frontiers: A Study of the Spanish-Indian Policy of Don Juan Bautista de Anza* (Norman, 1932), pp. 94; 101.

61. Concha to Ugarte, Santa Fe, June 20, 1788, AGN, Prov. *Int.*, 161.

62. Wendorf, "*Some Distributions of Settlement Patterns*," in Willey (ed.), *Prehistoric Settlement Patterns*, p. 22.

Beginning in the late seventeenth century, and led by Fray Eusebio Kino, Spanish colonial administration advanced into the northern regions and started a new century of expansion. Pimería Alta, portions of modern-day Arizona, Sonora and Baja California, presented unique challenges to Spanish colonial officials. Its harsh desert environment discouraged settlers. Only the most hardy settlers accepted the challenge. Resilient and resistant natives also contributed to the slow growth and relative underdevelopment of the region. Thomas E. Sheridan discusses how the regions were shaped by the intermingling of Indian and European elements during the eighteenth and nineteenth centuries of expansion and settlement. Emerging out of this past would be a multi-faceted frontier culture of subsistence farming, small ranching and an ethnically diverse population.

The Arrival of the Europeans
Thomas E. Sheridan

Before they learned to read and write in government schools, Akimel O'odham (River People, or Pima Indians) living along the Gila River recorded their history by carving notched symbols into the soft wood of willow or the ribs of the giant saguaro. Caressing these mnemonic marks, Piman keepers of the sticks would then "tell" the events of the past. The narratives do not march to the same rhythm as Western histories. There are no "great men," no prime movers, no sweeping sense of historical progress. Instead, isolated occurrences are simply described--a battle, a harvest, a strange plague.

Nevertheless, certain trends emerge from those terse recitations--trends that resonate with the fatalistic power of global forces glimpsed only at the local level. The earliest of the surviving calendar sticks begins in 1833, the year of a great meteor shower. Nearly seventy years later, when a tubercular anthropologist named Frank Russell wrote down the stick's telling, the only entry for 1901 and 1902 was the opening of a day school in a nearby Maricopa Indian village. In between, there are stories about Apache attacks and epidemics, battles with the Mohave and Quechan Indians of the Colorado River, and the arrival of telegraph lines and railroads. Seven decades of Arizona history are refracted through the lenses of people who began the century as proud and independent farmers, and who ended it as impoverished wards of the state. The notches on the calendar sticks are therefore both epigrams and elegies. The world they describe was already in the process of being transformed when the records begin. By the time the sticks were entombed in a museum collection, the world was gone..

Between the Conquests

The Columbian Exchange in Arizona

It was a world perched on the periphery of a periphery, a frontier between the colonial expansion of Europe and the last defiant stand of native North America. Even though they had never been conquered or missionized, the Akimel O'odham had been drawn into the European orbit. In 1837-38, for example, the oldest Pima calendar stick recorded the following incident:

> One cold night in the spring a Pima at Rso'tuk was irrigating his wheat field by moonlight. Without thought of enemies he built a fire to warm himself. This the Apaches saw and came about him in the thicket. Hearing the twigs cracking under their feet, he ran to the village and gave the alarm. The Pimas gathered in sufficient numbers to surround the Apaches, who attempted to reach the hills on their horses. Two horses stumbled into a gully and their riders were killed before they could extricate themselves. The others were followed and all killed.

There is no mention of white men in this short narrative. But the reasons the Pimas and Apaches were fighting, and the very way they fought, demonstrate how thoroughly the worlds of both had been transformed by what historian Alfred Crosby calls the Columbian Exchange. Take, for example, Apache methods of transportation. In 1541 the expedition of Francisco Vázquez de Coronado ventured onto the western fringes of the Great Plains after wintering among the Pueblo Indians of northern New Mexico. There Coronado and his men encountered Native Americans they called Querechos. The Querechos may have been Athapaskan-speaking ancestors of the Apaches, but they traveled on foot, their belongings pulled by dog train, as they pursued the great herds of bison across the plains. The daring Indian horsemen who struck terror into European settlers from Canada to northern Mexico were creations of the conquest. Like the Apaches who raided the Pimas, they did not exist until Indians learned how to steal or break wild Spanish horses.

And what of the lone Pima irrigating his wheat field that cold spring night? Neither he nor his Apache assailants had ever lived in a mission or paid homage to a Spanish king. Yet the very crop he cultivated came from seed introduced by missionaries like Padre Eusebio Francisco Kino in the seventeenth and eighteenth centuries. Prior to the arrival of the Europeans, the major Pima food crops had been corn, beans, and squash. Those cultigens could only be grown during spring and summer months when frosts were not a danger. Wheat, on the other hand, could be sown in December and harvested in June, enabling the Pimas to farm year-round. That allowed them to live in larger, more permanent settlements--a crucial defensive measure against their Indian enemies. Both the Pimas and the Apaches saw their lives transformed by Old World animals and Old World plants.

Those material changes were more important than the exploits of individual European military or religious leaders. The explorations of *conquistadores* like Coronado may capture our imaginations, but in terms of their historical impact, they were little more than ripples on the surface of a deep, dark lake. The events that truly revolutionized human society in Arizona took place quietly, without notice: the exchange of seeds, the theft of a horse herd, the introduction of an iron plow. Those were the acts that changed people's lives, even people who never lived under the flags of Mexico or Spain.

One of the most devastating consequences of European contact occurred unintentionally at the microbial level. When Columbus crossed the Atlantic in 1492, the peoples of North and South America had been biologically isolated for at least 10,000 years. Melting ice sheets and rising oceans had severed them from their Eurasian kinsmen, so they never participated in the genetic changes taking place in the Old World.

Perhaps the most important of these changes was the development of partial immunity against so-called childhood diseases, such as smallpox, measles, and influenza. Many of the plagues that swept across Europe, Asia, and Africa originated among animals, especially those that lived in herds. Old World peoples had grown up with horses, sheep, goats, and cattle for hundreds of generations. They had been infected by, and had developed relatively successful adaptations to, many of the microbes that spread from animals to humans and back again in an exchange that produced smallpox and cowpox; measles, distemper, and rinderpest; and the constantly mutating strains of influenza.

The people of the New World were not so resistant. The few animals they had domesticated--dogs and turkeys in North America, guinea pigs and llamas on the southern continent--did not host the sort of viruses that could ravage human populations. Consequently, epidemic disease was relatively unknown in the Americas before the Europeans arrived.

Once Eurasian epidemics arrived, however, they breached the genetic insularity of the New World with terrifying rapidity. Smallpox first broke out in the Caribbean in 1518. Two years later it spread to Mexico, where it pustulated into a great pandemic, sapping the strength of the Aztec and Tarascan empires and weakening the

Incas nearly a decade before Pizarro and his men ever reached Andean South America. The results were catastrophic: drastic population decline and the disintegration of many Indian societies. Indian populations declined by 66 to 95 percent during the sixteenth, seventeenth, and eighteenth centuries.

We may never know when the first wave of disease spread across Arizona. Because no Europeans lived among the Indians of Arizona for most of the sixteenth and seventeenth centuries, the documentary record remains largely mute. Nevertheless, Old World diseases like smallpox, measles, and influenza must have taken their toll. A few anthropologists even speculate that the collapse of supposedly pre-Hispanic civilizations like the Hohokam may have been caused, at least in part, by such epidemics. Most archaeologists contend that the Hohokam were gone by A.D. 1450, but Hohokam chronologies are notoriously imprecise. It is conceivable that some communities survived into the sixteenth century only to wither under pestilential winds.

The Early Spanish Entradas

Unfortunately the records left by Spanish explorers shed little light on the controversy. The narratives are vague, contradictory, and full of gaps. Fading memories, a faulty knowledge of geography, and a desire to tell superiors what they wanted to hear often worked against their historical reliability. And yet these early narratives have their own strengths and fascination. During the sixteenth century, tiny bands of conquistadores from the Iberian Peninsula toppled empires and spanned the globe. It was an explosion of conquest and exploration unparalleled in the history of the world, and it flashed across Arizona, creating legends that enticed other Europeans and Euro-Americans for generations to come.

The first visitors from the Old World may have been Alvar Núñez Cabeza de Vaca and his three companions, including a North African named Estevan. Shipwrecked off the Gulf coast of what is now Texas in 1528, the *náufragos* (shipwrecked ones) survived as slaves and shamans before trekking across half a continent. Some scholars believe they crossed Texas into New Mexico, perhaps nicking the southeastern corner of Arizona before turning south into Sonora. Others argue that they followed a more southerly route across Coahuila and Chihuahua. Regardless of where they went, however, Cabeza de Vaca and his comrades heard stories of Indian kingdoms to the north "where there were towns of great population and great houses." When they finally ran into a Spanish slaving party north of

Culiacán, Sinaloa, eight years later, they and their tales reached Mexico City. Those stories launched the first documented penetrations of Arizona.

Fray Marcos de Niza led the initial expedition. Because Viceroy Antonio de Mendoza wanted to find his own Tenochtitlán while keeping rival Hernán Cortés at bay, the Franciscan and his guide, Estevan, slipped quietly out of Mexico City and up the west coast of New Spain. As adventurous as the friar was cautious, Estevan plunged on ahead, traveling as far north as the Zuni pueblos. But the luck that had won him fame as a curer in Texas ran out among the Zunis, who pierced him with arrows. No one knows what Estevan saw or learned before he died.

Fray Marcos was more fortunate, but he may not have had as much to tell. The Franciscan claimed to have followed in Estevan's footsteps until he came to a hill across from the Zuni pueblo of Cíbola, which he described as "larger than the city of Mexico." A number of researchers, however, question whether he left Sonora at all. They agree with Coronado, who called Fray Marcos a liar.

Regardless of his veracity, the Franciscan's glowing description of Cíbola--just one of seven cities that he called "the greatest and best" of all Spanish discoveries in the New World--triggered the *entrada* of Francisco Vázquez de Coronado in 1540. Governor of Nueva Galicia in western Mexico, Coronado led more than 300 Spaniards, including at least three women, and more than a thousand Indians on a bold, well-organized venture that took them from southern Nayarit to central Kansas. And the excursions of his lieutenants extended Coronado's own travels. Melchor Díaz crossed the Colorado River into California. Pedro de Tovar fought a pitched battle with the Hopi Indians. García López de Cárdenas became the first European to see the Grand Canyon. Hernando de Alarcón sailed up the Gulf of California and navigated the shoals of the lower Colorado. Together or in small groups, Coronado's party made the first systematic European exploration of the Southwest.

Apparently Arizona did not fire their imaginations. With the exception of Alarcón, who quizzed the Yuman-speaking Indians along the Colorado about their methods of curing, their sexual practices, and their chronic warfare with one another, most members of the Coronado expedition showed little interest in the Native Americans there. It is also difficult to reconstruct their route through the state. Historian Herbert Eugene Bolton and geographer Carl Sauer believed that they ascended the San Pedro River, but Charles DiPeso argued that they crossed into Arizona near the modern town of Douglas. With no archaeological evidence to corroborate Coronado's passage through Arizona, the documentary evidence is like pieces of a puzzle without a frame.

Between the Conquests

What we do know is this: Coronado's failure to find great cities of gold and silver put an end to Spanish designs on the region for the next forty years. No other Europeans entered Arizona until the 1580s, and then they came from New Mexico, not Sonora. The fantasy of Cíbola could not compare with the fortunes being made in Zacatecas, Guanajuato, and San Luis Potosi. Because of those great silver strikes, Mexico's bonanza lay forever to the south.

Yet Spanish interest in Arizona still flickered. In 1583, Antonio de Espejo led nine soldiers and more than a hundred Zunis on a search for precious metals through the north central part of the state. Espejo traded with the Hopis and claimed their territory for Philip II of Spain. He also discovered silver and copper deposits in the vicinity of Jerome, east of Prescott. Both actions rekindled Spanish curiosity about Arizona, but neither resulted in a permanent Spanish presence here.

An expedition of more far-reaching consequences was Juan de Oñate's colonization of northern New Mexico in 1598. Oñate and his large party of men, women, and livestock left the mining communities of southern Chihuahua in late January of that year. By November the Spaniards were in Hopi country chasing after Espejo's ore. But a bitter northern Arizona winter drove them back to the Zuni pueblos and eventually to the Rio Grande. Oñate therefore commissioned one of his captains-- Marcos Farfán de los Godos--to search for the minerals instead.

Farfán and eight companions, along with some Hopi guides, rode southwest across the Little Colorado into the timbered country of the Mogollon Rim. There he and his party encountered Jumana Indians, who may have been Yuman-speaking Yavapais. The Jumanas daubed themselves with minerals of various colors, wore skins of deer and beaver, and lived on a diet of venison, wild plant foods, and maize. A stark contrast to the sedentary Hopis, with their multistoried pueblos and their abundant fields, the Jumanas led Fárfan to the valley of the Verde River.

The Verde enchanted Farfán, who waxed eloquent about its "splendid pastures, fine plains, and excellent land for farming." The river also passed within a few miles of the mineral deposits discovered by Espejo, which were being mined by the Indians themselves. Farfán wrote, "These veins are so long and wide that one-half of the people in New Spain could stake out claims in this land." His description made the Verde Valley sound like an Eden where Spaniards could find two of the things--water and silver--that they loved most. The legend of Arizona's fabulous mineral wealth was being born.

The Athapaskans

Despite Farfán's paean, the Verde Valley never became a part of the Spanish empire. Like the rest of Arizona north of the Gila River, it remained in the hands of Native Americans for the next three hundred years. By 1600, however, the Spaniards had encountered most of the Indians--Pais, River Yumans, and Hopis--who emerge more clearly in later historical records. But none of the early explorers recorded any contacts with two of Arizona's largest and most famous Native American peoples-- the Athapaskan-speaking Navajos and Apaches--at least not on Arizona soil. To Coronado, in fact, much of what later became the Apachería (Apache territory) was rugged *despoblado*--an unpopulated terrain of pine forests and rushing rivers the Spaniards were only too happy to leave.

It is possible that the ancestors of the Apaches and Navajos simply stayed out of the Spaniards' way. Coronado crossed paths with the Apachean Querechos in northeastern New Mexico, and Espejo fought people who were probably Athapaskans in northwestern New Mexico. But Apaches apparently did not move south of the Little Colorado until the 1600s. Like the Spaniards, the Athapaskans were relative latecomers to the Southwest.

They were also consummate opportunists. Linguists have shown that all Navajo and Apache groups spoke dialects of a single language, one related to those spoken by Athapaskan hunters and gatherers in northern Canada. In other words, the people who later became the Navajos and Chiricahua, Jicarilla, Lipan, Mescalero, Kiowa, and Western Apaches migrated south along the western edge of the Great Plains at about the same time. Trains of coyote- and wolf-sized dogs carried their belongings. Bison provided them with meat and hides. Because of their dependence on the huge "cows" of the prairie, Oñate dubbed them the "Vaquero Apache."

Once they reached the Southwest, however, the Athapaskans diverged as they absorbed many of the traits of their neighbors. Some groups established strong trading relationships with the Pueblo peoples, exchanging salt, bison hides, and deer skins for cotton blankets and agricultural produce. They also began farming in well-watered locations throughout the Four Corners area, including Arizona. By the 1630s, Spaniards in New Mexico were referring to them as Apaches de Nabajú.

Pueblo influences only deepened after the 1680 Pueblo Revolt, which temporarily drove the Spaniards out of northern New Mexico. When the Spaniards reconquered the area in 1694, many rebels took refuge among the Apaches de Nabajú, teaching them how to make pottery, weave close-coiled baskets, and perform complex ceremonies, and inspiring them to organize themselves into matrilineal clans. Puebloan and Athapaskan elements fused to create a new system of action and belief that became Navajo culture.

The Navajos also took much of value from the Spaniards, particularly a thorough knowledge of domestic animals. Horses enabled them to raid their neighbors. Sheep and goats allowed them to fan out across the mesa and canyon country of the Colorado Plateau. By the end of the eighteenth century, they were even carrying on a brisk trade in woolen blankets with Spanish communities in New Mexico. Hunters and gatherers by origin, the Navajos quickly transformed themselves into the greatest Indian pastoralists in North America.

Contact with the Pueblo peoples and the Spaniards revolutionized Apache society as well. During the seventeenth century, small Apache groups continued their southward migrations. As bands splintered and drifted away from one another, cultural and linguistic differences developed. The Western Apaches, who settled in the White Mountains, adopted matrilineal clans and ceremonial masked dancers from their Pueblo neighbors. The Chiricahua Apaches, on the other hand, never organized themselves into clans, indicating that their relations with the Pueblo Indians were more tenuous.

But the Chiricahuas did ally themselves with small groups of Uto-Aztecan hunters and gatherers in southeastern Arizona and northern Mexico known as the Sumas, Mansos, Janos, and Jocomes. When the Spaniards appeared, these groups and the Apache newcomers joined together to raid Spanish herds. The Sumas and Mansos died out or were absorbed into Apache society, but the Chiricahuas prospered. They became the specters that rode through Hispanic nightmares for the next two hundred years.

The Missionization of the Pimería Alta

By the late 1600s, the Apaches and their allies had begun preying upon the Piman communities of southern Arizona. In March 1699, the Jesuit missionary Eusebio Francisco Kino and Juan Mateo Manje, the second-highest civil official in Sonora, visited O'odham settlements in the Tucson Basin. Manje reported that O'odham along the San Pedro River had "just finished devastating a ranchería of Apaches, capturing some children and other booty.   This was in response to an Apache attack on the pueblo of Santa María three weeks earlier, when the enemies ran off the few horses the community had. The people of Humari [a Pima chief] had gone forth to avenge that raid, just as these Pimans would do now."

Earlier, the Spaniards had tried to bring the Hopis into their sphere of influence. In 1629 the Franciscans founded a mission at Awatovi, followed by additional missions at Shongopovi and Oraibi. But the Hopis soon began to resist the gray-robed friars in a variety of ways, poisoning one of the first missionaries and protesting the abuses of others. When the Pueblo Revolt broke out, the Hopis swiftly dispatched the four Franciscans living among them. Then, in 1700, to make sure the missionaries never regained a foothold in their territory they destroyed the Christian village of Awatovi and killed its men. Both the Franciscans and the Jesuits made sporadic attempts to return to the Hopi mesas, but their attempts failed.

As a result, the Sonoran Desert rather than the Colorado Plateau became the focus of missionary activity in Arizona for the rest of the colonial period. Missionaries and Spanish officials alike dreamed of extending the empire to the Gila River, to Hopi country and beyond, but Apache resistance halted the Spanish advance in what came to be called the Pimería Alta.

Even there the European presence was precarious. Beginning in 1687, Kino and his colleagues established missions among O'odham living in the river valleys of northern Sonora. Some of the new converts rebelled in 1695, but the missions weathered that storm and Kino pushed onward. He explored Tohono O'odham (Papago) country as far west as the Colorado River, visited the Sobaipuri Pimas along the Santa Cruz and San Pedro, and traveled as far north as the Salt River Valley, where he preached to the Gileños, as the Akimel O'odham living along the Salt and Gila rivers were called. Nearly everywhere he and his companions went, the O'odham welcomed them with food, arches made of branches, and simple wooden crosses. The tall Jesuit was as charismatic as he was energetic, and the Pimas responded to his warmth and his drive.

They also appreciated the material gifts he gave them: grain seeds, vegetables, fruit trees, and small herds of livestock. Kino and his fellow missionaries knew that in order to convert the Indians, they had to change the way they lived as well. The foundation of their efforts therefore became the policy of *reducción*, which involved "reducing" the Indians to village life, in which they could be catechized and controlled. The O'odham moved to gathering camps each year to harvest mesquite pods, cholla buds, saguaro fruit, and other wild foods. It was part of their seasonal round, but the Jesuits feared such movement because they believed that the Indians reverted to their "pagan" habits away from mission discipline.

Between the Conquests

In northern Sonora, most Pimas accepted, or were forced to accept, Spanish ideas about the way civilized people should live. In Arizona, on the other hand, missionization proceeded more slowly Kino founded missions San Xavier and San Miguel at the Piman communities of Bac and Guevavi along the Santa Cruz, but the Jesuits soon abandoned those northern outposts. They were not restaffed until 1732, twenty-one years after Kino died.

The rest of Pimería Alta never came under Spanish control. Nonetheless, both the Sobaipuris along the San Pedro River and the Gileños along the Gila became staunch allies of the Spaniards, fighting the Apaches and trading with the communities of Tucson and Tubac. In the words of historian Kieran McCarty, the Pimas served as "the perennial listening post during both the Spanish and Mexican periods for situations developing beyond the frontier." Without the O'odham allies, Hispanic Arizona would not have survived.

The Beginnings of Hispanic Arizona

Spaniards did not establish towns for themselves in southern Arizona until the second half of the eighteenth century. By the late 1600s, however, a few settlers were grazing their stock on the lush grasslands drained by the headwaters of the Santa Cruz. Ten years before Kino and Manje explored the Pimería Alta, José Romo de Vivar was running cattle at the southern end of the Huachuca Mountains. A prominent Sonoran rancher and miner, he may have been southern Arizona's first Hispanic pioneer.

More colonists trickled into the region after the Jesuits reestablished the missions of Bac and Guevavi in 1732. But the most important impetus to Spanish settlement was the discovery of large chunks *(bolas)* and slabs *(planchas)* of silver lying on the ground near a mining camp called Arizonac, which was located in Sonora a few miles southwest of modern Nogales. The name may have come from two Piman words, *ali* and *shonak,* which mean "small springs." Or prominent Basques in the area, including Juan Bautista de Anza the Elder, father of the founder of Alta California, may have called the camp "valuable rocky places" *(arritza onac)* or "good oaks" *(aritz onac).* Whatever its linguistic origin, the designation bequeathed both its name and its legend to the territory that took shape to the north more than a century later.

The discovery of the silver itself was made by a Yaqui Indian in 1736. Prospectors streamed into the region, creating Arizona's first mining boom. But Anza decided that the silver was buried treasure, not a natural deposit. He did so to defend the interests of his king, who was entitled to half of any treasure but only a fifth of the proceeds from any mine. Because Anza commanded the *presidio* (garrison) of Fronteras and also served as *justicia mayor*, or chief justice, of Sonora, his authority carried great weight. Disappointed miners soon left for other bonanzas, and Arizona sank back into obscurity. But the name and the images it conjured wormed their way into the lore of the time, tantalizing prospectors with the promise of veins so rich you could pick up the silver with your bare hands. Like Espejo's ore, that lure became part of Arizona's myth. The dream of lost Spanish mines even danced in the heads of the railroad speculators who pressured President James Buchanan to buy southern Arizona from Mexico in the early 1850s.

By its very nature, however, prospecting was a nomadic and evanescent occupation. Most of the pioneers who remained in Arizona made their living as subsistence farmers and small ranchers, not miners. These were the families that cleared the fields, built up the herds, and constructed homes for themselves along the Santa Cruz and its tributaries. The mission registers of Guevavi recorded their names--Ortega, Bohórquez, Gallego, Covarrubias. They also chronicled the ceremonies that marked the end of one generation and the beginning of another.

The generations faced extinction on several occasions. The first was in 1751, when O'odham led by Luis Oacpicagigua rebelled against the harsh discipline of several Jesuit missionaries. Luis and his followers killed two priests and more than a hundred Spanish settlers before the revolt dissipated and Luis surrendered to the Spaniards at the Pima community of Tubac along the Santa Cruz River. To prevent future uprisings among the O'odham, the Spanish Crown established a new *presidio* (garrison of professional soldiers) at Tubac in 1752. It was the first permanent Spanish settlement in Arizona and the northernmost military outpost of Spanish Sonora.

Like most frontier communities, Tubac was an ethnic melting pot, its population composed not just of Spaniards but also of *coyotes* (Spanish-Indian offspring), mulattos (Spanish-black offspring), *moriscos* (Spanish-mulatto offspring), and Indians from various tribal groups. The captains of the presidios may have been peninsular Spaniards or *criollos* (Spaniards born in the New World). Most *gente de razón* ("people of reason"; non-Indians), in contrast, were products of that fusion of the European, Indian, and African that made colonial Mexico such a vital and fluid society during the Spanish colonial period.

For the next century these Hispanic pioneers fought a grueling battle for survival along the Santa Cruz River. The dream of northward expansion still flickered. In

Between the Conquests

1775, Juan Bautista de Anza led a group of Spanish colonists from Tubac to San Francisco Bay. The Spaniards tried to secure that route five years later by settling along the lower Colorado, but the Yuman-speaking Quechan Indians soon grew tired of Spanish livestock trampling their fields and Franciscan missionaries telling them how to live. Veterans of countless battles against their Cocopa, Maricopa, and O'odham enemies, the Quechans bided their time until the morning of July 17, 1781. Then, in the heat of a desert summer, they surprised the Spaniards during mass and slaughtered them, including the Franciscan missionary Francisco Garcés. According to historian David Weber, the Yuma revolt turned California into an "island" and Arizona into a "cul de sac," severing the Arizona-California connection before it could be firmly established. José de Zúñiga, captain of the Tucson presidio, blazed a trail between Tucson and the Zuni pueblos in 1795, but Apache hostilities prevented that route from becoming well traveled. In the Southwest, Hispanic pioneers moved north-south, not east-west, sealing the isolation of the northwestern provinces.

The Apachería

The failure to open those routes left Arizona exposed and beleaguered on the edge of a twisted upthrust of mountain ranges and river gorges known as the Apachería. The region was both a homeland and refuge for the Apaches, to whom livestock raiding became as important as gathering agave or harvesting corn. The Apaches even referred to the people of northern Mexico as their "shepherds"--their arrogance the arrogance of all mounted warriors, whether Scythian, Mongol, or Comanche, who had been preying on farmers and pastoralists since plants and animals were first domesticated in the neolithic Near East.

Because of their bloodthirsty reputation, however, no other Native American group has been as misrepresented or misunderstood. Raiding--to search out enemy property in the language of the Western Apaches--was an economic activity, one usually carried out by five to fifteen men. Raids were designed to run off livestock, not to shed the blood of the stock raisers themselves. War, on the other hand, meant "to take death from an enemy," and Apaches waged it to seek revenge for the murder of a kinsman. Blood vengeance was a common theme in Native American cultures across North America. It set the Hurons against the Iroquois Confederacy in the Northeast and the Quechans and Mohaves against the Maricopas and Gila Pimas in the Southwest. It was also one of the few cultural mechanisms that united large numbers of Apaches in a common cause.

The differences between raiding and warfare shed considerable light on the structure of Apache society itself. Like most other Indian groups, kinship was the fundamental principle of Apache culture. There were no hereditary kings or priests, no formal councils of government. In contrast to the Spaniards, the Apaches did not think of themselves as a nation or an empire. On the contrary, the Apaches, like their O'odham enemies, resided in small local groups that were essentially independent of one another. Composed of people related by either blood or marriage, local groups controlled their own farming sites and hunting territories. They also chose their own chiefs, a political reality few Europeans understood. The Apaches recognized larger groupings among themselves, but those entities were more linguistic and geographic than political. Local groups carried out nearly all the important activities of Apache life, including raids.

Warfare, in contrast, transcended the local group. Apaches were matrilineal, meaning they traced their family lines through women. The Western Apaches also organized their matrilineages into clans, an extension of kinship that cut across the boundaries of local groups and bands. According to legend, each clan descended from women who had cleared land for cultivation in a certain area. Clan members could not marry each other, because they were relatives. For the same reason, they were obliged to avenge a clan member's murder. Consequently, many large-scale Apache attacks were organized for the purpose of blood revenge.

The fluidity of Apache society confounded the Spaniards, who had spent seven centuries forging a national identity during the Reconquista (the reconquering of the Iberian Peninsula from Islamic invaders). Like most people, the Iberians interpreted the actions of others through the lens of their own customs and beliefs. Hierarchical and bureaucratic, they attempted to impose hierarchy on the Native Americans they encountered. But the Apaches slipped through Spanish preconceptions as easily as they penetrated the Spanish line of presidios along the frontier. Treaties made with the chief of one local group were not binding on any other group, not to mention the Apaches as a whole. The Apaches broke apart and came together again in patterns of alliance that defied the comprehension of their Spanish adversaries. The Iberians may have considered themselves Basques, Andalusians, or Castilians, but they also swore allegiance to both Majesties--the Spanish Crown and the Roman Catholic Church-- whose authorities were absolute in temporal and spiritual affairs.

Apache autonomy ultimately proved to be a fatal weakness. Clan affiliations only partially counterbalanced intense loyalty to the local group. The stable pattern was raiding, not warfare. The various Apache bands never forged a common identity strong enough to drive the Spaniards, Mexicans, or Anglo Americans out of the Southwest. On the contrary, the Spaniards, and later the Anglo Americans, defeated the Apaches by exploiting divisions among the Indians themselves.

That strategy did not evolve until late in the colonial period, however. Throughout most of the eighteenth century, the Spaniards had to overcome other threats to their northwestern frontier: the Yaqui revolt of 1740, the Pima rebellion of 1751, and the bitter guerrilla warfare of the Seris and Lower Pimas during the 1750s and 1760s. Not until the Seris had been worn down by the largest military campaign in Sonoran colonial history, in fact, were the Spaniards able to turn their full attention to the Apaches. Even then, it took more than twenty years of intense military pressure before the Spaniards and the Apaches achieved a fragile peace.

The Bourbon Reforms

Spanish populated with Missions & helped expansion Military

The first thing the Spaniards did was to realign their presidios. In 1765, Charles III of Spain commissioned the marqués de Rubí to make a sweeping inspection of the northern presidios. Rubí's recommendations resulted in the Reglamento of 1772, a major reorganization of the presidial system carried out by Hugo O'Conor, one of the "Wild Geese" who fled English-occupied Ireland to fight for the Catholic kings of Spain. O'Conor transferred the presidio of Terrenate north to the west bank of the San Pedro in 1776. It survived for less than five years before the garrison limped back to Sonora, decimated by Apache attacks. O'Conor was more successful in 1775 when he relocated the presidio of Tubac forty miles to the north. There, at the new site of San Agustín de Tucson, the soldiers were closer to the Western Apaches, enabling them to mount offensive campaigns into Apache territory more easily. They also had good wood and water and the comforting presence of several nearby O'odham communities. Tucsonenses (Hispanic residents of Tucson) and Pimas fought Apaches together for the next hundred years.

But presidial realignments were only part of much broader shifts in Spanish policy that were known as the Bourbon Reforms (because they took place under the Bourbon kings of Spain). In 1776, Carlos III placed the *provincias internas* (the "interior" or northern provinces, including Sonora) under the direct jurisdiction of the Spanish Crown rather than the viceroy in Mexico City. The king then created the office of *comandante general* to streamline the administration of the provincias internas by giving one official broad civil and military powers. The comandante general was supposed to take decisive action against both Indian and European antagonists, including the Russians on the Pacific coast and the British in the Mississippi Valley. Spanish officials feared that the expansion of the Russians and the British might threaten not only the northern provinces but also the rich silver-mining areas of Zacatecas and San Luis Potosí. Militarization replaced missionization as the dominant philosophy of conquest along the frontier.

The expulsion of the Jesuits in 1767 foreshadowed that change. Missionaries from the Society of Jesus first entered northwestern New Spain in the 1590s. Believing that most soldiers and settlers were bad influences on Native Americans, they tried to establish autonomous mission communities where they could isolate and protect their Indian converts. In areas where they were successful, such as the valley of the Río Yaqui and the Pimería Alta, they also dominated Indian land and labor. But as Spanish ranchers and miners settled along the mission frontier, bitter competition for Indian resources broke out between the missionaries and the colonists. The Jesuits won many of the skirmishes with colonial officials, but in 1767 they lost the war.

The Spanish Crown allowed gray-robed Franciscans to replace the Jesuits, but the friars never had a chance to exercise the power their black-robed predecessors had enjoyed. Immediately after the expulsion of the Jesuits, in fact, Spanish officials toyed with the idea of abolishing the missions once and for all. They abandoned that scheme as soon as they realized that the missions were the cheapest and most effective way to control Christianized Indians. Nonetheless, a new order had arisen in northern New Spain, one that reflected a fundamental transformation of European society and the colonies Europe controlled. The world economy was growing more and more capitalistic as medieval privileges crumbled. Consequently, resources such as land and labor became commodities in the marketplace rather than rights and duties locked up in a feudal order. The Jesuit dream of independent missions contradicted the entrepreneurial dream of abundant land and a mobile labor force. With the Jesuits gone and the Franciscans weakened, it became much easier for Spanish settlers to exploit that land and labor for private gain.

Pacification and Expansion

For a time, the new order worked extremely well. Beginning in the 1770s, soldiers from presidios and "flying companies" *(compañias volantes)* scoured the Apachería. At Tucson, Captain Pedro Allande y Saabedra mounted nearly a dozen major forays against the Apaches between 1783 and 1785 alone. Haughty domineering, and wracked by wounds, Allande was a nobleman who had fought everyone from the Portuguese to the Seri Indians during his long career. He capped that career in Tucson by impaling the heads of his Apache enemies on the palisades of the presidio walls.

Juan Bautista de Anza was an even more successful adversary. As governor of New Mexico during the 1780s, Anza severed an alliance between the Navajos and the Western Apaches. He then employed Navajos as auxiliaries in his campaigns against Apache groups living along the headwaters of the Gila River. Other Spanish commanders formally incorporated Native Americans into the military as well, with Opatas manning the flying company at Bavispe and Pimas serving at the reinstated garrison of Tubac. Indeed, the use of one Indian group to fight another was a very old strategy in northern New Spain, one that dated from the Chichimec wars of the 1500s. But commanders like Anza raised it to an art form, persuading Navajos, Utes, and Comanches to stop fighting the Spaniards and carry the battle to their Apache foes.

Spanish officials did not rely on the sword alone, however. In 1786, Viceroy Bernardo de Gálvez instituted a cynical but effective policy of bribery, instructing his military commanders to offer Apaches who agreed to stop fighting "defective firearms, strong liquor, and such other commodities as would render them militarily and economically dependent on the Spaniards." This Machiavellian approach evolved into a full-fledged rationing system in 1792, when a native of the Canary Islands named Pedro de Nava became comandante general of the provincias internas. Apaches were already living in *establecimientos de paz*, or peace camps, near the garrisons of Janos, Fronteras, Bacoachi, Santa Cruz, and Tucson, but Nava made the peace camps one of the cornerstones of Spanish Apache policy. At the camps the Indians received beeves, flour, brown sugar, and tobacco. With the threat of fire and blood hanging over them, the Spaniards hoped that rations would take the place of raids.

Many Apaches never accepted the Spanish program, but a number of the peace camps were remarkably successful. In 1793, for example, more than a hundred Western Apaches from the Aravaipa band left their territory in the Galiuro Mountains and sued for peace at the Tucson presidio. José Ignacio Moraga, the officer in command, gave chief Nautil Nilché a suit of clothes in honor of the occasion. The Apache leader reciprocated by handing Moraga six pairs of enemy Apache ears. Common currency on the frontier, the grisly trophies symbolized Nautil Nilché's new loyalties. He and his kinsmen and kinswomen settled north of the presidio along the floodplain of the Santa Cruz River, where they formed the nucleus of an Apache

Manso (Tame Apache) community that remained a part of Tucson's frontier population for the next half century.

Because of the success of the Apache peace program, Hispanic Arizona flourished modestly during the last years of Spanish rule. A few adventurous pioneers grew crops, raised stock, or operated small gold and silver mines in outlying areas such as Arivaca and the San Pedro Valley but most Spaniards continued to live along the Santa Cruz. The total non-Indian population hovered around 1,000, with 300 to 500 people at Tucson, 300 to 400 at Tubac, and less than 100 at Tumacacori. The rest of Arizona remained in Native American hands.

Despite their small size, communities like Tucson and Tubac were as tenacious as the mesquite trees that provided most of their shade. Their appearance was not impressive: flat-roofed adobe buildings clustered beside a ragged patchwork of fields. As Tucson's Captain José de Zúñiga noted in an official report to the Real Consulado (Royal Board of Trade) in 1804, "We have no gold, silver, iron, lead, tin, quicksilver, copper mines, or marble quarries." He went on to say, "The only public work here that is truly worthy of this report is the church at San Xavier del Bac." Built by O'odham under the direction of Franciscans between 1779 and 1797, Bac was a baroque glory; Zúñiga dismissed the other missions along the Santa Cruz as mere chapels.

Beneath the dust and manure and sun-baked bricks, however, the roots of Hispanic Arizona spread wide and deep. Spanish frontiersmen were as tough as any pioneers on the North American continent. They knew the desert and they knew the Indians-fighting, sleeping, and dying with Tohono O'odham from the western deserts, Pimas from the San Pedro Valley, Apaches from the eastern mountain ranges, and even Yaquis from southern Sonora and Yumans from the Colorado River. Tucson, Tubac, Guevavi, and other settlements along the Santa Cruz were multi-ethnic communities in every sense of the term.

Nevertheless, divisions of class did exist. Soldiers may have belonged to every racial category under the Spanish sun, but most presidial officers were full-blooded Spaniards or their descendants. As anthropologist James Officer notes, the Elías González, Urrea, Comadurán, Zúñiga, and Pesqueira families belonged to a far-flung elite that linked Hispanic Arizona with Arispe, Altar, Alamos, and other important Sonoran centers of power. Members of this small but proud aristocracy intermarried, formed business partnerships, and helped one another fight for control over Sonora's military and economic affairs. One native Tucsonense, José de Urrea, nearly became president of Mexico itself during the civil wars following independence from Spain.

Most Hispanic residents of Arizona, on the other hand, found their lives circumscribed by river, desert, and the Apaches. Theirs was largely a subsistence economy, one wedded to the floodplain of a shallow intermittent stream. The most important crop was wheat, followed by corn, beans, and squash. The most important animals were cattle and horses, although a herd of 5,000 sheep at Tubac produced enough wool for 600 blankets in 1804. During times of relative peace, farming and ranching expanded along the Santa Cruz and spilled over into other watersheds. But whenever Apache raiding intensified, herds dwindled, fields were abandoned, and families took refuge behind presidio walls.

It was a harsh, hard scrabble way of life, one that swung like a pendulum between flood and drought, peace and war. Nonetheless, it endured. The people of Hispanic Arizona may not have been able to extend the empire, but they held on to their little piece of it in the face of great odds. Like rawhide, the sinews of their culture bound them together and bound them to the land.

Those sinews were to be strained to the limit in the years to come.

In response to Russian encroachments in the region, formal Spanish control of Alta California began with a four-pronged strategy. Two expeditions moved north by sea, two by land. Junípero Serra, Gaspar de Portolá, Fernando Rivera y Moncada and Fray Juan Crespi led several hundred colonizers into Alta California in 1769 to begin pacification of the natives through the missions and control of the northern frontier for Spanish colonial interests. Andrew Rolle summarizes these earliest Spanish expeditions, as well as the problems encountered along the way and during the first stages of the settlement.

Colonizers of the Frontier

Andrew Rolle

New Spain's northern border eventually extended, in an arc, from in present-day Louisiana to a remote chain of Jesuit missions spread throughout northern Mexico and both Californias. Along this vast frontier were located missions, mining camps, cattle ranches, and crude adobe *presidios,* or forts.

Three Jesuit clerics contributed to colonization of the approaches to California. Foremost of these was Eusebio Francesco Kino, a native of Trento in today's Italy. Father Kino was responsible, in the years 1678-1712, for the founding of missions on New Spain's northern frontiers. By his explorations, Kino proved in 1702 that California was not an island. Aiding him was another Italian Jesuit, the square-jawed, flinty Juan Maria de Salvatierra, who in 1697 founded the first of a chain of missions in Lower California. A third major "blackrobe," a term used by Native Americans to refer to the missionaries, was Father Juan de Ugarte who labored for years among newly converted Indians.

In 1763, after the defeat in North America of France by the British during the Seven Years' War, Spain feared more than ever that England might attempt to extend its New England colonization further west, possibly into Spanish territory. To prepare for such incursions, in 1765 Charles III, one of Europe's enlightened monarchs, appointed José de Gálvez *visitador-general,* or inspector general, of New Spain. In 1768 Gálvez, commissioned to reform colonization procedures, sailed to Lower California on an inspection tour of the peninsula's scraggly frontier missions.

While Gálvez, an avid expansionist, was in Baja California, he was ordered by King Charles to expel the Jesuits from the Spanish colonies. All over Europe there was then distrust of that order's political power. Fearing the Jesuits would eventually control Spain's colonial settlements, the King ordered the Jesuits replaced in distant Baja California. Gray-robed Franciscan friars arrived at La Paz to continue the work begun earlier by Father Kino and his fellow Jesuits. These Franciscan priests would become the key colonizers for Gálvez in Alta California.

Russian encroachments on New Spain from the north--particularly the voyages to the American Northwest by Vitus Bering and Alexei Chirikof in 1741--also disturbed the Spaniards. Furthermore, Russian sea otter-hunting ships were extending their cruises farther southward each year. Gálvez, therefore, felt a pressing need for Spaniards to occupy Alta California, although he personally would never see an outpost in the province.

As Spain's inspector general, Gálvez next arranged a vital four-pronged expedition into Alta California. Two divisions were to go by sea and two by land; if one party should fail, another might succeed. If all went well, the four groups would convene at San Diego before pressing onward to Monterey, so highly praised by Vizcaíno. Religious supervision of the expedition was entrusted to the Franciscan missionaries. The peninsular (Baja) missions contributed to the exploring parties all the horses, mules, dried meat, grain, cornmeal, and dry biscuits they could spare.

Gálvez took great care to select the right cleric to lead the Franciscans into the new land. His choice was Fray Junipero Serra, a fifty-five-year-old priest of great endurance. Selection of Gaspar de Portolá to head the military branch of the expedition was equally shrewd. Serra, a kind of zealot, and Portolá, the dutiful soldier, were to become the first colonizers of Alta California. Serra, a native of the Mediterranean island of Majorca, had first come to America in 1749 to labor among the Indians of the New World. Before he was called to take charge of the missions of both Californias, he served for nine years among the Pamé Indians in the Sierra Gorda mountains of Mexico.

Father Serra repeatedly brushed aside obstacles that would have stopped lesser men, including a lame leg, from which he suffered nearly all his life. When he set out on the 1769 expedition to Upper California, he was in such poor health that two men had to lift him onto the saddle of his mule; but when his friend Fray Francisco Palóu, discouraged by the sight, bade him a regretful farewell, Serra insisted that, with the aid of God, he would successfully reach Alta California.

Serra's military companion, Portolá, had served the king as a captain of dragoons, becoming Baja California's first governor. In addition to occupying San Diego and Monterey, Portolá and Serra hoped to establish five missions. Church ornaments and sacred vessels did not constitute all of Serra's cargo, however; he brought along seeds and implements with which to plant future mission gardens. The two land parties also herded along 200 head of cattle, the descendants of whom would roam the hills and valleys of Alta California, becoming the chief source of the province's pastoral wealth for several generations.

Two tiny vessels, the *San Carlos* and the *San Antonio,* were to form the sea expedition. On January 9, 1769, the *San Carlos* was ready to start at La Paz in Lower California. Added to her crew were 25 Catalan military volunteers, needed, it was felt, to overcome any native resistance encountered after landing. Five weeks later the *San Antonio* left the same port and shook out her billowing sails, likewise moving northward toward San Diego.

By the latter part of March, Captain Fernando Rivera y Moncada, in command of the first land division-his force strengthened by 25 seasoned leather-jacketed soldiers and 42 Christianized natives--was ready to start northward. Rivera was accompanied by Fray Juan Crespi. On March 22, 1769, their small army began to march up the spiny Baja peninsula. They would become the first overland party to reach Alta California. The other land contingent, commanded by Portolá, bronzed and bearded, riding at its head, set out for San Diego on May 15, 1769.

The *San Antonio,* though she had set sail a month later than her sister ship, was the first to arrive at the rendezvous in San Diego, on April 11. When she sailed into port, the natives at first mistook the *San Antonio* for a great whale. On April 29, to the joy of those on the *San Antonio,* the *San Carlos* nosed alongside her and dropped anchor. The 110-day voyage of the *San Carlos* had resulted in such severe scurvy on board that there were no men able to lower a shore boat when it finally arrived. A third ship, the *San José;* had also been dispatched by Gálvez but was lost at sea.

Ashore, tents of sails sheltered the crewmen, many of whom suffered from dysentery. Pedro Prat, who came on the *San Carlos* as surgeon, scoured the shore in search of green herbs with which to heal the sick. Because so many of the men had died, the further voyage to Monterey had to be postponed. All available men were busy caring for the sick. The dead were buried at a place that has since borne the name *La Punta de los Muertos,* or Dead Men's Point.

On May 14, 1769, the gloom was lightened by the appearance of Captain Rivera's land party from Baja California. To assure a better water supply, Rivera moved the entire camp nearer a stream at the foot of today's Presidio Hill. At the end of June his camp was joined by the arrival at San Diego of Portolá's and Serra's second land party.

More than a third of the 300 men who had set out for Alta California, by land and sea, had failed to survive the trip. Half of those still alive vere physically weakened by hunger, dysentery, and scurvy. After the founding of Mission San Diego de Alcala, Portolá left behind a small garrison of soldiers to care for those who were still too ill to travel.

Then, with the least-emaciated soldiers, he pressed on further northward. The 64 members of his expedition included those with surnames later prominent in California history--such as Ortega, Amador, Alvarado, Carrillo, Yorba, and Soberanes. These troops wore leather jackets of thick deerskin and carried bull-hide shields. Lances and broad-swords were among their weapons, as well as short muskets.

Portolá made frequent stops to rest his men and animals. Their route may be traced by the place names which Father Crespi carefully recorded in his daily journal--Santa Margarita, Santa Ana, Carpintería, Gaviota, Cañada de los Osos, Pajaro, and San Lorenzo. Portolá pressed on until he reached the shallow Salinas River.

Nearing Monterey Bay, he stood upon a hill and saw an open *ensenada*, or gulf. But the place he beheld did not seem to fit Vizcaíno's enthusiastic description of "a fine harbor sheltered from all winds". Indeed, Monterey can hardly be described as a well-protected port. Instead, the little company gazed at a long, curving beach. Where was the grand landlocked harbor Vizcaíno had described? Great swells from the ocean rolled in upon sandy beaches without obstruction, and there was no refuge from the wind except in a small shoreline indentation. Thus, for good reason, Portolá failed to recognize the bay of Monterey.

He now concluded that his only hope of finding Monterey or Point Reyes and other Vizcaíno landmarks, was by continuing further northward. Portolá's party, therefore, moved up the coast past today's Santa Cruz. By this point, eleven of his men were so ill that they had to be carried in litters swung between mules. Near Soquel they had their first sight of the "big trees," which Portolá named *palos colorados*, or redwoods, because of the color of their wood. At one stopping place they saw a giant tree of this species, which they called *palo alto* (high tree); the town located there still bears that name.

As Portolá's advance party moved northward, their path was hindered by *arroyos*, or gulches, which had to be bridged. Eventually an advance party reported seeing a "great arm of the sea." This was San Francisco Bay, which the whole group viewed for the first time on November 2, 1769. Astonished by the sight of so magnificent a body of water, the explorers now concluded that Monterey Bay must actually be behind them, for this splendid sight they now beheld must be a different large estuary. For decades ships had bypassed San Francisco Bay. Ironically, it remained for a land expedition to discover the greatest harbor on the Pacific coast.

Around this grand estuary; waterfowl were so abundant and gentle that they could be knocked down with long sticks. After his men had feasted on geese, ducks, and mussels, Portolá decided to return southward to Point Pinos. When his party reached Carmel Bay, they erected a large cross near the seashore, with a letter buried at its base; this missive informed any passing ships that Portolá's expedition had been there first. His men then crossed Cypress Point, and near the area which they still did not recognize as Monterey Bay, they erected another wooden cross. On its arms they carved these words: "The land expedition is returning to San Diego for lack of provisions, today, December 9, 1769."

On January 23, 1770, Portolá and his party returned to their base at San Diego. When they arrived, those who had stayed behind rushed out to greet them. In the years to come, Serra and his fellow Franciscans would develop missions near Portolá's camp sites. At the moment, survival was as stake. As provisions grew short, Portolá sent the *San Antonio* back to San Blas on the Mexican west coast for supplies. As the ship had not yet returned, on February 10, 1770, he ordered Captain Rivera and a small party of the strongest men back into Baja California to seek supplies from its missionaries. As for hunting wild game, scarce ammunition had to be saved for defense against possible native attacks.

Each day the missionaries knelt in prayer for the coming of a supply ship. Finally, on March 19, 1770, the San Diego encampment briefly spotted a sail. But then it disappeared. Four days after being sighted, the *San Antonio* reappeared and finally dropped her anchor. She carried the badly needed supplies.

With the San Diego base more secure, Portolá made a further trip northward by land. This time he finally recognized Monterey Bay, where he established a presidio. On June 3, 1770, Father Serra conducted mass there amid the ringing of bells and salvos of gunfire. Here was founded the second mission in Alta California, dedicated to San Carlos Borroméo. For convenience in obtaining wood and water, the mission was later removed to Carmel, four miles from Monterey. From Carmel, which became Serra's new mission site, he wrote his friend Father Palóu, "If you will come I shall be content to live and die in this spot."

On July 9,1770, Portolá turned his governorship over to Pedro Fages and sailed away on the *San Antonio*, later becoming governor of Puebla in New Spain. Portolá deserves to be remembered not only as the first governor of both Californias (1767-1770), but also as leader of the expedition over the thousand-mile trail from the peninsula that discovered San Francisco Bay. Father Serra, Portolá's trail companion, remained behind to begin a chain of mission establishments in the far-off province.

Selected Readings

The best portrayal of Kino is still Herbert Eugene Bolton's *Rim of Christendom* (1936). See also Rufus Kay Wyllys, *Pioneer Padre: The Life and Times of Eusebio Kino* (1935) and Bolton's *The Padre on Horseback* (1932), as well as Frank C. Lockwood, *With Padre Kino on the Trail* (1934). Kino's astronomical activities are discussed in Ellen Shaffer, "The Comet of 1680-1681," *Historical Society of Southern California Quarterly* 34 (March 1952),57-70. Finally, on Kino, consult Ernest J. Burrus, trans. and ed., *Kino Reports to Headquarters* (1954).

On Salvatierra see Miguel Venegas, Juan María de Salvatierra, translated and edited by Margaret Eyer Wilbur (1929). For other early Jesuit activity in the Southwest, see J. J. Baegert, *Observations in Lower California,* translated and edited by M. M. Brandenburg and Carl L. Baumann (1952); also Peter M. Dunne, *Pioneer Black Robes on the West Coast* (1940) and Dunne's *Pioneer Jesuits in Northern Mexico* (1944), *Early Jesuit Missions of the Tarahumara* (1948), and *Black Robes in Lower California* (1952). See also Theodore E.Treutlein, ed., *Pfeffirkorn's Description of Sonora* (1949).

On Gálvez see Herbert I. Priestley, *Jose de Gálvez, Visitador-General of New Spain* (1916). See also the translation of Father Javier Clavigero's *Storia della California* (1789) in Sara E. Lake and A. A. Gray, *The History of Lower California* (1937).

Regarding the Russian threat to California see Frank A. Golder, *Russian Expansion on the Pacific, 1641-1858* (1914), and Golder's *Bering's Voyages* (2 vols., 1922-25). Good accounts of the first colonization of California are Charles E. Chapman, *The Founding of Spanish California* (1916); Irving Berdine Richman, *California Under Spain and Mexico, 1535-1847* (1911); Douglas S. Watson, *The Spanish Occupation of California* (1934).

Missionary activity has been widely chronicled. *The diario of Fray Francisco Palóu* appears, in translation, in Herbert E. Bolton, ed., *Historical Memoirs of New California* (5 vols., 1926). See also Herbert I. Priestley, ed., *A Historical, Political and Natural Description of California by Pedro Fages* (1937). Lives of Serra include Abigail H. Fitch, *Junípero Serra* (1914); Agnes Repplier, *Junípero Serra: Pioneer Colonist of California* (1933) and Father Zephyrin Engelhardt, *The Missions and Missionaries of California* (4 vols., 1908-15).

The best work on Serra is Maynard J. Geiger's *The Life and Times of Fray Junipero Serra* (2 vols., 1959); see also Geiger, trans. and ed., *Palóu's Life of Fray*

Junipero Serra (1955) and Geiger, "Fray Junipero Serra: Organizer and Administrator of the Upper California Missions, 1769-1784," *California Historical Society Quarterly* 42 (September 1963) 195-220, as well as Geiger, *Franciscan Missionaries of Hispanic California, 1769-1848: A Biographical Dictionary* (1969). For Serra's successor see Francis Guest, *Fermin Francisco de Lausén (1736-1803): A Biography* (1973).

Regarding Portolá, see Robert Selden Rose, ed., *The Portolá Expedition of 1769-1770: Diary of Vicente Vila* (1911); also Costansó, *The Narrative of the Portolá Expedition of 1769-1770*, Frederick J. Teggart ed., (1910); Theodore E. Treutlein, "The Potolá Expedition of 1769-1770," *California Historical Society Quarterly* 47 (December 1968), 291-313; Janet R. Fireman and Manuel P. Servín, "Miguel Costansó: California's Forgotten Founder," *California Historical Society Quarterly* 49 (March 1970), 3-19; and *The Costansó Narrative of the Portolá Expedition* . . . trans. By Ray Brandes (1970).

Spanish claims are in Henry Raup Wagner, "Creation of Rights of Sovereignty Through Symbolic Acts," *Pacific Historical Review* 7 (December 1938), 297-326; Manuel P. Servín, "Symbolic Acts of Sovereignty in Spanish California," *Southern California Quarterly* 45 (June 1963), 109-21; and Servín's "The Instructions of Viceroy Bucareli to Ensign Juan Pérez," *California Historical Society Quarterly* 40 (September 1961), 243-46.

Antonia I. Castañeda's bold and provocative essay uncovers one of the untold stories of the settlement and conquest of Alta California: the sexual outrages committed by some Spanish soldiers on Amerindian women. So shocking was this behavior that some Spanish priests, Junipero Serra for example, sought new legislation which called for severe punishments for acts of sexual violence against native women. He blamed civil and military officials and was instrumental in the passage of the Reglamento Provisional, the first regulatory code drawn up for California. Spanish priests also viewed the attacks as detrimental to the mission program and considered them threatening to the success of the California province itself. Castañeda frames these actions within the context of conquering nations "wherein the sexual violation of women represents both the physical domination of women and the symbolic castration of the men of the conquered groups."

Sexual Violence in the Politics and Policies of Conquest: Amerindian Women and the Spanish Conquest of Alta California

Antonia I. Castañeda

In the morning, six or seven soldiers would set together. . . and go to the distant rancherías *(villages) even many leagues away. When both men and women at the sight of them would take off running . . . the soldiers, adept as they are at lassoing cows and mules, would lasso Indian women--who then became prey for their unbridled lust. Several Indian men who tried to defend the women were shot to death.*

Junipero Serra, 1773

In words reminiscent of sixteenth-century chroniclers Bernal Díaz del Castillo and Bartolomé de las Casas, the father president of the California missions, Junipero Serra, described the depredations of the soldiers against Indian women in his reports and letters to Viceroy Antonio María Bucareli and the father guardian of the College of San Fernando, Rafaél Verger. Sexual assaults against native women began shortly after the founding of the presidio and mission at Monterey in June 1770, wrote Serra, and continued throughout the length of California. The founding of each new mission and presidio brought new reports of sexual violence.

The despicable actions of the soldiers, Serra told Bucareli in 1773, were severely retarding the spiritual and material conquest of California. The native people were resisting missionization. Some were becoming warlike and hostile because of the soldiers' repeated outrages against the women. The assaults resulted in Amerindian

83

attacks, which the soldiers countered with unauthorized reprisals, thereby further straining the capacity of the small military force to staff the presidios and guard the missions. Instead of pacification and order, the soldiers provoked greater conflict and thus jeopardized the position of the church in this region.[1]

Serra was particularly alarmed about occurrences at Mission San Gabriel. "Since the district is the most promising of all the missions," he wrote to Father Verger, "this mission gives me the greatest cause for anxiety; the secular arm down there was guilty of the most heinous crimes, killing the men to take their wives."[2] Father Serra related that on October 10, 1771, within a month of its having been founded, a large group of Indians suddenly attacked two soldiers who were on horseback and tried to kill the one who had outraged a woman. The soldiers retaliated. "A few days later," Serra continued, "as he went out to gather the herd of cattle... and (it) seems more likely to get himself a woman, a soldier, along with some others, killed the principal Chief of the gentiles; they cut off his head and brought it in triumph back to the mission."[3]

The incident prompted the Amerindians of the coast and the sierra, mortal enemies until that time, to convene a council to make peace with each other and join forces to eliminate the Spaniards. The council planned to attack the mission on October 16 but changed the plan after a new contingent of troops arrived at the mission.[4] Despite this narrowly averted disaster, the soldiers assigned to Mission San Gabriel continued their outrages.

The soldiers' behavior not only generated violence on the part of the native people as well as resistance to missionization, argued Serra; it also took its toll on the missionaries, some of whom refused to remain at their mission sites. In his 1773 memorial to Bucareli, Serra lamented the loss of one of the missionaries, who could not cope with the soldiers' disorders at San Gabriel. The priest was sick at heart, Serra stated: "He took to his bed, when he saw with his own eyes a soldier actually committing deeds of shame with an Indian who had come to the mission, and even the children who came to the mission were not safe from their baseness."[5]

Conditions at other missions were no better. Mission San Luis Obispo also lost a priest because of the assaults on Indian women. After spending two years as the sole missionary at San Luis, Father Domingo Juncosa asked for and received permission to return to Mexico because he was "shocked at the scandalous conduct of the soldiers" and could not work under such abominable conditions.[6] Even before San Luis Obispo was founded in the early fall of 1772, Tichos women had cause to fear. The most notorious molesters of non-Christian women were among the thirteen soldiers sent on a bear hunt to this area during the previous winter of starvation at Monterey.[7]

The establishment of new missions subjected the women of each new area to sexual assaults. Referring to the founding of the mission at San Juan Capistrano, Serra wrote that "it seems all the sad experiences that we went through at the beginning have come to life again. The soldiers, without any restraint or shame, have behaved like brutes toward the Indian women."[8] From this mission also, the priests reported to Serra that the soldier-guards went at night to the nearby villages to assault the women and that hiding the women did not restrain the brutes, who beat the men to force them to reveal where the women were hidden. Non-Christian Indians in the vicinity of the missions were simply not safe. They were at the mercy of soldiers with horses and guns.[9]

In 1773, a case of rape was reported at San Luis Rey, one at San Diego, and two cases at Monterey the following year.[10] Serra expressed his fears and concern to Governor Felipe de Neve, who was considering establishing a new presidio in the channel of Santa Barbara. Serra told Neve that he took it for granted that the insulting and scandalous conduct of the soldiers "would be the same as we had experienced in other places which were connected with presidios. Perhaps this one would be worse."[11]

Native women and their communities were profoundly affected by the sexual attacks and attendant violence. California Amerindians were peaceable, non-aggressive people who highly valued harmonious relationships. Physical violence and the infliction of bodily harm on one another were virtually unknown. Women did not fear men. Rape rarely, if ever, occurred. If someone stole from another or caused another's death, societal norms required that the offending party make reparations to the individual and/or the family. Appropriate channels to rectify a wrong without resorting to violence existed.[12]

Animosity, when it did surface, was often worked out ritualistically--for example, through verbal battles in the form of war songs, or song fights that lasted eight days, or encounters in which the adversaries threw stones across a river at each other with no intent actually to hit or physically injure the other party. Even among farming groups such as the Colorado River people, who practiced warfare and took women and children captive, female captives were never sexually molested. The Yumas believed that intimate contact with enemy women caused sickness.[13]

Thus, neither the women nor their people were prepared for the onslaught of aggression and violence the soldiers unleashed against them. They were horrified and terrified. One source reported that women of the San Gabriel and other southern missions raped by the soldiers were considered contaminated and obliged to undergo an extensive purification, which included a long course of sweating, the drinking of herbs, and other forms of purging. This practice was consistent with the people's belief that sickness was caused by enemies. "But their disgust and abhorrence," states the same source, "never left them till many years after."[14] Moreover, any child born as a result of these rapes, and apparently every child with white blood born among them for a very long time, was strangled and buried.[15]

Father Pedro Font, traveling overland from Tubac to Monterey with the Anza expedition between September 1775 and May 1776, recorded the impact of the violence on the native people he encountered. Font's diary verifies the terror in which native Californians, especially the women, now lived. Everybody scattered and fled at the sight of Spaniards. The women hid. They no longer moved about with freedom and ease. The people were suspicious and hostile. The priests were no longer welcome in the living quarters.

The Quabajay people of the Santa Barbara Channel, Font wrote, "appear to us to be gentle and friendly, not war-like. But it will not be easy to reduce them for they are displeased with the Spaniards for what they have done to them, now taking their fish and their food. . . now stealing their women and abusing them."[16] Upon encountering several unarmed Indians on Friday, February 23, Font commented that "the women were very cautious and hardly one left their huts, because the soldiers of Monterey . . . had offended them with various excesses. "[17]

At one village, Font noted, he was unable to see the women close at hand because as soon as the Indians saw his party, "they all hastily hid in their huts, especially the girls, the men remaining outside blocking the door and taking care that nobody should go inside."[18] Font attempted to become acquainted with the people of another village on the channel. He went to the door, but "they shut the inner door on me . . . this is the result of the extortions and outrages which the soldiers have perpetrated when in their journeys they have passed along the Channel, especially at the beginning."[19] Font echoed Serra's concern that the sexual assaults and other outrages had severely retarded missionization in California.

Serra and his co-religionists had great cause for concern, because the missions were not meeting their principal objective of converting Amerindians into loyal Catholic subjects who would repel invading European forces from these shores. By the end of 1773, in the fifth year of the occupation of Alta California, fewer than five hundred baptisms and only sixty-two marriages had been performed in the five missions then existing.[20] Since the marriages probably represented the total adult converts, that meant that the remaining four hundred converts were children. These dismal statistics fueled arguments for abandoning the California missions. While various reasons may be cited for the failure to attract adult converts, certainly the sexual attacks and the impact of that violence on women and their communities were primary among them.

Few historians have recognized that the sexual extortion and abuse of native women gravely affected the political, military, religious, and social developments on this frontier. In 1943, Sherburne F. Cook commented that "the entire problem of sexual relations between whites and the natives, although one which was regarded as very serious by the founders of the province, has apparently escaped detailed consideration by later historians."[21] Cook tackled the issue in demographic terms and wrote about the catastrophic decline in the Indian population as a result of alien diseases, including venereal diseases, brought in by Europeans, as well as other maladies of the conquest.[22]

Almost thirty years later, Edwin A. Beilharz wrote that "the major causes of friction between Spaniard and Indian were the abuse of Indian women and the forced labor of Indian men . . . . Of the two, the problem of restraining the soldiers from assaulting Indian women was the more serious."[23] In his study of the administration of Governor Felipe de Neve, Beilharz notes that Neve recognized the seriousness of the problem and tried to curb the abuses.

Since the 1970s, the decade that saw both the reprinting of Cook's work and the publication of the Beilharz study, the development of gender as a category of analysis has enabled us to reexamine Spanish expansion to Alta California with new questions about sex and gender. Cook, Beilharz, and other scholars initiated but did not develop the discussion about the centrality of sex/gender issues to the politics and policies of conquest.

It is clear that the sexual exploitation of native women and related violence seriously threatened the political and military objectives of the colonial enterprise in California. Repeated attacks against women and summary reprisals against men who dared to interfere undermined the efforts of the priests to attract Amerindians to the missions and to Christianity. They also thwarted whatever attempts the military authorities might make to elicit political or military allegiance from the native peoples.[24]

From the missionaries' point of view, the attacks had more immediate, deleterious consequences for the spiritual conquest of California, because such actions belied significant principles of the Catholic moral theology they were trying to inculcate. As the primary agents of Christianization/Hispanicization, the missionaries argued that they could not teach and Amerindians could not learn and obey the moral strictures against rape, abduction, fornication, adultery, and all forms of sexual impurity while the soldiers persisted in their licentiousness and immorality. Their actions repudiated the very morality the friars were to inculcate.[25]

Early conflict between ecclesiastical and civil-military officials over deployment and discipline of the mission escort soon gave rise to constant bitter disputes centering on the question of authority and jurisdiction over the Indians in California. The conflict over control of the Indians revolved around the issue of their segregation from the non-Indian population. Rooted in the early conquest and consequent development of colonial Indian policy, the issue has been extensively discussed by other historians. The concern here is to examine it specifically from the point of view of sex/gender and to define a context for explaining why, despite strenuous efforts by church and state alike, there was little success in arresting the attacks on Indian women.[26]

Serra, for his part, blamed the military commanders and, once appointed, the governor. They were, he said, lax in enforcing military discipline and unconcerned about the moral fiber of their troops. They failed to punish immoral soldiers who assaulted native women, were flagrantly incontinent, or took Amerindian women as concubines. In California, he stated, secular authorities not only condoned the soldiers' assaults on Indian women but interfered with the missionaries' efforts to counter the abuse, and thereby exceeded their authority with respect to Amerindians.[27]

To argue his case against Lieutenant Pedro Fages, the military commander, and to muster political and economic support for the California establishments, Serra made the arduous trip to Mexico City for an audience with Viceroy Bucareli. He left California in September of 1772 and arrived in Mexico the following February. At the viceroy's request, Serra submitted a lengthy work entitled "Report on the General Conditions and Needs of the Missions and Thirty-Two Suggestions for Improving the Government of the Missions."[28] Serra addressed sex/gender issues as part of several grievances against Fages's command. His recommendations for curtailing the sexual violence and general malfeasance of the soldiers were that Fages should be removed and that Spaniards who married Indian women should be rewarded.

Once the viceroy had removed the lieutenant, Serra continued, he should give strict orders to Fages's successor that, upon the request of any missionary, "he should remove the soldier or soldiers who give bad example, especially in the matter of incontinence . . . and send, in their place, another or others who are not known as immoral or scandalous."[29]

Drawing on colonial tradition established much earlier in New Spain, wherein colonial officials encouraged intermarriage with Amerindian noblewomen in order to advance particular political, military, religious, or social interests, Serra suggested that men who married newly Christianized "daughters of the land" be rewarded.[30] In the second to last of his thirty-two suggestions, Serra asked Bucareli to "allow a bounty for those, be they soldiers or not, who enter into the state of marriage with girls of that faraway country, new Christian converts."[31]

Serra specified the three kinds of bounty to be given the individual: an animal for his own use immediately upon being married; two cows and a mule from the royal herd after he had worked the mission farms for a year or more; and, finally, allotment of a piece of land. Since soldiers were subject to being transferred from one mission or presidio to another, Serra further recommended that he who married a native woman should be allowed to remain permanently attached to his wife's mission.[32]

With this recommendation, which he discussed in more detail in a subsequent letter to the viceroy, Serra hoped to solve several related problems.[33] He sought to curb the sexual attacks on Indian women as well as to induce soldiers to remain and become permanent settlers in Alta California. Theoretically, soldiers would thereby remain on the frontier, and formal and permanent unions with Indian women would allay the natives' mistrust and help to forge a bond between them and the soldiers. These marriages would thus help to ease Indian-military tensions while also cementing Catholic family life in the region.[34]

It was equally important to remove temptation and opportunity for licentious behavior. Thus, in a second memorial to the viceroy, written in April of 1773, a little over a month after his report, Serra forcefully argued against the proposal that the annual supply ships from San Blas be replaced with mule trains coming overland. In addition to the greater expense of an overland supply line, he reasoned, the presence of one hundred guards and muleteers crossing the country would add to "the plague of immorality" running rampant in California.[35]

The document that resulted from the official review of Serra's memorial, the *Reglamento Provisional*--generally known as the *Echeveste Regulations*--was the first regulatory code drawn up for California. The *Echeveste Regulations* acted favorably on twenty-one of Serra's thirty-two original recommendations, including the removal of Fages as military commander.[36]

Implementation of the new regulations, however, did not stop the abuse of women or the immorality of the soldiers. Serra continued to blame the civil-military authorities. He charged Captain Fernando de Rivera y Moncada, who replaced Fages, with currying the soldiers' favor; and he subsequently accused the newly appointed governor, Felipe de Neve, of antireligiosity and anticlericalism. Thus, in the summary of Franciscan complaints against Neve, which Francisco Panagua, guardian of the College of San Fernando, sent Viceroy Mayorga in 1781, Father Panagua wrote that "another consequence... of the aversion which the said Governor [Neve] has for the religious, is that the subordinates...live very libidinously in unrestrained and scandalous incontinence as they use at will Indian women of every class and strata."[37] Serra further charged that Neve allowed fornication among the soldiers, "because, so I have heard him say,...it is winked at in Rome and tolerated in Madrid."[38]

Serra's charges against Fages, Rivera, and Neve were not well founded. As head of the California establishments, each was fully cognizant that the soldiers' excesses not only undermined military discipline, and thus their own command, but also seriously jeopardized the survival of the missions and the presidios. Fundamentally, the assaults against women were unwarranted, unprovoked, hostile acts that established conditions of war on this frontier. Although the native peoples by and large did not practice warfare, they were neither docile nor passive in the face of repeated assaults. The people of the South were especially aggressive. The country between San Diego and San Gabriel remained under Indian control for a long time.[39] It was in this region that the Indians marshaled their strongest forces and retaliated against the Spaniards. Some of the engagements, such as the one at San Gabriel in 1771, were minor skirmishes. Others were full-fledged attacks. In 1775 at Mission San Diego, for example, a force of eight hundred razed the mission, killed one priest and two artisans, and seriously wounded two soldiers. Women participated and sometimes even planned and/or led the attacks. In October 1785, Amerindians from eight *rancherias* united under the leadership of one woman and three men and launched an attack on Mission San Gabriel for the purpose of killing all the Spaniards. Toypurina, the twenty-four-year-old medicine woman of the Japchivit *rancheria*, used her considerable influence as a medicine woman to persuade six of the eight villages to join the rebellion. The attack was thwarted. Toypurina was captured and punished along with the other three leaders.[40]

Throughout their terms, Fages, Rivera, and Neve were keenly aware that Amerindians greatly outnumbered Spain's military force in the fledgling settlement and that, ultimately, the soldiers could not have staved off a prolonged Indian attack.

Neve's greatest fear, expressed in his request to Bucareli for more commissioned officers, was that "if an affair of this kind [disorders caused by soldiers] ever results in a defeat of our troops, it will be irreparable if they [the Indians] come to know their power. We must prevent this with vigor."[41]

Therefore, during their respective administrations, the military authorities enforced Spain's legal codes, as well as imperial policy regarding segregation of Amerindians from non-Indians as a protective measure for the former. They prosecuted soldiers for major and minor crimes, and they issued their own edicts to curb the soldiers' abuse of Amerindians in general and women in particular. Their authority, however, was circumscribed by Spain's highly centralized form of government.[42]

While the governor of the Californias was authorized to try major criminal cases such as those involving homicide and rape, judgment and sentence were decided at the viceregal level in Mexico City. With the separation of the Interior Provinces from the kingdom of New Spain in 1776, the commandant-general, who combined in his office civil, judicial, and military powers, became the final arbiter.[43]

A 1773 case illustrates the complexity of legal procedures. This case--in which a corporal, Mateo de Soto, and two soldiers, Francisco Avila and Sebastian Alvitre, were accused of raping two young Amerindian girls and killing one of them near the mission of San Diego--dragged on for five years. Fages, Rivera, and Neve all dealt with the case, which occurred while Fages was military commander. Fages received the official complaint from Mariano Carrillo, sergeant at the San Diego presidio, who had interviewed the young survivor at that presidio in the presence of four soldiers acting as witnesses. The girl was accompanied to the presidio by two mission priests and an interpreter, who was also present at the interview.[44]

Fages forwarded the documents to Viceroy Bucareli in Mexico City and, on Bucareli's order, subsequently sent a copy to Felipe Barri, then governor of the Californias, at Loreto. When Rivera replaced Fages, he complied with the viceroy's order to bind the men for trial and to send them to Loreto, the capital of the Californias, in Baja California. By 1775, when Rivera sent Avila and Alvitre to Loreto (Soto had deserted and was never apprehended), Neve had replaced Barri as governor of the Californias. It fell to Neve to hear testimony and conduct the trial, which he opened on October 19, 1775.

The trial, including testimony from six soldiers and comments from the accused after Carrillo's charges were read to them, produced voluminous documents. Neve concluded the trial on November 22 and sent a copy of the entire proceedings to the viceroy for final disposition, along with a statement noting certain discrepancies from proscribed judicial procedure. Upon receipt of the proceedings, Bucareli turned the file over to Teodoro de Croix, recently appointed commandant-general of the Interior Provinces, which included the Californias.[45]

Almost three years elapsed before Croix called in the case.[46] On August 26, 1778, his legal adviser, Pedro Galindo Navarro, submitted his opinion to Croix. In Navarro's opinion, the accusation of rape and homicide was not proven. The dead child's body, he argued, was not examined or even seen; the identification of the soldiers accused was unsatisfactory, since it appeared to have been prompted by the interpreter; the entire charge rested on the testimony of a child, "poorly explained by an interpreter." Finally, the accused denied the charge.[47]

Navarro recommended that the penalty for Avila and Alvitre, who had been detained during the five years of the trial, be commuted to time served and that they should be sentenced to remain and become citizens of California. Croix accepted these recommendations. He issued the order, and the two discharged soldiers were enrolled in the list of settlers at the new pueblo of San José de Guadalupe.[48]

Whether local officials would have convicted the soldiers of rape and homicide must remain a matter of conjecture. In any event, despite laws and prosecutions, the sexual exploitation of Indian women did not cease. The missionaries continuously reported that soldiers "go by night to nearby villages for the purpose of raping Indian women."[49] And while some cases were recorded, many more must surely have gone unreported. Nevertheless, it is clear that the commandants and the governors did prosecute and take disciplinary action when charges were filed against individual soldiers. Contrary to Serra's charges of laxity and complicity, Fages, Rivera, and Neve did exert the full measure of their authority in this and other reported cases of sexual violence or abuse. Abundant evidence details the dual policy of prevention and punishment implemented by the three seasoned frontier administrators in their ongoing effort to check the soldiers' excesses.[50]

Ever concerned that Amerindians would discover the real weakness of the Spanish position in California, Neve sought to prevent the sexual attacks, and thereby to defuse the military and political conflicts they gave rise to, by forbidding all troops, including sergeants and corporals, from entering Indian villages. Only soldiers escorting the priests on sick calls were exempt from this order, and then the soldier was not to leave the missionary's side. Escort guards were strictly admonished against misconduct and were severely punished if they disobeyed.[51]

In the same vein, he prohibited soldiers of the mission guard from spending the night away from the mission--even if the priests demanded it. Neve emphatically repeated this same order in the instructions he left to Pedro Fages, who succeeded him as governor in September of 1782. "It is advisable," Neve further instructed Fages, "that we muzzle ourselves and not exasperate the numerous heathendom which surround us, conducting ourselves with politeness and respect. . . . It is highly useful to the service of the King and the public welfare that the heathen of these establishments do not learn to kill soldiers."[52]

Governor Fages was equally emphatic when he issued the following order in 1785: "Observing that the officers and men of these presidios are comporting and behaving themselves in the missions with a vicious license which is very prejudicial because of the scandalous disorders which they incite among the gentile and Christian women, I command you, in order to prevent the continuation of such abuses, that you circulate a prohibitory edict imposing severe penalties upon those who commit them."[53]

A decade later, Viceroy Branciforte followed up Neve's earlier order with his own decree prohibiting troops from remaining overnight away from the presidios, because among other reasons this practice was "prejudicial to good discipline and Christian morals."[54] Governor Diego de Borica, who succeeded Fages in 1794, issued a similar order the following year. These edicts had little effect.

Soldiers and civilian settlers alike disregarded the civil laws against rape as well as military orders against contact with Amerindian women outside of narrowly proscribed channels. The records verify that sexual attacks continued in areas adjacent to missions, presidios, and pueblos throughout the colonial period. Amerindian women were never free from the threat of rapacious assaults.

Why, despite strenuous efforts by officials of both church and state, did the sexual attacks persist unabated? Why, despite the obviously serious political and military conflicts the assaults ignited, did they continue? In view of extensive legislation, royal decrees, and moral prohibitions against sexual and other violence, what, in the experience of the men who came here, permitted them to objectify and dehumanize Indian women to the degree that chasing and lassoing them from mounted horses and then raping them reveals?

Until recently, scholars attributed sexual violence and other concurrent social disorders in early California to the race and culture of the mixed-blood soldier-settler population recruited or banished to this frontier. Institutional historians concluded, with Bancroft, that the "original settlers, most of them half-breeds of the least

93

energetic classes . . . , were of a worthless character."[55] Institutional studies generally concurred with Serra's view that the soldiers were recruited from the scum of the society. Serra had repeatedly beseeched Bucareli to send "sturdy, industrious Spanish families" and asked him to advise the governor of the Californias "not to use exile to these missions as punishment for the soldier whom he may detest as insolent or perverse."[56]

In the last two decades, the conditions that shaped institutional development on this frontier have been reexamined. In addition, studies of the social history of the people recruited to Alta California have been undertaken. As a result, the earlier interpretations have been rejected. Scholars now conclude that the slow development of colonial institutions in California was attributable to limited resources, lack of uniform military codes, and other structural problems--and not to the racial or social-class origins of the soldier-settler population.[57]

Instead, the mixed-blood recruits--who themselves derived from other frontier settlements were admirably able to survive the harsh privations and onerous conditions. In so doing, they established lasting foundations of Spanish civilization in California and the Southwest. Although the cuera (leather-jacket) soldiers were indeed unruly and undisciplined, their behavior reflected a particular informality and a "peculiar attitude of both officers and men."[58] According to revisionist studies, the isolation and distance from the central government, a shared life of hardship and risk, and the fact that blood and marriage ties existed among officers and common soldiers--all contributed to this attitude of informality and independence. Oakah Jones, Jr., makes essentially the same argument for contentious frontier settlers and extends the analysis. In his view, the racially mixed settlers responded to the often brutal conditions on the far northern and Pacific frontiers by creating a distinct frontier culture, characterized by self-reliance, individualism, regionalism, village orientation, resistance to outside control, innovativeness, family cohesiveness, and the preservation of Roman Catholicism as a unifying force.[59]

But these revisionists do not address sex/gender issues. The informality of disciplinary codes does not explain the origins or the continuation of sexual violence against native women. Moreover, as the documents for Alta California clearly reveal, Spanish officials enforced colonial criminal statutes and punished sexual crimes to the extent of their authority. However, neither the highly regulatory Laws of the Indies (the extensive legislation enacted to protect the rights of Amerindians), which mandated nonexploitive relations with Amerindians, nor punishment for breaking the laws arrested the violence.[60]

To begin to understand the soldier-settler violence toward native women, we must examine the stratified, patriarchal colonial society that conditioned relationships between the sexes and races in New Spain; the contemporary ideologies of sex/gender and race; and the relations and structures of conquest imposed on this frontier. While rape and other acts of sexual brutality did not represent official policy on this or any other Spanish frontier, these acts were nevertheless firmly fixed in the history and politics of expansion, war, and conquest. In the history of Western civilization writ large, rape is an act of domination, an act of power.[61] As such, it is a violent political act committed through sexual aggression against women."

* "The practice of raping the women of a conquered group," writes historian Gerda Lerner, "has remained a feature of war and conquest from the second millennium to the present."[62] Under conditions of war or conquest, rape is a form of national terrorism, subjugation, and humiliation, wherein the sexual violation of women represents both the physical domination of women and the symbolic castration of the men of the conquered group. These concepts and symbolic meanings of rape, as discussed by Lamer; Susan Brownmiller, Anne Edwards, and others, are rooted in patriarchal Western society--in the ideology that devalues women in relation to men while it privatizes and reifies women as the symbolic capital (property) of men.[63] In this ideology, rape has historically been defined as a crime against property and thus against "territory." Therefore, in the context of war and conquest, rape has been considered a legitimate form of aggression against the opposing army--a legitimate expression of superiority that carries with it no civil penalty. In nonmilitary situations, punishment for rape and other crimes of sexual violence against women in Western civilization has, until very recently, generally been determined by the social condition or status of the women violated and by the status of the violator.[64] *

In eighteenth-century California, the status of Amerindian women--as members of non-Christian, indigenous groups under military conquest on Spain's northernmost outpost of empire-- made them twice subject to assault with impunity: they were the spoils of conquest, and they were Indian. In the mentality of the age, these two conditions firmly established the inferiority of the Amerindian woman and became the basis for devaluing her person beyond the devaluation based on sex that accrued to all women irrespective of their sociopolitical (race, class) status. The ferocity and longevity of the sexual assaults against the Amerindian woman are rooted in the devaluation of her person conditioned by the weaving together of the strands of the same ideological thread that demeaned her on interrelated counts: her sociopolitical status, her sex, and her gender.

From their earliest contact with Amerindian peoples, Europeans established categories of opposition, or otherness, within which they defined themselves as superior and Amerindians as inferior.[65] These categories were derived from the Aristotelian theory that some beings are inferior by nature, and therefore should be dominated by their superiors for their own welfare, and from the medieval Spanish concept of "purity of blood," which was based on religion and which informed the sense of national unity forged during the reconquest.[66] These ideas--which were fundamentally political concepts that separated human beings into opposing, hierarchical subject-object categories--prevailed during the era of first contact with Amerindians and the early conquests of the Americas.

By the late eighteenth century, a different political concept--racial origin defined place and social value in the stratified social order of colonial New Spain. Race was inextricably linked to social origin and had long been a symbol for significant cleavages in society; it was one primary basis for valuation--and devaluation--of human beings.[67] In the contemporary ideology and society, Amerindian women were thus devalued on the basis of their social and racial origins, which placed them at the bottom of the social scale, and as members of a conquered group.

Two aspects of the devaluation of Amerindian women are especially noteworthy. First and foremost, it is a political devaluation. That is, it is rooted in and driven by political considerations and acts: by war, conquest, and the imposition of alien sociopolitical and economic structures of one group over another. Second, the devaluation rationalized by conquest cuts across sex. At this level, women and men of the conquered group are equally devalued and objectified by the conquering group. Amerindian women and men were both regarded as inferior social beings, whose inferiority justified the original conquest and continued to make them justifiably exploitable and expendable in the eyes of the conqueror. The obverse, of course, also holds in this equation: women and men of the conquering group share the characterization and privileges of their group. In this instance, the primary opposition is defined by sociopolitical status, not sex.

Although the ideological symbols of sociopolitical devaluation changed over time--from religion to socioracial origins to social class--the changing symbols intersected with a sex/gender ideology that has remained remarkably constant from the fifteenth to the twentieth century.[68] As the term implies, the sex/gender ideology defines two categories of opposition--sex and gender--within which women are characterized as superior or inferior in relation to others.

With respect to sex stratification, women are placed in opposition and in an inferior position to men, on the assumption that in the divine order of nature the male sex of the species is superior to the female. In this conception, the ascribed inferiority of females to males is biologically constructed.

The opposition centering on gender revolves around sexual morality and sexual conduct. This opposition creates a level of superior-inferior or good-bad stratification based on social and political value-centered concepts of women's sexuality. This dichotomization provides a very specific, socially constructed, "sexual morality" category for valuing or devaluing women.

Rooted in the corollary patriarchal concepts of woman as the possession of man and of woman's productive capacity as the most important source of her value, this ideology makes woman a pivotal element in the property structure and institutionalizes her importance to the society in the provisions of partible and bilateral inheritance. It also places woman's value, also termed her "honor," in her sexual accessibility--in her virginity while single and, once wed, in the fidelity of her sexual services to the husband to ensure a legitimate heir.[69]

Within this construct, women are placed in opposition to one another at two extremes of a social and moral spectrum defined by sexuality and accessibility. The good woman embodies all the sexual virtues or attributes essential to the maintenance of the patriarchal social structure . . . sexual purity, virginity, chastity, and fidelity. Historically, the norms of sexual morality and sexual conduct that patriarchal society established for women of the ruling class have been the norms against which all other women have been judged. These norms are fundamentally rooted in questions of the acquisition and transference of economic and political power, and of women's relationship to that power base.

Since the linchpins of these ideological constructs are property, legitimacy, and inheritance, a woman excluded from this property/inheritance structure for socio-political reasons (religion, conquest, slavery, race, class), or for reasons based on sexual immorality (any form of sexual misconduct), is consequently excluded from the corresponding concepts and structures of social legitimacy. A woman so excluded cannot produce legitimate heirs because she is not a legitimate social or sexual being.

The woman who is defined out of social legitimacy because of the abrogation of her primary value to patriarchal society, that of producing heirs, is therefore without value, without honor. She becomes the other, the bad woman, the embodiment of a corrupted, inferior, unusable sex: immoral, without virtue, loose. She is common property, sexually available to any man that comes along.

A woman (women) thus devalued may not lay claim to the rights and protections the society affords to the woman who does have sociopolitical and sexual value.[70] In colonial New Spain, as in most Western societies until the very recent period, the woman so demeaned, so objectified, could be raped, beaten, worked like a beast of burden, or otherwise abused with impunity.

The soldiers, priests, and settlers who effected the conquest and colonization of Alta California in the last third of the eighteenth century perceived and acted toward Amerindians in a manner consistent with the ideology and history of conquest regarding them as inferior, devalued, disposable beings against whom violence was not only permissible but often necessary. For, despite the Laws of the Indies, the contradictions in the ideology and corresponding historical relations of conquest were great from the very beginning. These contradictions were generally exacerbated, rather than resolved, across time, space, and expansion to new frontiers.

From the very beginning, the papal bulls and scholarly (ideological) debates that affirmed the essential humanity of Amerindians and initiated the legislation to effect their conversion and protection sanctioned violence and exploitation under certain conditions. Loopholes in the royal statutes that were technically intended to protect Amerindians and guarantee their rights, but more specifically protected the crown's interest in Indian land and labor, had permitted virulent exploitation of Indians since the laws were first passed.[71]

More contemporary military and civil laws, such as those enacted by Neve, Fages, and Borica, carried severe penalties for illegal contact with or maltreatment of Indians; but these laws were especially contradictory because they were intended to curb certain kinds of violence by soldiers who were trained to kill Indians and who were sent to California to effect the temporal (military) conquest of this region.[72] Thus, violence against Amerindians was permissible when it advanced the particular interests of the Spanish Conquest, but punishable when it did not. Since the sexual violence that occurred in this region was but the most contemporary manifestation of a national history that included the violation of enemy women as a legitimate expression of aggression during conquest, it would seem that sexual violence became a punishable offense only when it was the source of military or political problems.[73]

Finally, perhaps the greatest contradictions were those of the greatest champion of Amerindian rights--the Catholic church. On the one hand, Catholic clergy sought to remove Amerindians from contact with Spaniards, in order to protect them from the exploitation and violence of conquistadores, soldiers, and colonists; on the other hand, Jesuits, Franciscans, and other religious orders relied heavily on corporal punishment in their programs to Christianize and Hispanicize native people. While proclaiming the humanity of Amerindians, missionaries on the frontier daily acted upon a fundamental belief in the inferiority of the Indian. Their actions belied their words.

Accordingly, in his lengthy memorial of June 19, 1801, refuting the charges of excessive cruelty to Amerindians leveled against the Franciscans by one of their own, Father President Fermín Francisco de Lasuén disputed the use of extreme cruelty in the missions of the New California. Force was used only when absolutely necessary, stated Lasuén; and it was at times necessary because the native peoples of California were "untamed savages. . . people of vicious and ferocious habits who know no law but force, no superior but their own free will, and no reason but their own caprice."[74] Of the use of force against neophyte women, Lasuén wrote that women in the mission were flogged, placed in the stocks, or shackled only because they deserved it. But, he quickly added, their right to privacy was always respected--they were flogged inside the women's dormitory, called the *monjero* (nunnery). Flogging the women in private, he further argued, was part of the civilizing process because it "instilled into them the modesty, delicacy, and virtue belonging to their sex."[75]

A key element in the missionaries' program of conversion to Christianity included the restructuring of relations between the sexes to reflect gender stratification and the corollary values and structures of the patriarchal family: subservience of women to men, monogamy, marriage without divorce, and a severely repressive code of sexual norms.

In view of the fact that the ideologies, structures, and institutions of conquest imposed here were rooted in two and a half centuries of colonial rule, the sexual and other violence toward Amerindian women in California can best be understood as ideologically justified violence institutionalized in the structures and relations of conquest initiated in the fifteenth century.[76] In California as elsewhere, sexual violence functioned as an institutionalized mechanism for ensuring subordination and compliance. It was one instrument of sociopolitical terrorism and control--first of women and then of the group under conquest.

NOTES

1. Fray Junipero Serra to Antonio María de Bucareli y Ursua, Mexico City, May 21,1773, in *Writings of Junipero Serra*, ed. Antonine Tibesar, O.F.M., 4 vols (Washington, D.C.:Academy of Franciscan History, 1955), 1:363.

2. Serra to Father Rafaél Verger, Monterey, August 8, 1772, in *Writings,* 1:257.
3. Serra to Bucareli, Mexico City, May 21, 1773, in *Writings,* 1:361.
4. George Harwood Phillips, *Chiefs and Challengers: Indian Resistance and Cooperation in Southern California* (Berkeley: University of California Press, 1975), p.22
5. Serra to Bucareli, Mexico City, May 21,1773, in *Writings,* 1:363.
6. Serra to Father Guardian [Francisco Pangua], Monterey, July 19, 1774, in *Writings,* 2:121.
7. Serra to Verger, Monterey, August 8,1772, in *Writings,* 1:259, 261.
8. Serra to Father Francisco Pangua or his Successor, Monterey, June 6, 1777, in *Writings,* 3:159.
9. José Francisco Ortega, Diligencias Practicadas por Sargento Francisco de Aguiar, 1777, Julio II, San Diego, *Archives* of *California,* 55:279, Bancroft Library, University of California, Berkeley.
10. Sherburne F. Cook, *Conflict between the California Indian and White Civilization* (Berkeley: University of California Press, 1976), p.24. (Originally published 1943.)
11. Serra to Father Juan Figuer, Monterey, March 30,1779, in *Writings,* 3:305.
12. Robert F. Heizer and Albert B. Elsasser, *The Natural World of the California Indians* (Berkeley: University of California Press, 1980), p. 25.
13. Hugo Reid, "Letters on the Los Angeles County Indians," in Susana Dakin, *A Scotch Paisano: Hugo Reid's Life in California, 1832-1852* (Berkeley: University of California Press, 1939), Appendix B, pp.215-216, 240; Heizer and Elsasser, *Natural World of the California Indians,* pp.52-53.
14. Reid, "Letters on the Los Angeles County Indians," p. 262.
15. Ibid.; see also Herbert Howe Bancroft, *History* of *California,* 7 vols. (San Francisco: A. L. Bancroft, 1984-1985), 1:180 and n. 29 (same page).
16. Herbert Eugene Bolton, trans. and ed., *Font's Complete Diary: A Chronicle of the Founding of San Francisco* (Berkeley: University of California Press, 1931), p. 256.
17. Ibid., p. 247.
18. Ibid.
19. Ibid., pp. 251-252.
20. Charles E. Chapman, *A History of California: The Spanish Period* (New York: Macmillan, 1930), pp. 246-247.
21. Cook, *Conflict,* p. 24.

22. Ibid., pp.25-30, 101-134.

23. Edwin A. Beilharz, *Felipe de Neve: First Governor of California* (San Francisco: California Historical Society, 1971), pp. 72-73.

24. This argument is based on my analysis of the documents.

25. Reverend Herbert Jone, *Moral Theology, Englished and Adapted to the Laws and Customs of the United States of America by Reverend Urban Adelman* (Westminster, Md.: Newman Press, 1960), pp.145-161.

26. The conflict between church and state in California, which Irving Richman calls the conflict between State Secular and State Sacerdotal, is extensively discussed in general histories of Spanish California. See Bancroft, *History of California,* vol.1; Irving Berdine Richman, *California under Spain and Mexico, 1535-1847* (Boston: Houghton Mifflin, 1911), pp. 142-158.

27. Serra to Father Fermín Francisco de Lasuén, Monterey, January 8, 1781, in *Writings,* 4:63; Beilharz, *Felipe de Neve,* p. 77; Richman, *California under Spain and Mexico,* pp.116-337.

28. Serra to Bucareli, Mexico City, March 13,1773, in *Writings,* 1:295-329; see also Bernard E. Bobb, The *Viceregency of Antonio Maria Bucareli in New Spain, 1771-1779* (Austin: University of Texas Press, 1962), p. 163.

29. Serra to Bucareli, Mexico City, March 13,1773, in *Writings,* 1:299, 301, 305, 307; Serra to Teodoro de Croix, Santa Barbara, April 28,1782, in *Writings,* 4:129.

30. Magnus Morner *(Race Mixture in the History of Latin America* [Boston: Little, Brown, 1967], pp.35-37) discusses interracial marriage in the early colonial period as part of the early social experiments of the sixteenth century. I discuss the promotion of intermarriage more specifically as an instrument of conquest in chapter 5 of "Presidarias y Pobladoras: Spanish-Mexican Women in Frontier Monterey, California, 1770-1821," Ph.D. diss., Stanford University, 1990.

31. Serra to Bucareli, Mexico City, March 13, 1773, in *Writings,* 1:325.

32. Ibid.

33. Serra to Bucareli, Monterey, August 24,1775, in *Writings,* 2:149,151, 153.

34. This is my interpretation of the documents.

35. Serra to Bucareli, Mexico City, April 22, 1773, in *Writings,* 1:341.

36. Bancroft, *History of California,* 1:206-219; Bobb, *Viceregency of Bucareli,* pp.162-163; Chapman, *History of California: The Spanish Period,* pp.289-291.

37. As quoted in Beilharz, *Felipe de Neve* p. 77.

38. Serra to Lasuén, Monterey, January 8, 1781, in *Writings,* 4:63.

39. Bancroft, *History of California,* 1:546-549; Phillips, *Chief and Challengers,* p.23.

40. Fages al Comandante General, 7 de noviembre de 1785, Monterey; 30 de deciembre de 1785, San Gabriel; 5 de enero de 1786, San Gabriel--all in *Archives of California*, 22:348-349. For the interrogation of Toypurina and her coleaders of the rebellion at Mission San Gabriel, see Diligencias que del órden del Gobernador practicó el Sargento Joseph Francisco Olivera . . . , *Archivos general de la nación: Provincias Internas*, vol. 120, microfilm, Bancroft Library, University of California, Berkeley. For a popular account of Toypurina's leadership role in the rebellion, see Thomas Workman Temple II, "Toypurina the Witch and the Indian Uprising at San Gabriel," *Masterkey* 32 (September-October 1958): 136-152. For a discussion of Amerindian rebellions in California, see Bancroft, *History* of *California*, 1:249-256; Cook, *Conflict*, pp.65-90; Phillips, *Chiefs and Challengers*.

41. As quoted in Beilharz, *Felipe de Neve*, p.83.

42. Bobb, *Viceregency of Bucareli;* Alfred Barnaby Thomas, *Teodoro de Croix and the Northern Frontier of New Spain,1776- 1783* (Norman: University of Oklahoma Press, 1941).

43. Thomas, *Teodoro de Croix*, pp. 16-57, 230-246; Max L. Moorhead, *The Presidio: Bastion of the Spanish Borderlands* (Norman: University of Oklahoma Press, 1975), pp. 27-160; Sidney B. Brinckerhoff and Odie B. Faulk, *Lancers for the King: A Study of the Frontier Military System of Northern New Spain, with a Translation of the Royal Regulations of 1772* (Phoenix: Arizona Historical Foundation, 1965), p.7.

44. Representación de Don Pedro Fages sobre el estupro violento que cometierón los tres soldados que espresa, año de 1774, Californias, *Archivos general de la nación: Californias*, vol.2, Part 1, microfilm. The five-year chronology of this case is from Beilharz, *Felipe de Neve*, pp.27-30.

45. Beilharz, *Felipe de Neve* p. 29.

46. Bobb, *Viceregency of Buscareli* pp. 128-171; Thomas, *Teodoro de Croix*, pp. 17-57, 230-246; Beilharz, *Felipe de Neve*, p.29.

47. Beilharz, *Felipe de Neve*, pp. 29-30.

48. Ibid.

49. Ortega, Diligencias, 1777, Julio 11, San Diego, *Archives of California*, 55:258-279; Cook, *Conflict*, pp.106-107.

50. Beilharz, *Felipe de Neve*, pp. 67- 84, 160-162.

51. Pedro Fages to Diego Gonzales, Monterey, July 1,1785, *Archives of California*, 54:175; Cook, *Conflict*, p.106.

52. As quoted in Beilharz, *Felipe de Neve*, p.73; see also Neve's instructions to Fages, his successor, in Appendices, same source, pp. 161-162.

53. Fages to Gonzales, July 1,1785, *Archives of California*, 54:175.

54. Branciforte al Gobernador de California, 'Sobre escoltas a los religiosos ...,' 5 de octubre de 1795, Mexico, *Archives of California*, 7:256; Gobernador a Comandantes de Presidios, "Excesos de la tropa con las indias, su corrección ...," 11 de abril de 1796, Monterey, *Archives of California*, 23:421-422.

55. Bancroft, *History of California*, 1:601.

56. Serra to Bucareli, Mexico City, June 11, 1773; Serra to Pangua, Monterey, June 6, 1777, in *Writings*, 1:383, 3:159.

57. Oakah L. Jones, Jr., *Los Paisanos: Spanish Settlers on the Northern Frontier of New Spain* (Norman: University of Oklahoma Press, 1979); Brinckerhoff and Faulk, *Lancers for the King*; Max L. Moorhead, "The Soldado de Cuera: Stalwart of the Spanish Borderlands," and Leon G. Campbell, "The First Californios: Presidial Society in Spanish California, 1760-1822," in *The Spanish Borderlands: A First Reader*, ed. Oakah L. Jones, Jr. (Los Angeles: Lorrin L. Morrison, 1974), pp.87-105 and 106-118, respectively. Moorhead's essay was originally published in the *Journal of the West* in January 1969, and Campbell's first appeared in the *Journal of the West* in October 1972.

58. Moorhead, "The Soldado de Cuera," p. 91.

59. Jones, *Los Paisanos*, pp. 252-253.

60. Juan de Solórzano y Pereyra, *Política indiana*, 5 vols. (Buenos Aires: Compañia Ibero-Americana de Publicaciones, 1972); José María Ots y Capdequi, *Instituciones* (Barcelona: Salvat Editores, S.A., 1959), and *Historia del derecho español en América y del derecho indiano* (Madrid: Ediciones S.A. de Aguilar, 1967).

61. The discussion about rape and other forms of sexual violence against women is based on the following sources: Gerda Lerner, *The Creation of Patriarchy* (New York: Oxford University Press, 1986); Susan Brownmiller, *Against Our Will: Men, Women and Rape* (New York: Bantam Books, 1976); Christine Ward Gailey, "Evolutionary Perspectives on Gender Hierarchy," in *Analyzing Gender: A Handbook of Social Science Research*, ed. Beth B. Hess and Myra Marx Ferree (Newbury Park, Calif.: Sage, 1987), pp. 32-67; Carole J. Sheffield, "Sexual Terrorism: The Social Control of Women," in *Analyzing Gender*, pp. 171-189; Jalna Hanmer and Mary Maynard, "Introduction: Violence and Gender Stratification," in *Women, Violence and Social Control*, ed. Jalna Hanmer and Mary Maynard (Atlantic Highlands, N.J.: Humanities Press International, 1987), pp. l-12; Anne Edwards, "Male Violence in

Feminist Theory: An Analysis of the Changing Conceptions of Sex/Gender Violence and Male Dominance," and David H. J. Morgan, "Masculinity and Violence," in *Women, Violence and Social Control* pp. 13-29 and 180-192, respectively.

62. Lerner, *Patriarchy*, p. 80.

63. Lerner, *Patriarchy*, p. 80; Brownmiller, *Against Our Will*, pp. 23-24; Edwards, "Male Violence in Feminist Theory," p. 19; Ramón Arturo Gutiérrez, "Marriage, Sex, and the Family: Social Change in Colonial New Mexico, 1690-1846," Ph.D. diss., University of Wisconsin-Madison, 1980, p.15.

64. Lerner, *Patriarchy*, p. 96; Brownmiller, *Against Our Will* pp. 18-20; Sheffield, "Sexual Terrorism," pp. 173-174.

65. Tzvetan Todorov, *The Conquest of America: The Question of the Other*, trans. Richard Howard (New York: Harper and Row, 1982).

66. Lewis Hanke, *The Spanish Struggle for Justice in the Conquest of America* (Philadelphia: University of Pennsylvania Press, 1949), pp. 111-132; Verena Martínez-Alier, *Marriage, Class, and Color in Nineteenth-Century Cuba: A Study of Racial Attitudes and Sexual Values in a Slave Society* (Cambridge, England: Cambridge University Press, 1974), p 76; Morner, *Race Mixture*, pp.3-5, 36; Health Dillard, "Women in Reconquest Castile: The Fueros of Sepulveda and Cuenca," in *Women in Medieval Society* ed. Susan Mosher Stuard (Philadelphia: University of Pennsylvania Press, 1976), p.86.

67. Martínez-Alier, *Marriage, Class, and Color in Nineteenth-Century Cuba*, p. 76.

68. Edwards, "Male Violence in Feminist Theory," p.28, n. 4. Although some feminist scholars prefer not to make an analytical distinction between sex (biological) and gender (sociocultural) categories, I believe that the distinction is important because of the distinct oppositions within which each category places women. The biological distinction of sex places women in opposition and in a subordinate position relative to men; the sociocultural distinction of gender places women in opposition and in an inferior position to other women. This sociocultural distinction is based on concepts of sexual morality and conduct that are informed by political and economic values. With few exceptions, however, the sociocultural construction of gender has not accounted for the political and economic dimensions that historically related (if not defined) a woman's sexual morality and gender value to her sociopolitical (religion, race, class) status-- and vice versa.

69. Lerner, *Patriarchy*, pp. 80-88; Sylvia Marina Arrom, *The Women of Mexico City, 1790-1850* (Stanford, Calif.: Stanford University Press, 1985), p. 71; Health Dillard, *Daughters of the Reconquest: Women in Castillian Town Society 1100-1300*

(Cambridge, England: Cambridge University Press, 1984), pp.12-35, see especially pp.30-32, and "Women in Reconquest Castile," pp.86, 91.

70. For a discussion of the concept of women's honor and dishonor drawn from codes of sexual conduct and used as a basis for devaluation of women in medieval Spain, see Dillard, *Daughters of the Reconquest,* pp. 168-212; for a discussion of the concept of family honor and the political issues inherent in the devaluation of women on the basis of class and race, see Martínez-Alier, *Marriage, Class, and Color in Nineteenth-Century Cuba,* pp. 11-41, 71-81; for a discussion of these issues in the northern frontier of colonial New Spain, see Ramón A. Gutiérrez, "From Honor to Love: Transformations of the Meaning of Sexuality in Colonial New Mexico," in *Kinship Idealogy and Practice in Latin America,* ed. Raymond T. Smith (Chapel Hill: University of North Carolina Press, 1984), pp.237-263; see also Gutiérrez, "Marriage, Sex, and the Family."

71. Hanke, *The Spanish Struggle for Justice,* pp.133-146.

72. Moorhead, "The Soldado de Cuera," p. 102.

73. For discussions of sexual violence in the national history of Spain, first during the reconquest and then during the conquest of Mexico, see Dillard, *Daughters of the Reconquest,* pp.206-207, and "Women in Reconquest Castile," pp.85-89; Todorov, *Conquest of America,* pp.48-49, 59,139,175.

74. Refutation of Charges, Mission of San Carlos of Monterey, June 19, 1801, in *Writings of Fermín Francisco de Lasuén,* 2 vols., trans. and ed. Finbar Kenneally, O.F.M. (Washington, D.C.: Academy of American Franciscan History, 1965), 2:194-234; quotes are from 2:220.

75. Ibid., 2:217.

76. Sheffield, "Sexual Terrorism," pp.171-189.

Raymund Paredes traces the origins of anti-Mexican sentiment from the 16th through the 18th centuries. Originating in Spanish-English religious rivalry and extending to early characterizations of Mexicans, these attitudes influenced early American colonists and shaped the nature of the earliest contacts between Anglo-Americans and Mexicans on the Mexican frontier in the early 19th century. Paredes provides an in-depth introduction into racial, religious and cultural antagonisms discussed later by Arnoldo De León in the next section.

The Origins of Anti-Mexican Sentiment in the United States

Raymund A. Paredes

Traditionally, when scholars have treated the development of anti-Mexican sentiment in the United States, they have focused on the first large-scale encounters between Mexicans and Americans in the early 19th century as the source of bad feelings."[1] The cultures of the two peoples, goes the conventional wisdom, were so dissimilar that misunderstanding and resentment grew rapidly and hardened into a tradition of prejudice. Samuel Lowrie, in his study of American-Mexican relations in Texas, found that a "culture conflict" developed immediately after American colonists entered Mexican Texas in 1821[2] while Cecil Robinson, the well known scholar of American literary images of Mexico, describes the "inevitable collision" between two nations competing for the same stretches of land.[3] The weakness of these studies, and others of their type, is that they have little to say about the attitudes American travelers and settlers carried into Mexican territory that largely determined their responses to the natives. The enmity between the two peoples may well have been inevitable but not exclusively for reasons of spontaneous culture conflict and empire building.

Rather, American responses to the Mexicans grew out of attitudes deeply rooted in Anglo-American tradition. Americans had strong feelings against Catholics and Spaniards and expected their evils to have been fully visited upon the Mexicans; after all, had not the Mexicans been subjected to nearly three hundred years of Catholic-Spanish oppression? The logic may have lacked a certain finesse but the fact of its application is inescapable. Secondly, although Americans in the early 19th century knew little about the contemporary people of Mexico, they held certain ideas about the aborigines -- and the natives of Latin America generally -- that affected their judgments.

The purpose of this essay is to trace the nature and history of those attitudes and images that shaped early American assessments of the Mexicans. Anti-Catholic

107

sentiment and hispanophobia will be considered first, inasmuch as these prejudices operated in Anglo-American culture from the earliest days and exerted the most immediate influence on American attitudes. Next, I will discuss the more desultory career of the Mexican aborigines in early American thought. Finally, I will consider how these notions merged, in effect forming a mode of perception which rendered unlikely the possibility that 19th-century Americans would regard the people of Mexico with compassion and understanding.

The English settlement of America commenced at a time when hatred of Catholicism and Spain had been building for over fifty years. Widespread dissatisfaction with the Roman Church, based on charges of corruption and complacency, appeared in England shortly after 1500, crystallized during the Reformation, and intensified as Protestantism drifted leftward.[4] Propagandists denounced the Mass as blasphemous, indicted the clergy for the encouragement of superstition and ignorance, and assailed the Pope as the anti-Christ. Eventually, resentment of Catholicism transcended religious issues. Englishmen came to regard the Roman Church as a supra-national power which sought to overthrow their government. Reports of Catholic plots circulated regularly in England after the mid-16th century, some warning of tangible dangers such as the Desmond revolts in Ireland and the fantastic Gunpowder Plot of 1605, while others -- the constant rumors of Jesuit intrigues, for example -- only demonstrated how closely English fears of Catholic political adventures verged on hysteria. It was in the context of this fear that English anti-Catholicism intersected and merged with a nascent hispanophobia. As every Englishman knew, Spain was the most powerful of Catholic nations and the self-proclaimed champion of the Roman Church. The Spanish military forces -- the "popist legions" -- were the very instruments of Catholic tyranny. The Catholic-Spanish alliance was regarded by many Englishmen as a partnership conjured by Satan himself and thus one that possessed an unlimited capacity for mischief. Englishmen were well aware of the most notorious product of this collaboration, the Spanish Inquisition.

Although Englishmen disliked Catholics in the lump, the Spaniard was considered the worst of the breed for reasons not altogether related to religion. The spirit of nationalism surged in the Elizabethan era and England's attempts to assert itself as an international power placed it directly across the gun barrel from Spain. Countless military engagements, the most spectacular of which was with the Armada in 1588, maintained animosities at a high pitch until well into the 18th century. During the Revolt of the Netherlands (1555-1609), an event closely followed in England, Dutch nationalists conducted an impassioned "paper war" against their Spanish rulers, vilifying them for their cruelty, avarice, arrogance, and immorality.[5] In 1583, *The Spanish Colonie* by Bartolomé de Las Casas appeared in England and reported how the Spaniards, in an astonishing display of brutality, managed to reduce the native population of America by twenty million souls. By the end of the decade, the "Black Legend" had been firmly planted in the English mind and the Spaniard had displaced the Turk as the greatest of English villains.[6]

There is one other feature of 16th-century English hispanophobia that bears mention here. As Englishmen traveled more widely -- particularly to Africa on slaving expeditions -- they became increasingly aware of human differences, the most obvious of which was complexion. The color "black" had already acquired a number of negative connotations in the English mind, and eventually, the Elizabethans formulated a scale of human beauty ranging from the blond perfection of the northern European to the ebony hideousness of the African.[7] The Spaniard was placed near the bottom of the scale. In an era when Englishmen increasingly esteemed purity not only in a religious sense but also in an incipient racial context, the Spaniard was manifestly "impure," being the product of European Moorish miscegenation which had proceeded for hundreds of years. This well-known phenomenon disturbed many Englishmen who used the terms "Moor" and "Negro" almost interchangeably.[8] Quite simply, the Moor was an African, so that in the mixture of bloods on the Iberian peninsula the odium of blackness was transferred to some extent to the Spaniard.

The colonial record provides ample evidence that prejudices against Catholics and Spaniards traveled across the Atlantic intact. Indeed, they may well have been more intense among the immigrants than in the general English public. After all, many of the colonists derived from the most anti-Catholic element in England, the radical Puritans, and to a man the settlers were ardent nationalists who regarded their role in the struggle with Spain with high seriousness. They saw themselves as guardians against Spanish penetration into the northern regions of the New World, as economic rivals intent on undermining the fragile structure of Spanish mercantilism, and as Protestant missionaries who would carry the Gospel unperverted to the American savages.

Always in contact with their homeland, the colonists received a steady influx of anti-Catholic and hispanophobic literature from England. One of the most popular works among the settlers was John Foxe's *Book of Martyrs,* a study of Catholic persecution which described vividly the numerous outrages of the Spanish Inquisition.[9] The collections of Richard Hakluyt and Samuel Purchas, the two great literary champions of English imperialism, were also well known to the settlers. By the late 17th century, the denunciations of Spanish activity in the New World by Las Casas and Thomas Gage had appeared on colonial booklists.[10]

The settlers themselves produced a conspicuous body of anti-Catholic and hispanophobic literature. In one of the earliest colonial works, *Of Plymouth Plantation,* William Bradford cited the corrupting influences of "popish trash" as a major reason for the Separatist emigration. He also railed against the jealousy and cruelty of the Spaniards and speculated that the colonists would have no greater trouble with the American savages. Bradford's history gave voice to Separatist hispanophobia which had been exacerbated during sojourns in Dutch sanctuaries where memorials to Holland's struggle with Spain were everywhere in evidence. During Bradford's tenure as governor of Plymouth Colony, the citizens allied with the Dutch settlers of New Amsterdam "the better to resist the pride of that common enemy, the Spaniard, from whose cruelty the Lord keep us both, and our native countries."[11] Like most of his co-religionists, Bradford believed that God protected Protestant true-believers from the evil designs of the Spaniards.

As it turned out, Bradford's invective was temperate when measured against other expressions of colonial anti-Catholicism and hispanophobia. The greatest denunciators were ministers who raged against their enemies from the pulpit and in religious tracts. The renowned John Cotton, for example, described the Roman Church as "worldly and carnal" and the Spaniards as a belligerent nation possessed by Satan. The Spanish Inquisition, he proclaimed, was "incomparably more bloody than any other Butchery."[12] Thomas Hooker outlined a history of Catholic treachery and corruption in the preface to his *Survey of the Summer of Church Discipline* (1648) and characterized the Pope as the incarnation of evil and his followers as "wretched rabble." Such assaults extended beyond religious literature. Colonists read anti-Catholic doggerel in their almanacs and heard anti-Spanish ballads on the streets.

A well-known poem in New England during the late 17th century was John Wilson's "Song of Deliverance." Wilson, a Boston minister, claimed, with appropriate modesty, no great merit for his verses but explained that they were intended to help children "learn and rehearse." One section of the "Song" treats the wicked intentions of the Spanish Armada and indicates how precisely and firmly Elizabethan prejudices were planted in the colonies:

> Besides, great store and company
> of tearing torturing Whips,

And instruments of cruelty,
    provided in their Ships;

As meaning not to be so kind,
    our blood at once to spill,

But by our lingering pain, their mind
    and bloody lusts to fill.

From seven years old (or if not so,
    from ten and so forth on)

All had been kill'd, both high and low
    their Sword could light upon.

Virgins had dyde, when they had first
    the Virgins honour lost:

Women unript, on Spears accurst,
    had seen their Infants tost.

The children, whom they meant to save,
    with brand of Iron hot,

Were in their face (like Indian slave,)
    to bear a seared spot.

Their Soul (alas) had been a spoyle
    to Soul-destroying Pope;

Their bodyes spent in restless toyle,
    without all ease or hope.[13]

It is difficult to say how widely Wilson's poem was used as a pedagogical tool but we can say that colonial schoolchildren were exposed to a barrage of anti-Catholic and anti-Spanish propaganda. One of the most popular of early American textbooks was the *New England Primer* which over a period of one hundred and fifty years sold three million copies. Early editions contained excerpts from *The Book of Martyrs* and poems which admonished their readers to "Abhor that arrant Whore of Rome,/ And all her Blasphemies." Children learned basic anatomy lessons by studying a figure of that "man of sin," the Pope, whose various body parts were indicated with such captions as "In his Heart,...Malice, Murder, and Treachery" and "In his Feet...Swiftness to shed Blood."[14]

The literary campaign against Rome and Spain continued throughout the colonial period and beyond, engaging some of the most able and influential figures in the settlements. Cotton Mather inveighed eloquently against the traditional enemies of the Puritans while publishers of popular almanacs such as Nathaniel Ames (both father and son) and Nathaniel Low issued a stream of anti-Catholic and anti-Spanish materials. In the mid-18th century, the first Anglo-American magazines appeared and took up the fight. The Dudleian lecture series was established at Harvard in 1750, a part of which was given over to "the detecting and convicting and exposing of the idolatry of the Romish church: their tyranny, usurpations, damnable heresies, fatal errors, abominable superstitions, and other crying wickedness in her high places."[15] One could easily recite the details of these various tirades, but to little purpose; suffice it to say that the character and vehemence of literary anti-Catholicism and hispanophobia continued virtually unchanged.[16]

Colonial resentment of Rome and Spain was not confined to the printed page but found expression in a number of statutory and military actions. As the settlers desired to see Catholicism removed from the continent, many of the colonial legislatures passed exclusionary and restrictive laws.[17] In 1641-42, the Virginia House of Burgesses ruled that no "Popish recusants" could hold colonial office. Massachusetts Bay banished priests and Jesuits under penalty of execution. In 1698, New York forbade Catholics to hold weapons and required that they deposit bond as security of good behavior. Even in Maryland, originally established as a Catholic settlement, Protestants became dominant, turned out the colony's founder, Lord Baltimore, and decreed that "none who profess to exercise the Popish religion...can be protected in this province."[18]

The colonists were no less vigorous in their campaigns against the Spaniards. In the 1630s, New Englanders helped to establish a Puritan colony off the Mosquito Coast to be used as a base for English penetrations into Central America. Many colonists, including John Cotton and Roger Williams, supported Cromwell's "Western Design," according to which the English would drive the Spaniards from the West

Indies. In 1655, colonists participated in the assault on Jamaica, the first recorded venture against the Spaniards by English-Americans.[19]

Soon thereafter, English- and Spanish-Americans were battling on the mainland, particularly as the English colonists pushed southward and westward and found themselves, as the saying went, "in the chops of the Spaniards."[20] The settlers of Jamestown lived under constant threat of attack and in 1686, the Spaniards razed the Scottish settlement at Port Royal; predictably, Carolinians vowed to redress this "bloody insolency." After 1700, hostilities intensified as the enemies became embroiled in lengthy, bloody disputes involving titles of possession, buccaneering, and runaway slaves. English colonists complained constantly that the Spaniards provoked the Indians against them; the Spaniards countered with similar charges. One episode in 1702 exemplifies the character of the rivalry. As an opening blow in Queen Anne's War, Governor James Moore of Carolina organized an attack on the Spanish garrison at St. Augustine. Moore himself led the naval contingent of the expedition while a force of some five hundred Englishmen and Indians approached St. Augustine overland, ravaging enemy outposts along the way. The town fell without resistance, the residents having retreated nearby to the Castillo de San Marcos. Moore then lay siege to the fort and waited for heavy artillery to arrive from Jamaica. Still without cannon after seven weeks, the colonial forces withdrew hastily when the sails of Spanish warships appeared on the horizon.[21] This engagement, like many others between English-Americans and Spaniards, was as significant as an exhibition of long-standing hostilities as for any inherent military importance.

It is no exaggeration to characterize the 18th century as a period of incessant military and political conflict between English-Americans and Spain. The establishment of Georgia in 1733 greatly agitated the Spaniards who laid plans to destroy the colony. England, for its part, was itching for a fight and found an excuse five years later when Captain Robert Jenkins appeared in the House of Commons to tell how the Spaniards had severed his left ear as punishment for a trumped-up charge of illegal trade in the West Indies. The wronged officer dramatized his tale by exhibiting the remnant of his humiliation, still remarkably well-preserved after several years.[22] The spectacle was too much for the politicians who, after the fashion of their breed, had an appreciation of the theatrical; after an extended debate, they finally declared war. English colonists leaped to the fray -- known, of course, as the War of Jenkins' Ear -- engaging the enemy along the Georgia-Florida frontier and in an abortive assault on the South American port of Cartagena. Moving to the revolutionary period, we find that many Americans were angered by Spain's delay in granting recognition of independence, stubbornly unsympathetic to Spain's fear that such an act would be considered an inducement to rebel by its own restive colonies. Perhaps the greatest controversy between the two peoples involved navigation rights on the Mississippi. Anglo-Americans traditionally had traveled the river freely but after 1782 Spain moved to interdict illegal trade and incursions into its northern territories. Americans responded with threats of war against their "natural and habitual enemy."[23] The dispute was settled by the Treaty of San Lorenzo in 1795 but bitterness and suspicion remained. Eleven years later, Thomas Jefferson surveyed the history of Anglo-American relations with Spain and concluded: "Never did a nation act towards another with more perfidy and injustice than Spain has constantly practiced against us."[24] To some extent, Jefferson's resentment was justified but it was also a product of a long tradition of hispanophobia. Like most of his compatriots, the great Virginian was more inclined to remember Spanish vices than Spanish virtues.

The political and military conflicts combine with the mass of literary evidence to reveal that prejudices against Catholics and Spaniards, transported to the New World at the end of the Elizabethan era, persisted among Anglo-Americans for two centuries without significant modification. The colonists believed the Roman Church to be corrupt and ostentatious, an institution that demanded blind allegiance and thus fostered ignorance and superstition. As for the Spaniards, they were the perfect adherents of Popery, cruel, treacherous, avaricious, and tyrannical, a people whose history was an extended intrigue. As Americans gazed southward with increasing interest, they saw yet another episode of that history unfolding and they could not but believe that the Mexicans had been blighted by their participation in it.

Concerning their impressions of the Mexican aborigines, the early English-American colonists had virtually nothing to say but such notions as they held were unquestionably those of their contemporary homebound compatriots. Although questions related to the character and culture of the Mexicans -- and of all the American Indians -- were not issues of pressing concern to 17th century Englishmen, information on these subjects had been accumulating since the 1550s. During that decade, Richard Eden, an obscure civil servant with a Cambridge education, tried to awaken his countrymen to the advantages of overseas exploration and settlement. Eden's method was to gather in two collections summaries of the early voyages of Columbus and Vespucci, portions of Peter Martyr's monumental chronicle of the New World, *De orbe novo*, and selections from the highly regarded histories of the Spaniards, Oviedo and Gómara.[25] Eden had one eye on the economic potential of distant lands, but the other on national glory; he earnestly believed that the conquest of the New World was an undertaking of such immense ambition and daring that no nation aspiring to greatness could risk exclusion from it. Unfortunately for Eden, his own ambitions for England were ahead of his time so that his works never achieved the desired impact. But they did alert later writers to the certain rewards of western travel.

In learning about Mexico and other regions of the New World, Englishmen were at a severe disadvantage when compared to citizens of other European countries. Continental interest in America had been mounting, not spectacularly but steadily, from the moment Columbus' celebrated letter on his first voyage to the Indies began circulating in 1493. Moreover, mainland Europeans were exposed not only to a selection of letters, histories, and narratives on American subjects but also to illustrations, New World artifacts, and an assortment of live aborigines kidnaped by travelers and delivered to Europe for public display.[26] Owing to an early series of unprofitable voyages to North America and a certain degree of cultural isolation, England had been virtually untouched by the first wave of continental interest in the New World.[27]

This situation began to change in 1577 when Richard Willes enlarged Eden's "Decades" to include, among other things, Martyr's account of the conquest of Mexico and published the volume as *The History of Travayle in the West and East Indies.* The following year, an English edition of Gómara's *Conquest of the Weast India* appeared, this too featuring a treatment of Cortés' destruction of the Aztec empire. The major breakthrough came in 1589 with the publication of Richard Hakluyt's *Principall Navigations...*, a collection of travel narratives touching on English exploration. Hakluyt, as indicated earlier, was the greatest literary champion of English imperialism and as he urged his compatriots across the Atlantic, he described what to expect on the other side. The "Voyages" (as Hakluyt's work was generally known) was extremely popular and undoubtedly provided many Englishmen with their first glimpse of Mexico and other American regions. Samuel Purchas, Hakluyt's successor as literary imperialist and hispanophobe, issued two works, *Purchas his pilgrimage* (1613) and *Hakluytus Posthumus...* (1625), which circulated widely and provided new information on Mexico. By the time their program of colonization was well underway, Englishmen had access to as much general information about Mexico as any people in Europe with the possible exception of the Spaniards.[28]

The image of Mexico that emerges from these works is marked by a distinctive cleavage characteristic of general European responses to the Mexicans. On the one hand, European writers expressed admiration for the relatively advanced civilization of the Mexicans as compared with other New World aborigines. The Mexicans generally eschewed nakedness -- a trait that most 16th and 17th century writers regarded as a certain sign of savagism -- and instead wore bright cotton garments. The Mexicans were gifted craftsmen and created exquisite pieces of jewelry from the plentiful supplies of gold, silver, and precious stones to be found in their country. A number of Spanish writers noted their astonishment upon approaching Mexican cities which were marvels of planning and architecture. Especially notable was Tenochtitlán, the capital city of the Aztecs which sat in a salt lake and supported more than half a million residents.[29] The conqueror Cortés was especially impressed by the numerous temples of the city, monuments, he wrote, that were built with perfect art.

Moreover, English readers learned that Mexican cities pulsed with a variety of civilized activities. The Mexicans had established a sound educational system and instructed their children affectionately in the virtues of humility and respect for authority. Using a distinctive system of pictographs, native scholars recorded the traditions of their people in books made from the leaves of the maguey plant. A number of Europeans noted that the Mexicans lived according to a body of laws while the learned Jesuit, José de Acosta, found that they selected their rulers through democratic elections.[30] Perhaps the most gratifying news about the Mexicans to reach English readers was their quick receptivity to Christian instruction. Pedro Ordoñez de Cevallos reported that the Mexicans "very much honored priests and monks" and "when the Bell rings to Sermon, the Indian Boyes run up and down the streets crossing their foreheads."[31]

As to other positive qualities of Mexican character, English readers learned that the natives were hospitable, courteous and understanding, possessed of an ingenuousness all but extinct among Europeans. Acosta observed a contemplative aspect in the Mexicans, while another Spaniard, Martin Pérez, applauded the Mexicans for their valor. The greatest champion of the Mexicans, as for all the Indians, was Las Casas, who particularly admired the aborigines of Yucatan for their prudence and the general "uprightness" of their lives.[32]

Las Casas' diligent, indeed obsessive, campaign notwithstanding, the preponderance of European and, consequently, English opinion weighed heavily against the Mexicans.[33] Virtually every writer declaimed on their indolence, while others reported that the Mexicans were given to drunkenness, polygamy, and incest.

The Mexicans were vilified for their hostility to the Spaniards and their refusal to acquiesce promptly in the moral and cultural superiority of their conquerors. Their rapid degeneration under colonial rule also adversely affected European judgments. Ultimately, the Mexicans were regarded as a depraved race whose defects were only slightly mitigated by the grandeur and opulence of their cultures. Acosta, whose history of the Indies evinces a combination of erudition and fair-mindedness remarkable for his time, nevertheless portrayed Mexican history as a grotesque interplay of tribal jealousies, warfare, and heathenism. Acosta sanctioned a widespread European belief when he observed that the Mexicans had developed "customs more superstitious and...inhumane" than any ever seen or spoken of.[34]

No European writer on Mexico failed to note the terrible forms that heathenism had assumed in that land. Witches, sorcerers, and other agents of Satan fairly overran the countryside and held the natives in thralldom. Believing that their deities lived on human blood, the Mexicans had devised elaborate rites of sacrifice. Sullen priests led children, virgins, and prisoners of war to altars where they ripped open the chests of their victims, removed the still-beating hearts, and smeared blood on the marble lips of their idols. The priests would next burn the entrails in the belief that their gods enjoyed the smoke from such offerings. Finally, the priests ate various parts of the victims' bodies, including the arms and legs.[35] English readers learned that human sacrifices in Mexico sometimes reached the astonishing total of fifty thousand a year.[36] López de Gómara, who was perhaps the harshest and most influential writer on Mexico in the 16th century,[37] seemed to find the perfect symbol of Mexican culture in the Great Temple of Tenochtitlán. As architecture, the structure was the equal of the finest buildings of Europe but the Mexicans created their greatest art in celebration of their implacable savagery. Inside the Temple, priests offered up their victims to insatiable gods. An unmistakable stench emanated from the sacrificial chambers where blood ran several inches deep on the floor and the walls were stained red. It was a spectacle to make so stout a warrior as Cortes -- who had his own genius for barbarism -- turn away in revulsion.

As a writer of history, Gómara possessed various qualities unlikely to enhance his objectivity. He was a sedentary scholar with no experience in the New World and a hero-worshiper who had served as private secretary to Cortés. As an ardent nationalist, he sought to justify the violence of the Conquest and the subsequent subjugation and exploitation of the natives. Finally, Gómara embodied all the defects of a Renaissance European absolutely certain of his cultural and moral superiority. Still, Gómara's assessments, and those of writers of similar persuasion, had their impact, and Europeans came to regard the Mexicans as the most depraved of American aborigines. How could one condone, after all, such uniquely massive and reprehensible practices of human sacrifice and cannibalism among a people obviously intelligent and creative? Human sacrifice occurred in other regions of the New World and, of course, cannibalism was rampant, but of all the Americans, the Mexicans should have known better. A European might more easily accept the pure savagery of the Brazilian Tupinambá who wore not so much as a fig leaf, mindlessly devoured their enemies, and displayed not a trace of civilization.

As I have said, English images of Mexico derived largely from general European notions, mainly Spanish. There was, to be sure, a small irony in Englishmen accepting rather uncritically the views of their greatest enemies. But Englishmen had little experience in Mexico themselves and they took information where they found it. A small number did travel and live in Mexico, however, and a few even wrote about their experiences. Some of these early reports were collected by Hakluyt; together they provide a somewhat different perspective on the Mexican situation from the Spanish.

These early accounts form a tissue of fantasy, distortion, and occasionally acute observation. Some of the visitors emphasized the physical greatness of Mexico while others were most immediately struck by its sheer strangeness. Henry Hawks, a merchant who spent five years in Mexico, described the recurrent earthquakes, the "burning mountains," and the remarkable fauna. He wrote of a "certain gnat or fly which they call a musquito, which biteth both men and women in their sleep" and caused death. He reported too the existence of a "monstrous fish" -- presumably a crocodile -- which was a "great devourer of men and cattle."[38] Other travelers insisted that lions and tigers roamed the forests of Mexico. Here was a land where anything seemed possible.

As the travelers made clear, the inherent exoticism of Mexico was conspicuous in the natives. John Chilton, another merchant with over seventeen years experience in Spanish America, observed that the Mexican aborigines went about naked, painted their bodies blue, and wore their hair "long downe to their knees, tied as women use to do with their haire-laces."[39] Miles Philips, a survivor of the Hawkins debacle at San Juan de Ulúa in 1568, confirmed Chilton's description, only adding that the Mexicans painted their faces green, yellow, and red as well as blue. The Mexicans seemed, all in all, a sight terrible to behold. Interestingly, Hakluyt's travelers had little to say about the Mexican customs of devil worship, human sacrifice, and cannibalism, all of which were already disappearing under the cruel efficiency of Spanish colonialism.

As to the character of the natives, the English travelers had little good to report. Miles Philips came to regard the aborigines as pleasant and compassionate, but none of his compatriots shared his affection. More typical was the reaction of Henry Hawks who described the Indians as "void of all goodness." More than one writer found the Mexicans to be cowardly and drunken. John Chilton observed that for a bottle of wine, an Indian would sell his wife and children. But the most persistent charge against the Mexicans was indolence. English travelers were appalled that the natives had so little exploited their land. In noting the great fertility of the area around Mexico City, Robert Tomson commented "that if Christians had the inhabitation thereof, it would be put to a further benefit."[40] It was not much of a step to conclude that because the Indians had so little utilized their land they hardly deserved to keep it, a principle that later generations of Englishmen and Anglo-Americans would invoke frequently.

The English travelers, writing in an age of rising hispanophobia, were quick to note that Spanish conduct was as reprehensible in the New World as the Old. Tomson, for example, described how he was slapped into a Mexican prison on false charges of heresy and released only after numerous humiliations. Miles Philips and Job Hortop, whose unintended sojourns in Mexico were caused by Spanish "treachery," found themselves subjected to the outrages of the Inquisition tribunals which had been established in Mexico in 1571. Still, Philips and Hortop at least survived their ordeals in the grip of the Holy Office, as other marooned veterans of the Hawkins expedition did not.[41] Philips and Hortop also fared better than the native Mexicans who, by English estimates, had been reduced to absolute misery. Significantly, the English writers never had much praise and sympathy for the Indians but when they compared them to the Spaniards.

Indeed, the Indians had been so terribly abused that insurrection hung in the Mexican air and hardly an English traveler failed to catch its scent. Henry Hawks, in a rare instance of understatement, remarked that the aborigines "loved not the Spaniards" but he doubted that their courage and military prowess matched their resentment. John Chilton, who witnessed two rebellions during his stay in Mexico, noted that the Indians killed their conquerors at every opportunity and liked to wear Spanish scalps around their necks. The travelers went so far as to suggest that the Indians would welcome any interventionists who delivered them from their oppressors. This sort of oblique propaganda appears throughout the "Voyages" and served Hakluyt's great purpose of arousing his countrymen to challenge the Spaniards' domination of the New World. In support of this goal, Hakluyt graciously provided information about defense fortifications throughout Spanish America.

Hakluyt's "Voyages" was very popular in England but the collections of Samuel Purchas were even more so. Purchas' major work, *Hakluytus Posthumus* (generally known as the "Pilgrimes"), considerably advanced English knowledge of Mexico. The long excerpts from Acosta's *Natural and Moral History of the Indies,* for example, provided Englishmen with their first close look at pre-colonial Mexican society. Again, the exoticism of the Mexicans stands out. Acosta described how native priests beat themselves and slashed their legs to the bone in heathen rites of penitence, smearing blood on their faces and temples. Englishmen learned that the gods of Mexico were half man and half beast with bizarre names like Quetzalcóatl and Vitzliputzli. In the original edition of his "History," Acosta had maintained that the Mexicans -- and all the Indians -- were descended originally from unknown Old World peoples who had wandered to America across an as yet undiscovered strait or land bridge.[42] But English readers of his work were unlikely to detect any trace of blood-ties between the Mexicans and themselves. As always, the Mexicans seemed an alien and degenerate race whose very humanity was an issue much in doubt.

Certainly the most dramatic treatment of Mexican subjects to appear in the "Pilgrimes" was the partial reproduction of the Codex Mendoza, the first example of Mexican picture writing to be published in England.[43] It provided no important new information but it vividly illustrated various aspects of Mexican history and culture. The Codex depicted such mundane matters as parents instructing and disciplining their children but also represented various aspects of native warfare, including the disembodied heads of slain warriors. The human figures in the Codex were drawn in a primitive style and were distinguished by the almost formless faces, at once aloof and inscrutable.[44]

Purchas presented various other accounts of Mexican life including brief narratives by Cabeza de Vaca, Martín Perez, and Pedro Ordoñez de Cevallos and longer excerpts from Gómara, Oviedo, and Las Casas.[45] The first group of reports, although minor, are interesting inasmuch as they reveal 16th-century Europeans vacillating in their assessments of the Mexicans and finally settling into a bewildered contempt. Although many English readers were already familiar with the major writers represented in the "Pilgrimes," their response to Las Casas deserves a further comment here. As we have seen Englishmen eagerly accepted his testimony regarding Spanish atrocities in the New World, largely because it confirmed their prejudices and suited their purposes. But the friar's equally adamant defense of the Mexicans and other Indians fell on deaf ears because it did neither. Purchas himself, although an admirer of Las Casas, was inclined to emphasize not Mexican virtues but their "Man-eatings, Sodomies, Idolatries and other vices."

Within a span of three-quarters of a century, English translators, scholars, and propagandists had presented to their countrymen a substantial body of literature on Mexican subjects. The images that emerged from these works were not distinctively English but belonged to a broader European tradition. In any case, they did little to enhance appreciation of the Mexicans, grounded as they were in distortion, fantasy, and simple confusion.[46] As Europeans passed through Mexico, they carried ideological equipment which essentially precluded true understanding of the natives. The Aristotelian perspective of many Spanish writers, for example, required that the Mexicans exhibit recognizable systems of laws and social organization lest they be deemed savages. Their classical training also led a number of Spaniards to conclude that the stout aborigines were created for hard labor, which is to say to be slaves. English and Spanish writers alike were handicapped in their evaluations of Mexicans by the prevailing European fashion of travel reporting. Travelers and scholars had long insisted upon the exoticism and inherent inferiority of foreign societies, the rule of thumb being the more distant the people, the more striking these qualities. The benighted state of European ethnology in this period was exemplified by the enduring popularity of the "Travels" of Sir John Mandeville (which Hakluyt extracted in the first edition of the "Voyages" but judiciously omitted in the second), a preposterous chronicle of races of giants and headless people with eyes in their chests. Many of the Mexican narratives, with reports of strange beasts and natural wonders, bear traces of the Mandeville legacy. When European writers were not declaiming on the strangeness and barbarism of Mexico, they occupied themselves by trying to force the natives into conventional contexts of understanding and belief. Thus we see that the descriptions of the Chichimeca tribe manifest a strong resemblance to the *wilder Mann* of medieval thought. We note too the powerful influence of Biblical authority which maintained that all men, no matter how depraved, were receptive to Christianity; as a consequence, Europeans dutifully reported -- sometimes against their better judgment - the Mexicans to be so. Unable to deal with the Mexicans on their own terms and surveying the Americas in a haze of ethnocentrism, European writers in effect "invented" a species compatible with their traditions of savagism.[47]

The evidence regarding early colonial images of the Mexicans is primarily inferential. As indicated earlier, the collections of Hakluyt and Purchas were well-known to many colonists, perhaps even a majority. Probably the same percentage was acquainted with Thomas Gage's *The English-American,* the first book-length treatment of America by an English eyewitness and a work which managed to excoriate simultaneously the Spanish conquerors, the Catholic missionaries, and the hapless aborigines of Mexico and Guatemala. Gage added nothing new to available knowledge about Mexico except his pervasive malice but his work was quite popular in England and the colonies nonetheless.[48] Las Casas was also known to many colonists while the works of other major Spanish historians, notably Acosta, were read by a few intellectuals. Two other considerations should be borne in mind here. As a group, the colonists -- particularly the New Englanders -- were unusually well educated and alert to intellectual fashions in England and on the Continent. Secondly, given their powerful hatred of Catholicism and Spain, they were unlikely to disregard completely so important an area of activity for their enemies. It seems reasonable to conclude, therefore, that the early settlers held images of the Mexicans such as were circulating in contemporary England. Unquestionably, these images were not so clear, widespread, or fixed as those of Catholics and Spaniards, but still they lived in the minds of the colonists and grew more vigorous as time passed.

The first signs of active colonial interest in Mexico emerge near the end of the 17th century in the papers of Samuel Sewall, a devout Puritan whose commercial interests were pushing him subtly towards secularism; not surprisingly, Sewall's interest in Mexico was partly religious, partly economic. His earliest mention of Mexico occurred in a telling diary entry for September 26, 1686. That day, Sewall had attended a sermon during which the preacher, a Mr. Lee, "said that all America should be converted, Mexico overcome, England sent over to convert the Natives, look you do it."[49] Sewall took the charge seriously, read Las Casas and Gage, and came to imagine that he had located the New Jerusalem in Mexico City. He listened to every report of revolt in Mexico in the hope that the aborigines would overthrow the Spaniards and thus leave the way clear for his intended pilgrimage. But such reports were invariably "shams"[50] and Sewall decided to move matters along himself. In 1704, he urged Henry Newman to "set on foot the printing of the Spanish Bible in a fair Octavo; Ten Thousand Copies: and then you might attempt the Bombing of Santo Domingo, the Havana, Porto Rico, and Mexico itself."[51] Sewall's grandiose, if foredoomed, scheme apparently had the support of other New Englanders including Cotton Mather, who set about learning Spanish when he too received word of revolution in Mexico.[52]

Sewall's recurrent disappointments never dissuaded him from his interest. He pounced upon any tidbit of information about Mexico and wrote letters asking about such matters as the tides on the lake surrounding Mexico City. As a merchant, Sewall was dazzled by the reputed wealth of Mexico and the possibility of trade. He wrote of the "magnificence" of the capital city in which were found "1500 Coaches drawn with Mules." Sewall prayed long hours for Mexico and beseeched God to "open the Mexican Fountain."[53] Clearly, his words carried a double meaning. After the banishment of the Spaniards, Sewall expected that indigenous regimes would be receptive not only to Protestantism but to English-American traders.

Sewall's excited pursuit after news from Mexico suggests some of the difficulties any colonist interested in the subject would encounter. For the dearth of colonial writing on Mexico was not so much a function of indifference as of the sheer inaccessibility of such information. Although by 1700 colonists had established trade relations -- mostly illegal -- with various Spanish-American regions,[54] Mexico remained almost impenetrable. Spain regarded Mexico as the jewel of its colonial empire and guarded it assiduously against foreign economic exploitation -- a task simplified by the concentration of shipping in the single port of Veracruz -- until the moment of independence in 1821. Furthermore, overland travel from the English colonies to Mexico was impracticable because of great distances, rugged terrain, and hostile Indians. When colonists managed to elude Spanish defenses, as they did in the early 18th century on log-cutting expeditions to Yucatan and later on trading sorties into Texas, their business was conducted quietly and quickly.[55] Such incursions were not likely to stimulate studious treatments of Mexican life. In any event, because their ventures were both illegal and profitable, traders were disinclined to publicize them for fear of Spanish reprisals and intensified competition.

With the advent of local newspapers, word of contemporary Mexican affairs began to circulate more actively among the colonists. Mostly, it treated mundane issues and shed little light on the Mexicans themselves. Reports of native insurrection, widespread among Englishmen since the initial publication of Hakluyt's "Voyages," appeared occasionally, and if Sewall's and Mather's enthusiasm is any indication, were followed closely. *The Boston News-Letter*, the earliest established newspaper in the colonies, published this item in its second issue of April 24, 1704: "There was an Indian come from the Mainland of New Spain, complaining to the Governour of Jamaica, of bad usage they had met with from the Spainards [sic] and if His Excellency would send Forces, that the Indians would joyn them, and destroy the Spainards."[56] Colonists read that the Jesuits, living up to their reputation for mischief, also fomented revolt. Other types of reports, generally of a commercial nature, appeared in colonial newspapers. *The Boston News-Letter*, which advocated the opening of trade with Mexico as early as 1704, published lists of Mexican exports and noted the exchange value of Mexican currency. Needless to say, the Mexican gold and silver mines aroused great curiosity among Anglo-Americans and colonial newspapers regularly noted the immense quantities of these minerals being loaded in Veracruz for shipment to Spain. Where there was Spanish treasure there also were English pirates ready to pounce. Colonial newspapers reported on such activity with thinly-disguised approval.[57]

Although commercial news predominated, colonial newspapers provided other types of information about Mexico. They told of earthquakes and plagues in the country and changes in the governmental hierarchy. Around the middle of the 18th century, several newspapers carried articles speculating on the origins of the Mexicans. A piece in *The New York Weekly Post-Boy* argued that the Mexicans had descended from ancient Chinese or Japanese voyagers.[58] In 1740, *The Boston News-Letter* printed an article entitled "The CROWN of England's Title to America prior to that of Spain..." which resurrected the Elizabethan legend of Madoc ap Owen, a Welsh prince who allegedly planted a settlement in Mexico in the 12th century.[59] The story was sheer fantasy but its publication in a major New England newspaper indicates the intensity with which the colonists sought to wrench away from the Spaniards a portion of Mexican and southern American riches.[60]

The significance of these newspaper accounts is three-fold. First, the willingness of newspapers to publish Mexican items, no matter how trivial, inaccurate, or fanciful, suggests a considerable curiosity among colonists about the country. Secondly, the nature of the reports reflects the abiding Anglo-American interest in the economic exploitation of Mexico. Figures such as Sewall and Mather may have been motivated to learn about Mexico primarily for religious reasons, but other settlers had a different priority; in any case, colonial concern for the salvation of the aborigines seems to have receded quickly. Finally, and most importantly, the information received by the colonists contained nothing to challenge traditional images of Mexico as established by Spanish and English writers in the Elizabethan and Jacobean ages.

Actually, traditional images of Mexico underwent a period of revitalization after the mid-18th century. In 1758, for example, *The English American* by Thomas Gage re-emerged not once but twice. Samuel Nevill, a notorious imperialist and hispanophobe, serialized the work in his *New American Magazine* while James Parker issued the first American edition of Gage's diatribe. Both reproductions appeared under the title "The Traveller" and they not only stirred up sentiment against the Spaniards[61] but vivified colonial images of Mexican depravity. Colonists read of Montezuma's harem of one thousand concubines, and his menagerie of crocodiles and great snakes nourished on human flesh and blood. Gage described the superstition of Mexico City as the greatest in the world, exceeding even that of Rome. And, of course, there was mention of the aboriginal rites of human sacrifice. Gage told how Aztec priests concocted a paste out of seeds and children's blood to be used in their ceremonies. Colonists learned that around the Great Temple of Tenochtitlán were displayed the skulls of sacrificial victims, Gage estimating the total at 136,000.[62] Under Spanish rule, the Mexicans had improved not at all but regressed, retaining many of their old vices and absorbing some from the Spaniards as well. Gage argued that the Professed conversion of the Indians was mere pretense to placate their masters. Away from Spanish eyes, the Mexicans practiced devil worship and witchcraft.

Over the next generation, other conventional treatments of Mexican character and culture came into Anglo-American hands, notably *The History of the Conquest of Mexico* by Antonio de Solís who relied heavily on the accounts of Cortés and Gómara and thus inevitably disparaged the Indians.[63] The travel collection of John Harris and Edmund Burke's *Account of the European Settlements in America* were other representative works found on colonial booklists which treated the Mexicans with varying degrees of antipathy.[64]

By all odds, the most important study of Mexico to reach English Americans in the 18th century was William Robertson's *History of America*. This work, originally issued in London in 1777, remains with William Prescott's books the classic treatment of the Spanish Conquest in the English language. The "History" made an immediate impact in Britain and was soon transported to the United States where its influence was enormous.

Robertson gracefully recounted an historical episode which he regarded as one of the greatest of human adventures. He chronicled the exploits of the heroic Columbus, the ambitious Cortés, and the villainous Pizarro, all the while condemning what he perceived as the tragic flaw of Spanish character, an avarice so boundless that it compelled the conquerors to an unprecedented succession of outrages. Robertson allowed that the Conquest was effected for the most part by the dregs of Spanish society, an army of scoundrels all but banished from their homeland, and he warned about drawing unfair inferences about Spanish character from their actions. But Robertson's qualifications were unconvincing and the reported barbarism of the

Conquerors spoke for itself. In any event, Robertson's low estimate of the American performance of the Spaniards was no surprise, coming as it did from a Scottish Presbyterian and a licensed minister at that. More interesting, and ultimately of greater importance, were Robertson's comments on the Mexican aborigines.

Robertson moved to his assessment of the Mexicans from a broader consideration of the character of the New World aborigines. Writing in an age when the idea of the noble savage had gained wide currency, he vigorously rejected the concept.[65] He found nothing in his researches to conclude that the Americans were innocent and generous, a race that had luxuriated in a western paradise before the intrusion of the Spaniards. Instead, Robertson argued that their pre-Columbian way of life was less an example of dignified repose than a case of extraordinary indolence. A strict environmentalist influenced by Buffon and de Pauw, Robertson believed man was particularly affected by climate. All the great peoples and cultures, he noted, were found in the temperate zones; other factors being equal, the closer one lived to the equator, the less likely the possibility of human development. Thus, Robertson described the North American Indians as being "more robust, more active, more intelligent and more courageous" than those in the southern regions where the sultry climate had stifled the native molecules into a perpetual lethargy.[66] But such praise as he offered the northern aborigines was only relative; as a group, the Americans were brutal, treacherous, and cruel: in a word, "savages" without any mitigating adjectives. They were given to drunkenness and cannibalism and the only activity likely to shake them from their indolence was war. In sum, the Americans exhibited few of the traits that distinguish man from beast.[67]

Robertson's aborigines were not only defective morally and intellectually but physically. The Americans lacked robustness and sexual desire and were decimated by the ordinary diseases of the Old World. Here again, the Americans were victimized by the environment. Because of the constant heat, the Americans could not summon the energy to cultivate the land. This in turn caused the air to stagnate, the water to give off "putrid exhalations" and the land to be full of "noxious maladies." The climate of America was consequently "remarkably unhealthy" and the "principle of life" necessarily "less active and vigorous than in the ancient continent."[68]

While Robertson characterized the Americans as altogether a bad lot, some were worse than others and the supreme villains, by any measure, were the Mexicans. Unlike earlier writers such as Acosta, Robertson did not soften his denunciations with concessions to the cultural achievements of the Mexicans. He argued instead that their institutions "did not differ greatly from those of other inhabitants of America."

They fought incessantly, were vengeful, and never learned to temper their rage, a certain sign of savagism. Robertson concluded that "we cannot but suspect their degree of civilization to have been very imperfect."[69]

What did distinguish the Mexicans was their sophisticated religious system which contrasted with the primitive rituals of other Indians. But it was sophisticated essentially in its capacity for a brutality and sordidness which shaped the very character of the Mexican natives:

From the genius of the Mexican religion we may...form a most just conclusion with respect to its influence upon the character of the people. The aspect of superstition in Mexico was gloomy and atrocious. Its divinities were clothed with terror, and delighted in vengeance. They were exhibited to the people under detestable forms, which created horror. The figures of serpents, of tigers, and of other destructive animals, decorated their temples. Fear was the only principle that inspired their votaries. Fasts, mortifications, and penances, all rigid, and many of them excruciating to an extreme degree, were the means employed to appease the wrath of their gods, and the Mexicans never approached their altars without sprinkling them with blood drawn from their own bodies. But, of all offerings, human sacrifices were deemed the most acceptable. This religious belief mingling with the implacable spirit of vengeance, and adding new force to it, every captive taken in war was brought to the temple, was devoted as a victim to the deity, and sacrificed with rites no less solemn than cruel. The heart and head were the portion consecrated to the gods; the warrior by whose prowess the prisoner had been seized, carried off the body to feast upon it with his friends. Under the impression of ideas so dreary and terrible, and accustomed daily to scenes of bloodshed rendered awful by religion, the heart of man must harden and be steeled to every sentiment of humanity. The spirit of the Mexicans was accordingly unfeeling; and the genius of their religion so far counterbalanced the influence of policy and arts, that notwithstanding their progress in both, their manners, instead of softening, became more fierce. To what circumstances it was owing that superstition assumed such a dreadful form among the Mexicans, we have not sufficient knowledge of their history to determine. But its influence is visible, and produced an effect that is singular in the history of the human species. The manners of the people in the New World, who had made the greatest progress in the arts of policy, were, in several respects, the most ferocious, and the barbarity of some of their customs exceeded even those of the savage state.[70]

Later in his study, Robertson compares the other great civilization of the Americas, the Incan, to the Mexican. In nearly every respect the Incas are described as more civilized and more humane. Particularly in that notable American institution, the art of war, the Peruvians were less barbarous: "the wars in which the Incas engaged were carried on with a spirit very different from that of other American nations. They fought not, like savages, to destroy and exterminate; or, like the Mexicans, to glut blood thirsty divinities with human sacrifices. They conquered in order to reclaim and civilize the vanquished, and to diffuse the knowledge of their own institutions and arts."[71]

Ultimately, Robertson presented an extremely gloomy assessment of the Mexicans, greatly underestimating their cultural achievements while exaggerating the uniqueness of their barbarism.[72] In his mind, the Mexicans stood as the fiercest and most detestable of the New World peoples, inferior culturally to the Incas and in qualities of character to the North American natives.[73] By also arguing that the Spaniards who were attracted to America were the most undesirable elements of their society, Robertson offered to his readers a Mexico populated by two extraordinary breeds of scoundrels already mixing their bloods.[74] In an era when revolutionary movements in Latin America were at last beginning to gather real support, Robertson's Mexico seemed an unlikely setting for the flourishing of humane, republican institutions. To those readers acquainted with traditional portraits of Mexican life, Robertson's depictions were all too familiar; his claims of objectivity and originality notwithstanding, he essentially took old images and couched them in a variety of 18th-century scientism.

The History of America had its critics of course, both in Europe and in America. Francisco Clavigero, another historian of Mexico but one with broad experience in the country, attacked Robertson for his biases and his imperfect use of available sources.[75] Thomas Jefferson, who disagreed not with his depictions of the southern aborigines but with his generalizations about the American environment, rebuked Robertson for his slavish reliance on Buffon and de Pauw. Still, the "History" withstood such attacks and remained the most popular and influential study in its field until the publication of Prescott's *Conquest of Mexico* in 1843. It was serialized in numerous American journals and sold briskly in several editions, including a paperback. Prescott himself called Robertson "the illustrious historian of America" and prominent writers such as Joel Barlow, Washington Irving, and William Gilmore Simms came under Scot's influence. Indeed, Frederick Stimson wrote that for early American writers both historical and fictional, Robertson "seems to have been the chief source for all things pertaining to the Spanish in the New World."[76] Confirming traditional prejudices and vague premonitions, *The History of America* found a broad readership in the young republic.

The popularity of Robertson's "History" served to bring into play the final component necessary to form an ideological prism through which Americans would view contemporary Mexicans in the 19th century. As we have seen, anti-Catholicism and hispanophobia were clearly defined and pervasive in Anglo-American culture long before 1777; more than any previous event or literary work, *The History of America* helped to codify and disseminate anti-Mexican sentiment and raise it to a more nearly equal level of importance. These various antipathies eventually linked and merged as Americans came to recognize the phenomenon of cultural and racial fusion between Indian and Spaniard which had been proceeding since the Conquest.

When Americans began actually to encounter Mexicans in Texas, Santa Fe, and other Mexican territories after 1821, their initial responses were conditioned primarily by the traditions of hispanophobia and anti-Catholicism. Many American travelers in Mexico called the natives "Spaniards" and assigned to them, almost reflexively, the familiar defects of the Black Legend.[77] Josiah Gregg, a trader on the Santa Fe Trail, observed that the New Mexicans "appear to have inherited much of the cruelty and intolerance of their ancestors and no small portion of their bigotry and fanaticism."[78] Other travelers called the Mexicans "priest-ridden." Richard Henry Dana, a visitor to California, attributed Mexican indolence to their Catholicism which subordinated work to the celebration of an interminable series of religious holidays. The primacy of hispanophobia and anti-Catholicism in early American treatments of the Mexicans was partly the result of their sheer tenacity in the national consciousness but it was also a function of the traditional European belief that advanced cultures (which is to say their own) invariably overwhelmed primitive ones. Robertson lent support to this view when he contrasted the awesome hegemony of the Spaniards with the languid acquiescence of the Mexicans.

About 1840, racialist thought emerged to focus attention on the "inherent" characteristics of the Mexicans rather than those acquired during their long subjugation to the Catholic Spaniards. Here again, we note a natural line of development and the force of traditional images. The core of Anglo-American notions about the Mexicans had always been an assumed depravity and certainly the racialists retained this idea. It is striking how closely their depictions of contemporary Mexicans resemble Robertson's portrayal of pre-Conquest aborigines: there is the same indolence, duplicity, melancholy, violence, and cruelty. I am not suggesting that racialists generally bore the direct influence of Robertson but that his views of the Mexicans represent a traditional mode of perceiving them that persisted into the mid-19th century with only slight modifications. To be sure, racialists discarded Robertson's environmentalism as an insufficient explanation of human differences just as he had rejected earlier concepts of savagism. But his fundamental assumptions about Mexican character, some of which are traceable to Gómara, endured.

Of all racialist theories, the doctrine of miscegenation, which held that the progeny of racially-different parents inherited the worst qualities of each, had the greatest impact on American views of Mexicans. Racialists regarded mixed-breeds as impulsive, unstable, and prone to insanity.[79] The Mexicans, as the most conspicuous products of mass miscegenation, inevitably were assigned these qualities. Still, we recall that Gage had attributed part of the aborigines' decline to their intermarriage with the Spaniards and Robertson had noted that the Mexicans were given to sudden springs of violence. Moreover, in its emphasis on the vices of the Mexicans' progenitors, the doctrine of miscegenation led back to hispanophobia. Other 19th-century responses to Mexicans reveal the same process: old images received new justifications and lived on. Some are with us still.

NOTES

1. I am grateful to the American Council of Learned Societies for a research grant during 1976-77 which allowed me to complete this study.
2. *Culture Conflict in Texas, 1821-1835* (New York: Columbia University Press, 1932).
3. *Mexico and the Hispanic Southwest in American Literature*, 2nd ed. (Tucson: University of Arizona Press, 1977), pp. 17-18. A longer but still incomplete view of anti-Mexican sentiment in the United States is presented in Karl M. Schmitt, *Mexico and the United States, 1821-1973* (New York: John Wiley & Sons, 1974). pp. 11-31.
4. The literature on anti-Catholic attitudes in England is voluminous but particularly useful to this study are Sister Mary Augustina (Ray), *American Opinion of Roman Catholicism in the Eighteenth Century* (New York: Columbia University Press, 1936), pp. 11-35; Arnold O. Meyer, *England and the Catholic Church under Queen*

Elizabeth (London: Paul, Trench, Trubner, 1916); and William Haller, *Foxe's Book of Martyrs and the Elect Nation* (London: Cape, 1963).

5. See a condensation of the "Apologia" by William of Orange in Charles Gibson, ed., *The Black Legend: Anti-Spanish Attitudes in the Old World and New* (New York: Alfred A. Knopf, 1971), pp. 42-47.

6. The term "Black Legend" refers to a system of beliefs which holds that Spaniards are uniquely depraved. For a more extensive discussion of this phenomenon see William S. Maltby, *The Black Legend in England* (Durham, N. C.: Duke University Press, 1971); and Philip Wayne Powell, *Tree of Hate* (New York: Basic Books. 1971).

7. See Winthrop Jordan, *White Over Black* (Chapel Hill: University of North Carolina Press, 1968), pp. 3-43 for a thorough treatment of this phenomenon.

8. Ibid., p. 5. See also Robert R. Cawley, *The Voyagers and Elizabethan Drama* (Boston: D. C. Heath, 1938), p. 31 and Marvin A. Breslow, *A Mirror of England: English Puritan Views of Foreign Nations, 1618-1640* (Cambridge: Harvard University Press. 1970). p. 73.

9. Louis B. Wright commented that "no one can calculate the enormous influence of Foxe's descriptions of persecutions by Catholics in keeping alive hatred of Romanism in the breasts of American Protestants." See his *The Cultural Life of the American Colonies, 1607-1763* (New York: Harper & Row, 1957), p. 133.

10. See Thomas G. Wright, *Literary Culture in Early New England, 1620-1730* (New Haven: Yale University Press, 1920) and C. A. Herrick, "The Early New Englanders: What Did They Read?," *The Library*, 3rd series, 9, No. 33 (1918), 1-17.

11. *Of Plymouth Plantation*, ed. Samuel E. Morison (New York: Knopf, 1952), p. 380.

12. *The Powring Out of the Seven Vials: or, An Exposition of the Sixteenth Chapter of the Revelation, With an Application of It to Our Times* (London: n.p., 1645), p. 44.

13. "The Song of Deliverance" in *Handkerchiefs from Paul*, ed. Kenneth B. Murdock (Cambridge: Harvard University Press, 1921), p. 32.

14. See Paul L. Ford. *The New England Primer* (New York: Dodd, Mead, 1897), pp. 45, 90, 247-48.

15. Quoted in Ray Allen Billington, *The Protestant Crusade, 1800-1860* (1938; reprinted, Chicago: Quadrangle Books. 1964). p. 16.

16. There are several excellent studies of early American attitudes toward Catholicism and Spain. In addition to Billington and the Sister Augustina study cited

earlier, see Arthur J. Riley, *Catholicism in New England to 1788* (Washington, D.C.: Catholic University of America, 1936) and Stanley T. Williams, *The Spanish Background of American Literature* (New Haven: Yale University Press, 1955), I, 3-20.

17. See Augustina, pp. 212-61, Billington, pp. 4-19, and Riley, pp. 217-60.

18. Quoted in Billington, p. 6.

19. Harry Bernstein, *Origins of Inter-American Interest, 1700-1812* (Philadelphia: University of Pennsylvania Press, 1945), p. 2. See also Charles M. Andrews, *The Colonial Period of American History* (New Haven: Yale University Press, 1934), 111, 6-34.

20. For examples of hispanophobic documents from the Southern colonies, see Alexander S. Salley, ed., *Narratives of Early Carolina, 1650-1708* (New York: Charles Scribner's, 1911), pp. 185-86, 204-09, and Alexander Brown, *The Genesis of the United States,* 2 vols. (New York: Houghton-Mifflin. 1890), *passim.*

21. Charles W. Arnade, *The Siege of St. Augustine in 1702* (Gainesville: University of Florida Press, 1959).

22. J. Leitch Wright, *Anglo-Spanish Rivalry in North America* (Athens: University of Georgia Press, 1971), p. 87.

23. See G. L. Rives, "Spain and the United States in 1795," *American Historical Review,* 4 (1898), 62-79; for other treatments of American-Spanish problems in the period, see Arthur P. Whitaker, *The Spanish-American Frontier: 1783-1795* (Boston: Houghton-Mifflin, 1927) and Whitaker, *The Mississippi Question, 1795-1803* (New York: Appleton, 1934).

24. *The Writings of Thomas Jefferson,* ed. H. A. Washington (New York: Riker, 1857). V, 64.

25. Eden's major works, *A treatyse of the newe India* (1553) and the *Decades of the newe worlde* (1555) are reprinted in *The First Three English Books on America,* ed. Edward Arber (Birmingham: Turnbull & Spears, 1885).

26. See Hugh Honour's marvelous study, profusely illustrated, *The New Golden Land* (New York: Pantheon, 1975), esp. pp. 3-83.

27. See David Beers Quinn, *England and the Discovery of America, 1481-1620* (New York: Alfred A. Knopf. 1974). *passim.*

28. There are several useful studies of English responses to America during the period under consideration: Franklin T. McCann, *English Discovery of America to 1585* (New York: King's Crown Press, 1952); John Parker, *Books to Build an Empire* (Amsterdam: N. Israel, 1965); and Colin Steele, *English Interpreters of the*

New World from Purchas to Stevens (Oxford: Dolphin Books, 1975). A bibliography of books related to the New World published in England to 1600 may be found in George B. Parks, *Richard Hakluyt and the English Voyages,* 2nd ed. (1928; reprinted, New York: Ungar. 1961), pp. 270-76.

29. See Eden, "Decades," p. 342. Here, Tenochtitlán is called "Temixtitan."

30. José de Acosta, *The Natural and Moral History of the Indies,* ed. Clements R. Markham (1604; reprinted, London: Hakluyt Society, 1880), II, 411. The impact of the 1604 English edition of Acosta's monumental study was greatly enhanced by Purchas who extracted long sections in *Hakluytus Posthumus.*

31. "Notes of the West Indies," in *Hakluytus Posthumus, or Purchas His Pilgrimes* (Glasgow: MacLehose, 1906), XVII, 213.

32. "A briefe Narration of the destruction of the Indies by the Spaniards," in Purchas, XVIII, 120.

33. Howard Mumford Jones treats in admirable fashion the ambiguity of general European images of the Americans in *O Strange New World* (New York: Viking, 1964), pp. 1-70.

34. "Mexican Antiquities," in Purchas, XV, 240.

35. See Eden, "Decades," p. 189.

36. Francisco López de Gómara, *The Conquest of the Weast India* (1578; reprinted, New York: Scholars' Facsimiles & Reprints, 1940), p. 110.

37. See Benjamin Keen, *The Aztec Image in Western Thought* (New Brunswick, N.J.: Rutgers University Press, 1971), pp. 49-172, for a broad treatment of European attitudes towards the Mexicans in this period.

38. See Hawks, "A relation of the commodities of Nova Hispania," in Hakluyt, *Principall Navigations* (Glasgow: MacLehose, 1904), IX, 378-97. This modern publication of Hakluyt's work is based on the second edition which began appearing in 1598. The later edition dropped a narrative by a traveler in Mexico, David Ingram. This holds no importance for the present study because Ingram's report contains virtually no information on Mexico

39. "A notable discourse of M. John Chilton..." in Hakluyt, IX, 371.

40. "The voyage of Robert Tomson Marchant..." in Hakluyt, IX, 357.

41. At least two of the Hawkins party were burned at the stake and many others—of over a hundred put ashore—were punished for heresy. See Richard Greenleaf, *The Mexican Inquisition in the Sixteenth Century* (Albuquerque: University of New Mexico Press, 1969), pp. 163-67.

42. The origins of the Mexicans and other New World aborigines became a subject of considerable debate among European intellectuals and theologians soon after the Discoveries. Generally speaking, Europeans, like Acosta, sought to develop theories consistent with the biblical doctrine of monogenesis. Oviedo speculated that Americans were descended either from Carthagenians or ancient Spaniards; Las Casas argued for an East Indies origin. Gómara offered the mythical continent of Atlantis as the homeland of the Americans. Ever the nationalists, Hakluyt and Purchas both published the whimsical legend of Madoc ap Owen, a Welsh prince who allegedly planted an American colony about A.D. 1170. See Lee Huddleston, *Origins of the American Indians: European Concepts, 1492-1729* (Austin: University of Texas Press. 1967).

43. Steele, p. 43.

44. The portions of the Codex are presented in Purchas, XV, 412-504. For a look at the way sixteenth-century European artists depicted the Mexicans, see Honour, pp. 59-62.

45. For a survey of Mexican materials in the "Pilgrimes," see Steele, pp. 40-49.

46. The following remarks draw heavily from these works: J. H. Elliott, *The Old World and the New, 1492-1650* (Cambridge, Eng.: Cambridge University Press, 1970), pp. 1-53; Margaret Hodgen, *Early Anthropology in the Sixteenth and Seventeenth Centuries* (Philadelphia: University of Pennsylvania Press, 1964); and John H. Rowe, "Ethnography and Ethnology in the Sixteenth Century," *Kroeber Anthropological Society Papers*, 30 (1964), 1-19.

47. See Edmundo O. Gorman, *The Invention of America* (Bloomington: Indiana University Press, 1961).

48. In discussing the Spanish Conquest of Mexico, Gage plagiarized long passages from Gómara. See J. Eric S. Thompson's introduction to Gage's work in *Thomas Gage's Travels in the New World* (Norman: University of Oklahoma Press, 1958), xix.

49. *The Diary of Samuel Sewall,* ed. M. Halsey Thomas (New York: Farrar, Straus, Giroux. 1973). I, 122.

50. Ibid., pp. 397-98.

51. "Letter-Book of Samuel Sewall," *Collections of the Massachusetts Historical Society,* 6th series, 1 (1886), 297.

52. See "Diary of Cotton Mather, 1681-1708," *Massachusetts Historical Society Collections,* 7th series, 7 (1911), 284. Mather eventually published a Protestant pamphlet in Spanish, "La Fe del Christiano."

53. "Diary," I, 462. For further discussion of Sewall's interest in Mexico, see Harry Bernstein, *Making an Inter-American Mind* (Gainesville: University of Florida Press. 1961). pp. 6-10.

54. See Bernstein, *Origins of Inter-American Interest*, pp. 15-32.

55. Ibid., esp. pp. 16-19, and J. Leitch Wright, p. 118. The trade to Campeche in Yucatan was especially significant. Bernstein reports that in one month in 1714, twenty ships weighed anchor from Boston to Campeche. A number of years later, New Englanders were cutting so much Campeche wood that they drove down the English price by as much as eighty percent.

56. For another typical example of this type of report see *New York Gazette*, 31 January 1737, p. 3.

57. See, for example, *New York Weekly Post-Boy*, 25 April 1743, p. 1.

58. *New York Gazette*, 11 March 1754, p. 1. The same article, reprinted from *The London Daily Advertiser*, also appeared in *The Boston News-Letter*, 7 February 1754, p. 1.

59. *The Boston News-Letter*, 12 June 1740, p. 1.

60. The legend was reprinted in the second issue of Benjamin Franklin's *General Magazine*, February 1741, pp. 80-83. For a brief discussion of the Madoc legend, see Samuel Eliot Morison, *The European Discovery of America: The Northern Voyages* (New York: Oxford University Press, 1971), pp. 84-87.

61. Towards this end, Nevill published another series in his magazine, "The History of the Continent of America," which drew from Hakluyt and Purchas to celebrate the English presence in the New World.

62. *The Traveller* (Woodbridge, N. J.: James Parker, 1758). See pp. 34-40.

63. For an evaluation of Solis' treatment of the Mexicans see Keen, pp. 176-79.

64. Harris' work, *Navigantium arque Itinerantium Bibliotheca*, drew its Mexican material from Solis. See Keen. p. 258.

65. See Honour, pp. 118-37. A standard, although flawed study on the subject of the romantic primitive is Hoxie N. Fairchild's *The Noble Savage* (New York: Columbia University Press, 1928). See also Edward Dudley and Maximilian Novak, eds., *The Wild Man Within* (Pittsburgh: University of Pittsburgh Press, 1972).

66. See *The History of America* (1777; reprinted, New York: J. Harper, 1832), pp. 195-96.

67. As a devout Christian, Robertson was obliged to accept the Americans as fellow humans but he occasionally characterized them as "melancholy animals" (p. 188).

68. Robertson, p. 127. For a brilliant treatment of the ideas of Buffon and de Pauw and Robertson's adherence to them, see Antonello Gerbi, *The Dispute of the New World*, trans. Jeremy Moyle (Pittsburgh: University of Pittsburgh Press, 1973), esp. pp. 165-69. Buffon posited the inferiority of animals in the New World because of climatic influences while de Pauw extended the theory to the aborigines.

69. Robertson, p. 324.

70. Ibid., p. 329.

71. Ibid., p. 333.

72. Other scholars, Hugh Honour and Benjamin Keen for example, would not agree with my assessment of Robertson's depictions. Honour (p. 132) calls Robertson "more judicious" than many of his predecessors while Keen (pp. 275-85) argues that he paid respect to the Mexicans' cultural achievements. The issue is complicated by Robertson's habit of contradiction. As indicated before, he accepts the aborigines as fellow humans yet calls them animals. Certainly, Robertson notes the cultural superiority of the Mexicans over other aborigines but the admiration is purely relative, always qualified and not deeply felt. His truer feelings seem to emerge in the long passage quoted here in which he, a highly disciplined rationalist, nevertheless comes close to passionate excoriation.

73. The notion of the superiority of the North American Indians to the Mexicans in Anglo-American thought goes back to Hackluyt who in a letter to Walter Raleigh described the northern Indians as being of "better wittes" than the Mexicans. See Hakluyt, VIII, p. 443. This idea received great currency in the United States during the nineteenth century and has become part of the national mythology. See, for example, Walter Prescott Webb's remark that compared to that of the Plains Indians the blood of Indians in Mexican territory was "as ditch water." See Webb, *The Great Plains* (Boston: Ginn, 1931), pp. 125-26.

74. Robertson correctly identified the product of Spanish-Indian miscegenation as the *mestizo*. The term was not unknown to American readers. Miles Philips used it in his sixteenth-century narrative as did Thomas Gage in the next century. The phenomenon of miscegenation was to have a highly negative effect on American attitudes toward Mexico after 1840. See my "The Mexican Image in American Travel Literature, 1831-1869," *New Mexico Historical Review*, 52 (January 1977): 5-29.

75. Clavigero's work, *The History of Mexico* (1787) is far more balanced than Robertson's. Clavigero does not condone Mexican atrocities but juxtaposes them with the many humane and meditative aspects of Mexican life that Robertson ignores.

Clavigero's book was also known in the United States but its influence was restricted to intellectual and scholarly circles.

76. See Stimson, "William Robertson's Influence on Early American Literature," *Americas,* 14 (1957), 37-43. Surprisingly, Robertson's influence on American attitudes toward Mexico has been all but overlooked by scholars. One exception is David J. Weber in his *Foreigners in Their Native Land* (Albuquerque: University of New Mexico Press, 1973). pp. 52-61, 68-69.

77. As Harry Bernstein and Stanley Williams explain, there was a small group of scholars and intellectuals who sought to enhance appreciation of Spanish culture, to stimulate, as it were, "a white legend." But the movement was small and had no significant effect on popular attitudes in the period under consideration.

78. *Commerce of the Prairies* (1844; reprinted, Norman: University of Oklahoma Press, 1954), p. 154.

79. The legacy of the doctrine of miscegenation has persisted into the present century. In explaining the rash of Mexican rebellions in the Santa Anna era, the respected historian Wilfrid Callcott wrote: "For one thing, the Mexican was a new ethnic combination and as such had not become standardized as a product either physically or mentally. No plant or animal breeder will risk his cash or reputation by guaranteeing standard results as to types, color or characteristics of plants or animals secured from a new blend. The more emotional and less stable new racial blend, the new Mestizo, had vague longings for equality and justice, but as a class lacked the stamina and courage of his own convictions. He would start out boldly, but, at the first reverse, his old fear of the 'master' would return, and panic-stricken, he would give up the contest." See *Santa Anna* (Norman: University of Oklahoma Press, 1936), p. 116. In American fiction there are numerous Mexican characters who, suddenly and inexplicably, go temporarily crazy. One thinks, for example, of "Spanish Johnny" in Willa Cather's *The Song of the Lark* and Danny in Steinbeck's *Tortilla Flat.*

II

1800-1850

I

The Mexican Independence Movement, The Committee of Correspondence, Miguel Hidalgo y Costilla, José Maria Morelos y Pavon, Chilpancingo, Liberalismo, Secularization, The Northern Provincias, The Mexican Constitution of 1824, The United States Constitution, Adams-Onis Treaty of 1819.

At the beginning of the 19th century Spanish sovereignty had been extended into most of the regions of the northern frontier, today's American Southwest. By this time its population, as a result of intensified racial mixture, had become the most heterogenous group within the entire Spanish colonial empire. They were uniquely self-sufficient colonists due to their distance from Spain's power core center at Mexico City. In some ways they were freer than their countrymen to the south. Their frontier experience was not unlike that of the American frontiersmen. They were freer than their southern counterparts to create agricultural and urban communities adapted to local conditions. This required a healthy regard for the nomadic indigenous groups and a rational allocation of precious natural resources. In some ways, indicated by the presence of communalism in land and resource distribution in the New Mexico region, they developed distinct frontier practices and discarded old ones. The labor and land control institutions imposed throughout the Mexican colony, the *encomienda* and *repartimiento*, never took hold in the northern frontier. The frontiersmen were more concerned with survival in the demanding conditions of the frontier.

In central Mexico problems of a different sort surfaced at the turn of the century. Despite many efforts by Spanish colonial officials to maintain a sort of Mexican isolationism, news of events in Europe and among the thirteen American colonies slowly found their way into Mexico and provoked intense debate. Mexicans became aware of the American colonial rebellion against British rule. And they became increasingly interested in revolutionary developments in France which culminated in the first French Revolution. Smuggled copies of the American Declaration of Independence surfaced in Mexico and became the major subject of interest to the emerging 'literary clubs.' One of the most important of these was the Committee of Correspondence. Among its members were Miguel Hidalgo y Costilla, Juan Aldama and Ignacio Allende, prominent participants during the Independence movement's early years. They advanced a harsh critique of the Spanish colonial institutions and gave valuable assistance to the Mexican revolutionary movement about to erupt.

The Mexican Independence movement of 1810-1821 was the first major international political event on the North American continent in the early 19th century. It culminated decades of discontent with distant and oppressive Spanish rule.

141

say over & over
instill
impart

Gradually a sense of Mexican nationalism and anti-Spanish privilege had emerged as the overwhelmingly mestizo nation evolved an identity separate from Spain.

For decades prior to these events, mounting discontent with centuries of Spanish oppression had been infused with an unexpected jolt as a result of late eighteenth century colonial reforms. Bourbon reforms of the late eighteenth century had liberalized trade restrictions, opened previously closed areas of the economy to *Criollos* (Spaniards born in the New World) and unexpectedly nourished a rebellious and independent spirit. With the successful French invasion of Spain and the crown in disarray, some believed, particularly *Criollos,* that Mexico's independence had already arrived. The *Peninsulares* (Spanish immigrants in Mexico) maintained that the Spanish crown kept its authority over its colonies. Also of particular interest was the implementation of Spain's new liberalism, and its redefinition of human rights and the fundamental equality of men. Privileged social positions on account of race or birth were undermined and had been targets of the European and American rebellions. Mexican revolutionary leaders followed these events closely.

The Committee of Correspondence, Mexico's first anti-colonial conspiracy, secretly met to discuss these historic victories against tyranny. The French Revolution offered Mexican intellectual leaders the possibility to eliminate government by privileged elites and the American Declaration of Independence, particularly its proclamations against colonial rule, inspired Mexican rebels against colonial rule. Convinced of their need to declare against Spanish colonial rule, members of the conspiracy planned for the uprising to begin in late 1810. The *Criollo* class, the majority within the Committee of Correspondence, hoped to establish an equal footing with the despised *Peninsulares.* As a group they cared little for the interests of Mexico's non-Spanish classes and castes. But leaders with more ambitious goals, including massive social and political reorganization, emerged to force the movement into new and radical directions. *class, social group*

Miguel Hidalgo y Costilla emerged as the unlikely leader of the conspiracy to end Spanish colonial rule. Hidalgo, a village priest from Dolores, had contemplated the implications of the American and French Revolutions as a member of the original Committee of Correspondence. And as a fiery opponent of Spanish privilege and an ally of Mexico's countless dispossessed, he rallied the colonial outcasts against the hated *gauchupines* (derogatory for *Peninsulares*). Needing little encouragement the *castas* (non-Spaniards) erupted into vengeful violence against centuries of Spanish oppression. Hidalgo's plan declared for the complete repudiation of Spanish colonial rule and massive social reform including an end to racial privilege and massive

denial
negation

distributions of church and privately owned lands. Both proposals were enthusiastically embraced by Mexico's *castas* but fierce opposition from the privileged colonial elite. Following Hidalgo's capture and execution in 1811, an even more unlikely rebel, José María Morelos y Pavón, burst on the scene.

With momentum on his side and thousands of the dispossessed, Morelos streamlined the movement and articulated a set of radical proposals. He called for massive social, economic and political reforms. Not only content to rid Mexico of Spanish authority, he wanted to revolutionize the nation's institutions through a massive reform agenda. At its core was a complete repudiation of all vestiges of Spanish colonial privilege. At the Independence Convention at Chilpancingo in 1813, Morelos and his supporters advocated massive land redistributions, elimination of the racial caste system, expropriation and distribution of the haciendas, republican government with effective suffrage, secularization of Catholic Church properties and taxation of its capital assets. Morelos' grand plan was to lay the basis for an elusive equality at all levels of society for countless generations in the future.

In 1821, after more than a decade of devastating civil war, Spain reluctantly conceded to Mexican Independence in El Plan de Iguala. And in 1822, Juana Machado Wrightington witnessed the changing of the guard and the transition from Spanish to Mexican rule in Alta California. She saw Father Agustin Fernandez de San Vicente order the soldiers to lower the Spanish flag and raise the Mexican tricolor. Amid the assembled soldiers and great fanfare in San Diego's presidio, Wrightington was one of the few eyewitnesses to this momentous occasion. The transition to Mexican rule was official. Juana was now a Mexican, along with millions of others on Mexican territory, from California to Yucatan. In the northern regions, Mexicans began the arduous task of implementing the new ideas unleased during the decade of civil war, embodied in *liberalismo.* To them it meant more regional autonomy, modernization of the economy through freer trade, elimination of the independent authority and power of the Catholic institutions and trade with foreigners.

Perhaps the single most important result of the new *liberalismo* was the secularization of church lands, authorized by Mexico's decree of August 17, 1833. The plan to expropriate and distribute church owned properties and lands, underway by the 1830s throughout the northern regions, undermined centuries of Catholic privilege, power and wealth. By the middle of the 19th century secularization had resulted in the distribution of millions of acres of church owned land and elevated hundreds of private citizens to a level of a new landed elite.

Receiving inspiration and direction from the framers of the American Declaration of Independence and the United States Constitution, Mexico fashioned its first Constitution in 1823. Like the American Constitution it included the principle of the balance of powers. The executive, judicial and legislative branches of the federal government were adopted. Mexico also embraced the bicameral legislature, the upper and lower houses, together comprising the Congress. The notion of absolute and proportional representation also became a part of the first Mexican experiment in democracy. And like the Constitution of the United States, Mexicans displayed their fundamental mistrust of the popular will by leaving the election of the Presidential and Vice Presidential offices in the hands of the Electoral College. In sharp contrast to the American Constitution, Mexico sanctioned the designation of Roman Catholicism as its official religion. In addition, the Mexican President was granted unprecedented authority during declared emergencies.

The new Mexican nation inherited sovereignty of Spain's former territories from northern California in the north, to Texas in the far northeast, to the Yucatan Peninsula in the south. Mexico took official possession of the northern frontier zones as a result of the 1831 Treaty of Limits, an international treaty with the United States which reconfirmed the terms of the Adams-Onis Treaty of 1819. The Adams-Onís Treaty of 1819, also known as the Transcontinental Treaty, had previously clarified the western extent of United States possessions acquired through the Louisiana Purchase in 1803 while simultaneously designating the northern extent of Spain's North American territories. In exchange for the United States agreement to relinquish claims to Texas, Spain ceded Florida to the United States. The first Mexican Constitution in 1824 absorbed the northern territories and created the Federal Republic.

The first Mexican Republic originally incorporated 19 states and 4 territories or *provincias*. The *provincias* were Tlaxcala in central Mexico, New Mexico in the north, Old California (Baja California) and New California (Alta California). The Texas region, the focus of considerable attention by Mexico and the United States, was absorbed as a part of the state of Coahuila. One of the great tasks before the new nation was the modernization and incorporation of its vast northern territories.

"To people is to govern" was the first Mexican approach to its far northern frontier, a long neglected region under Spanish rule. In response to various domestic and foreign pressures Mexico embraced a number of strategies to modernize the region and encourage settlement into its frontier zones. Some Mexicans encouraged decisive colonization plans to solidify Mexico's grip.

In response to increased international pressure and Mexico's acute interest in protecting the zone, a number of immigration strategies were adopted. First, settlers from the south were offered generous land grants and a chance to begin again in a relatively sparsely populated region. Second, colonization efforts, such as the Hijar-Padres effort, were undertaken during the early 19th century to encourage a Mexican migration into the region. With only modest success in California, the effort was brief. Third, to the dismay of California's previous waves of immigrant settlers, exiled criminals were sent to California during the 1830s and 1840s. Fourth, various careful attempts in both New Mexico and California were made to attract limited numbers of foreigners through land grants and other privileges. Ultimately Mexico decided to support a plan for the settlement of American-born Catholics in Texas beginning in 1824. That same year Mexico passed its first decree permitting foreign immigration into the upper regions of the state of Coahuila, in a region later known as Texas. David Weber explores the various Mexican strategies aimed at the northern territories in greater detail in an article in this section.

II

The 1824 Decree, Haden Edwards, Fredonia, General Manuel Mier y Terán, Tadeo Ortiz de Ayala, Law of 1829, Law of 1830, Counter-Colonization, Anahuac, Lipantiitlan, Tenoxtitlan, The Texas Declaration of Independence, Antonio López de Santa Anna, San Jacinto, The Treaty of Velasco, General José María Tornel y Mendivil, Pedro Bautista Pino, Nueces River, Rio Grande, President James K. Polk, Juan Seguin.

For the first time, through the 1824 decree, Mexico permitted each of the northern regions to accept foreign-born immigrants. Offering generous land and tax concessions Mexico's ambitious plan aimed to populate, develop and protect its frontier zones. Immigrants were required to become Mexican citizens, obey Mexican law and become Catholics. With an eye on American expansionism, Mexico's objective was to erect a barrier in the path of United States expansion. It brought Mexico's northerners in contact with American-born citizens for the first time. And for the first few years, despite vast linguistic, cultural, religious and racial differences, the mestizo population of the frontier and the mostly Anglo Saxon Protestants of North America, cooperated in the first stages of settlement. At first there was little competition over land or resources. The need for common defense also functioned to mitigate against potential conflicts. There was a period of brief and helpful cooperation as they settled the frontier.

However, the period of peaceful coexistence was brief. Tensions between American colonists and the Mexican government surfaced as early as 1826. Haden Edwards, incensed at the Mexican government's unfavorable ruling in a land dispute, declared for a general uprising and Texas independence. It was the first sign of trouble with the American colonists and sent a clear message to authorities in Mexico City. This incident, the "Fredonia Revolt," reminded the Mexican government that the colonists could be dangerous and provoked a reevaluation of the 1824 decree.

In 1827 General Manuel Mier y Terán was ordered to Texas to inspect the region and advise Mexico on a policy that would protect it. He concluded that Mexico should end foreign immigration, counter-colonize with Mexicans and Europeans and enact legislation which would direct more Texas trade to the Mexican Republic. He asserted that the American settlers were pushing for a separate territorial government apart from the state of Coahuila. His warnings of the potential for an American inspired rebellion were taken seriously by Mexican authorities. The Terán report precipitated the Mexican government's passage of its 1830 decree, curtailing American immigration into the northern frontier. It also called for plans to begin to counter-colonize with Mexican immigrants, economic policies leading to stronger trade with Texas and a stronger military presence in the region.

Slavery in Mexico had already been declared illegal in Mexico through the 1829 decree. Mexican officials expressed hope that this measure would also discourage Americans from coming to Texas. Some Mexican officials, such as Tadeo Ortíz de Ayala, informed Mexican authorities of Texas' vast economic potential. Its natural resources and agricultural potential were unmatched any where in the Mexican Republic. The region was an indispensable part of Mexico's long-term modernization. Its loss could be devastating to the Mexican economic future and forever relegate Mexico economically subordinate to the United States, wrote Ortíz de Ayala.

The 1829 and 1830 decrees polarized Mexicans and Americans, a condition exacerbated by questions of loyalty and other political differences. Mexico's growing concern about its new immigrants and looming United States expansionism is explored by Gene Brack in an article in this section. Mexico took another step and used counter-colonization strategies aimed at the zone through the creation of three cities, Lipantitlan, Anáhuac and Tenoxtitlán, in southern Texas. The plan called for a northern migration of southern Mexicans in order to create a more balanced population of Mexicans and Americans. From the Mexican view this would discourage or prevent American rebellion from going any further. But the plan failed to attract a large northern migration. For Mexicans the frontier was not an attractive alternative and offered little advantage over their home regions.

According to Arnoldo De León, the American immigrants rebelled against Mexico for reasons unrelated to specific political questions. They had determined that Texas was run and inhabited by a people who were incapable or unwilling to progress beyond the present state of "disorder and primitivism." Mexicans were a particularly lethargic and unremarkable people that could not measure up to the Anglo American. And Mexico, in particular Texas, were plagued by political and economic indolence. The need to invert the political order from a people unwilling to progress and civilize the wilderness was a common concern on the minds of many *Texians* (American-born Texas settlers). And the Americans kept arriving, despite the new restrictive legislation and their well documented discomfort with alleged flaws in the Mexican character. American-born *Texians* numbered nearly 35,000 by the middle 1830s, while Mexicans numbered 5,000. For the first time Mexicans in the northern frontier were outnumbered by foreign-born immigrants. Consequently the need for counter-colonization and other measures.

In direct violation of Mexican law, Texas rebels organized conferences at Washington-on-the-Brazos in March, 1836, and wrote their Declaration of Independence. At first they had hoped to negotiate differences with the Mexican government including repeal of the 1829 and 1830 decrees. The 1829 decree was especially troubling to the *Texians*. They regarded it as a violation of their private property, even though Mexican law made no such guarantees. They had also determined that it violated the 1824 law which had permitted *Texians* to bring their slaves. For a complete summary of the *Texians'* grievances against the Mexican government see the Texas Declaration of Independence in this section. Mexico remained firm. The foreign immigrants had agreed to obey Mexican law and defiance of Mexican law amounted to sedition. The *Texians* claimed that they lacked political representation in the Coahuila state legislature. Rebellious *Texians* also charged Mexico with a failure to provide civil and constitutional protections. The Mexican government claimed that such guarantees were never a part of the 1824 immigration law. The *Texians*, the Mexican government argued, had traveled to a foreign country with copies of their American Constitution and blatantly defied Mexico's authority.

The rise to power by Centralist Antonio López de Santa Anna was an important development for relations with the rebellious *Texians*. Determined to eliminate the Texas insurgency, Santa Anna advanced to the Texas frontier at the head of an army estimated at 3,000-6,000 men to destroy the seditionists. In San Antonio he found about two hundred *Texians* and several *Tejanos* (Spanish-speaking Texans) had taken refuge in the old mission site called the Alamo. After defeating them he moved on to Nacogdoches and Goliad where the poorly organized Texians were wiped out. The *Texians* retreated and the brief war appeared to be over. But at San Jacinto, Santa Anna's troops, in a surprise attack led by Texas revolutionary leader Sam Houston, were defeated. Santa Anna was taken prisoner by Houston. Under the threat of execution, he was forced to sign the Treaty of Velasco.

The Treaty enumerated the conditions of the Mexican surrender and withdrawal from Texas. A copy of the Treaty is included in this section. The Treaty, highly controversial and disputed by many Mexican political leaders, virtually assured Texas autonomy in 1836. As a result of internal chaos and nationalistic opposition to the conditions of the treaty, it was never officially ratified by the Mexican Congress. To many major Mexican newspapers, intellectuals, political opponents of Santa Anna and the military the notion of Texas independence was unthinkable. Other opponents would question its constitutionality under Mexican law. They argued that no Mexican authority could alienate the national territories. Furthermore, Santa Anna had signed the Treaty under the threat of execution. approve

Despite the Mexican refusal to ratify the Treaty of Velasco, Texas independence was virtually assured. Many of Mexico's most prominent political voices, such as General José María Tornel y Mendívil, not only believed that the Treaty of Velasco was invalid but that the Texas secessionary movement was part of a larger United States conspiracy to realize its Manifest Destiny, issues explored in greater detail in the Gene Brack article in this section. The Tornel commission in 1836 concluded that more Mexican territories would be lost if Texas continued to remain independent. Tornel had predicted a sort of nineteenth century domino effect if Texas independence was not reversed. Other important territories, Tornel surmised, could fall to American expansionism.

For decades prior to the Texas Revolt, Mexicans had been alerted to United States expansionistic designs on their northern territories. As early as 1812 prominent northern officials, such as Pedro Bautista Pino, a strict Spanish protectionist, made repeated appeals to the central government for financial and military support to prevent the loss of the northern territories. Pino had also predicted that the Mexican failure to enact and enforce stringent protectionist measures in the north could result in territorial loss to the United States or some other European power. Despite the warnings of the American scheme for conquest and appeals by the Mexico's northern officials, Texas became the Lone Star Republic in 1836. Between 1836 and 1845 statehood within the United States was delayed because of its status as a slave state. Mexican opposition under the threat of war was an additional factor which may have delayed Texas statehood. Gene Brack, in an article in this section, summarizes the tense relationship between the two nations in the two decades prior to the outbreak of the Mexican American War.

Further complicating relations between the Texas Republic and the Mexican government was the conflict regarding Texas' southern boundary. According to Mexican surveys and maps dating to 1767, the southern boundary of Texas was at the Nueces River, approximately 120 miles north of the Rio Grande (called the Rio Bravo del Norte by Mexico). Despite evidence to the contrary Texas maintained its largely insupportable claim for the Rio Grande, based on Article 4 of its secret agreement in the Treaty of Velasco with Antonio López de Santa Anna. The disputed territories represented approximately one-third of the current state of Texas. The United States, upon admission of Texas as a state, agreed to support Texas claims to the Rio Grande. This disputed territory was the focus of numerous diplomatic exchanges and the site of the principal military confrontation which prompted President James K. Polk to request a declaration of war against Mexico. Not until 1848 and the signing of the Treaty of Guadalupe Hidalgo was the Rio Grande validated as the boundary separating northern Mexico and southern Texas.

Why then would Mexico invite and encourage foreign immigration into a region so vulnerable and coveted by competing foreign nations? The answer rests in the Mexican conviction that if strict adherence to the provisions of the law were respected including the adoption of Roman Catholicism, Mexican citizenship, regard for Mexican traditions and the law, colonists would be sufficiently 'Mexicanized' in order to erect a barrier in the path of American expansionism. Mexico believed that these *hijos del país* (sons of the country) would help to diversify the Texas economy, orient trade toward Mexico and most of all, remain loyal Mexican citizens.

The hopes of the Mexican government were shattered when American-born *Texians* began a campaign of blatant disregard for Mexican authority. In this section Arnoldo De León explores the nature of disputes with the Mexican government and motivations of American-born *Texians* in their effort to separate Texas from Mexico. The disputes with Mexicans and their government included racial, sexual, political, class and ethnocentric dimensions which colored the earliest contacts between the two people. And according to De León, a complete accounting of the relationship between Anglo Americans and Chicanos in the northern frontier must include these aspects of their earliest contact. These disputes, in part due to historic anti-

Mexicanism, continued unabated throughout the nineteenth century and were a primary feature of the relationship between Mexicans and Anglo *Texians* for decades to come.

Chicanos in the region undoubtedly endured a multitude of mixed emotions as events unfolded around them. Some Texas Mexicans such as José Antonio Navarro, Ignacio Zaragoza and Juan Seguín were open and public about their political differences with the Mexican government. Although they did not originally advocate an open defiance of Mexican authority, ultimately they came to support the revolutionary cause. But this position emerged only after attempts for Texas statehood within the Mexican Republic had failed. For the most part, the majority of *Tejanos* became victims of the Mexican and American conflict. Some like Juan Seguín repeatedly proved their allegiance to the Texas revolutionary cause. He was forced to leave, under the threat of a lynch mob, on the allegation of disloyalty when Mexico tried to retake Texas in 1842.

III

The Lone Star Republic, Thomas Catesby Jones, James K. Polk, hijos del paiz, John Slidell, General Zachary Taylor, Spot Resolution, General Winfield Scott, General Stephen Kearney, The Bear Flaggers, Andres Pico, Nicholas Trist, The Treaty of Guadalupe Hidalgo, Article V, VIII, IX, and X, The Protocol of Querétaro, McKinney v. Saviego, Texas-Mexico Railroad v. Locke, California Land Act of 1851, Court of Private Land Claims.

Events over the next decade following the Texas Revolt drew the United States and Mexico invariably closer to armed conflict. The struggle for sovereignty over Texas and the suspicion of the inexorable expansion of the United States into regions of the Mexican Republic quite naturally contributed to increased international polarization. Chicanos, by virtue of the signing of the Treaty of Guadalupe Hidalgo, the Protocol of Querétaro and the Supreme Court's systematic erosion of the intent of these documents would be the ultimate losers in the confrontation. For the most part the residents of the Mexican frontier remained apart from the major diplomatic and war maneuvers. But within a short time their lives would be enveloped by developments after the middle 19th century. Conflicts over territory and colliding interests would have serious ramifications for the first generation of Chicanos in the United States. The Mexican American War, which culminated decades of Mexican and American conflict, is the defining event of the Chicano experience. The Treaty of Guadalupe Hidalgo promised unprecedented civil, political, religious and property to the newly adopted citizens of the United States following the war.

Despite the Texas Declaration of Independence and the defeat of the Mexican army at San Jacinto in 1836, many issues remained unsolved. Texas established the Lone Star Republic and maintained its sovereignty until its admission into the United States in 1845. The Texas boundary question continued to remain a major irritant to relations between the Lone Star Republic and Mexico. While the Lone Star Republic claimed territories to the Rio Grande, Mexico continued to insist on a boundary 120 miles to the north, at the Nueces River. The United States administration of President James K. Polk agreed to support Texas territorial claims. The admission of Texas as a slave state into the United States in 1845, despite Mexico's insistence that this was tantamount to an act of war, caused Mexico to break off diplomatic relations with the United States and brought the nations to the brink of war. The United States had always supported Texas territorial claims to the Rio Grande. It now moved to go to war to make it official.

Mexican and American relations, prior to the admission of Texas to the United States, had periodically reached crisis levels. In 1842, Thomas Catesby Jones, based on misinformation that the United States and Mexico had gone to war, captured the California provincial capital at Monterey. He declared California an American protectorate. He lowered the Mexican flag and raised the American. Later he realized his mistake and shamefacedly removed the American flag and apologized to Mexican officials. The seriousness of this brief episode, and warnings from California officials led to the enactment of a new law in 1843 authorizing the expulsion of foreigners from the northern regions, including California, Sonora, Sinaloa and Chihuahua. But northern Mexican officials moved slowly or not at all. In 1842, Texas filibusterers attempted to "liberate" New Mexico but were promptly defeated and arrested. That same year the Mexican army invaded Texas and briefly occupied the city of San Antonio and areas to its south. The United States government had made no secret of its desire to obtain Mexio's northern regions and Mexico made it clear it would defend them.

The direct threats to Mexican sovereignty in the region caused alarm but few effective measures which solidified Mexican control over the northern provinces. Mexico encountered aggressive negotiations as well as additional occupations of portions of its northern frontier. David Weber, in an article in this section, explores the Mexican attempt to strike a delicate balance between the necessity to populate the region while insisting upon the political loyalties of foreign immigrants. Northern officials, such as New Mexican provincial governor Manuel Armijo, undertook the delicate task of encouraging a controlled flow of foreign immigrants while simultaneously ensuring the continuation of Mexican political authority. Similar problems emerged in the California province where officials tried various solutions, including, to the distress of the native population, the forced exile of convicts from various Mexican prisons in the 1820s and 1830s. Mexico had also permitted a small number of Americans and Europeans to reside there.

Mexican political instability also contributed to the deterioration of relations with the United States. The struggle for power between Centralists and Federalists bred internal political chaos and hindered an effective campaign to reclaim Texas. Effective diplomatic responses to problems with the United States became nearly impossible. The Mexican political strategy of concentrating political authority in the hands of the federal authorities may have also contributed to growing political discontent which contributed to open rebellion.

The election of Democrat James K. Polk for President of the United States in 1844, a southerner with grand plans for American expansion, brought matters to a critical point. The Polk administration would epitomize the climax of American expansionism during the 19th century. Elected on pro-slavery and pro-expansion platform, Polk had decided to seek the admission of Texas as a slave state and support Texas claims for the Rio Grande boundary. Polk also pursued the acquisition of the Oregon Territories from Great Britain, a feat accomplished in 1846.

Polk made no secret of his desire to acquire or seize California from Mexico. He had unsuccessfully proposed to purchase it through diplomatic exchanges. He formulated two more belligerent plans to realize his objective. He had instructed United States Consul to California, Thomas Larkin, to fashion his "California Plan," a scheme to encourage *Californio* (Spanish-speaking Californians) support for an American military occupation. The *hijos del paiz*, a collection of early California settlers principally from the United States, functioned as a seditionary front line for the plan. That same year John Slidell was sent to Mexico City on a secret mission to present various American demands, including the purchase of Mexico's vast northern provinces, California and New Mexico.

The John Slidell mission in 1845 created the illusion of a United States strategy to pursue a diplomatic resolution to the Texas boundary question. He hoped to convince Mexico to agree to the Rio Grande boundary. And Slidell was prepared to offer up to $25 million for the purchase of the California and New Mexico provinces, virtually the entire American Southwest. Incensed by Slidell's audacious proposals and an American sponsored Texas Independence, Mexican officials rejected the Slidell scheme.

Mexico was aware of reports which placed American General Zachary Taylor in southern Texas. While Slidell was in Mexico trying to negotiate an end to the territorial dispute, the American forces had already prepared to seize it. But the Slidell mission was a daring political maneuver for the Polk administration. Polk's strategy had worked. The United States Congress could now be persuaded to believe that the administration was attempting a diplomatic resolution of its troubles with Mexico. Mexico, in contrast, appeared to reject peaceful negotiation .

Mexico's most immediate concern was the presence of American General Zachary Taylor in the disputed region in southern Texas. Taylor was poised to launch an attack on northern Mexico. By March, 1846, under specific instructions from President Polk, Taylor advanced south of the Rio Grande and blockaded the Mexican port city at Matamoros, an act which not only violated international law but also caused an armed Mexican response which resulted in American bloodshed.

When news of the incident reached Washington D.C., Polk prepared his war message to Congress. He asserted that the United States had no choice but to declare war since Mexico had invaded American territory and "shed American blood on American soil." Sensing a conspiracy of Southern slave states and attempting to prevent a war declaration against Mexico, Congressman Abraham Lincoln introduced the "Spot Resolution." Lincoln's proposal demanded the identification of the exact spot where American blood had been spilled. Unable to muster a majority vote, the initiative failed. Polk, some historians argue, had already unfolded his war strategy. The exchange of fire between American and Mexican troops provided the ground for Polk's plea for war with Mexico. He used the incident to convince Congress of a Mexican invasion of American territory. On May 13, 1846, Congress accepted Polk's argument and declared war. Polk's war of territorial conquest had begun.

The Polk war strategy advanced along three fronts. General Winfield Scott arrived in Mexico by sea at Vera Cruz and he began an arduous and costly march toward Mexico City. After several decisive battles on southern Mexican soil he would eventually force peace terms on the Mexican government through the Treaty of Guadalupe Hidalgo. What remained of the Mexicans troops near Texas were cleared out of northeastern Mexico by General Zachary Taylor. General Stephen Kearney, in command of the Army of the West, occupied New Mexico and moved west to merge with the "Bear Flaggers," as they sat poised off the California coast prior to the war.

In New Mexico and California American military forces met stern armed resistance from Mexican citizens as they tried to prevent American occupation. At San Pascual Pass, in southern California, Stephen Kearney's troops confronted fierce resistance from loyal *Californios* led by Andres Pico and were forced to retreat to New Mexico in 1847. In New Mexico, opposition to American occupation surfaced frequently during and after the war, primarily in the north. Despite the promises of a bright American future many displayed their strongest apprehensions toward the American occupiers. The natives had come to view themselves as occupying a homeland and had evolved a strong identification with the region. They displayed their loyalty to Mexico by organizing resistance to American occupation. Perhaps their vivid displays of loyalty to the Mexican Republic are better understood in light of the uncertain future they faced in a nation already influenced by anti-Mexicanist thought. Periodic resistance was almost certainly a sign of their disenchantment with the prospects of an American takeover of Mexico's northern frontier zone.

By September, 1847 General Winfield Scott drove into Mexico City and made peace offers to Mexico. Nicholas Trist, sent to Mexico as peace commissioner, opened negotiations with Mexico. Despite being recalled by President Polk, due to Polk's insistence on more Mexican territory and a reduced financial settlement, Trist began negotiations which ultimately resulted in the Mexican ratification of the Treaty of Guadalupe Hidalgo on February 2, 1848. Polk, furious with Trist and sensing growing opposition to the war and the Treaty, had no choice but to submit the treaty to the Senate for its approval. On March 10, 1848, the United States Senate, by a 28-14 vote, ratified the treaty.

For Chicanos the treaty is the most important document defining their constitutional, civil and property rights in the United States. Richard Griswold del Castillo, in an article in this section, documents the complex task involved in the negotiations among the national representatives which resulted in the final document. Article V forced Mexico to surrender its vast northern provinces including California and New Mexico. It also redefined the border between Texas and northern Mexico at the Rio Grande. Through Article V the United States had acquired the Southwest. This region comprises the current states of California, Arizona, Nevada, Colorado, and New Mexico. It also included regions of the current states of Texas, Utah and Wyoming. These new boundaries would remain unchanged until the United States, under the threat of seizure and occupation, forced the sale of Mexico's Mesilla Valley, known as the Gadsden Purchase. It extended southern Arizona's territory beyond the Gila River, 120 miles farther south.

For Mexico this was a bitter humiliation and the subject of considerable political debate. Some Mexican political analysts believed the territorial surrender was unconstitutional. The Mexican Constitution, in their view, did not authorize the alienation of the national territories. In their view, Article V violated the Mexican Constitution. Some Mexican politicians such as Benito Juarez and Manuel C. Rejón encouraged a protracted guerilla war to resist the Treaty and save the Mexican Republic. To others it meant the economic, political and cultural subordination of Mexico to the United States. To them, Mexico would forever remain a defeated nation with bitter memories of United States imperialism. It also forced Mexicans to examine the shortcomings of their leaders. Others reminded Mexico that resistance or continued warfare could mean the complete obliteration of the Mexican nation. The United States, they argued, could strike back and absorb the entire Mexican nation. The issue was settled when Mexico, in a state of unprecedented disarray, ratified the Treaty and it was forwarded to the United States Senate.

Mexicans in favor of the Treaty pointed to the unprecedented political, civil, religious and cultural protections extended to the former Mexican citizens now residing on the lost lands. Under Article VIII, approximately 120,000 former Mexican citizens living in the acquired regions were allowed to continue to reside in their old homelands or move south into Mexico. They could retain Mexican citizenship or accept United States citizenship. But they had to make their decision within one year of the exchange of ratifications of the treaty, or around May, 1849. A "substantial number," principally New Mexicans, decided to declare their intent to retain Mexican citizenship. And according to studies by Richard Griswold del Castillo, approximately five thousand people returned to Mexico, principally due to a planned Mexican repatriation campaign to create a defensive border buffer against further American expansionism.

The vast majority decided to stay and take their chances with the new American administration. For the first time in the history of the United States, citizenship was granted to non-whites. Proponents of the treaty, Miguel Atristain and Bernardo Couto, were optimistic that the new United States citizenship as well as property and civil provisions would protect the former Mexican citizens. The Treaty also appeared to offer attractive guarantees for their properties, including civil and religious protections.

Article VIII permitted the new citizens to retain their properties of all kinds. Many of the former Mexican citizens possessed lands and properties granted to them under Mexico's secularization decrees of the early 19th century. As many as thirty million acres of land had been distributed to private land holders in the twenty years following Mexican Independence. According to the Treaty they could retain these properties, or sell them without any restriction. In addition they were also protected in the free exercise of their Catholic faith.

Article IX expanded upon the guarantees confirmed through Article VIII. Not only was United States citizenship guaranteed, Article IX extended all the rights of citizenship according to the principles of the Constitution to the new Americans. But these guarantees only became effective when the territories were incorporated as states. Until then citizenship provisions were in force but any additional rights would remain unmet until Congress authorized the inclusion of the territories as states. For the *Californios* this occurred in 1850, soon after the Treaty was signed. For others, in the regions which eventually became the states of Arizona and New Mexico, the extension of all the rights of citizenship was delayed until 1912. In theory this meant that the fully incorporated new citizens enjoyed the right to vote, run for public office, testify in court and sue on their behalf. These were unprecedented guarantees which were withheld from most residents of the United States. In practice, however, Mexicans faced constant challenges to these protections. In California, for example, considerable time and debate was spent trying to exclude Mexicans from voting on the grounds that they had Indian ancestry. And as late as the 1920s attempts were made to classify Mexicans as Indians in order to legally segregate them in public schools in the Southwest. Indians were virtually without rights in the United States and excluded from citizenship protections of the Treaty.

In other regions of the Southwest, particularly in Texas, these guarantees were never seriously considered or upheld. Texas had previously declared, during the 1830s, that Mexicans who had not voluntarily taken an oath of allegiance to the Republic of Texas had forfeited their land rights. In general, they were never considered citizens of the Republic or the state. Texas officials had taken the position that provisions and protections under the Treaty of Guadalupe Hidalgo did not apply to their state. This argument was based upon their unique history as an independent republic and Texas admission to the United States prior to the Treaty of Guadalupe Hidalgo. According to the state of Texas citizenship protections did not apply. Texas officials hinged their belief on a Supreme Court decision known as *McKinney v. Saviego* (1856). In this case, the justices determined that Texas was not part of the Treaty of Guadalupe Hidalgo since its independence and statehood had both occurred prior to the Mexican American War. Later rulings, such as *Texas-Mexican Rail Road v. Locke* (1889), challenged this decision and pointed to specific references to Texas in the Treaty of Guadalupe Hidalgo and the Protocol of Querétaro. For Mexicans in Texas these rulings, exacerbated by prevailing anti-Mexicanism, quickly evaporated any hopes of equal treatment as citizens or property holders in the state of Texas.

Important to Mexican negotiators in the Treaty of Guadalupe Hidalgo were protections of Spanish and Mexican land grants. Estimated at between twenty and thirty million acres across the Southwest, the grants had been obtained by private citizens principally through Mexico's early 19th century secularization decrees. The original version of Article X had asserted that all land grants made by the Spanish and Mexican authorities were considered valid. However, under heavy pressure by President James Polk, who insisted that Article X would complicate land disputes in Texas, the United States Senate omitted it. Mexican officials protested and demanded an explanation. American and Mexican officials agreed to place in writing the substance of their understanding with regard to the omission of Article X. This language, known as the Protocol of Querétaro, contains the statements of clarification regarding the legal status of land grants in the Southwest. The Treaty could not validate land titles, argued the American negotiators, only the courts could.

As a result, the California legislature passed the California Land Act of 1851. The law empowered a panel of judges, the California Land Commission, to decide on the validity of Mexican owned land grants. Mexican land owners were required to present their case for ownership within three years. But the process never worked as smoothly as anticipated. Within twenty years, due to the tremendous cost of litigation, fraud, thievery and organized bands of squatters, the *Californios* had lost millions of acres of their ancestral lands. Richard Griswold del Castillo, in an article in this section, documents how this process worked in more detail. The Mexicans in New Mexico and Arizona had a similar experience with the American courts. The Court of Private Land Claims, established in 1891, decided on the validity of land claims in these two regions. Prior to 1891 land grant validation was directed by the Office of the Surveyor General of the Territory of New Mexico. The record clearly indicates that the United States courts, over the course of at least fifty years, seriously eroded not only the purpose of the Treaty but its spirit as well. The systematic erosion of the guarantees contained in the Treaty is the core of the Chicano experience in the United States following the Mexican American War.

SELECTED READING LIST

1. Acuña, Rudolfo. *Occupied America: A History of Chicanos*. New York: Harper and Row, 1981.

2. Barker, Eugene C. *Mexico and Texas, 1821-1835.* University of Texas Research Lectures on the Causes of the Texas Revolution. New York: Russell & Russell, 1928; reprint ed., New York: Russell & Russell, 1965.
3. Bowden, J.J. *The Spanish and Mexican Land Grants in the Chihuahuan Acquisition.* El Paso: Texas Westernlore Press, 1971.
4. Brack, Gene M. *Mexico Views Manifest Destiny, 1821-1846; An Essay on the Origins of the Mexican War.* Albuquerque: University of New Mexico Press, 1975.
5. Chávez, John R. *The Lost Land: The Chicano Image of the Southwest.* Albuquerque:University of New Mexico Press, 1984.
6. De León, Arnoldo. *They Called them Greasers.* Austin: University of Texas Press, 1983.
7. -----------. *The Tejano Community, 1836-1900.* Albuquerque: University of New Mexico Press, 1982.
8. Merk, Frederick. *Manifest Destiny and Mission in American History:A Reinterpretation.* New York: Alfred A. Knopf, 1963.
9. Montejano, David. *Anglos and Mexicans in the Making of Texas, 1836-1986.* Austin: University of Texas Press, 1987.
10. Peña, Enrique de la. *With Santa Anna in Texas: A Personal Narrative of the Revolution.* Translated and edited by Carmen Perry. Introduction by Llerena Friend. College Station: Texas A&M University Press, 1975.
11. Pitt, Leonard. *Decline of the Californios: A Social History of the Spanish Speaking Californians, 1846-1890.* Berkeley: University of California Press, 1970.
12. Price, Glenn. *Origins of the War Against Mexico: The Polk-Stockton Intrigue.* Austin:University of Texas Press, 1963.
13. Ruiz, Ramon, ed. *The Mexican War: Was It Manifest Destiny?* New York: Holt Rhinehart and Winston, 1963.
14. Santa-Anna, Antonio López de; Martínez Caro, Ramón; Filisola, Vicente; Urrea, José; and Tornel, José María. *The Mexican Side of the Texas Revolution, 1836: By the Chief Mexican Participants.* Translated with Notes by Carlos E.Castañeda. Dallas: P. L. Turner Co., 1928; reprint ed., *The Chicano Heritage,* New York: New York Times, Arno Press, 1976.
15. Spicer, Edward H. *Cycles of Conquest: The Impact of Spain, Mexico, and the United States on the Indians of the Southwest, 1533-1960.* Tucson: University of Arizona Press, 1962.
16. Weinberg, Albert K. *Manifest Destiny: A Study of Nationalist Expansion in American History.* 1935. Reprint, Chicago: Quadrangle Books, 1963.

For José Maria Tornel, Texas was Mexico's most precious territory. Its enormous size and vast potential did not go unnoticed by prominent Mexican authorities. In response to disturbing signs by rebellious American immigrants during the 1820s, Mexican political leaders urged stern measures and counter-colonization to offset seditionary activity. Gene Brack offers a fascinating glimpse of Mexico's first impressions of the United States, its discovery of fundamental differences between Mexico and Americans and growing concern for the safety of its northern frontier regions prior to the Texas revolution.

Texas, "This Most Precious. . .Territory"

Gene M. Brack

Above all it was the growing menace of American pressure upon Texas that caused a definite change in Mexican attitudes toward the United States in the years immediately following Poinsett's departure. It now seemed clear that the United States was not to be benevolent ally of Mexico but sought instead, like some European powers, only to exploit the frailty of the struggling nation. By 1830 Mexico had already reacted to this dawning realization by assuming a policy of isolationism. She expelled the remaining Spaniards in 1828, passed stringent passport laws in 1826 and 1829, and in 1830 tried vainly, through enactment of a new colonization law, to curtail American immigration to Texas. Aliens, especially those from the United States, were therefore not warmly received in Mexico, and Mexicans, apart from a number of exiles who resided in New Orleans, did not travel much in the United States. An important exception was Lorenzo de Zavala, who made an extensive tour of the United States in 1830, but his account of the journey was not published until 1846 and therefore had no effect upon earlier opinion in Mexico. Dispatches from Mexican ministers in Washington kept Mexican officials relatively well informed of affairs in the United States, but added nothing to the public's store of information. A conservative administration curtailed freedom of the press in 1830; some papers ceased publication, denying the public during an especially crucial period even this dubious source of information. Only in Texas, where circumstances seemed designed to establish mutual animosity, was there much contact between the people of the two nations.

Lack of information and declining curiosity meant that Mexicans really knew very little about the people they were rapidly coming to regard as enemies. This is not to say that they were completely inattentive to domestic affairs in the United States, but only to suggest that after about 1830 Mexicans viewed the northern republic differently than before. They now seemed much less concerned with defining the institutional strengths of the United States, and rather more concerned with

159

identifying flaws in the American structure. It happened that the change in Mexican attitudes from ambiguity to hostility came at a time when the United States was troubled by sectional disputes. Luis de Onís had written his *Memoria* while the Congress of the United States debated the issues leading to the Missouri Compromise; he noted that the federal system seemed to promote sectionalism and predicted that it would lead ultimately to destruction of the union. During the 1820s Mexican newspapers sometimes mentioned sectional tensions in the United States, but the subject arose more frequently after 1830. By that time sectionalism had indeed become a paramount issue in American politics, for the tariff of 1828 had caused serious unrest in the South, and the subsequent tariff of 1832 was nullified by South Carolina, a crisis solved by President Andrew Jackson's firm opposition and by a compromise tariff bill passed in 1833. These were dramatic events that naturally attracted attention in Mexico, especially as they coincided not only with Mexico's own sectional problems stemming from the continuous discord between federalists and centralists, but also with the rapid development of Mexican animosity toward the United States. The weaker nation would view with much interest any sign of instability in its potential antagonist.

The Mexican minister at Washington, José María Tornel, reported in December 1830 that sectionalism in the United States would probably lead to a division between North and South. The impulse toward separation was felt most strongly in South Carolina where there had arisen "a strong party of nullifiers" whose greatest concern was the recently enacted tariff that seemed to grant unfair advantages to the Northern states. Georgians also were unhappy because they had been denied jurisdiction over Indians in their state. Tornel observed that President Jackson had in a recent message indicated his concern over the sectional difficulties that plagued his administration.[1]

As early as the spring of 1829 *El Correo* carried a story describing the theory of nullification and explaining why Southern states opposed the tariff of 1828.[2] Then in 1832 South Carolina invoked nullification. *El Fénix de la Libertad* made the interesting comment that it very rarely gave notice to political matters in the United States, preferring instead to concentrate upon "topics of importance to the South American republics," but that the nullification crisis was of sufficient importance to merit the attention of Mexicans. The editors of *El Fénix* praised the United States for its power, prosperity, and liberalism, and criticized the South Carolinians for attempting to destroy this great nation with their radical principles of states' rights. The next issue of *El Fénix* printed a translation of the ordinance of nullification.[3] A few days later *El Telégrafo* remarked that the federal system was the "essence" of the "grandeur" of the United States and that it would be a pity were it to be destroyed by the South Carolinians.[4] In the spring of 1833 *El Fénix* announced the reelection of Andrew Jackson and reported that because Henry Clay had "recognized his errors and modified his stand on the protective tariff" the nullification controversy had been resolved by a compromise.[5]

to strive to equal; especially by emulating

That these newspaper criticized South Carolina and spoke favorably of the American union indicates that Mexicans had not turned totally against the United States during the early 1830s. Until the time of the Texas revolution, Mexican papers continued occasionally to express friendship toward the northern neighbor. In 1831 an *El Fénix* editorial compared conditions in the United States just after it obtained independence---the large public debt, insufficient currency, and economic torpor--- with the unparalleled prosperity that came after the adoption of a constitution that guaranteed religious, political, and economic freedom.[6] *El Telégrafo* declared in 1833 that the United States was a "monument to civilization, a model that all people ought to emulate."[7] Later in 1833 the same paper printed a biographical sketch of Thomas Jefferson, praising him as the father of American federalism and lauding his democratic successors, Madison, Monroe, and Jackson. The only interruption in this liberal regime had occurred with the election of John Quincy Adams in 1824, but even he had been "very moderate."[8] Apart from printing some diplomatic correspondence and other official notices the official *Diario* rarely mentioned the United States prior to 1836. An exception came in 1835 when it carried a series of articles on the United States, one of which theorized that the northern republic had grown powerful largely because it was not plagued by unfriendly neighbors, concluding, somewhat ironically, that Mexico's advantage was even greater for having the Anglo-Americans as a "neighbor and natural ally."[9] By and large, however, the Mexican press during these years treated the United States either with indifference or outright hostility.

One Mexican who did not become disenchanted with the United States was Lorenzo de Zavala. As a liberal and federalist who had played a leading role in creating the 1824 constitution, Zavala had been a close friend and ally of Poinsett and an active York Rite mason. At various times he represented Yucatán in the Mexican senate and served as governor of the state of Mexico and as minister of hacienda. Appointed minister to France in 1833, he returned from that mission to reside in Texas where he owned land. Zavala would become an active participant in the Texas revolution, which he viewed as a struggle to defend Mexican federalism against the centralizing efforts of Santa Anna. He died a natural death in 1836. Zavala's account of his tour of the United States in 1830 was not published in Mexico until a decade after his death, but it provides an interesting view of the United States as seen by an articulate and sophisticated Mexican liberal in 1830.

Zavala was predictably sympathetic to the United States. He, like other Mexican liberals, admired its institution and, in many ways, its people. But his *Viage a los Estados Unidos* reveals that Zavala discerned profound differences between Americans and Mexicans, and his portrayal of American society demonstrates that even a sympathetic Mexican viewed the United States with a certain degree of misgiving . He found Americans neither gracious nor friendly, but "selfish, reticent and suspicious." A certain abruptness of manner made traveling in their company very disagreeable. Zavala had often shared a coach with Americans who failed to speak a single word throughout an entire journey. American businessmen devoted themselves totally to their work in order to improve their stations. It appeared to Zavala that their lives consisted only of an endless exchange of goods and money in pursuit of profit. Still, the morality of Americans exceeded that of all other people. Constant application to their work made them "virtuous and independent," but left them "overbearing and dull."[10]

The false modesty observed by Americans in mixed company Zavala found disconcerting. When dining, for example, one requested a "chicken leg," lest the naked word "leg" offend the "chaste and virtuous ears of the ladies." An American who used such profane words as "skirt," "petticoat," or "corset," when speaking of women's clothing, would be considered extremely indelicate.[11] The sophisticated Zavala noted that Americans seldom discussed abstract matters or displayed much enthusiasm for any subject not calculated to advance their pecuniary interests. This preoccupation with mercenary affairs, he thought, went far toward explaining the fundamental difference between Americans and Mexicans. An American would be most likely to ask a Mexican whether there were steamboats in Mexico, or factories, or mines; "he would want to know whether it was easy to make money in this or that state." A Mexican, on the other hand, when discussing the United States with an American, would probably want to know about government and religion; he would ask about the customs of the people in various regions, and "whether there were theaters in this or that place." Englishmen when dining discussed the quality of the wine, the seasoning of the food, the elegance of the table setting, and various other trivial but genteel matters pertaining to the meal itself. Americans talked about the price of cotton, or perhaps of butter.[12]

Slavery disturbed Zavala. He did not dwell at length on the subject, nor did he appear very concerned about the black victims of the institution, though he did cite some of the harsher aspects of the "black codes" in the slave states. He observed that the Protestant churches either excluded blacks altogether or confined them to a designated, segregated place, that they might not avoid their degradation even in worship.[13] He believed that slavery had an adverse effect upon American society at large, and that it exercised an "extroadinary influence" upon the morality and civilization of the Southern states. Zavala felt that he might demonstrate the insidious effect of slavery upon the intellectual life of the South by comparing the press in the free states with that in the slave states. He observed that between 1810 and 1830 the number of periodicals published in New York increased from 66 to 212; in Pennsylvania from 61 to 185; and in Ohio from 40 to 69. But no such proliferation of printed material occurred in the slave states. In South Carolina, ten periodicals had been published in 1810 and sixteen in 1830; in Georgia three in 1810 and three in 1830; and in Louisiana, ten in 1810 and nine in 1830.[14]

But in most respects Zavala seemed pleased by what he saw in the United States, and even in his treatment of slavery he appeared far less critical than most of his countrymen, for after 1830 Mexicans increasingly justified their dislike of the United States by pointing to the hypocrisy with which Americans proclaimed principles of freedom while condoning slavery. Mexico was of course no haven for the underprivileged; even after independence, society there retained the vestiges of a rather rigid class system, Indians were a downtrodden caste, and peonage was common practice. Although slavery had once existed in Mexico it had been abolished just after independence and another such edict had gone out in 1829. While abolition may have been directed chiefly at the slave-owning colonists in Texas, it nevertheless seemed to reflect a national temper of repugence toward what Mexicans genuinely considered an inhuman institution. And because blacks were so scarce in Mexico, abolition affected no important vested interest and might therefore be a popular cause that offended virtually no one.[15] In any event, emancipation was enthusiastically supported in all parts of Mexico but Texas, where authorities revealed the weakness of their jurisdiction by admitting their inability to enforce the measure. But the point to be emphasized is that Mexicans, though themselves capable of violence and cruelty, appeared honestly appalled at the institution of slavery. Even before the decree of 1829 the English chargé Henry Ward had observed that Mexican attitudes toward race and slavery differed remarkably from that of their neighbors in the United States and Latin America. Following an indictment of the United States for its subjugation of blacks, Ward declared that Mexico seemed "exempt" from similar evils.[16]

Slavery alone cannot explain why Mexican attitudes turned so decisively against the United States. Texas remained the overriding cause of hostility and slavery only reinforced the wicked image of Americans that developed in Mexico after about 1830. In what remains the best study of the antecedents of the revolution in Texas, Eugene Barker concluded that slavery was not a direct cause of the event.[17] He did observe that the "racial inheritances" of the two peoples profoundly affected relations between Mexicans and the American colonists in Texas.[18] Barker apparently referred to a conflict of cultures in a broad sense, as analyzed by Herbert Bolton in relation to an earlier period. It simply goes without saying that diversity of language, institutions, religion, and customs contributed to mutual animosity between Mexicans and Americans once they divided on such a critical issue as Texas.[19] And three hundred years of Anglo-Spanish rivalry no doubt also contributed to Mexican-American hostility. But Barker also referred to racial attitudes in a more specific sense when he wrote that Texans "believed themselves morally, intellectually, and politically superior" to Mexicans, declaring that this "racial feeling" had affected American relations with Mexico since 1821.[20] Mexicans naturally resented the ethnocentrism of Americans, and though Barker did not elaborate upon the point it is a very important one, for it may explain why Mexicans gave so much attention to American slavery as the issue of Texas approached a critical stage. They viewed slavery in the United States as the most obvious and cruel manifestation of an intense Yankee ethnocentrism that would have tragic effects upon Mexico should she not persevere in Texas.

This ethnocentrism also carried over to the day-to-day relations between the two countries. Mexican representatives in the United States observed and experienced first-hand the condescending, arrogant attitude of many Americans toward Mexico and her people. Both Juan Almonte and Manuel de Gorostiza were so deeply offended by their experiences and observations in Washington that they became bitter, life-long, and influential enemies of the Americans. And American diplomatic representatives in Mexico often made no secret of their disdain for all things Mexican. Most came from Southern slave states and seemed to regard Mexicans as being scarcely superior to blacks. Some, such as Anthony Butler and William Parrott, of whom more will be said later, were outrageously open in their condescension. Even those American diplomats who sympathized with Mexico tended to give offense, because they carried instructions from Washington to pursue objectives in Mexico that could have no other effect.

One of Poinsett's objectives had been to negotiate a treaty of limits, and in doing so to reassert his country's claim to Texas, which it had surrendered in the 1819 treaty with Spain. But soon after his arrival in Mexico Poinsett informed his government that Lucas Alamán the foreign secretary, was very suspicious of the United States, that Alamán cited the 1819 treaty as evidence of an American disposition to encroach upon foreign territory, and that there was "great apprehension in the minds of the people" that the United States would seek to recover Texas.[21] In preparing for the negotiations the Mexican government conducted a systematic search of its archives for all documents relating to the boundary between Mexico and the United States. It consulted the papers of Luis de Onís, the Spanish diplomat who negotiated the treaty of 1819 and who warned of American territorial ambitions, and in their own correspondence the Mexican negotiators revealed a decided mistrust of American motives.[22] Mexico further prepared for the pending negotiations by establishing a commission to survey the unmarked boundary of 1819. The government named General Manuel Mier y Terán, an able man, deeply anti-American, to lead the commission in Texas.

But nothing was done about sending the commission on its way until events in Texas heightened concern. The Fredonian rebellion, an uprising led by an American residing near Nacogdoches in eastern Texas, occurred in December 1826. Mexican authorities easily crushed the rebellion, but it had the effect of ending Mexican lassitude toward Texas, increased suspicions of American designs on the territory, and prompted the government to activate its plans concerning the Terán commission. *El Sol* declared in an editorial that the government of the United States had sponsored the Fredonian affair and demanded that it renounce its claims on Texas and agree to a well-marked boundary.[23] Poinsett reported that several members of the Mexican congress agreed with the allegations in *El Sol*. On the other hand President Victoria informed the American minister that he regretted that such an opinion had appeared in the public papers, but expressed an "earnest desire" for the president of the United States to give "some public manifestation of his disapprobation" of the rebellion.[24] No such disavowal came, of course, and the Mexican government, now deeply concerned, authorized the Terán commission in September 1827 not only to survey the boundaries of Texas but also to report fully on conditions there. Its subsequent reports provided Mexicans with much previously unknown information about the distant province.[25]

Terán later become military commander of the eastern interior provinces, a district including Texas. Until his death by suicide in 1832 Terán would remain, according to his biographer, the "eyes, ears and possibly the brains of Mexican officialdom in Texas."[26] His reports and suggestions provided the basis for Mexican policy toward Texas during those years. Poinsett reported in the summer of 1829 that Terán almost single-handedly kept the Mexican government "excited" over the situation in Texas.[27]

Terán's observations convinced him that American immigration into Texas composed the chief threat to its security. In frequent communications to the Mexican government, he advised it to adopt measures designed to prevent the United States from gaining further influence in Texas. Late in 1829 he sent his government an analysis of American expansionism that would be widely quoted and often paraphrased by Mexicans during the turbulent period that lay ahead. Americans, he wrote, pursued by devious means their territorial objectives. Instead of employing conquering armies they used methods that would be absurd were they not so effective. To support their designs upon Texas, for instance, they claimed rights based upon dubious and irrelevant historical facts; they were much more concerned with obtaining advantages than with the justice of their methods. But they must not be allowed to have Texas, because the territory was vital to the economic independence of Mexico; Terán believed that Texas might produce food enough for the entire population of the Mexican republic. To stem the tide of emigration from the United States he suggested that troops be stationed in Texas, that forts be built there, and that American colonization be strictly limited.[28]

Reports from Mexican observers in the United States tended to support Terán's allegations concerning American designs upon Texas. In a letter that found its way to the agency in the Mexican government that regulated colonization, Pizarro Martínez wrote from New Orleans to the foreign secretary that because of its size, wealth, and location Texas excited the ambition of the "overbearing, enterprising and intrepid" northern republic. Americans, "restless and arrogant," considered Texas a "patrimony" that would come naturally into their possession. Therefore, it was dangerous to admit more Americans, and Mexico should appeal instead to European immigrants in an attempt to neutralize the influence of those Americans already there.[29] Nicolás Bravo, the exiled vice-president of Mexico, noted while traveling in the United States in 1829 that American public opinion favored acquisition of Texas, if not by purchase, then by force. Bravo, like Terán and others, was appalled by the callous disregard of Americans for the territorial rights of Mexico. He wrote that they either opposed or favored its acquisition "on grounds of its usefulness or uselessness," but that they gave absolutely no attention to the "justice of the matter."[30]

Bravo's letter, accompanied by a group of chauvinistic articles extracted from American newspapers, appeared in *El Sol*. One of the articles, from the Nashville *Republican*, said that Mexico was too poor to support an army or navy and that her citizens were discontented and divided. Mexico therefore could not defend Texas, which appeared in imminent danger of attack (from an unnamed enemy). Thus the United States should assume the burden of protecting the region, and in return for her efforts it was only reasonable that the United States should acquire Texas, which, in any event, was suitable for only agriculture, of which Mexicans had not the least understanding. At this point the editor of *El Sol* remarked that he preferred for Texas to be seized openly by enemy invasion rather than have it usurped by the clever machinations of such "false friends."[31]

José María Tornel, Mexican minister at Washington, reported to his foreign secretary in the spring of 1830 that American newspapers seemed preoccupied with the subject of Texas. He observed that they invariably failed to take Mexico's rights into consideration when debating the convenience of acquiring Texas. Tornel also warned that the new American president, Andrew Jackson, appeared determined to acquire Texas and that Anthony Butler, the American minister sent to replace Poinsett, doubtless carried instructions to continue pressing for the territory. Tornel believed that Mexico should refuse to part with "this most precious part of our territory," and urged that immigration from the United States be halted and measures taken to secure the safety of the province.[32]

Early in 1830 a pamphlet appeared in Mexico City expressing concern for the future of the Mexican nation should the United States acquire Texas. It said that France and Spain might safely cede Louisiana and Florida to the United States, because these territories had only secondary importance to European nations, just as Mexico, should it possess colonies in Africa or Asia, might part with them without endangering the future of the republic. But Texas was a different matter. The area comprised an integral part of the national domain. On its borders existed an enemy which would without compunction mutilate the Mexican nation in order to gain its territorial objectives. Texas, if developed, offered Mexicans the means of halting the American advance. But if the province were lost or sold to the United States, then Mexico would be humiliated and degraded, her opportunities for gaining economic independence would be destroyed, and she would be relegated forever to the rank of a second-class power. The pamphlet closed with a plea to the government to prevent such a disaster by taking all necessary measures to preserve the norther province.[33]

Taking these ominous warnings into account, the government in the spring of 1830 attempted to neutralize American influence in Texas. Relying almost totally upon Terán's suggestions, the Mexican congress passed a law providing for military occupation of the province, counter-colonization by Mexicans and Europeans, and the development of stronger economic ties by means of coastal trade between Texas and other Mexican states.[34] The law was framed by Lucas Alamán the foreign secretary who had returned to that office with the conservative resurgence of 1830. In a preamble to the bill in which he explained the necessity for such a measure, Alamán paraphrased directly from Terán's many dispatches.[35] And the government of the United States was fully informed of Mexico's determination to retain Texas and of its reasons for taking such a position. Alamán sent Anthony Butler, the American chargé, a copy of his message which Butler in turn passed on to Washington.[36]

But American immigration into Texas continued, and military occupation was the only provision of the new law actually put into effect. Such lax enforcement may have resulted in part from the good relations between Stephen F. Austin, the chief colonizer of Texas, and Lucas Alamán. More importantly, the continuing struggle between centralists and federalists may also have contributed to the failure of the 1830 law. For powerful state leaders may have been reluctant to support such national projects as the 1830 colonization law, especially when these measures were undertaken by such prominent centralists as Alamán and Terán.[37] And perhaps internal cleavages such as this help to explain why the nation did not respond more effectively, public opinion notwithstanding, when revolution came to Texas in 1835-36. In any event, after 1830 the Texas colonists grew steadily more restless under a regime that became increasingly arbitrary. Misunderstanding and conflict arose from the tense situation and violence frequently erupted as Texas drifted inexorably toward the climax of 1836. And while the Mexican government sought vainly to deal with the menacing situation in Texas, its relations with the United States remained uneasy.

Anthony Butler, the American chargé, was an arrogant, vulgar, and calculating person, completely devoid of those qualities normally expected of a diplomat. *El Sol* had announced upon his arrival that Butler carried instructions to attempt the purchase of Texas, and from that moment until his recall in 1835 Mexicans suspected Butler of instigating unrest there. Never popular in Mexico, Butler climaxed his incredible career there by publicly insulting José María Tornel, threatening to cane or to whip the Mexican upon next encountering him. At this point the Mexican government insisted that Butler leave the country.[38]

Meanwhile the Mexican political scene grew ever more turbulent, leading in 1834 to Santa Anna's seizure of dictatorial power. This in turn, heightened discontent in many parts of Mexico, weakening the central government's already tenuous control of such outlying regions as Texas and Yucatán.[39] Yet the government continued to receive communications urging it to provide for the security of Texas. Tadeo Ortíz de Ayala, a civil servant familiar with the province, frequently warned that the loss of Texas with its rich resources would be disastrous. In 1833 he wrote that Texas alone might produce more cotton than the total amount harvested in the United States annually, besides cattle and foodstuffs, but that the Americans were avidly pursuing their efforts to rob Mexico of the fertile region.[40]

Ortíz's accounts of the economic resources of Texas, together with Terán's earlier reports, reveal a certain irony in the Mexican attitude toward the threatened province. Before Terán's commission was sent to Texas, that is, before Mexicans became very seriously alarmed over the security of the region, they knew very little about its resources. The reports of the commission erased that ignorance, however, and made Mexicans aware that Texas might be a potential source of wealth for the economically troubled republic. As a result, Mexicans became even more reluctant to part with Texas, yet they saw it slipping ever more rapidly from their insecure grasp. Thus a sort of cycle emerged: concern for Texas caused Mexico to take measures, such as Terán's trip, which resulted in increased regard for the threatened province, but which did little or nothing to alleviate the concern, and thereby only served to heighten it. Anthony Butler reported as early as 1830 that the difficulties to be overcome in acquiring Texas had multiplied when the Mexican government learned from its agents in Texas of the "intrinsic and positive value" of that region.[41] Butler also described how quickly Texas had become a pivotal issue in Mexican politics when he reported in 1831 that "popular sentiment" seemed unalterably opposed to American acquisition of Texas, and therefore no government dared to entertain such a proposal. Butler had gone on to say that when Vicente Guerrero had been president his opponents had only to publish reports that he intended to sell Texas to bring demands for his removal.[42]

The cycle was repeated in 1835. Rendered virtually helpless by internal discord, yet intensely anxious about the threatening cloud that seemed forever to blow over Texas from the United States, the government ordered Juan Almonte to Texas to provide as best he might for the security of the province until Mexico could recover from the internal divisions that prevented her from devoting greater attention to the preservation of Texas.[43] The product of Almonte's trip was a lengthy statistical report on the population, flora and fauna, commerce and topography of Texas.[44] Almonte, as had Terán and Ortíz, emphasized the immense wealth that might be anticipated from the region. He was not able to prevent the loss of Texas or even to delay it, but he did remind Mexicans, on the very eve of the disaster, that their loss would be a grievous one.

And the United States would be responsible. In the fall of 1835 Almonte received a letter from an American abolitionist, David Lee Child, informing the Mexican that land speculators in the United States were to a great degree responsible for instigating the unrest in Texas and that President Andrew Jackson favored their activities. Americans had taken advantage of Mexico's "mild and hospital" laws in order to facilitate the conquest of Texas, "or to plant slavery there and to be enemies" in the Mexican camp. The activities of abolitionists in the United States had served "to inflame the desire of southerners to possess" Mexican territory. Child told Almonte to use the letter as he pleased, "if by doing so you can further the object we have in common, the preservation of the integrity of the Mexican Republic."[45]

As early as January 1834 the liberal, pro-American newspaper *El Fénix* had said that it disbelieved reports of a pending American-inspired revolution in Texas, but the editors did feel that Texas was too valuable for Mexico to surrender and that her territorial integrity was worth fighting for, if things should come to that point.[46] *El Mosquito Mexicano* urged Mexicans to unite on the issue of Texas, for to remain divided would only guarantee the success of rapacious and cruel Americans whose purpose was to enrich themselves by stealing Texas.[47] *El Mosquito Mexicano* first appeared in 1834 and remained the most rancorously anti-American newspaper of the entire period. Bitterly critical of the American immigrants in Texas, *El Mosquito* declared that it would not be fair to future generations of Mexicans, whose forefathers had fought so bravely for independence, to allow any part of the national domain to fall under the control of the United States.[48]

Although the newspaper *El Anteojo* began publication in the summer of 1835 it ignored the Texas issue until November of that year. The revolution in Texas was now in its preliminary stage, and *El Anteojo* said that Americans were the "natural enemies" of Mexico. It asserted that abundant evidence existed to prove that Americans had fomented the unrest in Texas, and that they promoted Mexico's ruin in order to enrich themselves, for gold was the only god in the United States. Mexicans should not tolerate this attempt by Americans to advance their cause by armed forced against a people they considered inferior.[49] *El Anteojo's* editorials continued in this vein throughout the winter of 1835-36. Its editors took pride, they said, in being among the first to point out the hypocrisy with which Americans claimed moral supremacy when in their laws, politics, and even in their uses of religion they trampled upon the rights of those they regarded as their inferiors.[50] The author of a letter to *El Anteojo* said that it was not certain that the United States sought to acquire *all* of Mexico; Americans *did* want Texas, however, and were motivated to a great extent by their desire to expand slavery. This alone made it necessary for Mexicans to fight to retain the province.[51] In December 1835 the editors stated that a war against the Texans would be a *national* affair between Mexico and the United States, rather than a domestic war as claimed by the American government. American support and encouragement of the Texans proved this, and Mexicans should know the identity of the true enemy.[52] A few days earlier there had appeared in *El Anteojo* a lengthy article entitled "Tranquility," advancing the thesis that social equality guaranteed by law provided the foundation for the orderly advance of society and civilization. A large percentage of those living in the United States did not enjoy such equality. Many black victims of this discriminatory system were not slaves; yet, due only to their dark skins, they suffered under tyranny of white Americans. These victims of American oppression might be lured to Mexico, where they would enjoy equality and serve a stabilizing influence in the northern departments, helping to provide a buffer against the American advance. This long article revealed a sophisticated grasp of the effects of a caste system upon free blacks in the United States, and the editors of *El Anteojo*, at least, seemed willing to accept blacks, as social equals in Mexico. The article closed with the suggestion that Americans in Texas would not remain content with merely gaining their independence, but might be relied upon to establish a caste system affecting Mexicans much as it had blacks in the United States.[53]

By the beginning of 1836 it was widely assumed in Mexico that the United States had provoked the disturbances in Texas. Many Mexicans furthermore feared that should Americans succeed in Texas they would soon seek even more territory from Mexico. A Matamoros newspaper summarized these views when it asserted that Mexicans, from the richest proprietor to the humblest laborer, were preoccupied with the awful implications of the obvious fact that the United States had turned against Mexico. Americans supplied the malcontents in Texas, and the United States government would violate fundamental principles of international law if it did not suppress this contraband trade. The enrichment of a few Americans who speculated in Texas lands threatened the very existence of Mexico. Should the Yankees succeed in Texas, they would eventually overrun the entire Mexican republic.[54]

NOTES

1. Tornel to Foreign Secretary (Lucas Alamán), December 18, 1830, Archivo General de la Nación (hereafter cited as AGN), Mexico, Relaciones Exteriores, "Internacional, Estados-Unidos, 1806-1840," Barker transcript 564, University of Texas Archives, Austin, pp. 32-38.
2. *El Correo de la Federación Mexicana*, April 16, 1829.
3. *El Fénix de la Libertad*, February 15, 16, 1833.
4. *El Telégrafo*, February 24, 1833.
5. *El Fénix de la Libertad*, April 19, 1833. Clay was, of course, an ardent protectionist, but authored the bill of 1833 which revised the tariff downward and eased the way toward settling the crisis.
6. Ibid., December 14, 1831.
7. *El Telégrafo*, September 3, 1833.
8. Ibid., September 2-4, 1833.
9. *Diario del Gobierno*, March 29, 1835.
10. Lorenzo de Zavala, *Viage a los Estados Unidos* (Mérida, 1846), pp. 80-81.
11. Ibid., p. 85.
12. Ibid., pp. 164-65.
13. Ibid., p. 26.
14. Ibid., pp. 39-42.
15. Waddy Thompson, American minister to Mexico during the early 1840s, saw no more than a half dozen blacks during two years' residence in Mexico City, *Recollections*, pp. 5-6.
16. Ward, *Mexico in 1827*, 1: 36-38.
17. Eugene C. Barker, *Mexico and Texas*, 1821-1835 (Dallas: P.L. Turner & Co., 1928), p. 147.
18. Ibid., p. iv.
19. This view is supported by Samuel Lowrie, *Culture Conflict in Texas, 1821-1835* (New York: Columbia University Press, 1932).
20. Barker, *Mexico and Texas*, pp. 148-49.
21. Poinsett to Secretary of State Henry Clay, July 27, August 10, 1825, MDM.
22. Request for correspondence, March 29, 1826, AGN, Relaciones Exteriores, Manning transcript 554, University of Texas Archives, Austin, p. 99. The entire volume of transcripts concerns preparations for the boundary negotiations.

23. *El Sol*, February 20, 1827.

24. Poinsett to Secretary of State Henry Clay, February 21, March 8, 1827, MDM.

25. Ohland Morton, *Terán and Texas: A Chapter in Texas-Mexican Relations* (Austin: University of Texas Press, 1948), pp. 42-82.

26. Ibid.

27. Poinsett to Secretary of State Martin Van Buren, August 2, 1829, MDM.

28. Terán to Secretary of War and Marine (Francisco Moctezuma), November 14,1829, AGN, Guerra y Marina, Operaciones Militares, 1830, fracción 1, legajo 14, Barker transcript 329, pp. 240-44; Morton, *Terán and Texas*, p. 197.

29. Pizarro Martínez to Foreign Secretary (Juan José Espinosa de los Monteros), April 16, 1827. AGN, Archivo de Secretaría de Fomento. Colonización, Año de 1831, legajo 6, Bolton transcripts, pt. 1, no. 673, Bancroft Library, California, p.3.

30. *El Sol*, November 3, 1829.

31. Ibid., November 4, 1829.

32. Tornel to Foreign Secretary (Lucas Alamán), March 6, 1830, AGN, Relaciones Exteriores, Barker transcript 554, pp. 42-43.

33. "Espedición de los Anglo-Americanos sobre el estado de Texas," *Voz de la Patria* (Mexico City), February 8, 1830.

34. Alleine Howsen, "Causes and Origin of the Decree of April 6, 1830," *Southwestern Historical Quarterly* 16 (April 1913): 378-422; Eugene C. Barker, *The Life of Stephen F. Austin* (Chicago: Cokesbury Press, 1925), pp. 296-328; Bancroft, *North Mexican States and Texas*, 2: 113-14.

35. Lucas Alamán, "Iniciativa de ley proponiedo al gobierno las medidas que se debian tomar para la seguridad del Estado de Tejas y conservar la integridad del territorio mexicano, de cuyo proyecto emanó la ley de 6 de Abril de 1830," *Obras*, 12 vols. (Mexico City: Editorial Jus, 1942-45), 10: 523-43.

36. Butler to Secretary of State Martin Van Buren, March 9, 1830, MDM.

37. Morton, *Terán and Texas*, pp. 316-17; Stanley Green, "Lucas Alamán: Domestic Activities, 1823-1835" (Ph.D. diss., Texas Christian University, 1970), pp. 236-37.

38. Robert A. Carter, Jr., "Anthony Butler and His Mission to Mexico" (M.A. thesis, University of Texas, 1952); Rives, *The United States and Mexico*, 1: 234-61.

39. Wilfred Hardy Callcott, *Santa Anna: The Story of An Enigma Who Once Was Mexico* (Norman: University of Oklahoma Press, 1936), pp. 108-21.

40. Edith Louise Kelly and Mattie Austin Hatcher, eds., "Tadeo Ortíz de Ayala and the Colonization of Texas, 1822-1833," *Southwestern Historical Quarterly* 32 (April

1929): 311-43; W.H. Timmons, "Tadeo Ortíz and Texas," *Southwestern Historical Quarterly* 71 (July 1968): 21-33.

41. Butler to Secretary of State Martin Van Buren, March 9, 1830, MDM.

42. Same to President Andrew Jackson, May 25, 1831. William R. Manning, ed., *Diplomatic Correspondence of the United States, InterAmerican Affairs, 1831-1860*, vol. 8 (Washington: Carnegie Endowment for International Peace, 1937), p. 243.

43. Helen Willits Harris, "The Public Life of Juan Nepomuceno Almonte" (Ph.D. diss., University of Texas, 1935), pp. 30-32.

44. Juan N. Almonte, *Noticia estadística sobre Texas* (Mexico City, 1835).

45. Child to Almonte, September 15, 1835, AGN, Archivo de Secretaría de Fomento. Colonización, legajo 9, Bolton transcripts, pt. 1, no. 673, folder 7, pp. 9-10. The same group of papers contains a collection of translations of articles on Texas taken from American newspapers, one of which said that it would be difficult for Mexicans to "contain Colonel Crockett." Almonte, the translator, identified Crockett in a footnote as a "lunatic Politician ." Ibid., folder 5, p. 88.

46. *El Fénix de la Libertad*, January 4, 1834.

47. *El Mosquito Mexicano*, August 4, 1835.

48. Ibid., November 3, 1835.

49. *El Anteojo*, November 4, 1835.

50. Ibid., November 6, 1835.

51. Ibid., November 15, 1835.

52. Ibid., December 9, 1835.

53. Ibid., November 20, 1835.

54. *Mercurio del Puerto de Matamoros*, January 1, 15, 1836.

According to Arnoldo De León, an understanding of the manifestations of American racism on the northeastern Mexican frontier is crucial for a complete understanding of the Texas Revolt. Mexicans, thought many Texans, were a particularly depraved people, on a par with Indians and Blacks, with little right or will to tame the wilderness. Americans carried with them the moral responsibility to tame the frontier and rescue it from primitivism. Revolt from the Mexican Republic was their only solution.

Initial Contacts:
Redeeming Texas from Mexicans, *1821-1836*

Arnoldo De León

Most whites who first met Tejanos in the 1820s had never had prior experiences with Mexicans nor encountered them anywhere else. Yet their reaction to them upon contact was contemptuous, many thinking Mexicans abhorrent. What caused pioneers to feel this way? Why were their attitudes bigoted instead of neutral? What did they find in Mexicans that aroused xenophobic behavior, or what was it within themselves that generated that response?

According to one Texas historian, Anglo settlers who entered Texas accepted Mexicans on the basis of equality initially and did not react scornfully toward the native Tejanos until the Texas wars for independence of 1836. Relationships before then, according to him, were characterized by a marked tolerance, lack of basic antipathy between the two races, and an almost total lack of friction traceable to racial problems.[1] In the opinion of another student of Anglo attitudes during the period 1821-1845, white feelings toward Mexicans were very complex, at times contradictory, and constantly in flux.[2]

The latest scholarship on the subject of racial and cultural attitudes, however, does not sustain these arguments. Americans moving to the west, recent studies indicate, had much more in mind than settling the land and creating prosperous communities. Cultural heirs to Elizabethans and Puritans, those moving into hinterlands sensed an "errand into the wilderness" and felt a compelling need to control all that was beastly--sexuality, vice, nature, and colored peoples. Order and discipline had to be rescued from the wilds in the name of civilization and Christianity. Moving westward with this mission uppermost in their minds, whites psychologically needed to subdue the external world--forests, beasts, and other peoples--for the rational had to be ever in command. Coming into constant encounter with peoples of color in wilderness settings, these sensitive whites struggled against noncivilization. To allow an inverse order and a concomitant surrender of themselves and their

ancient, pre-historic

liberties to primitive things was to allow chaos to continue when God's will was to impose Christian order.[3] *obedience* *originate*

The desire to bring fields and Indians under submission did not emanate solely from religious passion but was also a product of the individual compulsion to repress instinctual urges. Within humanity were encased base impulses (e.g., sexuality, savagery) that were just as primitive and animalistic as the things of the forest which demanded domination. Killing, destruction, subordination, and appropriation of lands not only brought the external wilderness under control but also served as a form of release for the animal within. In prevailing over primitive things through violence, whites found regeneration, but their efforts also resulted in the uglier manifestations of racism.[4] Therein lay the seed for the perverse responses toward Mexicanos in the first encounter.[5]

Waves of Anglo settlers first entered Texas when the Mexican government in 1821 granted colonization rights in the province to a Missouri entrepreneur named Moses Austin. Hundreds more followed thereafter, coming to Mexican Texas under the aegis of Moses' son, Stephen, and other empresarios. Most were not radically different from the pre--nineteenth-century pioneers. Like them, they entertained a strong belief in themselves and the superiority of their way of life.

Why, asked the historian Samuel M. Lowrie in his study of culture conflicts in Texas, were Americans as narrow and freedom loving as frontiersmen willing to settle in a country as religiously intolerant and undemocratic as Mexico?[6] Perhaps because they felt it their duty to make order of what they perceived as chaos. Certainly they uttered such sentiments many times, though Lowrie did not discern it, given the state of scholarship in the 1930s when he wrote his study. As William H. Wharton, one of the more radical agitators for independence from Mexico, put it in an appeal for American support as the revolution went on in Texas,

> The Justice and benevolence of God, will forbid that the delightful region of Texas should again become a howling wilderness, trod only by savages, or that it should be permanently benighted by the ignorance and superstitious, the anarchy and rapine of Mexican misrule. The Anglo-American race are destined to be for ever the proprietors of this land of *promise* and *fulfillment*. *Their* laws will govern it, *their* learning will enlighten it, *their* enterprise will improve it. *Their* flocks will range its boundless pastures, for *them* its fertile lands will yield their luxuriant harvests: its beauteous rivers will waft the products of *their* industry and enterprise, and *their* latest posterity will here enjoy legacies of

"price unspeakable," in the possession of homes fortified by the genius of liberty, and sanctified by the spirit of a beneficent and tolerant religion. This is inevitable, for the wilderness of Texas has been redeemed by Anglo-American blood and enterprises. The colonists have carried with them the language, the habits, and the lofty love of liberty, that has always characterized and distinguished their ancestors. They have identified them indissolubly with the country.[7]

But none was more articulate than Stephen F. Austin, who several times before the war for independence confessed, almost stereotypically, that his intent was "to redeem Texas from the wilderness." In one of his most eloquent expressions, he averred: "My object, the sole and only desire of my ambitions since I first saw Texas, was to redeem it from the wilderness--to settle it with an intelligent honorable and enterprising [sic] people.[8]

To Austin, redemption could come by "whitening" Texas--or, phrased differently, by making it a cultural and racial copy of the United States. In August 1835, he wrote that the best interests of the nation required "that Texas should be effectually, and fully, Americanized--that is--settled by a population that will harmonize with their neighbors on the *East*, in language, political principles, common origin, sympathy, and even interest." It was well known, he continued, that his object had always been to fill up Texas with a North American population. "I wish a great immigration from Kentucky, Tennessee, *every where*, passports, or no passports, *any how*. For fourteen years I have had a hard time of it, but nothing shall daunt my courage or abate my exertions to complete the main object of my labors--to *Americanize Texas*. This fall, and winter, will fix our fate--a great immigration will settle the question."[9]

At the national level, Americans had never been oblivious to the prospects of rescuing Texas from its alleged primitive status. At all times, there had been those in Washington who had similar thoughts and expressed them publicly. Among them was Henry Clay, who asked in 1821: "By what race should Texas be peopled?" Lest it be settled by others who would make it a "place of despotism and slaves, of the inquisition and superstition," it should be taken over by settlers from the United States who would transplant to it the free institutions of Anglo-Americans. Should Texas then break off from the United States for some reason, Clay affirmed, at least it would have been rescued from a race alien to everything that Americans held dear.[10]

Clay did not stop at rhetoric. While he was Secretary of State, he and President John Quincy Adams instructed Joel R. Poinsett, the United States Minister to Mexico, to attempt to purchase Texas. Mexico, which had never put Texas up for sale, squarely rejected the proposal, only to see it repeated. When Andrew Jackson assumed office in 1829, he urged Poinsett to renew his efforts, authorizing the minister to offer $5 million for whatever amount of Texas Mexico would surrender. Similar futile attempts at negotiating the purchase of Texas continued until the time of the revolution.[11]

What whites refused to accept was a state of affairs in which chaos presided over them. But what exactly was it that they considered as disorder? Texas was already settled and under the rule of government, heir to centuries of Spanish civilization. Something else disturbed them, for to them, a connection existed in the new land between the state of civilization and chaos. Thus all the discussion about rescuing Texas from primitivism. The newcomers saw the Tejanos as mongrels, uncivilized, and un-Christian--a part of the wilderness that must be subdued. Living in Mexico and Texas were the sort of people who threatened the march of white civilization.

Incontrovertibly, as far as whites were concerned, order and discipline were missing. For Anglo settlers who arrived in Texas imported certain ideas from the United States, which regarded the native Mexican population as less than civilized. These attitudes ranged from xenophobia against Catholics and Spaniards to racial prejudice against Indians and blacks. Thus Mexicanos were doubly suspect, as heirs to Catholicism and as descendants of Spaniards, Indians, and Africans.

In England, hostile feelings toward the Roman Church originated in the sixteenth century with Henry VIII's religious and political break with the Pope and were hardened by conflict with Catholic Spain. The English mind readily thought in terms of a Catholic-Spanish alliance, conjured by Satan himself, from which nothing less than demonic designs could be expected. Additionally, the English associated the Spanish with cruelty and brutality. Alleged Spanish tyranny in the Netherlands during the latter half of the sixteenth century as well as atrocities toward the Indians in Latin America produced an image of the Spaniard as heartless and genocidal. And, finally, the English saw the Spanish as an embodiment of racial impurity. For hundreds of years, racial mixing or *mestizaje* had occurred in the Iberian peninsula between Spaniards and Moors. At a time when Elizabethans were becoming more and more sensitive to the significance of color--equating whiteness with purity and Christianity and blackness with baseness and the devil--Spaniards came to be thought of as not much better than light-skinned Moors and Africans.

English immigrants to the North American colonies probably brought those ideas with them and were certainly exposed to them through anti-Catholic and anti-Spanish literature constantly arriving in the new society. Men of letters, ministers, and propagandists helped in disseminating such notions. Military clashes along the Georgia-Florida border in the eighteenth century only intensified the hatred.

As for the Mexican aborigines, the English conceived of them as degenerate creatures--un-Christian, uncivilized, and racially impure. From letters, histories, and travel narratives, English writers put together a portrait that turned the people of Mexico into a degraded humanity. The natives subscribed to heathenism, and witches and other devilish agents permeated their culture. They partook of unholy things like polygamy, sodomy, and incest and rejected Christianity outright. Furthermore, they practiced savage rituals like human sacrifice and cannibalism. Of all the Latin American inhabitants, the Mexican Indians seemed the most beastly, for though they were in many ways the most advanced of all the New World peoples, they exercised the grossest violation of civility by these practices. Stories of Aztec gods like Quetzalcoatl who were half man and half beast and accounts of exotic Aztec rites only convinced the English of the Indians' place on the fringes of humankind, with dubious claims to existence, civilization, and Christian salvation.

While such images of the Mexican natives may not have been as widespread as those held of Spaniards, they were nonetheless familiar to many colonists. In newspapers,, recent histories, and re-editions of old propaganda materials, furthermore, colonists were able to read things about the origins of the Mexicans which perpetuated enriched images acquired from the mother country.[12]

In addition to ideas that had been fashioned vicariously, there were those that arose from intimate contact with other peoples whom whites esteemed no more than the Mexican aborigines or the Spaniards. The long history of hostilities against North American Indians on the frontier and the institution of Afro-American slavery molded negative attitudes toward dark skin, "savagery," "vice," and interracial sex. The majority of those who responded to empresario calls most assuredly thought along those lines, for they came from the states west of the Appalachians and south of the Ohio River--Louisiana, Alabama, Arkansas, Tennessee, Missouri, Mississippi, Georgia, and Kentucky. A significant number were Eastern born, but had been part of the frontier movement before their transplantation into Texas.[13] From the Southern and frontier-orientated culture they had acquired a certain repulsion for dark-skinned people and a distaste for miscegenation. Believing that the mores of their own provincial institutions should apply in the new frontier, they assumed a posture of superiority and condescension toward the natives. By conditioning, they were predisposed to react intolerantly to people they found different from themselves but similar to those they considered as enemies and as inferiors. Along with dislike for Spaniards and the Indians of Latin America, these perceptions produced a mode of thinking that set the contours of the primordial response.

And what particularly provoked this reaction? Most Tejanos were descendants of Tlascalan Indians and *mestizo* soldiers from Coahuila. Additionally, a few in Nacogdoches were the offspring of people from Louisiana and reflected that area's racial amalgam, including Indians and blacks. Throughout the province, Tejanos had intermarried among themselves and with Christianized Indian women from local missions so that the colonists continued as a mixed-blood population.[14] Their contrast to "white" and salient kindred to "black" and "red" made Mexicans subject to treatment commensurate with the odious connotations whites attached to colors, races, and cultures dissimilar to their own.

Manifestly, Americans who immigrated to Texas confronted the native Mexicans with certain preconceptions about their character. Whites believed that the inhabitants of the province had descended from a tradition of paganism, depravity, and primitivism. Mexicans were a type of folk that Americans should avoid becoming.

The fact of the matter was that whites had little contact with Tejanos up to 1836, for most of the Mexican population was concentrated in the San Antonio and La Bahía areas, quite a distance from the Anglo colonies. But whites knew what they would find in Texas before contact confirmed their convictions. They encountered biologically decadent and inferior people because their thoughts had been shaped by the aforementioned circumstances. Thus, Mexicans lived in ways that Anglos equated with an opprobrious condition. They inhabited primitive shelters. William F. Gray, a land agent from Virginia, comparing Mexicans with the black American culture he knew, pronounced some of the Mexican homes "miserable shabby *jacales*" scarcely equal in appearance to the Afro-American houses in the suburbs of his state.[15] Mexicans adhered to a different religion: they were completely the "slaves of Popish superstitions and despotism" and religion was understood not as an affection of the heart and soul but as one requiring personal mortification on such superficialities as penances and other rituals.[16] If Anglos and Mexicans were not inherently different peoples, editorialized the *Texian and Emigrant's Guide* in 1835, habit, education, and religion had made them essentially so.[17]

Additionally, Texians thought that Mexicans' cultural habits clashed with American values, such as the work ethic. Mexicanos appeared a traditional, backward aggregate, an irresponsibly passive people dedicated to the present and resigned not to probe the universe about them. An American arriving in Nacogdoches in 1833 found the citizens there the most "lazy indolent poor Starved set of people as ever the Sun Shined upon." He could not comprehend their lethargy by day, nor their inclination to play the violin and dance the entire night.[18] J. C. Clopper of Ohio reasoned in 1828 that Mexicanos were "too ignorant and indolent for enterprises and too poor and *dependant* were they otherwise capacitated."[19] Mexicanos habitually succumbed to indolence and ease and indulged themselves in smoking, music, dancing, horse-racing, and other sports, noted David Woodman, a promoter for a New York and Boston land company, while activity, industry, and frugality marched on in the new American settlements.[20] "The vigor of the descendants of the sturdy north will never mix with the phlegm of the indolent Mexicans," Sam Houston (the future hero of the war for independence) argued in January 1835 in an address to the citizens of Texas, "no matter how long we may live among them."[21] In contrast to the newcomers, Tejanos were chained by custom to complacency, and instead of committing themselves to progress, they preferred fun and frolic. Some three years after Mexico opened Texas to Anglo-American settlement, Anthony R. Clark complained that Spaniards in the District of Nacogdoches, "generally of the lower sort and illiterate [*sic*]," would rather "spend days in gambling to gain a few bits than to make a living by honest industry."[22] William B. Dewees, who lived in San Antonio in the late 1820s, found Bexareños totally hedonistic. "Their whole study seems to be for enjoyment. Mirth and amusement occupy their whole time. If one is fond of the balls and theaters, he can here have an opportunity of attending one every evening. Almost every species of dissipation is indulged in, except drinking."[23] In Goliad, the Mexicans had such a strong predisposition for gaming that almost all the inhabitants in 1833 were gamblers and smugglers, said empresario Dr. John Charles Beales.[24] And Alexander McCrae, touring Texas in 1835 under the auspices of the Wilmington Emigrating Society, remarked in astonishment: "I for the first time saw females betting at a public gambling table; I do not suppose they were of respectable standing in society, from the company they kept; but I am told that it is not all uncommon for Mexican *ladies* to be seen gambling in public."[25]

Acting further to stimulate negative attitudes was the racial composition of Tejanos, who, in the white mind, were closely identified with other colored peoples. For two hundred years, ideas that black men lusted for white women and notions that slaves were of a heathen or "savage" condition had played upon Americans' fantasies; the result had been the institutional debasement of blacks because of their race. Images of the Indian as fierce, hostile, and barbaric similarly affixed themselves in the thoughts of white settlers, and the constant confrontation over land led more to the reaffirmation of these images than to their dissolution. Consequently, when whites arrived in Texas, they unconsciously transferred onto the new "colored" folk they encountered a pseudo-scientific lore acquired from generations of interaction with blacks and Indians.

Travelers, who frequently came in contact with Tejanos, plainly discerned the Mexicans' relation to the black and red peoples. At no time did Americans hold up Frenchmen, or Germans, or themselves for that matter, as a people who physically resembled Mexicans--comparison invariably was with Indians and blacks. Several factors steered discussion in that direction: Anglos were not about to elevate Mexicans to the level of European whiteness; their own sense of superiority turned Tejanos into a people lesser than themselves; and obviously, in any comparison, Mexicans were going to resemble their progenitors. Thus, whites often likened Mexicans to Africans and Native Americans. When Clopper mentioned the complexion of the Tejanos, he thought it "a shade brighter than that of the aborigines of the country."[26] On the other hand, the land agent Gray stamped Tejanos as a "swarthy looking people much resembling our mulattos, some of them nearly black."[27] Sam Houston asked his compatriots (in the aforementioned address) if they "would bow under the yoke of these half-Indians,"[28] while abolitionist Benjamin Lundy, in Laredo in 1834, remarked that the Mexicans in the town looked like mulattoes.[29] Even when commentators omitted drawing comparisons about color, they nonetheless made reference to the Mexicans' dark complexion. One traveler asserted that because of it they were "readily designated at first sight."[30]

The same association with Indians and Africans was also apparent in caustic comments about the Mexicans' ancestors. A Texan identifying himself as "H. H." in a letter to the *New Orleans Bee* in 1834 pronounced the people of Mexico the most "degraded and vile; the unfortunate race of Spaniard, Indian and African, is so blended that the worst qualities of each predominate."[31] Two years later, when the Texans were locked in a fateful struggle with the Mexican nation, leaders of the rebellion appealed to their comrades by reminding them that Mexicans were "the adulterate and degenerate brood of the once high-spirited Castilian."[32]

In addition to all their other discoveries about Mexicans, whites in the period between 1821 and 1836 thought Tejanos lax in virtue. A number of aspects of Mexican morality bothered them, including the native *fandango*, a dance of a sinuous sort with sexually suggestive moves. George W. Smyth from Tennessee witnessed it in Nacogdoches upon his arrival in 1830, and was surprised "that the priest and all participated, so contrary to all my pre-conceived notions of propriety."[33] Asahel

Langworthy, a New York lawyer and land speculator, found the dance somewhat uncivilized, identifying it with lack of culture and refinement. "I witnessed one afternoon," he wrote, "a Spanish *fandango* danced in the open air by a party of these people, evidently of a low class."[34]

Because of the apparent revelry of such recreational forms, whites began early on to assume Mexicans had a defective morality, and Mexican attitudes toward sexuality strengthened the white images of Mexicans as sensuous and voluptuous. Despite the close supervision given unmarried girls to prevent intercourse with their male counterparts, Clopper alleged, "soon as married they are scarcely the same creatures--giving the freest indulgence to their naturally gay and enthusiastic dispositions, as if liberated from all moral restraints."[35] To the Ohioan, Mexicans were not cut from the same moral fabric as Americans.

But even if Mexicans as a race were sexually degenerate, some exception might be made for the females, especially by those men wandering into areas like Béxar where white women were scarce, and thus where Mexican women might be attractive, even if they were of mixed blood. Among those venturing into San Antonio at this early date was Clopper, who considered the local women handsome of person and regular in feature, with black, sparkling eyes and "a brighter hue" than the men.[36] Like others of this era, he had a preference for those who came close to the American ideal of female beauty and purity. Becoming friendly with one of the Castilian *señoritas,* Clopper wrote a meticulous description of his acquaintance. "She was of the middle size, her person of the finest symmetry," he noted, "moving through the mazes of the *fandango* with all the graces that distinguished superiority of person of mind and of soul. Her features were beautiful forming in their combination an expression that fixed the eye of the observer as with a spell, her complexion was of the loveliest, the snowy brightness of her well turned forehead beautifully contrasting with the carnation tints of her cheeks. A succession of smiles were continually sporting around her mouth," he elaborated, "her pouting cherry lips were irresistible and even when closed seemed to have utterance--her eye--but I have no such language as seemed to be spoken by it else might I tell how dangerous was it to meet its lustre and feel its quick thrilling scrutiny of the hearts as tho' the very fire of its expression was conveyed with its beamings." The admirer admitted in closing: "I felt lonely and sad as a stranger in that place and a vision so lovely coming so unexpectedly before me could not fail to awaken tender recollection and altogether make an impression not to be forgotten."[37]

Though not much else was said on the issue of interracial sex, at least one Texan brought up a theme that would preoccupy white males after 1836. Mexican women, he thought, manifested a "decided preference" for foreigners, and would willingly consent to marriage should they be approached. "Where a Mexican woman becomes attached there are few who can love more warmly," he added.[38] And it would probably be safe to conjecture that at least some of those women that the future hero of the Alamo, William Barrett Travis, "chingó," were Mexicans.[39]

Despite their comments about passionate Mexican women, whites did not say much about sexually virile males. During the revolution, however, hysterical Texians did inject a sexual dimension into the war--crying out that Mexican soldiers were sexual threats to white women. "What can be expected for the *fair Daughters* of chaste *white women* when their own country women are prostituted, by a licensed soldiery, as an inducement to push forward into the Colonies, where they may find fairer game!" feared James W. Fannin, who later was killed in the Goliad massacre.[40] John W. Hall, a spirited mover of independence, asked the public to imagine what would happen if Mexican soldiers gained a foothold in Texas soil? Beloved wives, mothers, daughters, sisters, and helpless innocent children would be given up to the dire pollution and massacre of the barbarians, he claimed.[41] And from the Alamo, Travis also raised the specter of "the pollution of [the Texans'] wives and daughters" by the Mexican soldiers of General Antonio López de Santa Anna.[42]

The vision of Mexican rapists seemingly reflected white men's state of mind as of 1836. Probably, they saw in Mexicans the same threat that horrified them in black males, and it was too early then for them to have formulated other perceptions. As it turned out, no violations were reported and the rape theme practically disappeared, rarely to crop up again, even though in subsequent times Texans faced other threats of Mexican violence. After the episode, Anglos seldom saw Mexicans as a danger to white women.

The events of 1836 brought forth charges of Mexican depravity and violence, a theme which became pervasive once Anglos made closer contact with the state's Hispanic population following the war. In the crisis of the moment, firebrands spoke alarmingly of savage, degenerate, half-civilized, and barbarous Mexicans committing massacres and atrocities at Goliad and the Alamo.[43] Even worse, whites conjured up ideas of slave uprisings and possible alliances between slave rebels and Mexicans whom whites considered to be infused with African blood anyway. Entrepreneur James Morgan reported that slaves high upon the Trinity were daringly seeking to enlist the Coshatti [Coushatta] Indians and come down and murder the inhabitants of the Galveston region and join the Mexicans.[44] A resolution adopted by citizens meeting in Brazoria in March 1836 warned in consternation: "We have moreover been appraised of the horrid purpose of our treacherous and bloody enemy, to unite in his ranks, and as instruments of his unholy and savage work, the Negroes, whether slave or free, thus lighting the torch of war, in the bosoms of our domestic circles."[45]

Such talk may have been part of the hysteria that ordinarily accompanies war propaganda anywhere. But in any case, some whites were already regarding Mexicans as cruel enough to be considered less than human, and thus dispensable, like Indians, Africans, and animals. Reminiscing about his role in the struggle between Texas and Mexico, Creed Taylor recalled: "I thought I could shoot Mexicans as well as I could shoot Indians, or deer, or turkey; and so I rode away to war."[46] Similarly, eighty-year old Sion R. Bostick of San Saba County reminisced in 1900 that, although he did not know the real causes of the conflict, he joined it as "I thought I could kill Mexicans as easily as I could deer and turkeys."[47]

What whites found in the Texas experience during these first fifteen years was that Mexicans were primitive beings who during a century of residence in Texas had failed to improve their status and environment. Mexicans were religious pagans, purposelessly indolent and carefree, sexually remiss, degenerate, depraved, and questionably human. The haunting prospect of being ruled by such people indefinitely explains in part the Texian movement for independence in 1836.

Historians, however, have not paid due attention to these attitudes as factors in the movement for independence, for to do so is to come close to labeling the first generation of Texans as racists. White racism toward the indigenous Mexican population, some would maintain, did not develop until after an extended period of interaction between Texans and Mexicans. Not until decades later, others contend, did science postulate the biological inferiority of certain peoples, thereby begetting racist practices. Yet such arguments have ignored the baneful ubiquity of race in the forging of the American national character, have neglected the psychological implications of its presence, and are unattentive to the deep-seated resentments whites felt toward darker-skinned people whenever they came in contact with them. They have overlooked the motivating force of white supremacy and the compelling need of white America to press ahead with the task of "civilizing" colored peoples and what they stood for.

Dismissing racial prejudice means not taking account of Americans' psychic character as they came to interact with Mexicans in Texas. Admittedly, racism was not *the* cause of the Texas revolution, but very certainly, it was *very* prominent as a promoting and underlying cause. Its roots were planted in the unique psychohistorical experience of the white Texas pioneers and settlers.

And indeed, in the heat of the crisis, leaders of the revolution revealed feelings about race that surely contributed to their strike for independence. Stephen F. Austin, despite his capacity to understand a culture "different" from his and assimilate into that culture with versatility, nevertheless revealed latent racist feelings as the combat raged. It was, he said, one of barbarism waged by a "mongrel Spanish-Indian and negro race, against civilization and the Anglo American race."[48] David G. Burnet, president and the *ad interim* revolutionary government, wrote to Senator Henry Clay: "The causes which have led to this momentous act are too numerous to be detailed in a single letter; but one general fact may account for all; the utter dissimilarity of character between the two people, the Texians and the Mexicans. The first are principally Anglo Americans; the others a mongrel race of degenerate Spaniards and Indians more depraved than they."[49] Much later, it was admitted that among the main reasons for the origins of the conflict was the "insuperable aversion" to social amalgamation between whites and Mexicans: "the colonists from the North were somewhat homogenous in blood and color; the Mexicans, a mongrel breed of negroes, Indians and Spaniards of the baser sort."[50]

Thus, beneath the talk of oppression lingered the underpinnings of white supremacy and racial antipathy. In truth, the Texans never experienced oppression like that of others who have risen in rebellion. The Mexican government was thousands of miles away, afflicted with internal problems, and unable to pay proper attention to what was transpiring in Texas. Culturally, the Americans got along well with the *criollo* elite. In fact, after the revolution, the *criollos*, who closely resembled Anglos in racial makeup, were comfortably fitted into white society. Moreover, wherever Anglos went individually, and found themselves in a minority, they adjusted adequately to Mexican culture (despite harboring racist feelings). This was the case in the next decades in El Paso, Santa Fe, and Los Angeles.

But in Coahuila y Tejas, Anglos were dealing primarily not with *criollos*, but with mixed-blood (or "mongrel") Mexicans. And, by 1836, Texas was very different from later Southwestern settings. Though Texas was not legally American, it might as well have been. It was "white" spiritually, attitudinally, politically, socially, economically, and demographically--an American entity all to itself. These circumstances, in which Texians of diverse social standing thought of themselves as "white people" instead of individuals, incited the daring and massive quest for supremacy over barren wastes and Mexicanos.

Which is to say that the Texas Revolution was one of racial adjustment. For Anglo-Texans to have accepted anything other than "white supremacy and civilization" was to submit to Mexican domination and to admit that Americans were willing to become like Mexicans. The prospect of being dominated by such untamed, uncivil, and disorderly creatures made a contest for racial hegemony almost inevitable.

NOTES

1. Seymour V. Connor, *Texas: A History,* p. 120.
2. Crisp, "Anglo-Texan Attitudes toward the Mexican," p. 5.
3. Select works advancing this argument include Ronald T. Takaki, *Iron Cages: Race and Culture in Nineteenth Century America,* pp. 11-15; Drinnon, *Facing West,* p. 465; Gary B. Nash, *Red, White, and Black: The Peoples of Early America,* ed., pp. 81-82; David Brion Davis, *The Problem of Slavery in Western Culture,* p. 4; and Robert F. Berkhoffer, Jr., *The White Man's Indian: Images of the American Indian from Columbus to the Present,* p. 27. See also Bernard W. Sheehan, *Savagism and Civility: Indians and Englishmen in Colonial Virginia.*
4. Richard Slotkin, *Regeneration through Violence: The Mythology of the American Frontier, 1600-1860,* p. 5.
5. The same need to subjugate others at whatever cost would mold Anglo/Mexican relations after that and would continue westward to find further expression in California, in the "white man's burden" in the Pacific, and finally in Vietnam (Takaki, *Iron Cages,* p. xvii; Drinnon, *Facing West,* p. xvii).
6. Samuel H. Lowrie, *Culture Conflict in Texas, 1821-1836,* p. 68.
7. William H. Wharton, Address, April 26, 1836, in *The Papers of Mirabeau Buonaparte Lamar,* ed. Charles Adams Gulick, Jr., and Winnie Allen (cited hereafter as *Lamar Papers*), I:365 (emphasis in original).
8. Stephen F. Austin to Thomas F. Learning, July 23, 1831, in *The Austin Papers,* ed. Eugene C. Barker, 2:414, 427, 678.
9. Stephen F. Austin to Mrs. Mary Austin Holley, August 21, 1835, in *Austin Papers,* 3:101-103 (emphasis in original).
10. Cited by Mattie Alice Hatcher, *The Opening of Texas to Foreign Settlement, 1801-1821,* p. 277.
11. John William O'Neal, "Texas, 1791-1835: A Study in Manifest Destiny" (M.A. thesis, East Texas State University, 1969), pp. 90-93.
12. Paredes, "The Origins of Anti-Mexican Sentiment in the United States," pp. 139-166. Others supporting Paredes' position are S. Dale McLemore, "The Origins of Mexican American Subordination in Texas," *Social Science Quarterly 53* (March 1973): 663; David J. Weber, ed., *Foreigners in Their Native Land,* pp. 59-61, 89; and idem, "'Scarce More than Apes': Historical Roots of Anglo-American Stereotypes of Mexicans in the Border Region," in *New Spain's Far Northern Frontier: Essays on Spain in the American West, 1540-1821,* ed. David J. Weber, pp. 295-307.
13. Eugene C. Barker, *The Life of Stephen F. Austin: Founder of Texas, 1793-1836,* p. 149.
14. Andrew Anthony Tijerina, "Tejanos and Texas: The Native Mexicans of Texas, 1820-1850" (Ph.D. dissertation, University of Texas at Austin, 1977), pp. 10-14, 37-39, 44-45; Alicia V. Tjarks,

"Comparative Demographic Analysis of Texas, 1777-1793," *Southwestern Historical Quarterly* 77 (January 1974): 291-338.

15. William F. Gray, *From Virginia to Texas...*, p. 92.

16. J.C. Clopper, "Journal of J.C. Clopper, 1828," *Southwestern Historical Quarterly* 13 (July 1909): 72, 76.

17. *Texian and Emigrant's Guide* (Nacogdoches), December 26, 1835, p. 4. See as well the *Telegraph and Texas Register* (San Felipe de Austin), January 23, 1836, pp. 102-118.

18. Quoted by Crisp, "Anglo-Texan Attitudes toward the Mexican," p. 22.

19. Clopper, "Journal," p. 76 (emphasis in original).

20. David Woodman, *Guide to Texas Emigrants*, p. 35.

21. Houston to Soldiers, January 15, 1836, in *The Papers of the Texas Revolution, 1835-1836,* gen. ed. John H. Jenkins, 4:30.

22. Ernest W. Winkler, ed., *Manuscript Letters and Documents of Early Texians*, 1821-1845, p. 32.

23. William B. Dewees, *Letters from an Early Settler of Texas*, p. 56.

24. Dr. John Beales' Journal, 1833, in William Kennedy, *Texas: The Rise, Progress, and Prospects of the Republic of Texas*, p. 396.

25. Joshua James and Alexander McCrae, *A Journal of a Tour in Texas*, p. 15. Emphasis is McCrae's. See also Dewees, *Letters from An Early Settler*, p. 57, for remarks on the Mexican passion for gambling.

26. Clopper, "Journal," pp. 71-72.

27. Gray, *From Virginia to Texas*, p. 89.

28. Houston to Soldiers, January 15, 1836, in *Papers of the Texas Revolution* 4:30.

29. Benjamin Lundy, *The Life, Travels, and Opinions of Benjamin Lundy*, p. 95.

30. Amos Andrew Parker, *Trip to the West and Texas*, p. 122; see also Asahel Langworthy, *A Visit to Texas,* p. 15.

31. *New Orleans Bee,* November 5, 1834, p. 2.

32. Thomas J. Green to the Friends of Liberty throughout the World, April 5, 1836, in *Lamar Papers* I:348.

33. George W. Smyth, "The Autobiography of George W. Smyth," ed. Winnie Allen, *Southwestern Historical Quarterly* 36 (January 1933): 202.

34. Langworthy, *Visit to Texas*, p. 217.

35. Clopper, "Journal," p. 72.

36. Ibid.

37. Ibid., pp. 72-73.

38. *New Orleans Bee,* November 5, 1834, p. 2.

39. William Barrett Travis, *The Diary of William Barrett Travis*, August 30, 1833-June 26, 1834, ed. Robert E. Davis, pp. 15, 68, 85, 91, 142, 154, 170. The Spanish verb *chingar* (to have sexual relations with) is Travis' own term.

40. James W. Fannin to J.W. Robinson, February 7, 1836, in *Official Correspondence of the Texan Revolution, 1835-1836,* ed. William C. Binkley, I:402 (emphasis in original). See also R.C. Morris to J.W. Fannin, February 6, 1836, in ibid. I:400; Council to the People of Texas, February 13, 1836, in ibid. I:419.

41. John W. Hall to Public, February 1836 (?), in *Papers of the Texas Revolution* 4:470.

42. W.B. Travis to Henry Smith, February 12, 1836, in *Official Correspondence of the Texan Revolution* I:416.

43. Thomas J. Green to the Friends of Liberty throughout the World, April 5, 1836, in *Lamar Papers* I:348; David G. Burnet to Henry Raguet, April 7, 1836, in *Official Correspondence of the Texan Revolution* 2:602.

44. James Morgan to S.P. Carson, March 24, 1836, in *Official Correspondence of the Texan Revolution* I:534.

45. Meeting at Brazoria, March 17, 1836, in *Lamar Papers* I:345.

46. Creed Taylor, *Tall Men with Long Rifles,* narrated by James T. De Shields, p. 9.

47. Sion R. Bostick, "Reminiscences of Sion R. Bostick," *Quarterly of the Texas State Historical Association 5* (October 1901): 95.

48. Stephen F. Austin to Mary Austin Holley, August 21, 1835, in *Austin Papers* 3:101-103.

49. D. G. Burnet to Henry Clay, March 30, 1836, in *Official Correspondence of the Texas Revolution* 2:561.

50. "Compendium of the Early History of Texas," in *The Texas Almanac, 1857-1873,* comp. James M. Day, p. 180.

In 1824 Mexico permitted mass foreign immigration into its northern frontier for the first time. The immigrants had agreed to become Mexican citizens, convert to Catholicism, and obey Mexican laws. Within ten years Anglo-American immigrants, principally from the American south, filtered into Texas and began a campaign of blatant disregard for Mexican sovereignty through local seditions, contempt for Mexican laws and conducting illegal trade. In March, 1836, fifty-nine Texas rebels, now at war with Mexico, met at Washington-on-the-Brazos and declared their independence from Mexico. This culminated nearly a decade of growing political difficulties with the Mexican republic dating to Mexico's abolition of slavery in 1829. Since that time Texas rebels called attention to a number of political issues including demands for more political representation in the Coahuila state legislature, the recognition of slavery and free trade, among others. Mexico viewed the rebels as the seditionary front line of American-sponsored expansionism.

Texas Declaration of Independence

When a government has ceased to protect the lives, liberty, and property of the people, from whom its legitimate powers are derived, and for the advancement of whose happiness it was instituted, and, so far from being a guarantee for the enjoyment of those inestimable and inalienable rights, becomes an instrument in the hands of evil rulers for their oppression: When the Federal Republican Constitution of their country, which they have sworn to support, no longer has a substantial existence, and the whole nature of their government has been forcibly changed, without their consent, from a restricted federative republic, composed of sovereign states, to a consolidated, central, military despotism in which every interest is disregarded but that of the army and the priesthood--both the eternal enemies of civil liberty, the ever-ready minions of power, and the usual instruments of tyrants. When, long after the spirit of the constitution has departed, moderation is, at length, so far lost by those in power that even the semblance of freedom is removed, and the forms themselves, of the constitution discontinued; and so far from their petitions and remonstrances being regarded the agents who bear them are thrown into dungeons; and mercenary armies sent forth to force a new government upon them at the point of the bayonet: When in consequence of such acts of malfeasance and abdication, on the part of the government, anarchy prevails, and civil society is dissolved into its original elements---In such a crisis, the first law of nature, the right of self-preservation---the inherent and inalienable right of the people to appeal to first principles and take their political affairs into their own hands in extreme cases---enjoins it as a right towards themselves and a sacred obligation to their posterity to abolish such government and create another, in its stead, calculated to rescue them from impending dangers, and to secure their future welfare and happiness.

Nations, as well as individuals, are amenable for their acts to the public opinion of mankind. A statement of a part of our grievances is, therefore, submitted to an impartial world, in justification of the hazardous but avoidable step now taken of severing our political connection with the Mexican people, and assuming an independent attitude among the nations of the earth.

The Mexican government, by its colonization laws, invited and induced the Anglo-American population of Texas to colonize its wilderness under the pledged faith of a written constitution that they should continue to enjoy that constitutional liberty and republican government to which they had been habituated in the land of their birth, the United States of America. In this expectation they have been cruelly disappointed, inasmuch as the Mexican nation has acquiesced in the late changes made in the government by General Antonio López de Santa Anna, who, having overturned the constitution of his country, now offers us the cruel alternative either to abandon our homes, acquired by so many privations, or submit to the most intolerable of all tyranny, the combined despotism of the sword and the priesthood.

It has sacrificed our welfare to the state of Coahuila, by which our interests have been continually depressed through a jealous and partial course of legislation carried on at a far distant seat of government, by a hostile majority, in an unknown tongue; and this too, notwithstanding we have petitioned in the humblest terms, for the establishment of a separate state government, and have, in accordance with the provisions of the national constitution, presented to the general Congress a republican constitution which was, without just cause, contemptuously rejected.

It incarcerated in a dungeon, for a long time, one of our citizens, for no other cause but a zealous endeavor to procure the acceptance of our constitution and the establishment of a state government.

It has failed and refused to secure on a firm basis, the right of trial by jury, that palladium of civil liberty, and only safe guarantee for the life, liberty, and property of the citizen.

It has failed to establish any public system of education, although possessed of almost boundless resources (the public domain) and, although it is an axiom, in political science, that unless a people are educated and enlightened it is idle to expect the continuance of civil liberty, or the capacity for self-government.

It has suffered the military commandants stationed among us to exercise arbitrary acts of oppression and tyranny; thus trampling upon the most sacred rights of the citizen and rendering the military superior to the civil power.

It has dissolved by force of arms, the State Congress of Coahuila and Texas, and obliged our representatives to fly for their lives from the seat of government; thus depriving us of the fundamental political right of representation.

It has demanded the surrender of a number of our citizens, and ordered military detachments to seize and carry them into the interior for trial; in contempt of the civil authorities, and in defiance of the laws and the constitution.

It has made piratical attacks upon our commerce, by commissioning foreign desperadoes, and authorizing them to seize our vessels, and convey the property of our citizens to far distant ports for confiscation.

It denies us the right of worshiping the Almighty according to the dictates of our own conscience; by the support of a national religion calculated to promote the temporal interests of its human functionaries rather than the glory of the true and living God.

It has demanded us to deliver up our arms, which are essential to our defense, the rightful property of freeman, and formidable only to tyrannical governments.

It has invaded our country, both by sea and by land, with intent to lay waste our territory and drive us from our homes; and has now a large mercenary army advancing to carry on against us a war of extermination.

It has, through its emissaries, incited the merciless savage, with the tomahawk and scalping knife, to massacre the inhabitants of our defenseless frontiers.

It has been, during the whole time of our connection with it, the contemptible sport and victim of successive military revolutions; and has continually exhibited every characteristic of a weak, corrupt, and tyrannical government.

These, and other grievances, were patiently borne by the people of Texas until they reached that point at which forbearance ceases to be a virtue. We then took up arms in defense of the national constitution. We appealed to our Mexican brethren for assistance. Our appeal has been made in vain. Though months have elapsed, no sympathetic response has yet been heard from the Interior. We are, therefore, forced to the melancholy conclusion that the Mexican people have acquiesced in the destruction of their liberty, and the substitution therefor of a military government--- that they are unfit to be free and incapable of self-government.

The necessity of self-preservation, therefore, now decrees our eternal political separation.

We, therefore, the delegates, with plenary powers, of the people of Texas, in solemn convention assembled, appealing to a candid world for the necessities of our condition, do hereby resolve and declare that our political connection with the Mexican nation has forever ended; and that the people of Texas do now constitute a free sovereign and independent republic; and are fully invested with all the rights and attributes which properly belong to independent nations; and, conscious of the rectitude of our intentions, we fearlessly and confidently commit the issue to the decision of the Supreme Arbiter of the destinies of nations.

This agreement, signed in Velasco, Texas, on May 14, 1836, ended military hostilities between Mexico and the Texas secessionists. It culminated nearly a decade of mounting tensions and resulted in further complicating relations with the United States. Of particular interest, and troublesome for future relations with Texas and the United States was Article 4, a secret agreement by Antonio López de Santa Anna to make the Rio Grande the southern boundary of Texas. Mexico repudiated the treaty and considered Santa Anna's alienation of the national territory unconstitutional. Texas proceeded to declare itself the Lone Star Republic in 1836. In 1845 Texas was admitted to the United States as a slave state, further testing relations with Mexico. The James K. Polk administration used this agreement to assert its rights to the Texas region extending to the Rio Grande. The Texas assertion of the Rio Grande as its southern boundary, despite Mexican insistence on the Nueces, partly contributed to the outbreak of the Mexican American War.

Treaty of Velasco

PUBLIC AGREEMENT

Articles of Agreement entered into between His Excellency David G. Burnet, President of the Republic of Texas, of the one part, and His Excellency General Antonio López de Santa Anna, President-General-in-Chief of the Mexican Army, of the other part:

Article 1. General Antonio López de Santa Anna agrees that he will not take up arms, nor will he exercise his influence to cause them to be taken up, against the people of Texas, during the present war of independence.

Article 2. All hostilities between the Mexican and Texan troops will cease immediately, both on land and water.

Article 3. The Mexican troops will evacuate the territory of Texas, passing to the other side of the Rio Grande del Norte.

Article 4. The Mexican army, in its retreat, shall not take the property of any person without his consent and just indemnification, using only such articles as may be necessary for its subsistence, in cases where the owners may not be present, and remitting to the commander of the army of Texas, or to the commissioners to be appointed for the adjustment of such matters, an account of the property consumed, the place where taken, and the name of the owner, if it can be ascertained.

Article 5. That all private property, including horses, cattle, negro slaves, or indentured persons of whatever denomination, that may have been captured by any portion of the Mexican army, or may have taken refuge in the said army, since the commencement of the late invasion, shall be restored to the commander of the Texan army, or to such other persons as may be appointed by the government of Texas to receive them.

Article 6.   The troops of both armies will refrain from coming into contact with each other; and to this end, the commander of the army of Texas will be careful not to approach within a shorter distance of the Mexican army than five leagues.

Article 7.   The Mexican army shall not make any other delay on its march than that which is necessary to take up their hospitals, baggage, &c., and to cross the rivers. Any delay, not necessary to these purposes, to be considered an infraction of this agreement.

Article 8.   By express, to be immediately despatched, this agreement shall be sent to General Filisola, and to General T. J. Rusk, commander of the Texan army, in order that they may be apprized of its stipulations; and, to this end, they will exchange engagements to comply with the same.

Article 9.   That all Texan prisoners now in possession of the Mexican army, or its authorities, be forthwith released, and furnished with free passports to return to their homes; in consideration of which a corresponding number of Mexican prisoners, rank and file, now in possession of the government of Texas, shall be immediately released. The remainder of the Mexican prisoners, that continue in possession of the government of Texas, to be treated with due humanity; any extraordinary comforts that may be furnished them to be at the charge of the government of Mexico.

Article 10.   General Antonio López de Santa Anna will be sent to Vera Cruz, as soon as it shall be deemed proper.
    The contracting parties sign this instrument for the above-mentioned purposes, by duplicate, at the port of Velasco, this the 14th day of May 1836.

DAVID G. BURNET
ANT°. LÓPEZ DE SANTA ANNA.

Secret Agreement

Antonio López de Santa Anna, General-in-Chief of the Army of Operations, and President of the Republic of Mexico, before the Government established in Texas, solemnly pledges himself to fulfill the Stipulations contained in the following Articles, so far as concerns himself:

Article 1.   He will not take up arms, nor cause them to be taken up, against the people of Texas, during the present war for independence.

Article 2.   He will give his orders that, in the shortest time, the Mexican troops may leave the territory of Texas.

Article 3.   He will so prepare matters in the cabinet of Mexico, that the mission that may be sent thither by the government of Texas may be well received, and that by means of negotiations all differences may be settled, and the independence that has been declared by the convention may be acknowledged.

Article 4.   A treaty of commerce, amity, and limits, will be established between Mexico and Texas, the territory of the latter not to extend beyond the Rio Bravo del Norte.

Article 5.   The present return of General Santa Anna to Vera Cruz being indispensable for the purpose of effecting his solemn engagements, the government of Texas will provide for his immediate embarkation for said port.

Article 6.   This instrument, being obligatory on one part as well as on the other, will be signed in duplicate, remaining folded and sealed until the negotiations shall have been concluded, when it will be restored to his excellency General Santa Anna; no use of it to be made before that time, unless there should be an infraction by either of the contracting parties.

Port of Velasco, May the 14th, 1836.

ANT°. LÓPEZ DE SANTA ANNA,
DAVID G. BURNET.

James Collingsworth, *Secretary of State*
Bailey Hardeman, *Secretary of the Treasury*.
P.H. Grayson, *Attorney-General*

David Weber explores the Mexican government's attempts to manage its vast northern frontier. Inheriting an expansive underpopulated and underdeveloped northern region following independence, Mexican strategists launched a variety of migration strategies and reluctantly invited North American colonists. A two-fold strategy emerged which encouraged Mexican immigrants from the south combined with immigrants from the United States. Mexican officials hoped to create a barrier before the tide of American expansionism underway during the early nineteenth century. The strategy to Mexicanize the frontier is best exemplified by New Mexican Governor Manuel Armijo's thoughtful and cautious approach.

The "Texas Game" Again?
Peopling California and New Mexico

David J. Weber

The principal wealth of a country consists of its population.
Manuel Castañares, *California, 1845*

The march of emigration is to the West, and naught will arrest its advance but the mighty ocean.
Alfred Robinson, *California, 1845*

While Anglo-Americans poured into Texas in the 1820s and 1830s, New Mexico and California attracted modest but significant numbers of foreign settlers. The number of American colonists in New Mexico remained relatively small throughout the Mexican era, but in the early 1840s norteamericanos began to settle in California, at a rate that alarmed Mexican officials. To many observers, both Mexican and American, this new wave of immigration seemed a repeat of events in Texas--a prelude to Mexico's loss of California. A newspaper in New York City in 1845 could not have put the matter more plainly: "Let the tide of emigration flow toward California and the American population will soon be sufficiently numerous to play the Texas game."[1] That American settlers did not flow into California and New Mexico and repeat the "Texas game" prior to the 1840s, owed more to happenstance that it did to a concerted Mexican effort to keep American colonists out.

With the opening of the Santa Fe trade in 1821, Americans visited New Mexico in large numbers. Hundreds of traders and trappers arrived in some years, but few remained. No exact account of foreigners who settled in New Mexico exists. A census of 1839 revealed only thirty-four *extranjeros* living in the province, and another count, taken about 1840 at Taos, the center of the province's foreign-born population, showed twenty-three Americans, seven of whom had become Mexican citizens.[2] These statistics certainly err on the low side, but even so, the number of foreign residents in New Mexico could not have amounted to more than a few hundred.

California attracted more foreign settlers than did New Mexico in the 1820s and 1830s, but there, too, only a small percentage of foreign traders or trappers remained to make California their home. In 1830 some 120 foreigners lived in California, and that number doubled to 240 by 1835 and reached about 380 in 1840. As in New Mexico, these figures are approximations and may be low. California officials acknowledged that they had no accurate count of the number of foreigners scattered throughout the province.[3]

Compared to Texas, few foreigners settled in California or New Mexico, but their commercial and, in many cases, their education or training, made them highly influential. Moreover, most were adult males, making them more important numerically than might seem to be the case in an era when men dominated decision making in the political and economic arenas. In California, at least two-thirds of the 3,200 gente de razón in 1821 were women and children, so even several hundred adult male immigrants would count heavily.[4]

That few North Americans settled permanently in New Mexico or California during the 1820s and the 1830s is easily understood. First, westering Anglo-Americans needed to go no farther into northern Mexico than Texas to find cheap land. Second, Anglo-Americans who moved beyond Texas, west of the 100th meridian and the timber line, often found the land uninviting. The treeless plains country was then depicted on maps as "The Great American Desert," and conventional wisdom held that farms only prospered where trees grew.[5] Then, too, ignorance of geography and the formidable barriers presented by Comanches, Apaches, and other tribes kept settlers from venturing too far west.

The few foreigners who did make their way into New Mexico and California found they could not obtain land as easily as in Texas. The Colonization Law of 1824, which permitted individual states to draw up regulations for colonization, provided that procedures for territories, such as California and New Mexico, would come from Congress. Lacking pressure from would-be landowners, Congress took no action until it approved the colonization regulations of November 21, 1828, which spelled out the method whereby territorial governors, with approval of the diputaciones, could grant land to Mexican as foreigners. Those procedures continued to be used erratically in California and New Mexico until the end of the Mexican era, with only slight modifications. Wary, perhaps, of the carelessness of local officials after its experience with Coahuila, Congress required that empresario grants in the territories received final approval in Mexico City; legislation passed earlier in 1828 required congressional approval for noncitizens to obtain land.[6]

The November 21, 1828 regulations opened New Mexico and California to colonization by foreigners, but a land rush did not follow. Foreigners found the most desirable lands already occupied. In New Mexico, gente de razón and Pueblo Indians ranched and farmed the best-watered, most centrally located, and most secure lands. Moreover, steady growth of population brought New Mexicans into keen competition with one another for choice farmland and pasturage, leaving little room for foreigners.[7]

In California, missions occupied the choice coastal lands until secularization in the mid-1830s, and mission lands were inviolable under the 1828 colonization regulations. Sandwiched in between the mission properties were perhaps thirty private rancho grants that had been made under Spain. Until the mid-1830s, Mexican officials issued only a few grants, none of which apparently went to foreigners. The real land boom in California, then, awaited the secularization of the missions.[8]

Not only was desirable land scarcer in California and New Mexico than it was in Texas, but federal officials discouraged foreigners from colonizing in the territories in the late 1820s and 1830s. Federal officials had no desire to repeat the Texas experience and open other parts of northern Mexico to what the secretary of foreign relations termed in 1829 "a disguised invasion."[9] To officials such as Tadeo Ortiz, the threat to the security of California and New Mexico was "identical" to that of Texas, and one state legislature, alarmed at the Haden Edwards revolt in Texas, went so far as to urge the government to "set aside a band fifty leagues wide from Texas to Alta California" to populate as a barrier against the North Americans.[10] Not surprisingly, then, would Col. John Davis Bradburn of Virginia, a naturalized Mexican who would later win infamy among his former countrymen as a revenue officer in Texas, petitioned Congress in 1829 for an empresario grant in New Mexico, a congressional committee noted the deteriorating situation in Texas and recommended against his request, arguing that "it would not be wise to expose New Mexico to a like fate."[11] The following year, Mexico's minister in Washington published notices in American newspapers warning would-be immigrants that the law of April 6, 1830 applied to New Mexico as well as Texas.

On the local level, too, officials expressed reluctance to welcome American settlers. New Mexicans were pleased to receive merchandise from the United States, but showed less enthusiasm for the North Americans themselves. Santiago Abreú of Santa Fe, a delegate to Congress and future territorial governor, noted in 1826 that

Americans had a propensity "to settle, buy land, and even marry" in New Mexico, and could be of great benefit to the province, but New Mexicans had to "avoid abuse to our generous character."[12] Only those foreigners who were honorable and who had a useful trade, he argued, should be permitted to stay.

In California, too, officials at all levels discouraged Anglo-Americans from settling. As Carlos Carrillo of Santa Barbara put it, it was widely known that the United States policy was "to recognize no other right to lands than that of occupation."[13] Indeed, prior to the passage of the 1828 colonization regulations, local officials had explicit orders not to grant land to foreigners, and on at least two subsequent occasions, in 1830 and 1832, Secretary of State Lucas Alamán ordered the governor of California to take care that American and Russian families remained a minority. Alamán did not intend to stop Anglo-Americans from colonizing in California entirely, as he tried to do in Texas with the controversial April 6, 1830 law, for California needed more people. Alamán expressed special interest in creating communities north of San Francisco Bay as a bulwark against the Russians at Fort Ross, and criticized California officials for making it too difficult for foreigners to acquire land. He instructed Governor Figueroa in 1832 to implement the colonization laws of 1824 and 1828.[14]

In the 1820s and early 1830s, while Texas was being subdivided by foreign empresarios, no colonization grants were given to foreigners in New Mexico or California. The man who came closest to receiving one was John G. Heath, a Missouri lawyer who had been among the first Americans to enter New Mexico after the opening of the Santa Fe trade in 1821. Heath received permission from the ayuntamiento of El Paso to colonize twenty-five square leagues on the Rio Grande in the Mesilla Valley in 1823. The New Mexico diputación revoked the grant, however, on the grounds that the overthrow of Iturbide had invalidated the Imperial Colonization Law under which the grant was made. The same law that worked for Stephen Austin in Texas failed to serve John Heath in New Mexico. The decision ruined Heath financially, for he did not learn of the cancellation of his grant until he returned to El Paso in 1824 with 150 colonists from Missouri. Denied permission to settle, most of the colonists returned to the United States to the apparent regret of the citizens of El Paso.[15]

Although empresario grants were not made in New Mexico and California prior to the late 1830s, foreigners managed to purchase house lots or small farms directly from Mexicans. Others squatted on unoccupied land and tried to keep out of sight. In contrast to Americans in Texas, most of the foreign-born residents of New Mexico and California in the 1820s and 1830s assimilated into the majority culture, at least in external matters, and did not form separate enclaves. As a young American noted in California in 1841, the foreigners "are scattered throughout the whole Spanish population, and most of them have Spanish wives . . . they live in every respect like the Spaniards."[16]

Thus, a small number of foreigners began to make their homes in New Mexico and California in the 1820s and 1830s, but none settled in the vast despoblado that today comprises the states of Nevada, Utah, western Colorado, and Arizona. All this immense area was vaguely considered part of New Mexico or California, except for Arizona below the Gila, which fell under the jurisdiction of Sonora. Americans explored, trapped, and established occasional trading posts in this region, but made no permanent settlements.

Most of the region between the Rio Grande settlements of New Mexico and the California coast was too remote and too firmly under Indian control to recommend it to immigrants. Nonetheless, a variety of ideas for colonizing the region were discussed, including a plan by California's future governor and would-be empresario, José Figueroa, to build a chain of settlements along the Colorado River to the Great Salt Lake.[17] Nothing came of these ideas, however, and the Mexican frontier failed to push into this region except for a brief period of expansion in Arizona.

Southern Arizona saw a surge of mining activity, ranching, and population growth in the 1820s, before the Apache offensive resumed full force. At Tucson, then the largest center of Mexican population in what is today Arizona, the number of settlers living near the presidio had declined in the late colonial period, but between 1819 and 1831 their number trebled from 62 to 193. These settlers, together with soldiers and their families, brought Tucson's total population to 465 in 1831, counting men, women, and children. Tubac, the second largest settlement in the area, had 303 inhabitants that same year and still more pobladores were scattered on ranches and mining camps that had begun to proliferate during the Apache peace.[18]

As Arizona's population grew, so too did the number of private rancho grants. Nearly all of the so-called Spanish land grants in Arizona date from 1820 to 1833, the early Mexican era, and nearly all were located south of the Gila. Many, of course, were in the Santa Cruz Valley, near the urban centers of Tucson and Tubac, but others were in the San Pedro Valley to the east, where settlers had spilled over in search of new lands.[19] The *tucsonenses*, for example, soon found that the limited irrigable lands near the presidio, three-fourths of which belonged to Indians from the mission of San Xavier, would not support the growing population. They began to ranch and farm at Tres Alamos on the San Pedro River, over thirty miles east of Tucson. Working the land in this area meant constant vigilance over livestock and, as one contemporary put it, working with "the plowhandle in one hand and the musket or lance in the other."[20]

Occasional victories notwithstanding, the ill-equipped and outnumbered Mexican settlers could not block the tide of nomadic Apaches who threatened to overrun their fields and pastures. Beginning in the 1830s the Mexican frontier retreated in Arizona. Only one land grant was made in the area after 1833. By the mid-1840s Apaches had driven Mexican settlers out of the San Pedro Valley and had forced them off isolated ranches and out of small communities in the more populous Santa Cruz Valley. Hamlets such as Sopori and Canoa, and even Calabazas with its rich mines, had been abandoned. Thus, although the non-Indian population of Sonora apparently grew by some 25 percent between 1822 and 1845, the northern edge of the state that is today's Arizona lost population. Mexicans remained only at Tucson and Tubac in 1848, and late that year Apaches forced the complete abandonment of Tubac.[21] Unlike Texas, New Mexico, or California, the number of gente de razón in Arizona fell rather than rose in the Mexican era.

During the first two decades of Mexican independence, then, Anglo-American immigrants posed no challenge to Indian or Mexican hegemony in the frontier areas west of Texas. Due to a combination of geographical accident and Mexican policy, relatively few foreigners settled in New Mexico or California. Keeping Anglo-Americans in small, manageable numbers, however, did not solve the perennial problem of how to bolster the population of the beleaguered frontier provinces. The paucity of pobladores seemed especially acute in vulnerable Alta California where, as Governor Juan Bautista Alvarado noted in 1840, "due to insufficient population there is a great dearth of defenders and laborers."[22] The need for more workers had become even more intense after the secularization of the missions spurred the growth of private ranches.

From San Francisco north to Oregon no Mexican settlements existed. Russians, however, had planted Fort Ross on Bodega Bay and refused to move, making it clear that they wanted to acquire San Francisco Bay and much of northern California. The Russian presence in California had troubled Mexican officials from the first months of independence, just as it had vexed Spanish policy makers. Much ink flowed as officials penned warnings about the need to settle Mexicans in the region to check Russian expansion. Not until 1833, however, did serious plans take shape. Those plans led to the government's most serious effort to colonize any portion of the far northern frontier with Mexicans.

In 1833 the liberal Gómez Farías administration appointed José María Híjar of Guadalajara as director of colonization for California. This appointment, which occurred simultaneously with the sending of Tadeo Ortiz to Texas as director of colonization, was part of a concerted effort to bolster the frontier's exposed eastern and western flanks.

Híjar started for California with considerable political power. In addition to overseeing the colonization he was to replace the ailing José Figueroa as governor. Moreover, Híjar's sub-director of colonization, José María Padrés, was to become commanding general of California should General Figueroa wish to be relieved of military as well as civil command. Híjar and Padrés had money as well as titles to support the project because the government dipped into the Pious Fund, a special trust for the California missions that had no counterpart in Texas. Although the program was never fully budgeted, Híjar and Padrés had authorization to pay for transportation, food, lodging, supplies, and one year's maintenance of a group of colonists who would build a settlement in northern California.

In April 1834 a group of pioneers, recruited mainly from the Mexico City area, set out from the nation's capital. Canvas-covered wagons carried women, children, and supplies, while the men rode alongside on horseback. The expedition journeyed by way of Querétaro and Guadalajara to the port of San Blas, from which they set sail in early August for the month-long voyage to Alta California.

Two hundred and thirty-nine colonists left from San Blas and a few more would eventually join them in California. Like American pioneers, they were a youthful group with an average age of twenty. Among them were fifty-five women and seventy-nine children age fourteen and under. Many of the colonists had a profession or trade, such as teacher, lawyer, doctor, carpenter, distiller, tailor, and shoemaker; perhaps 20 percent of the group consisted of farmers. The professionals and tradesman would be especially useful in California where foreigners were beginning to fill those functions.[23]

Although the enterprise seems to have been well-planned and the colonists well-chosen, plans went awry upon arrival in California. First, Híjar learned that Santa Anna had overthrown Gómez Farías and had sent orders to Figueroa not to permit him to assume the governorship. At the same time, Figueroa declined to turn the military command of California over to Padrés. Although their political base had crumbled, Híjar and Padrés went ahead with the task of establishing their colony.

Soon, however, they found themselves locked into a complex dispute with Governor Figueroa and the *californios,* which doomed the establishment of the colony.[24]

Híjar and Padrés failed in California in large part because their program seemed to threaten the economic interests of the *californios.* Among Híjar's responsibilities as director of colonization was the distribution of the mission lands, and exceedingly sensitive issue as we have seen. Imbued with the classical liberalism of the day, Híjar promised land to mission Indians, along with freedom to live where they chose, and payment for all the work that they did. Híjar even attempted to convey his egalitarian views to the so-called pagan Indians. Híjar's message threatened the social order in California where Indians constituted a cheap labor force and upset Figueroa who privately expressed concern that "legal equality would unhinge society," and that Indians might revolt.[25] Figueroa also assumed, incorrectly, that Híjar intended to distribute mission lands to Indians and to outsiders from Mexico, blocking opportunity for the *californios* to acquire that desirable property. Finally the *californios* suspected that Híjar and the Padrés were linked to a private stock company that had obtained monopoly privileges over California's export and import trade--a further threat to California's small but growing oligarchy.

Their self-interest apparently in jeopardy and their fears fed by a skillful propaganda effort by Governor Figueroa, the usually factious *californios* united to oppose Híjar and Padrés. An impasse was reached when Figueroa and the California diputación refused to turn mission lands over to Híjar and when the governor professed inability to lend material support to the colonists. Finally, Figueroa came to fear that Híjar and Padrés might overthrow him with the aid of the disgruntled and unpaid military, and he seems to have seized upon a pretext to get rid of his supposed rivals. When a minor *pronunciamento* against his government occurred in Los Angeles in 1835, Figueroa linked it to Híjar and Padrés and had them arrested at Sonoma, 600 miles from the scene of the crime. Without filing formal charges against them, he shipped Híjar, Padrés, and some other leaders of the colony back to San Blas. Somewhere he found 4,000 pesos to cover this emergency.

So ended Mexico's one effort to plant a subsidized colony on the northern frontier. Most of the colonists who came with Híjar and Padrés stayed in California. Although relatively few in number, they settled throughout the territory and used their special skills to gain prominence in provincial life. The teachers among them seem to have been especially influential.

With the failure of the Híjar-Padrés colony, the great void of Mexican settlement to the north of San Francisco Bay remained. Governor Figueroa, who had come to

California with orders from Lucas Alamán to populate this region as a check on Russian expansion, tried to fill the gap. In 1835, after the departure of Híjar and Padrés, he ordered a settlement founded at Sonoma and placed Mariano Vallejo in charge, naming him "Military Commander and Director of Colonization on the Northern Frontier."[26] Ironically, Figueroa could not find sufficient colonists for the town and it grew slowly, leaving the area open to a steam of Anglo-Americans who had begun to flow in the Sacramento Valley in the 1840s. Indeed, it was under Figueroa that the Americans first attained land and influence in this area. Perhaps the most far-reaching effect of the collapse of the Híjar-Padrés project, then, was that it left northern California open to the norteamericanos.[27] Meanwhile, the Russian threat vanished. The Russian traders and their families, plagued with internal problems, abandoned their handsome log homes and chapel at Fort Ross of their own accord in 1841.

Although they had opposed the Híjar-Padrés colony, prominent California officials continued to express the hope that Mexican colonists would be brought to California at government expense to offset the American and Russian influences and to make the area prosper.[28] No significant numbers of colonists from central Mexico settled elsewhere on the far northern frontier.

Many officials saw the need for countercolonization of the frontier by Mexicans, but few could explain satisfactorily why it failed to occur. It was commonplace to assume that "the Mexican character is not suited for colonization," as one Mexican intellectual put it in 1845.[29] Such an assumption seems to have been behind an editorial published in Mexico City which praised the Híjar-Padrés colonists because they had "overcome the disinclination of their upbringing and the laziness left us by the Spaniards, and had decided to leave behind the comforts of the capital."[30]

Rather than look to Mexican character to explain failure to settle the far northern frontier before 1846, however, it seems more fruitful to ask what might have prompted Mexicans to migrate. Opportunities on the remote frontier were limited and constant warfare between Indians and Mexicans did nothing to enhance the region's reputation. Moreover, as contemporaries recognized, there was no need to incur the heavy expense or hardship of travel to settle on distant frontiers when vacant land existed closer to the Mexican heartland. As we have seen, the population of Mexico was neither dense, nor growing rapidly. Demographic pressures simply did not exist. Finally, if what historians have learned from the American frontier experience applies to Mexico, prosperity stimulated migration, depression retarded it, and "the cost of migrating kept the very poor at home."[31]

On occasions when opportunity presented itself, Mexicans did move. *Sonorenses* and *nuevomexicanos* were drawn to California's temperate climate to ranch and farm (internal migration accounted for nearly one sixth of the population in Los Angeles in 1844); Mexicans moved into southern Arizona during the mining boom of the 1820s; others went to California after the gold discovery of 1848. Those were exceptional cases, however, for the far northern frontier was generally not an easily accessible land of opportunity for Mexicans in these years. When demographic pressure did increase in the early twentieth century, and when technological changes made the border region a land of opportunity, Mexican *campesinos* proved themselves as adept at migration and colonization as any other people.[32]

Mexican thinkers such as Tadeo Ortiz and Miguel Ramos Arizpe argued that if substantial countercolonization of the Far North by Mexicans or by Europeans were to take place, the government would have to sponsor it. Mexico seemed to be in an impossible position. While the expanding United States population moved west into northern Mexico without government support, Mexico's more static population would have to be induced onto the same frontier through the use of scarce national resources, or European immigration would have to be subsidized. Mexico could neither afford, nor properly carry out such programs so long as the nation remained in political turmoil, as one prestigious Mexico City newspaper editorialized in 1842.[33] Hence, the Híjar-Padrés experiment stands as a singular episode, rather than as part of a sustained program.

Mexico's failure to lure colonists onto the frontier led to continuation of the Spanish policy of sending convicts north as settlers. This practice was more extensive in California than in Texas, and caused dismay among some *californios* who charged the government with attempting to make the area a "penal colony."[34]

The use of convicts as colonists on the frontier enjoyed broad support among high government officials in Mexico City. The policy seemed wise, practical, and humane. The frontier would benefit by having its manpower shortage alleviated while convicts who were languishing in prisons at Vera Cruz and other unhealthy places could became rehabilitated and, as Gen. Manuel Mier y Terán put it, "become of real value to that society which now casts them out."[34]

Under independent Mexico, the first convicts sent to the frontier seem to have arrived in Californian in 1825. Not until 1829, however, was a systematic program launched. Then the secretary of justice notified courts and governors throughout the republic that convicted criminals and their families should be sent to California instead of Vera Cruz. The arrival of perhaps 150 convicts in California in 1829 and 1830 brought such a storm of indignation and protest that in 1831 the secretary of justice ordered the flow directed toward Texas. This order was in keeping with the law of April 6, 1830, which had not only closed Texas to further Anglo-American immigration, but had also authorized the government to settle convicts and their families there. Although convicts were to be given transportation, land, tools, and supplies for a year, the number who went to Texas was inconsequential, as we have seen.[36] After Texas became the nation's official penal colony even those from California could be sent there. One man convicted of hanging his wife, for example, was sent to Texas in 1835 after serving three years in jail in California.[37]

No significant number of convicts arrived in California again until 1842 when the government authorized sending 300 "criminals" who possessed some trade or skill. In exchange for good conduct and "services," they were to be given land and tools.[38] Recruited from jails in Mexico City, 150 convicts and their women reached California in August 1842, all apparently forming part of the military force that accompanied the new governor, Gen. Manuel Micheltorena. Dressed in tattered uniforms, unsalaried, and poorly supplied, the hapless "soldiers" raided gardens, orchards, and chicken coops in order to survive. Many *californios* viewed these *cholos*--a term they applied to lower class mestizos from Mexico--as ne'er-do-wells and contemptible, incurable thieves who lived on the public payroll. Micheltorena's failure to discipline them apparently contributed to the *californios'* revolt against him in 1845, and it is often suggested that the behavior of the convicts in California caused the *californios'* growing alienation from the rest of Mexico. Clearly alienation intensified during these years, to the point that some *californios* favored separation from Mexico, as we shall see. It seems doubtful, however, that the conduct of the convicts alone provoked this reaction.[38]

Some of the convicts behaved badly in California, but most seem to have become useful citizens as the government hoped. About fifty convicts who arrived in 1830, for example, were distributed among families in San Diego and Los Angles where, according to Heinrich Virmond, a German merchant who knew California well, "They planted more in one day than had ever been done before." The families for whom the prisoners worked gave them food, shelter, and six pesos a month: "Both parties were content with this," Virmond noted, "and the public treasury is not burdened...if there had been 100 more they all would have been provided employment in the town of Los Angeles."[39] The exaggerated charges that some *californios* made against the prisoners were probably more a result of wounded dignity--that Mexico would use California as a kind of Siberia or a penal colony--than a reaction to overt acts that the "cholos" committed.[40] It may be, too, that growing alienation from Mexico was a cause as much as a result of the antipathy toward the newcomers from Mexico.

Plans to colonize California with Europeans--which included schemes to ease the Mexican debt by turning over vacant lands all across the Far North to British bondholders, and selling California to a Prussian empresario--also came to nothing.[41] Meanwhile, the central government seems to have made no serious effort to colonize either Arizona or New Mexico with Europeans or Mexicans, for those areas seemed less threatened by American expansion than either California or Texas. Thus, counter colonization of the Far North, from San Antonio west to the Pacific, failed as it had in Texas and left the way open for immigration from the United States.

In the early 1840s, governors of both New Mexico and California began to open unprecedented amounts of public land to private development. In part, they hoped to attract colonists in order to promote development and bolster the defense of their respective regions. Then, too, they used land grants to award political supporters and to repay loans or gifts, which kept their sinking departmental treasuries afloat. Land was one of the few commodities with which the last governors of New Mexico and California could bargain. At the same time, land in the 1840s looked increasingly alluring to some foreign and Mexican entrepreneurs because of the prospect that the United States might acquire California and New Mexico and cause property value to rise.[42]

By placing vast tracts of public land in private hands, the last Mexican governors of New Mexico and California shaped settlement patterns and economic structures in their regions for decades to come. In California, about a third of the land that was given away went to Anglo-Americans in what seemed to be a replay of the "Texas game." In New Mexico, officials adopted a more cautious policy toward foreign-born residents.

Manuel Armijo, as governor of New Mexico during most of the period from 1837 to 1846, approved an extraordinary number of land grants, including nearly all of the so-called Spanish land grants in what would have become the state of Colorado. One historian has calculated that between 1837 and 1846 Armijo gave away over half of the 31,000,000 acres of lands granted by all New Mexico officials under Spain and Mexico. Armijo was not as profligate, however, as this figure suggests. As a result of litigation following the United States conquest of New Mexico, many of Armijo's land concessions stretched to dimensions far larger than he had intended, or than Mexican law and custom permitted. Moreover, many of these grants required that the recipient fulfill certain conditions, such as actual occupancy of the land, settling a certain number of families, and cultivation of the soil, before the final title could be issued. Some of these lands were also designated for community use and not intended to fall into private hands.[43]

Not nearly as reckless as some critics have suggested, Armijo appears to have granted lands to encourage private enterprise to create a barrier against Indians, Texans, and norteamericanos. To accomplish this, he judiciously permitted a few naturalized Mexicans, as well as *nuevomexicanos*, to develop lands in river valleys on the northern and eastern peripheries of the department, extending northward to the Mexican-United States boundary on the Arkansas River, and eastward toward the newly independent Republic of Texas.[44]

One of the first of Armijo's large grants went to his secretary, Guadalupe Miranda, and to Canadian-born Charles Beaubien. Partners, Miranda and Beaubien requested lands in 1841 on the plains east of the Sangre de Cristos along the Cimarron and Canadian rivers. They said they planned to ranch, grow sugar beets and cotton, and exploit timber and minerals. Their grant later became part of the celebrated and much enlarged claim of Beaubien's son-in-law, Lucien Maxwell, to some two million acres (2,680 square miles) of what is today northeastern New Mexico and southeastern Colorado.[45]

In 1843 Armijo gave out at least four more sizeable grants to foreign-born residents of New Mexico. First, Charles Beaubien's thirteen-year-old son, Narciso, together with Stephen Louis Lee, a former trapper from St. Louis, received the Sangre de Cristo grant in the San Luis Valley straddling the present New Mexico-Colorado border.[46] Second, a tract along the San Carlos River in today's southern Colorado went to Gervasio Nolán, an illiterate French Canadian. In partnership with two New Mexicans, Nolán also received a grant on the Canadian River to the south of the Beaubien-Miranda grant in 1845.[47] Third, land along the Cucharas, Huerfano, and Apishapa rivers in eastern Colorado south of the Arkansas, known as the Las Animas Grant, went to a former fur trader, Cerán St. Vrain, and his partner, Cornelio Vigil, alcalde of Taos. Fourth, Armijo granted ten leagues of land on the eastern plains to the northwest of Las Vegas to a Santa Fe merchant, John Scolly, and a group of American and Mexican partners.[48]

Although a considerable amount of the land that Armijo granted went to foreign-born residents, he was careful not to repeat the mistakes made in Texas. He seems to have selected foreigners cautiously, generally choosing men who had lived in the department since the 1820s, had married Mexican women, and had been

Mexican citizens for at least a decade. Only John Scolly, an Irishman, was not a naturalized citizen, but Scolly had a Mexican wife and had applied for citizenship in 1843.[49] Perhaps it was no coincidence that Armijo's grants went to an Irishman, two Canadians (Nolán and Beaubien), and to an American of French Ancestry (St. Vrain), rather than to Anglo-Americans alone. Finally, Armijo took the precaution of including Mexican partners in most of these grants.

Armijo might have chosen foreign-born recipients of land carefully, but he could not exercise control over subsequent sale of interest in that land. For example, although he was not a citizen, Charles Bent, co-owner with Cerán St. Vrain of Bent's Fort on the Arkansas, acquired a fourth interest in the Beaubien-Miranda grant, along with interest in two other grants.[50]

Opposition to Armijo's land policy, and to the Beaubien-Miranda grant in particular, soon surfaced. Led by Cura Antonio José Martínez of Taos and leaders of Taos Pueblo, critics argued that the Beaubien-Miranda was too large, impinged upon the communal lands of Taos Pueblo, and included Charles Bent as an illegal partner. Some writers have suggested that Martínez's objections to the grant amounted to little more than a personal vendetta against Bent, but the priest seems to have been genuinely alarmed at the implications of growing American influence in the department.[51]

Apparently in response to Martínez's complaint, interim governor Mariano Chávez, who briefly replaced the ailing Armijo, annulled the Beaubien-Miranda grant in February 1844. Beaubien then lied to protect his interests, saying that Bent was not one of his partners, and succeeded in persuading the departmental assembly to restore the grant. Victory was brief. Gen. Mariano Martínez, who assumed the governorship in May 1844, ordered Beaubien to abandon the grant. Martínez defended his action by citing a law of March 11, 1842, which permitted foreigners to acquire property anywhere in Mexico except in departments contiguous to foreign nations where specific permission of the central government was required. This law did not apply to naturalized citizens such as Beaubien, but it did apply to foreigners such as Charles Bent, who, Governor Martínez must have believed, still owned a share of the grant. At the same time that he revoked the Beaubien-Miranda grant, Martínez abrogated John Scolly's grant, citing the same law (Apparently Scolly's citizenship papers had not yet arrived, but his grant, diminished in size, was reissued and confirmed by Armijo in March 1846.)[52]

Pleased with the turn of events, Padre Martínez praised the new governor whose intervention, he said, had prevented Armijo from carrying out his "mean and ambitious desire of delivering a portion of this Department into the hands of some foreigners."[53] By May 1845, however, Governor Martínez had left office and José Chávez took the governor's chair for a few months. Chávez, a native New Mexican, permitted Beaubien, Bent, and St. Vrain to settle foreigners on the Beaubien-Miranda grant. In allowing foreign colonization, local officials came into conflict again with an official representing the central government. In autumn 1845, Gen. Francisco García Conde inspected New Mexico and ordered foreign settlers in the Cimarron area to leave their farms. The colonists and Manuel Armijo, who had assumed the governorship again on November 16, ignored this order. Armijo's leniency toward Charles Bent and the foreign settlers on the Beaubien-Miranda grant may have been influenced by the fact that he, too, owned a one-fourth interest in that grant.[54]

Governor Armijo's land grant policy did not win complete approval of officials representing the central government, nor did it please nationalistic New Mexicans such as Padre Martínez, but the governor appears to have acted prudently. Certainly, foreigners tried to take advantage of him by obtaining vast tracts of potentially valuable land, much of it intersected by the major trails that connected the United States with Taos and Santa Fe. At the same time, however, Armijo sought to utilize the foreign-born entrepreneurs to settle and hold an area that his own military could not control and his own countrymen could not colonize. If he saw personal profit in these arrangements, or if they resulted in loans to the government, so much the better.[55] National interest and self-interest seemed to coincide; there is no reason to suppose that he acted solely out of self-interest as has been suggested.

Armijo seems to have understood the risks inherent in granting too much land to foreigners. As early as 1827 he had lamented that "every day the foreigners are becoming more influential," and his desire to limit foreign influence remained alive until the 1840s.[56] By the 1840s, however, the governor had nowhere else to turn except to the foreign-born. The military and economic situation in New Mexico had become chaotic; nomadic Indians assaulted the province more boldly than ever before, and Anglo-Americans and Texans threatened attack. Caught in this desperate situation, with little more than the promise of aid from the federal government, Armijo enlisted the help of a select group of outsiders such as Beaubien, Lee, and Nolán, to whom he granted lands and whose loyalty he presumably felt he could trust.[57]

In the early 1840s, then, a few foreigners took possession of choice pieces of public land on the northern and eastern flanks of New Mexico, but prior to 1846 efforts to settle those remote grants met staunch resistance from Indians, who refused to acknowledge that a stroke of the pen gave outsiders the right to intrude upon them.

Indian resistance succeeded partly because demographic pressure from New Mexico never became so intense that large numbers of people spilled over onto Indian lands. Despite Armijo's liberal land policy, New Mexico did not become a magnet for large numbers of immigrants, either foreign-born or Mexican, prior to 1846.

Nonetheless, a trickle of immigrants and natural increase pushed New Mexico's population upward, from 42,000 in 1821 to some 65,000 in 1846, counting foreigners and Pueblo Indians as well as gente de razón. The average annual rate of population growth in New Mexico in these years was 2.1 percent, or double the rate of growth for Mexico as a whole, and it nudged the edges of settlement farther from the narrow band along the Rio Grande and prompted the creation of new communities. Compared to the soaring rates of growth in Texas or along the American frontier, however, New Mexico's demographic expansion was modest. Even the isolated Department of California grew at a faster rate and drew people away from New Mexico in the 1840s.[58]

Trappers and traders from New Mexico, foreigners and *nuevomexicanos* alike, had visited California regularly throughout the 1830s. A few, such as Julian Chávez, Jonathan Warner, and George Yount, had settled permanently on the coast, where the communities of Chávez Ravine (today the home of the Los Angeles Dodgers), Warner Springs, and Yountsville still bear their names. In the 1840s, California's reputation began to attract groups rather than individual settlers from New Mexico. In 1841, for example, two old-time residents of New Mexico, John Rowland and William Workman, led a party of twenty-five men, some with families, from Santa Fe to Los Angeles. Included in the group were some *nuevomexicanos*.

By 1845 at least thirty families of *nuevomexicanos* had migrated to the Los Angeles area alone, and many settled near San Bernardino under the leadership of the respected Lorenzo Trujillo. One reason for the New Mexicans' departure for California was to escape the ravages of Indian attack. Ironically, their reputations as Indian-fighters made them welcome in the San Bernardino area where rancheros hoped that a colony of hardy New Mexicans would be able to protect local livestock from Indians. Most *nuevomexicanos* seem to have settled in Southern California, but others, such as Manuel Vaca, for whom today's Vacaville in the Sacramento Valley is named, must have been scattered throughout the department by 1846.[59]

People left New Mexico for California in the early 1840s for a variety of reasons, including a growing anti-American sentiment, but California's climate was also a major attraction. Louis Robidoux, for example, who had lived in New Mexico for twenty years, in 1844 settled permanently in Southern California near Riverside where he found the fertile land was "not ungrateful like the land of New Mexico." He wrote to a friend who had stayed behind at Santa Fe: "I compare the people of New Mexico to the ants, who shut themselves in during the winter to eat what they have worked so hard for all summer." Robidoux went on to say that he did not live in California's most desirable area. Northern California, he said, "is the promised land where the arroyos run with virgin honey and milk. Another Texas."[60]

By the 1840s the lure of California reached well beyond New Mexico to the Mississippi Valley, where it held immense appeal to an expanding population of land-hungry Americans, many of whom sought an escape from debt and depression that still lingered along the American frontier after the Panic in 1837. It is impossible, of course, to generalize with confidence about the motives of a variety of individuals, but it seems reasonable, as one historian has suggested, that "pull factors" assume greater importance than "push factors" in prompting migrations over great distances.[61] For wanderers such as Nicholas Dawson the "pull" might simply have been a desire "to see and to experience,"[62] but the chief cause of the "fever" that drew men and women to the Pacific Coast in the early 1840s was cheap land--the same attraction that Texas had held two decades before. Hardheaded reports of the privations and obstacles of a journey over plains, mountains, and deserts, were offset in the minds of true believers by glowing accounts stressing both the ease of the journey and the heroism and nobility of those who made it. Few seemed to notice the contradiction.[63]

California held special opportunities for American immigrants in the early 1840s. First, the recent secularization of the missions had set thousands of Indians adrift, creating a pool of cheap labor and freeing choice coastal lands for private development. Second, recently forged commercial connections with the outside world had created a market for the products of California ranches, especially hides and tallow. These events set off a land rush among *californios* and foreigners alike. Between 1834 and 1846 some 700 private rancho grants were made, representing over 90 percent of all ranches granted in California under both Spain and Mexico. Private ranchos soon covered the former mission lands along the coastal plain and some would-be rancheros, chiefly Americans, began to petition for property in the great Central Valley, to the east of the coastal range along the San Joaquin and Sacramento rivers. The Central Valley had been the exclusive domain of Indians and the few British and American trappers and horse thieves who ventured among them, but an especially virulent malaria epidemic swept through the Valley in 1833. It killed perhaps three-fourths of the native American population, and weakened the survivors' ability to withstand encroachment by outsiders.[64]

Anglo-American awareness of opportunities to acquire cheap land on the Pacific Coast was heightened by the publicity surrounding the diplomatic crisis between the United States and Britain over Oregon, the growing conflict with Mexico, and by "boosters" in Oregon and California who sang the praises of their areas. In the early 1840s the Oregon "boosters" seemed most successful and lured a disproportionate number of overland migrants to the Pacific Northwest, but California publicists, such as John Marsh and John Sutter, also succeeded in drawing a significant number of overlanders to California's Central Valley.[65]

The first successful rancher in the Central Valley, Massachusetts-born, Harvard-educated "Dr." John Marsh had come to California by way of Santa Fe in 1836, leaving an extraordinary series of misadventures in his wake, including a warrant for his arrest for running guns to the Sioux. In California, Marsh looked to his future by becoming a Catholic, a citizen, and posing as a medical doctor. For credentials he flashed his Harvard bachelor's diploma, written in Latin. Within a year he had acquired enough capital to purchase Rancho Los Meganos. Although it was isolated on the San Joaquin, some forty miles beyond San Jose, the ranch prospered as Marsh traveled about exchanging medical services for cattle.[66]

In 1839 Marsh gained a neighbor when John Sutter began building a settlement on the Sacramento River, at the site of the present state capital. A fugitive like Marsh, Sutter had abandoned an unhappy marriage, five children, and debtor's prison in his native Switzerland to flee to the United States. At Taos, New Mexico, French-Canadian Trapper Charles Beaubien had told Sutter of California's "perpetual summer."[67] Reaching California in 1839 by a circuitous route, this perennial optimist and energetic confidence man immediately asked Governor Juan Bautista Alvarado for an empresario grant to settle Swiss families in California. Alvarado advised him to obtain a private rancho instead, and Sutter chose a superb site. His eleven league grant, formally approved in 1841 after he became a citizen, was watered by the Sacramento and Feather rivers, dominated all inland navigation through San Francisco Bay, and lay along the route to Oregon and the future immigrant trail over the Sierras. Alvarado apparently hoped that Sutter's settlement would help to block Anglo-American colonists, but officials such as Gen. Mariano Guadalupe Vallejo saw Sutter himself as a threat. As a British visitor in 1842 said of Sutter: "If he really has the talent and the courage to make the most of his position, he is not unlikely to render California a second Texas."[68]

Sutter, through his hospitality, and John Marsh, who wrote widely circulated letters praising California to Americans in the East, each played important roles in attracting Anglo-American immigrants to California. Marsh provided the immediate catalyst. John Bidwell, one of the leaders of the first immigrant group to set out for California from the United States, later recalled that he had been encouraged to emigrate by a letter "Dr." Marsh had written to a friend in Missouri describing California in glowing terms. Also tantalizing, Bidwell remembered, was a speech by Antoine Robidoux, a New Mexico-based trapper and trader, whose description of California "made it seem like a paradise." "He said that the Spanish authorities were most friendly and that the people were the most hospitable on the globe."[69]

Negative reports offset these glowing stories, however, and the so-called Bidwell-Bartelson party became the only immigrant group to make the journey overland to California in 1841. This small, inexperienced group was lucky to find its way west. As Bidwell later recalled, with no exaggeration: "Our ignorance of the route was complete . . . no one knew where to go, not even the captain."[70] They had the good fortune, however, to be in the path of a group of missionaries and trappers headed for Oregon, led by Father Pierre-Jean De Smet and the able mountain man, Thomas "Broken Hand" Fitzpatrick. Bidwell and his fellow immigrants tagged along. They followed the Platte River, crossed South Pass, and then on the Bear River the two groups separated. Half of Bidwell's companions prudently chose to go on to Oregon, leaving Bidwell and thirty-three others to find their way across northernmost Mexico to California alone.

Plodding westward beyond the Great Salt Lake, where they had to abandon their wagons in the soft sand, they followed the Humboldt to the Sierra Nevada, then stumbled across that formidable barrier lost and hungry much of the time, and fearful that winter snows would trap them. Finally they followed the Stanislaus River into the San Joaquin Valley and made their way to John Marsh's ranch. A woman, Nancy Kelsey, and her infant daughter, Ann, had made the extraordinary journey all the way. One of the men later recalled that on an especially treacherous path in the Sierras "I looked back and saw Mrs. Kelsey a little way behind me, with her child in her arms, barefooted, I think, and leading her horse--a sight I shall never forget."[71]

After the Bidwell party showed that it could be done, other Anglo American homeseekers made the arduous trek. As John Marsh argued: "A young woman with a child in her arms came in the company. . . . after this, the men ought to be ashamed to think of the difficulties."[72] No overland immigrants came in 1842, but more arrived in 1843 guided by Joseph Reddeford Walker through the pass in the Sierras that still bears his name. In 1844 Elisha Stevens captained the first group to make it through with wagons and the first to use what would become the main immigrant trail over

Donner Pass. That pass would not receive its present name, however, until the winter of 1846-47 when a snowstorm sealed the pass to the Donner party and tragedy followed. Whereas only 50 overland immigrants arrived in California in 1844, 250 came in 1845 and over 500 reached California in 1846, many hoping that their nation's flag would follow them west.[73]

The push of the American settlers overland to California alarmed officials and the press in Mexico City. The United States had made no secret of its interest in acquiring Alta California. President Andrew Jackson offered to buy San Francisco Bay from Mexico in 1835, and in 1842 Commodore Thomas Catesby Jones, commander of the United States fleet in the Pacific, demonstrated that the United States would take it by force if it could. Upon hearing rumors that the United States and Mexico had gone to war, Jones seized the port of Monterey, then shamefacedly gave it back again when he learned of his mistake. The episode outraged officials and the press in Mexico City, who surmised that Jones must have acted under orders, and apparently led to an 1843 decree authorizing the governors of Chihuahua, Sonora, Sinaloa, and California to expel all North Americans from their departments. In California, where indignation at Jones' blunder was not as intense as in Mexico City, local officials did not enforce that law.[74]

American settlement in California seemed especially alarming because the troubles in Texas had begun in a similar manner. That was recognized quite clearly by Mexico's minister in Washington, Juan N. Almonte, who had toured Texas and warned his government of dangers there in 1834. In 1840, upon learning that a group of American colonists were planning to settle in California, Almonte reported to the minister of war that although their stated intentions were "peaceful and friendly, your excellency should remember that this is no different than language used by Austin's colony and other immigrants who occupied Texas."[75] The minister of war had received similar warnings against granting land to Americans from the comandante general in California, Mariano Vallejo.[76]

The idea that American immigration was a prelude to the United States takeover of California was not a product of Mexican paranoia or of Almonte's or Vallejo's imaginations. Informed observers from many nations recognized the demographic and political forces at work. As early as 1839, for example, one French visitor to California reported to his government that the

> restless population [of the United States] is moving across the continent
> to the shores of the Pacific Ocean; it will not be long before we shall see

them marching with great strides toward the domination of these same shores where they seem so weak today.[76]

As in the case of Texas, American desire to acquire California by populating it with Americans was openly discussed by American politicians and journalists, and Almonte had only to read United States newspapers to learn of the danger. Indeed, residents of Mexico City could read the same articles in Spanish, for many soon appeared in translation, and the message was clear. "American immigration," one Mexico City paper warned, "will snatch all of our departments from us, one by one."[77]

The diagnosis was accurate, but the remedy remained elusive. Preoccupied with efforts to regain Texas in the 1840s, and bedeviled by frequent changes of government, policy makers in Mexico City could do little to stop the flow of illegal aliens from the United States. The government sent repeated instructions to officials in California to expel Americans who arrived without proper papers, and to prevent more from entering. Meanwhile, Mexican minister Almonte tried to dissuade Americans from going to California by publishing notices in the American press in 1841 and 1842 that said cheap land in California would not be forthcoming.[78]

In 1845, when it became evident that words would not stop the *norteamericanos*, the government entered into negotiations with a Jesuit, Eugene McNamara, to settle 10,000 Irishmen in California. At the same time, a large military force was ordered to the province, but lack of funds for transportation and pay delayed the expedition's departure interminably. "When will it cease to leave?" one Mexico City newspaper asked.[79] It never did.

Efforts by the central government to block the flow of immigrants into California were also undermined by officials there, just as had occurred earlier in Texas. Even as it became apparent that the United States and Mexico would go to war, *californios* continued to receive North Americans cordially and permitted them to settle despite orders from Mexico City. The contradiction between national policy and local practice did not go unnoticed by contemporaries. As Dr. Marsh wrote in early 1846:

> While Col. Almonte...in Washington, is publishing his proclamations in the newspapers of the United States forbidding people to emigrate to California and telling them that no lands will be given them; the actual Government here is doing just the contrary.[80]

If the law were to be followed to the letter, California officials would have to send newly arrived immigrants back over the Sierras to an almost certain death. Officials such as Mariano Vallejo and José Castro expressed reluctance to do that. Castro, then serving as military commander, alluded to the conflict between "duty" and "the sentiment of hospitality which characterizes the Mexican people."[81] California officials granted passports that permitted foreigners to stay temporarily, and in practice those temporary permits became permanent and Americans became citizens and obtained land. Reluctance to enforce the law more vigorously in California might have had less to do with hospitality or humanitarian motives, however, than with the recognition that immigrants would be good for the local economy. Many *californios* might have agreed with a remarkable comment made in 1840 by twenty-one-year-old Pablo de la Guerra of one of Santa Barbara's most powerful families. The foreigners, he said, "are about to overrun us, of which I am very glad, for the country needs immigration in order to make progress."[82] De la Guerra's pragmatic attitude, which placed regional concerns above national interest, resembled the response of the *tejanos* a decade before.

Most *californios* must have mixed emotions about the arrival of norteamericanos. General Vallejo, for example, an outspoken opponent of American immigration, repeatedly warned the government against the danger that it posed to Mexican sovereignty over California. On a personal level, however, Vallejo seems to have liked Americans (he had three American brothers-in-law and all but one of his children married foreigners). He did not use his troops to drive them from the country, although he blamed his failure to take military action against the foreigners on his chronic shortage of soldiers. He could not fight Americans and maintain defense against Indians simultaneously, he said.[83] Meanwhile, foreigners in the Sacramento Valley grew stronger by the day.

Instead of forming a barrier against Anglo-American settlement in the interior, as Governor Alvarado had hoped, Sutter's New Helvetia had become a magnet for them. Generous to a fault, Sutter gave them jobs and sold them land. In his capacity as a Mexican official (Alvarado appointed him "representative of the government" in the Sacramento Valley in 1840),[84] Sutter even issued passports and other documents to the Americans in violation of federal orders. These activities incensed Vallejo, who had long regarded Sutter as dangerous. By 1845 Vallejo correctly perceived that Sutter's fort had become "the gateway of communication between the United States and this country which they [the North Americans] covet so much."[85] By then Vallejo probably lacked the force to dislodge Sutter from his thick-walled fort. Certainly

Sutter felt secure form Mexican troops. As early as 1841 he expressed confidence that "it is too late now to drive me out of the country....I am strong now." If California forces moved against him, Sutter wrote, "I will make a declaration of Independence and proclaim California for a Republique."[86]

There was no need for Sutter to take such a dramatic step. Instead, he found security in an alliance with Governor Micheltorena. In exchange for the promise of military aid to prop up Micheltorena's shaky governorship, Sutter received twenty-two more square leagues of land, adjacent to his original New Helvetia. Only after the overthrow of Micheltorena in 1845, as war with the Unites States loomed over the Texas question, did the *californios* attempt to dislodge the troublesome Sutter. Then they chose peaceful means. They offered to buy him out, but he price was too high. As Vallejo woefully noted, however, "it is the security of the country that is to be bought, and that is priceless."[87]

Sutter's sale of land to unnaturalized Americans, in clear violation of the law, contributed substantially to the Anglo-American colonization in California.[88] At the same time, however, California officials themselves encouraged Americans to settle by making it easy for them to obtain citizenship and land.

The land boom that had begun in the mid-1830s reached its height in the 1840s. Governor Alvarado (1836-42) gave out 170 rancho grants; Micheltorena (1842-45) made some 120 grants; and Pío Pico (1845-46) about 80. As in New Mexico, nearly half of the grants made in California in the Mexican era were less than six years old in 1846. Foreigners, mainly Americans, received a large number of grants from all three governors. Micheltorena seems to have adopted an especially generous policy toward Americans, whose support he needed to buoy his sinking regime. Perhaps one third of the 120 grants that Micheltorena made went to foreigners.[89] His policy brought a few protests from *californios*, but Pico, a native governor, seems to have been equally generous. The *californios'* hospitality toward *norteamericanos* continued right to the end. On July 16, 1846, Pío Pico issued strongly worded orders that Americans living in California not be mistreated, even though war existed with the United States.[90]

The preponderance of land grants made to *norteamericanos* in the 1840s were in the Central Valley. By 1845 a branch of the Sacramento River was already being called the *Río de los americanos*, today's American River.[91] The immigrants of the 1840s remained geographically isolated from the *californios*, just as American immigrants had lived apart from *tejanos* two decades before. They did not blend in California society as had the merchants and trappers who settled in coastal California prior to 1840. As Juan Bautista Alvarado ruefully recalled, "would that the foreigners that came to settle in California after 1841 had been of the same quality as those who preceded them."[92]

The outlook of the new post-1840 immigrants differed so markedly from that of the older settlers that one historian suggested that Americans in California formed two distinct groups: "maritime interests" and "pioneering interests."[93] The distinction is useful, but by 1846 both groups had a common goal: both wanted California to "play the Texas game." The chief disagreement between the two groups was how and when to begin. While the maritime groups maneuvered behind the scenes and sought support of prominent *californios,* impatient "hot-heads" in the Sacramento Valley staged a coup. Known as the Bear Flag Revolt, this outbreak began at Sonoma in June 1846 before news of war between the United States and Mexico reached California. Even if that war had not occurred, then, it appears that Americans in California had become numerous enough to think they could play the "Texas game" and win.

Through natural increase and immigration, California had grown from 3,320 in 1821 to about 7,300 gente de razón in 1845. Much smaller than New Mexico, which had some 65,000 in 1846, California nevertheless had grown more rapidly in the Mexican era, at an average annual rate of 5 percent per year compared to 2.1 percent for New Mexico or 1.1 for Mexico as a whole. Foreigners, predominantly Americans, numbered conservatively 680 and constituted 9 percent of the California population in 1845, with 500 more American settlers on the overland trail to California in 1846 as war between Mexico and the United States broke out.[94]

As had happened in Texas, then, Mexico failed to people California and New Mexico with substantial numbers of loyal subjects, either Europeans or Mexicans, or to establish effective barriers to keep Anglo-Americans out. That failure contributed mightily to her loss of both provinces in 1846. More important, however, was the steady political, economic, and social drift of the frontier away from the metropolis. That drift undermined the will of frontiersmen to follow orders from Mexico City, to oppose American immigration, and to stop distributing land to citizens of a nation that had become what California's delegate to Congress in 1844 termed "our natural enemy."[95]

NOTES

1. Alfred Robinson to Thomas Larkin, New York, May 29, 1845, in George P. Hammond, ed., *The Larkin Papers: Personal, Business, and Official Correspondence of Thomas Oliver Larkin, Merchant and United States Consul in California*, 10 vols. (Berkeley, 1953), III, 205. Robinson put this phrase in quotes, saying "our papers are filled with such kinds of stuff."

2. "Relacíon de los Estrangeros que Existen en este Departamento. . . March 20, 1839," Ritch Papers, no. 175, HEH. Charles Bent to Manuel Alvarez, no date [ca. 1840], Alvarez Papers, NMSRC.

3. Hubert Howe Bancroft, *History of California*, 7 vols. (San Francisco, 1884-90), IV, 115-17. Whereas Bancroft placed the number at 380 in 1840, an official census counted only 48 permanent foreign residents of California that year. Theodore H. Hittell, *History of California*, 4 vols. (San Francisco, 1885-97) II, 275. José Figueroa to Secretario del Estado, June 5, 1834, Monterey, in *Political, Military, and Ecclesiastical Correspondence. . .* (San Francisco, 1958), pp. 5-7.

4. My estimate that two-thirds of the population consisted of women and children is conservative. Census figures from Los Angeles for 1830, 1836, and 1844 consistently show such a ratio. See, for example, J. Gregg Layne, "The First Census of the Los Angeles District. . .," SCQ, XVIII (September-December 1936), p. 83, and Marie E. Northrup, ed., "The Los Angeles Padrón of 1844," SCQ, XLII (December 1960), p. 360. The Los Angeles figures, however, define adults as those age twelve and above. Using age sixteen and above to define adults, one finds in Santa Fe that the male adult population was about 26 percent of the total population. This is based on computations from the barrios of San Francisco, Torreón, San Miguel, and Guadalupe, using the 1823 census in Virginia Langham Olmsted, trans. and ed., *New Mexico Spanish and Mexican Colonial Census*, 1790, 1823, 1845 (Albuquerque, 1975), pp. 129-135, 140-53, 156-74.

5. W. Eugene Hollon, *The Great American Desert, Then and Now* (New York, 1966), pp. 64-67.

6. Reglamento para la colonización de los territorios de la República, November 21, 1828, in Francisco F. de la Maza, *Código de colonizacion y terrenos baldios de la República Mexicana* (Mexico, 1893), pp. 237-40. See, too, the laws of March 12 and April 14, 1828, in ibid., pp. 222, 224.

7. The expansion of gente de razón at the expense of the Pueblos has been explored by Myra Ellen Jenkins, "Taos Pueblo and its Neighbors, 1540-1847," *NMHR*, XLI

(April 1966), pp. 85-144, and "The Baltasar Baca Grant: History of an Encroachment," *El Palacio,* LXVIII (Spring 1961), pp. 47-68.

8. Robert G. Cleland, *Cattle on a Thousand Hills* (1st ed., 1941; 2nd ed., San Marino, 1951), pp. 19, 286, n. 4. See, too, Robert G. Cowan, *Ranchos of California. A List of Spanish Concessions, 1775-1822, and Mexican Grants, 1822-1846* (Fresno, 1956), p. 139. W.W. Robinson, *Land in California* (Berkeley, 1948), finds that "at least" 30 rancho grants had been made prior to 1822.

9. Juan de Dios Canedo, *Memoria de la Secretaria de Estado y del Despacho de Relaciones Interiores y Exteriores...*(Mexico, 1829), p. 13.

10. Ortiz to Anastasio Bustamante, Bordeaux, October 31, 1830, in Edith Louise Kelly and Mattie Austin Hatcher, eds. and trans., "Tadeo Ortiz de Ayala and the Colonization of Texas, 1822-1833," *SWHQ,* XXXII (October 1928), pp. 159-60. See, too, pp. 153, 320. Congress of the state of Nuevo León, secret session, February 20, 1827, Monterrey, ASFC, legajo I, 1827-1830, expediente 28, West Transcripts, UT.

11. Quoted in Lansing B. Bloom, "New Mexico Under Mexican Administration, 1821-1846, "*Old Santa Fe,* I (January 1914), pp. 262-63. *Arkansa Gazette,* December 22, 1830. Bradburn is usually thought to be from Kentucky, but C. Alan Hutchinson, who has been collecting material on him, finds he was Virginia-born.

12. Santiago Abreú to the diputación of New Mexico [Mexico City], January 18, 1826, Ritch Papers, no. 86, HEH.

13. Herbert Ingram Priestly, ed. and trans., *Exposition Addressed to the Chamber of Deputies of the Union by Señor Don Carlos Antonio Carrillo, Deputy for Alta California, Concerning the Regulation and Administration of the Pious Fund* (1st ed., 1831; San Francisco, 1938), p. 8.

14. Bancroft, *History of California,* III, 176-80. Alamán to the governor of California, Mexico [February 2, 1830], ASFC, legajo 4, expediente 117, folder 29, transcript, BL. Alamán to Governor Figueroa, May 17, 1832, Archives of California, Bancroft Transcripts, vol. 57. (Superior Goverment State Papers), pp. 88-90, BL, called to my attention by C. Alan Huthchinson, *Frontier Settlement in Mexican California: The Híjar-Padres Colony and Its Orgins, 1769-1835* (New Haven, 1969), p. 157. Alamán instructed Figueroa to give grants to Heinrich Virmond and Henry Fitch in this area; Fitch was an American. I have not located any record of a foreigner who received a grant in California prior to this time. William Willis, an Englishman, and Abel Stearns, an American, were denied grants in 1828 and 1830 respectively (Bancroft, *History of California,* II, 663-64). Some writers have

incorrectly interpreted article 11 of the April 6, 1830 law as applying to California (see, for example, ibid., 663 and Jessie Davies Francis, "An Economic and Social History of Mexican California" [Ph.D. diss., University of California, Berkeley, 1934], p. 130).

15. J.J. Bowden, *Spanish and Mexican Land Grants in the Chihuahuan Acquisition* (El Paso, 1971), pp. 77-84, provides much new information on Heath's activities. A somewhat out-dated biography is "John G. Heath," by William H. H. Allison, *NMHR*, VI (October 1931), pp. 360-75.

16. *A Journey to California, 1841 . . .The Journal of John Bidwell*, Francis P. Farquhar, ed. (Berkeley, 1964), p. 45.

17. Figueroa made this proposal about 1824, before becoming personally familiar with the region. See C. Alan Hutchinson, "General José Figueroa in Mexico, 1792-1832," *NMHR*, XLVIII (October 1973), p. 284. See, too, Ignacio Zúñiga, *Rápida ojeada al Estado de Sonora, dirigida y dedicada al Supremo Govierno de la Nación* (Mexico, 1835), pp. 60-66, facsimile in David J. Weber, ed., *Northern Mexico on the Eve of the United States Invasion. . .* (New York, 1976).

18. See Karen Sykes Collins, ed., "Fray Pedro Arriquibar's Census of Tucson, 1820 [1797]," *JAH, XI* (Spring, 1970), pp. 14-15. Henry F. Dobyns demonstrated that Collins "1820" census is actually one of 1797, see his notes in the *JAH, XIII* (Autumn 1972), pp. 205-9. The vecino population of Tucson seems to have dropped from 79 in 1797 to 36 in 1804, then risen again. Tucson and Tubac censuses of 1831, respectively, document 127 and 128 of Cartas de Sonora II, Antiguo Archivo del Colegio de la Santa Cruz de Querétaro, Convento Franciscano, Celaya, Guananjuato, Mexico. The discovery, dating, and transcriptions of these documents have been done by Fr. Kieran McCarty, who kindly made them available to me. Analysis of this census data might reveal the source of the growing population: former soldiers, assimilated Indians, or newcomers from farther south.

19. Ray H. Mattison, "Early Spanish and Mexican Settlements in Arizona," *NMHR*, XXI and their disposition under American rule in *Early Arizona, Prehistory to Civil War* (Tucson, 1975), chap. 7.

20. Manuel Escalante y Arvizu, to Governor José María Gaxiola, December 9, 1828, AHES, Apaches, cabinet 2, drawer 3, McCarty Transcripts, AHS, film H-12. Juan Nepomuceno González, juez de paz, to the governor, Tucson, March 16, 1834 in ibid., film H-13.

21. José Francisco Velasco, *Noticias estadísticas del Estado de Sonora* (Mexico, 1850), pp. 54-55. Wagoner, *Early Arizona*, p. 168. Henry F. Dobyns, "Tubac

Through Four Centuries: An Historical Resume and Analysis" (MS, Arizona Sate Parks Board, 1959), pp. 593, 611. Antonio Comadurán to José María Elías González, Tucson, December 14, 1848, AHES, Apaches, Cabinet 2, drawer 3, filled under date of January 24, 1849, McCarty Transcripts, AHS, films H-15.

22. Alvarado to the diputación, quoted in Francis, "An Economic and Social History," p. 503. Insufficient population in California was noted by many officials. See, for example, Governor Manuel Victoria to the Secretary of Foreign Relations, June 7, 1831, Archives of California, Bancroft Transcripts, vol. 49 (Departmental Records), p. 135, BL. Woodrow James Hansen, *The Search for Authority in California* (Oakland, Ca., 1960), p. 21.

23. This account of the Híjar-Padrés colony is based upon C. Alan Hutchinson's detailed, judicious, and revisionist study: *Frontier Settlement in Mexican California.* Hutchison subsequently located a more detailed list of the colonists: "An Official List of the Members of the Híjar-Padrés Colony for Mexican California, 1834," *PHR,* XLII (August 1973), pp. 407-18.

24. Most historians have follwed Figueroa's version of the events, which he ably set forth in his *Manifiesto a la República Mejicana* (Monterey, 1835). The other side of the story has been largely unknown until painstakingly assembled by Hutchinson. I am following the interpretation set forth in his *Frontier Settlement in Mexican California,* pp. 268, 382 ff., and his fresh translation and editing of *A Manifesto to the Mexican Republic* (Berkeley, 1978).

25. Quoted in Hutchinson, *Frontier Settlement in Mexican California.* pp. 386-87, 274-78.

26. George Tays "Mariano Guadalupe Vallejo and Sonoma: A Biography and a History," *CHSQ,* XVI (September 1937), pp. 242-43. Alamán to Figueroa, May 17, 1832. Archives of California, Bancroft Transcripts, vol. 57 (Superior Governor States Papers), pp. 88-90, BL.

27. This interpretation is suggested by Hutchinson, *Frontier Settlement in Mexican California,* pp. 381-82, 374.

28. See, for example, Vallejo, quoted in ibid., p. 402, and Manuel Castañares, "Exposición," September 1, 1844, in Castañares *Colección de documentos relativos al departamento de Californias* (Mexico, 1845), p. 34, facsimile in Weber, ed., *Northern Mexico.*

29. Manuel Payno, "Puerto de Monterey, Alta California, *Revista científica y literaria de Méjico,* I (1845), p. 83, facsimile in Weber, ed., *Northern Mexico.* See, too, Constantino de Tarnava to the Minister of War and Navy, January 6, 1830, quoted

in Alleine Howren, "Causes and Origin of the Decree of April 6, 1830, "*SWHQ*, XVI (April 1913), p. 411; José Agustín de Escudero, *Noticias estadísticas de Sonora y Sinaloa* (México, 1849), p. 4, and Juan N. Almonte, *Proyectos de leyes sobre colonización* (Mexico, 1852), p. 5. A recent expression of this view is Dieter George Berninger, *La inmigración en México, 1821-1857* (Mexico, 1975), p. 81.

30. *El Telégrafo*, April 15, 1834, quoted in Hutchinson, *Frontier Settlement in Mexican California*, p. 208.

31. Ray Allen Billington, *America's Frontier Heritage* (New York, 1966), p. 29. Castañares, "Exposición," in *Colleccion de documentos*, p. 34, mentions the low density and plentiful land elsewhere in Mexico. Juan N. Almonte, *Noticia estadística sobre Tejas* (Mexico, 1835), p. 8, facsimile in Weber, ed., *Northern Mexico*, mentions the problem of distance.

32. See the interesting commentary on this question by Pablo Herrera Carrillo, "Las siete guerras por Texas," in Luis Chávez Orozco, ed., *Colección de documentos para la historia de las guerras entre México y los Estados Unidos* (Mexico, 1959), p. 37. Marie E. Northrup, ed. "The Los Angeles Padrón of 1844," *SCQ*, XLII (December 1960), pp. 360-417.

33. "La constitución y la guerra de Tejas," *El Siglo Diez y Nueve*, December 15, 1842, called to my attention by Gene Brack, *Mexico Views Manifest Destiny, 1821-1846. An Essay on the Orgins of the Mexican War* (Albuquerque, 1975), p. 115.

34. Juan Bautista Alvarado, "Historia de California," 5 vols., MS, IV, p. 9, BL. The term *presidiarios* was used in contemporary documents to indicate convicts sentenced to labor in a presidio. This term could also mean presidial soldier, and it has resulted in confusion among contemporaries (see Antonio Barreiro, *Ojeada sobre Nuevo-México. . .* [Puebla, 1832], in H. Bailey Carroll and J. Villasana Haggard, trans. and eds., *Three New Mexico Chronicles* [Albuquerque, 1942], p. 79n), and among historians, some have mis-translated the term as "convict-soldiers" (Howren, "Causes and Origin of the Decree of April 6, 1830," p. 409).

35. Quoted in Howren, "Causes and Origin of the Decree of April 6, 1830," pp. 410-11.

36. Bancroft, *History of California*, III, pp. 16-17, 47-50, and: Order of October 21, 1829; Circular of July 30, 1831: Resolution of April 23, 1833; and the Reglamento of May 6, 1833 in Maza, *Código de colonización*, pp. 240, 245, 248-50.

37. Ferdinand P. Wrangel traveled on the same ship with this man (*De Sitka a San Petersburgo al través de México* [Mexico, 1975], p. 52) who might have been

Eugenio Murrillo, sentenced to ten years in Texas according to Bancroft, *History of California*, III, p. 674, n. 5.

38. Resolution of February 22, 1842, in Maza, *Código de colonización*, p. 315. Bancroft, *History of California*, IV, pp. 287-91, 404-5, 420, 455-57. For the term *cholo*, see Antonio Blanco S., *La lengua española en la historia de California* (Madrid, 1971), pp. 152, 195, 559.

39. David J. Weber and Ronald R. Young, eds., and trans., "California in 1831: Heinrich Virmond to Lucas Alamán," *JSDH*, XXI (Fall 1975), p. 4. Angustias de la Guerra Ord, *Occurrences in Hispanic California*, Francis Price and William H. Ellison, trans. and eds. (Washington, 1956), p. 15. Francis, "Economic and Social History of Mexican California," p. 94.

40. Bancroft takes such a position in regard to the prisoners who came with Micheltorena in 1842, and judges that the *californios* "have grossly exaggerated the deeds of the cholos." *History of California*, V, 456. See, too, Thomas Oliver Larkin's favorable position as a penal colony is suggested in a law of October 25, 1828, prohibiting secret meetings and threatening a four year exile to the Californias for the third offense. Manuel Dublán and José María Lozano. eds., *Legislación mexicana*, 34 vols. (Mexico, 1876-1904), II, 86.

41. Lester Gordon Engelson, "Proposal for the Colonization of California by England in Connection with the Mexican Debt to British Bondholders, 1837-1846," *CHSQ*, XVIII (June 1939), pp. 136-48. John A. Hawgood, "A Projected Prussian Colonization of Upper California," *SCQ*, XLVIII (December 1966), pp. 352-68.

42. As early as 1840, one merchant who thought Texas might acquire New Mexico wrote to a friend at Taos: "It would be a good time to get grants from Armijo." David Waldo to John Rowland, May 1 and May 10, MS, California Historical Documents Collection, HEH. See, too, Harold Dunham, "New Mexico Land Grants with Special Reference to the Title Papers of the Maxwell Grant," *NMHR*, XXX (January 1955), pp. 4-6, and Abel Stearns to Thomas Oliver Larkin, June 12, 1846, in Hammond, ed., *The Larkin Papers*, V, 20.

43. See Victor Westphall's revisionist article: "Fraud and the Implications of Fraud in the Land Grants of New Mexico," *NMHR*, XLIX (July 1974), pp. 199-200. Westphall estimates that Armijo granted over 16,500,000 acres between 1837 and 1846, or "more than half of of the some 31,000,000 acres of land granted by all authorities of both Spain and Mexico in 160 years." Review of Morris F. Taylor, *O. P. McMains...*, *AW*, XX (Spring 1980), p. 84. The extension of six Mexican land grants into the area of today's Colorado is ably summarized in LeRoy R. Hafen,

"Mexican Land Grants in Colorado," *Colorado Magazine*, IV (May 1927). pp. 81-93, and by Marianne L. Stoller, "Grants of Desperation, Lands of Speculation: Mexican Period Land Grants in Colorado," *JW*, XIX (July 1980), pp. 22-39, who along with Janet Lecompte, "Manuel Armijo and the Americans," ibid., p. 58, argues that historians have exaggerated the size of Armijo's grants.

44. Armijo never explicitly stated defense as his motive for dispensing land to foreigners during these years, but many writers have surmised that he had defense against foreigners in mind. See, for example, Ralph Emerson Twitchell, *The Leading Facts of New Mexican History*, 2 vols. (Cedar Rapids, 1911-12), II, 196-97, and Ward Alan Minge, "Frontier Problems in New Mexico Preceding the Mexican War, 1840-1846" (Ph.D. diss., University of New Mexico, 1965), p. 306.

45. For the beginnings of the "Maxwell" grant see Lawrence W. Murphy, "The Beaubien and Miranda Land Grant, 1841-1846," *NMHR*, XLII (January 1967), pp. 27-46, and Murphy's "Charles H. Beaubien," in LeRoy R. Hafen, ed., *The Mountain Men and the Fur Trade of the Far West*, 10 vols. (Glendale, 1965-72), VI, 23-25. The grant has received book-length treatment, most authoritatively by William A. Keleher, *Maxwell Land Grant: A New Mexico Item* (Santa Fe, 1942), and Jim Berry Pearson, *The Maxwell Land Grant* (Norman, 1961). Both works focus on the post-Mexican War era. A grant to José Sutton of 16 square leagues on the Pecos near San Miguel del Bado, made in 1838, may represent the beginnings of Armijo's policy of granting large estates to foreigners. This question needs further study.

46. Weber, "Stephen Louis Lee," in Hafen, ed., *The Mountain Men*, III, 181-87. The most detailed study of this grant is in Hebert O. Brayer, *William Blackmore: The Spanish-Mexican Land Grants of New Mexico and Colorado, 1863-1878* (Denver, 1949), but Brayer treats the Mexican Period in a sketchy manner (pp. 59-62).

47. Weber, "Gervais Nolan," in Hafen, ed., *The Mountain Men*, IV, 225-29. Morris F. Taylor. "The Two Land Grants of Gervacio Nolán," *NMHR*, XLVII (April 1972), pp. 151-84.

48. Harold H. Dunham, "Cerán St. Vrain," in Hafen, ed., *The Mountain Men*, V, 310-11, and Ralph Emerson Twitchell, *The Spanish Archives of New Mexico*, 2 vols. (Cedar Rapids, 1914), I, 276-77.

49. Minge, "Frontier Problems in New Mexico," p. 222. Benjamin Read, *Illustrated History of New Mexico* (Santa Fe, 1912,) 411-14. Angélico Chávez, "New Names in New Mexico," *El Palacio*, LXIV (November-December 1957), p. 375.

50. Murphy, "Beaubien and Miranda," p. 32. Harold Dunham, "Charles Bent," in Hafen, ed., *The Mountain Men*, II, 46-47.

51. Martínez's objection to the grants are disscussed in Murphy, "Beaubien and Miranda," pp. 32-33, and in Myra Ellen Jenkins, "Taos Pueblo and its Neighbors, 1540-1847," *MNHR,* XLI (April 1966), pp. 107-8.

52. Murphy, "Beaubien and Miranda," pp. 32-33, "Minge, "Frontier Problems," pp. 224-27. Article 9 of the March 11, 1842 law, in Maza, *Código de Colonización,* pp. 215-18. Twitchell, *Spanish Archives,* I, 276-77. The most extensive discussion of Scolly's grant is in J.J. Bowden, "Private Land in the Southwest," 6 vols. (LLM thesis, Southern Methodist University, Dallas, 1969), III, 775-76.

53. Antonio José Martínez to Mariano Martínez, Taos, August 22, 1844, in Santiago Valdez, "Biografia del Rev. P. Antonio José Martínez," MS, 1877, Ritch Papers, No. 2211 (English Translation), pp. 38-40, HL.

54. Francisco Javier Conde to the governor, September 20, 1845, cited in Murphy, "Beaubien and Miranda," p. 35. A portion of the letter is quoted in Dunham, "New Mexico Land Grants," p. 22. Murphy, "Beaubien and Miranda" p. 32. Armijo also had a share of the St. Vrain-Vigil grant. David Lavander, *Bent's Fort* (New York, 1954), p. 403, n. 11.

55. Dunham, "New Mexico Land Grants," implies this, and there is evidence that grants to José Sutton and Carlos Beaubien represented payment for loans to the government. Daniel Tyler, "Anglo-American Penetration of the Southwest: The View from New Mexico," LXXV (January 1972), p. 337.

56. Armijo to the Ministro de Relaciones, July 31, 1827, quoted in David J. Weber, "Mexico and the Mountain Men, 1821-1828," *JW,* VIII (July 1969), p. 373. David J. Weber, *The Taos Trappers: The Fur Trade in the Far Southwest, 1540-1846* (Norman, 1971), p. 9.

57. This thesis is suggested by Tyler, "Anglo-American Penetration of the Southwest," pp. 325-38.

58. These figures do not include El Paso, which ceased to fall under New Mexico's jurisdiction after 1824. Bloom, "New Mexico Under Mexican Administration," I, 27-30. "Note on the Population of New Mexico, 1846-1849," *NMHR, XXXIV* (July 1959), pp. 200-202, which summarizes estimates from various souces from 1800-1846 and concludes that the population ranged between 60 and 70,000 in 1846. I am using a 1.1 percent average annual growth rate for Mexico. See chapt. 9, n. 67. Angélico Chávez, "New Names in New Mexico, 1820-1850," *El Palacio,* LXIV (November-December, 1957), pp. 291-318, 367-80, provides an idea from church records of both Mexican and foreign newcomers to New Mexico in these years, many of whom were transients.

59. LeRoy R. and Ann W. Hafen, *Old Spanish Trail: Santa Fé to Los Angeles* (Glendale, 1954), pp. 195-225. For the reception of New Mexicans in California see George William Beattie, "San Bernardino Valley Before the Americans Came," *CHSQ*, XII (June 1933), p. 116; Harold A. Whelan, "Eden in Jurupa Valley. The Story of Agua Mansa," *SCQ*, LV (Winter 1973), pp. 413-30 and Joyce Carter Vickery, *Defending Eden: New Mexico Pioneers in Southern California, 1830-1890* (Riverside, 1977). For Manuel Vaca, see Iris Higbie Wilson {Engstrand}, *William Wolfskin, 1798-1866* (Glendale, 1965), p. 130, and for Julian Chávez see J. Gregg Layne, "The First Census of the Los Angeles District....1836," *SCQ*, XVIII (September-December 1936), p. 94, and Don Devereaux, "Julian Chávez, an Early Río Arriba Immigrant," *El Palacio*, LXXIV (Winter 1967), pp. 35-36.
60. Robidoux to Manuel Alvarez, Rancho Jurupa, May 1, 1848 quoted in David J. Weber, ed. and trans., "Louis Robidoux: Two Letters from California, 1848," *SCQ*, LIV (Summer, 1972), pp. 109, 110.
61. This thesis of Dorothy Johansen is discussed briefly in John D. Unruh, Jr., *The Plains Across: The Overland Emigrants and the Trans-Mississippi West, 1840-60* (Urbana, 1979), pp.93-94. See, too, Billington's summary of theory in *America's Frontier Heritage*, pp.26-29.
62. Nicholas Dawson, *California in '41: Texas in '51* (Austin, 1969), pp. 12-13.
63. Unruh, *The Plains Across*, pp. 28-61, provides a fine account of the contradictory descriptions that would-be emigrants received in the 1840s. For the motives of the emigrants, see also Billington, *The Far Western Frontier, 1830-1860* (New York, 1956), pp. 89-91 and Earl Pomeroy, *The Pacific Slope: A History of California, Oregon, Washington, Idaho, Utah, & Nevada* (New York, 1965), pp. 27-35.
64. Cleland, *Cattle on a Thousand Hills*, p. 23. Sherburne Friend Cook, "The Epidemic of 1830-1833 in California and Oregon," *University of California Publications in American Archaelogy and Ethnology*, XLIII (May, 1955), pp. 303-26.
65. In 1945, for example, 3,000 immigrants reached the Willamette country compared to 250 who entered California, although some who settled in Oregon moved on to California and vice versa. Pomeroy, *The Pacific Slope*, pp. 30-31.
66. The standard biography is George D. Lyman, *John Marsh, Pionner: The Life Story of a Trail-Blazer on Six Frontiers* (New York, 1930).
67. Erwin G. Gudde, ed., *Sutter's Own Story* (New York, 1936), pp. 9-10. The most authoritative biography of Sutter remains James P. Zollinger, *Sutter, the Man and His Empire* (New York, 1939). Richard Dillon has written a sprightly popular biography

which contains some new information regarding Sutter's military career: *Fool's Gold. The Decline and Fall of Captain John Sutter of California* (New York, 1967). Sutter's character and historians' interpretations of it have been examined by John Hawgood, "John Augustus Sutter, A Reappraisal," *AW, IV* (Winter, 1962), pp. 345-56.

68. George Simpson, *Narrative of a Journey Round the World*, 2 vols. (London, 1847), I, 326. Called to my attention by Zollinger, *Sutter*, p. 92.

69. John Bidwell, *Echoes of the Past* (1st ed., 1914; New York, 1973), pp. 6-7. Marsh's efforts to promote immigration between 1840-46 are described at length in Lyman, *John Marsh*, chapts. 34-38. In 1845, apparently, Sutter sent agents to Fort Hall, a point just prior to where the trails to Oregon and California diverged, to entice overlanders to California. Unruh, *The Plains Across*, p. 339.

70. Bidwell, *Echoes*, pp. 7, 11.

71. Dawson, *California in '41*, p. 30.

72. Marsh to his parents, April 3, 1842, quoted in Lyman, *John Marsh*, p. 249.

73. There is a vast literature on overland migration to California during these years. George P. Stewart has produced a reliable and readable popular account in *The California Trail: An Epic With Many Heroes* (New York, 1962).

74. The best treatment of this episode is George M. Brooke, Jr., "The Vest Pocket War of Commodore Jones," *PHR*, XXI (August 1962), pp. 217-33. For the reaction in Mexico City see Frank A. Knapp, Jr., "Preludios de la pérdida de California," *Historia Mexicana*, IV (octubre-diciembre 1954), pp. 235-49, and Brack, *Mexico Views Manifest Destiny*, pp. 101-3. American interest in acquisition of California is discussed in many sources, see especially Robert Glass Cleland, "The Early Sentiment for the Annexation of California: An Account of the Growth of American Interest in California, 1835-1846," *SWHQ*, XVIII (July 1914), pp. 13-17, 29-30. Norman A. Graebner, *Empire on the Pacific: a Study in American Continental Expansion* (New York, 1955).

75. Almonte to the Minister of War, March 28, 1840, quoted in Guadalupe Vallejo, "Documentos para la historia de California," X, no. 146, MS, BL. See, too, Vallejo, Monterey, April 25, 1840, in Archivo Histórico de Defensa Nacional, expediente 532, microfilm, roll 2, BL.

76. P. T. Cyrille La Place, "The Report of Captain La Place on his Voyage to the Northwest Coast and California in 1839," George Vernon Blue, ed. and trans., *CHSQ*. XVIII (December 1939), p. 322.

77. *El Patriota Mexicano*, October 5, 1845, quoted in Frank A. Knapp, Jr., "The Mexican Fear of Manifest Destiny in California," in *Essays in Mexican History*, Thomas E. Cotner and Carlos E. Castañeda, eds. (Austin, 1958), p. 201.

78. Bancroft, *History of California*, IV, 271-73, 379-80. Orders from the central government designed to block Anglo-American immigration into California were issued in May 1841, July 1843, and July 1845.

79. *El Siglo Diez y Nueve*, October 16, 1845, quoted in Knapp, "Mexican Fear of Manifest Destiny in California," p. 207. Bancroft, *History of California*, V , 215-33.

80. "Letter to Dr. John Marsh to Hon. Lewis Cass [January 20, 1846]," *CHSQ*, XXII (December 1943), p. 317.

81. Castro, "Orden....," Sonoma, November 6, 1845, quoted in Bancroft, *History of California*, IV, 606. Ibid., IV, 274-75, 385-86; V, 56-57, 76. José Castro to Vallejo, November 11, 1845, in Vallejo, "Documentos para la historia de California," XII, no. 150, MS, BL. George Tays, "Revolutionary California: The Political History of California from 1820 to 1848" (Ph.D. diss. University of California, Berkeley, 1932; rev., 1934), p. 678.

82. Pablo de la Guerra to Vallejo, Santa Barbara, April 16, 1840, quoted in Hansen, *Search for Authority*, p. 33.

83. Tays, "Mariano Guadalupe Vallejo and Sonoma," pp. 56-58, 151-63. *Cinco Documentos sobre la Alta California* (Mexico, 1944), contains some of Tays' correspondence regarding the Bidwell party.

84. Quoted in Zollinger, *Sutter*, p. 80.

85. Vallejo to Anastasio Bustamante, Sonoma, November 22, 1845, in Vallejo, "Documentos para la historia de California," XII, no. 157.

86. Sutter to Jacob Leese, New Helvetia, November 8, 1841, quoted in Tays, "Mariano Guadalupe Vallejo and Sonoma," p. 69. Ironically, Leese was Vallejo's brother-in-law and Vallejo obtained a copy of this letter.

87. Quoted in Zollinger, *Sutter*, p. 177. See, too, pp. 134, 145-46. Bancroft, *History of California*, IV, 612-16 argues that Sutter initiated the sale. Other evidence suggests that an agent from Mexico came to California with authorization to purchase the fort (Tays, "Revolutionary California," p. 618), and there may be no incompatibility between these versions.

88. See, for example, Wilson, *William Wolfskill*, pp. 116-19, and Bancroft, *History of California* V, 57, n. 4.

89. All of these figures are rough. I am following Rose Hollengaugh Avina, "Spanish and Mexican Land Grants in California" (Ph.D. diss. Berkeley, 1932), p. 71. She

finds that 35 of 120 grants made by Micheltorena went to foreigners. Another writer finds that 46 of 131 grants by Micheltorena went to foreigners: Lela M. Weststeyn, "The Expansion of the Land Grant System Under the Last Two Mexican Governors..." (M.A. thesis, University of Southern California, 1937), p. 82. For an especially concise and lucid overview, see David Hornbeck, "Land Tenure and Rancho Expansion in Alta California, 1784-1846," *Journal of Historical Geography*, IV (1978), pp. 371-90, who finds that nearly 30 percent of the grantees in the 1840s had Anglo surnames.

90. Manuel Castañares to Vallejo, October 31, 1843, quoted in Bancroft, *History of California*, IV, 386, and Vallejo to Sutter, December 18, 1844 in Tays, "Vallejo," p. 159. Pico to the justices of the jurisdiction of Jurupa, Los Angeles, July 27, 1846, in California Historical Society Documents Collection, HEH.

91. Vallejo to Anastasio Bustamante, Sonoma, November 22, 1845, in Vallejo, "Documentos para la historia de California," XII, no. 157. Robinson, *Land in California*, p. 64.

92. Quoted in Hansen, *Search for Authority*, p. 35. This point has been made by various writers. See, for example, Rodman W. Paul's interesting essay: "The Spanish-Americans in the Southwest, 1848-1900," in John G. Clark, ed., *The Frontier Challenge: Responses to the Trans-Mississippi West* (Lawrence, Kansas, 1971), p. 42.

93. John A. Hawgood, "The Pattern of Yankee Infiltration in Mexican Alta California, 1821-1846," *PHR*, XXVII (February 1958), pp. 27-38.

94. The most careful presentation of data for this period is in Francis, "An Economic and Social History of Mexican California," pp.152-68. Although I do not agree with all of her analysis, I have utilized her figures. Thomas Oliver Larkin and others put the number of foreigners much higher. See Larkin's description of California, April 20, 1846, in Hammond ed., *The Larkin Papers*, IV, 305.

95. Castañares, "Exposición," in Castañares, *Collección de documentos*, p. 37.

The 1820s through the 1840s were the most pivotal years in the long history of diplomatic relations between the United States and Mexico. During these decades, Mexico attempted to control its northern borders and protect its territories from a people and a nation that had coveted some of its most important regions. Mexican officials were convinced that they faced a nation and a people that disparaged them and felt entitled to absorb their territories. Mexico faced aggressive expansionists from virtually every region of the United States. Americans, at least those in important positions with considerable political clout, made their desire for Mexican territory clear. President James K. Polk, a southerner sympathetic to slavery interests and an ardent believer in Manifest Destiny, embodied all of the qualities of the American ambition during the early and middle nineteenth century and wanted to "expand the area of freedom." He was willing to go to war with Mexico to do it. As a result, Mexico suffered a humiliating defeat at the hands of a superior army and the United States had completed its goal of continental conquest through the Mexican-American War and the Treaty of Guadalupe Hidalgo. Gene Brack summarizes United States-Mexico relations during these critical decades.

The Diplomacy of Racism:
Manifest Destiny and Mexico, 1821-1848

Gene Brack

"Poor Mexico: so far from God and so near to the United States." This lament, attributed to Mexican President Porfirio Diaz in the late nineteenth century, was especially applicable to the first quarter century of Mexican independence. Chaos and poverty prevailed, and Mexico's political, social and economic failures reinforced the belief, widely shared in the United States, that Mexicans, barbaric, irresponsible, and superficial (and Catholic) were not only incapable of self-government but also inherently inferior as human beings. Through apparent sloth and ineptitude Mexicans failed to make productive use of their national resources, and it therefore seemed reasonable to many Americans that these descendants of Spanish civilization ought to give way to the superior moral and material force of the Anglo-Saxon United States. The war that eventually resulted cost Mexico about one-half of her national domain and shattered the bright prospects with which she had launched her independence only twenty-five years earlier. Mexicans sometimes refer to this sense of unfulfilled promise as a "castration complex" believing the United States to be the perpetrator of the deed.

One may regret but not undo the past. Viewed retrospectively, it was perhaps inevitable that the United States, given the absence of strong foreign opposition, would expand its borders to the Pacific, acquiring Mexican territory in the process. But the methods of expansion betrayed the nation's expressed ideals, while the racist assumptions which seemed to justify those methods placed an ugly and perhaps permanent scar on future relations between the two peoples.

An important reason why many nineteenth-century Americans withheld sympathy, tolerance, and understanding from Mexico is that, then as now, they did not sufficiently take into account the role of historical factors in shaping a nation's destiny. The easy way to explain American success and Mexican failure was to attribute the former to Anglo-Saxon superiority and the latter to Latin inferiority, claiming for good measure that the United States, uniquely in all the world, was the instrument of God's will (thus the term "Manifest Destiny," coined in 1845 to justify imposing our [God's] will upon Mexico). However, a more reasonable though complicated and difficult, explanation lay in the colonial origins of the two nations.

Although English blundering had touched off the revolution that resulted in American independence, it is nonetheless true that for over a century prior to the revolution the British had allowed Americans a remarkable degree of political and economic freedom. ("American" properly refers to all peoples and nations in the western hemisphere, but for convenience it is used here to refer to the United States and its citizens.). We had therefore begun our nationhood with rather mature political institutions, thereby avoiding a long and tumultuous process of trial and error in establishing a workable government. From having governed ourselves we possessed from the outset a body of experienced leaders, such as Washington, Jefferson, Franklin, and John Adams. Social mobility (among white Americans) and equality of economic opportunity flourished in the absence of rigid class divisions, breeding prosperity and optimism. The Atlantic Ocean provided a barrier against more powerful European nations. Thus Americans avoided the troubled infancy that most "developing" nations have undergone. Even so, despite our numerous advantages, the establishment of independence was difficult: economic depression set in shortly after independence; violence broke out in Massachusetts and elsewhere; finally, the Articles of Confederation were discarded amid much domestic discord and replaced with the Constitution.

Therefore it should not be surprising that Mexico, in setting out upon what was for her a totally unchartered sea of independence, would fail to enjoy success either as quickly or as completely as the United States. As a colony Mexico had been ruled autocratically and often despotically. Her people had no experience in self government, and a rigid social structure preserved the highest places for European Spaniards, keeping most others in poverty and misery, while the Church taught the masses to accept suffering as the way to heavenly reward. Drained of capital by her

Spanish masters, Mexico was further handicapped economically by the ravages of eleven years of bloody warfare leading to Independence. Lacking experience in self-government and economic know-how, with poverty and ignorance the rule, Mexico would require decades to develop stability. Yet the new nation was immediately confronted by the most perplexing problem of all: a powerful, energetic, prosperous, and ambitious nation to the north from which she soon learned to expect neither sympathy nor understanding, but scorn, deceit, and finally, armed intimidation in pursuit of territorial objectives.

By the time Mexico gained independence in 1821 the United States was already a well-established republic. Three decades of constitutional government had been brilliantly successful, and the War of 1812 had demonstrated American ability to survive a major war against a powerful rival. The Louisiana Purchase of 1803 and the Adams-Onis Treaty of 1819 had already accomplished much of an expansionist program that within a seventy-two year period (1776-1848) would see thirteen English colonies, huddled in a narrow strip along the eastern seaboard, becoming a national power of continental proportions.

Indeed, it was this rapid expansion of the United States that caused Mexicans to view their northern neighbor with fear and suspicion from the very beginning of relations. Mexico's first diplomatic representative to the United States, soon after his arrival in Washington, wrote that Americans were not to be trusted; their haughty attitude toward Mexicans, whom they viewed as inferiors, caused Americans to believe that they should rule the entire hemisphere. Nor did our first minister to Mexico, Joel R. Poinsett, ally these fears.

It was ironic that Poinsett's mission to Mexico heightened tensions and left behind a legacy of mistrust and hatred, for he was one of those few Americans who not only was very well informed about Mexican conditions but also was deeply sympathetic to the people of that new but troubled country. Fluent in Spanish, Poinsett had become familiar with Latin America during two years' residence in Chile (1812-14) and had visited Mexico in 1822, writing a book, *Notes on Mexico*, based on his observations. In 1825 the sophisticated, elegantly-minded South Carolinian returned to Mexico where he found, to his dismay, a conservative group of Mexicans, unsympathetic to democratic institutions, dominating the political scene. Furthermore, the able English minister, Henry Ward, had convinced Mexican leaders that Britain, not the United States, was Mexico's true friend. The controlling clique had utterly excluded the liberal, pro-American faction from power and influence. Poinsett set out to revise these conditions partly because of his idealistic desire to see

Mexico governed democratically, but also because the United States government hoped to gain "most favored nation" commercial concessions and a boundary that would restore American claim to Texas.

Poinsett did not obtain the economic advantages he sought, and in the manner of negotiating a permanent boundary he shocked Mexican officials by insisting that Mexico should cooperate in detaining runaway slaves. He argued among other points that the border ought to be settled by a law-abiding population, asserting that slave owners were an especially orderly and desirable class of citizens. Mexicans had emancipated the few black slaves in their country when independence came, and thus they were startled to discover in these very first negotiations a relationship between slavery and American territorial objectives.

But it was in seeking to overcome the political influence of the anti-American, pro-English, conservative faction that Poinsett most grievously offended. These Mexican conservatives were so closely associated with Freemasonry of the Scottish Rite variety that their lodges served as their means of political organization similar to political parties in the United States. The liberal opponents of the *Escoceses* were hardly organized at all -- a problem Poinsett sought to solve by obtaining for them a York Rite masonic chapter. This new *Yorkino* group soon succeeded in winning election after election in the states and thus obtained control of the central government. Thrust from power, the displaced conservatives believed the American minister to be the agent responsible for their decline. Despite Poinsett's lofty motives, his actions made him vulnerable to exaggerated and distorted accusations of meddling in Mexican affairs in pursuit of American interests. A bitter controversy followed, reaching a crisis in 1828 when the liberals, upon losing the presidential election of that year, took matters into their own hands and overthrew the conservative victor. The resulting furor was so intense that by 1829 the liberal president, Vicente Guerrero, whose career Poinsett had helped advance, asked the United States to recall its minister. Guerrero declared that because of widespread distrust of Poinsett, "relations between the two republics have not been attended with that success which had been anticipated." It is not surprising that Mexicans of all political persuasions resented the efforts of a foreigner to manipulate their affairs. In 1793 Americans themselves had exhibited similar indignation when "Citizen" Genêt came to the United States seeking aid for revolutionary France. After President Washington rejected Genêt's appeals the Frenchman proceeded to issue military licenses and commissions to Americans in defiance of the government. This intervention into the affairs of a sovereign nation caused even those Americans who had originally supported Genêt to turn against him.

Many of Poinsett's Mexican friends reacted to the American minister's activities in much the same way. For years to come, Mexicans would associate Poinsett's name with treachery. His replacement would report in 1830 that Mexicans attached "great odium" to Poinsett and that they transferred that odium to the nation he represented.

While Mexican-American relations were beginning on this discordant note, an even more troublesome situation arose in the Mexican province of Texas. Apart from a few missions and military outposts, this enormous territory had remained undeveloped and underpopulated during the Spanish colonial period. The leaders of independent Mexico, aware of American interest in acquiring the region, attempted to promote its development by soliciting foreign colonists. The Mexican government reasoned that such a policy would provide a buffer zone between Mexico's interior and the expansionist-minded United States. To Mexico's ultimate misfortune, it was Americans who most enthusiastically responded, migrating in large numbers, primarily from the southern and western United States. A serious conflict of cultures and interests soon occurred. The American colonists assumed the life-style they had known in the United States, growing cotton with slave labor. They viewed with contempt the poverty-ridden and poorly governed native Mexicans. By 1830, authorities in Mexico City, alarmed at the increasing evidence of American land hunger and disturbed by Poinsett's activities, enacted a new colonization law designed to curtail further American migration to Texas and to force those Americans already there to conform to Mexican law and custom.

But the Mexican government was simply too weak to enforce its authority in Texas, and the 1830 regulations were openly defied as Americans continued streaming into the province. Violent incidents, bred of mutual misunderstanding and differences in language, religion, customs, and taste, began to occur. The crisis came in 1835 when a number of Mexican states revolted against the dictatorship of General Antonio López de Santa Anna who had seized power during the previous year. The Texans joined the revolt, and by early 1836, Santa Anna, accompanied by a sizeable army, had marched to San Antonio and destroyed a small garrison at the Battle of the Alamo. In the meantime Texans formally declared their independence from Mexico, and in April, 1836, routed Santa Anna at San Jacinto. Captured by the Texans, the Mexican leader, under duress, agreed to recognize their independence.

Several events accompanied the Texas revolution which seemed to prove American involvement and confirmed Mexican suspicions upon their territory. The Texans had freely enlisted recruits and raised money and supplies in the United States to aid their struggle against Mexico. These activities were an open defiance of existing neutrality agreements, yet the administration of President Andrew Jackson had rudely and contemptuously dismissed official Mexican protests. It thus became clear to Mexicans that the United States openly supported and encouraged the Texas revolutionaries and seemed more interested in obtaining Texas, by any means necessary, than in treating Mexico with justice and decency. After Santa Anna's defeat, a large detachment of American troops entered Texas on the pretext of guarding the Louisiana border against Indians and remained until December, 1836. The Mexicans interpreted this measure to mean that the United States was determined to safeguard the results of the revolution. American recognition of Texas independence served to underscore further the role of the United States in depriving Mexico of this large and valuable part of her national domain. Mexican authorities lost no time in claiming that Santa Anna's recognition of Texas independence was invalid and that Texas remained a part of Mexico. For almost a decade, Texas remained a republic, its independence supported by the United States and threatened by Mexico, an ambiguous focus of troubled Mexican-American relations.

A side issue which aggravated the strained relationship between the two countries involved American financial claims against Mexico. Many American citizens had entered Mexico after 1821 to undertake commercial ventures. The profits from such business activities could be great, but, given Mexico's instability, the risks were also great. When an American in Mexico suffered financial loss, for example, through legal or illegal seizure of his property or through non-payment of loans, he insisted that the Mexican government should assume responsibility. Mexican officials rejected such claims, declaring that their government was not responsible for the actions of individuals; Americans in Mexico were subject to Mexican regulations and conditions and could not claim special consideration. It is interesting to note that in similar fashion the United States government had disclaimed responsibility for the actions of those Americans who had openly violated neutrality agreements with Mexico by raising men, money, and arms in support of the Texan revolutionaries. And during the late 1830s a number of state governments in the United States defaulted on millions of dollars in debts owed to foreign creditors. Yet the United States insisted that the Mexican government was indeed responsible for the financial affairs of its citizens and should therefore pay claims which by the late eighteen thirties amounted to some twelve million dollars. The dispute was submitted to an international board of arbitration which awarded the United States some two million dollars. Mexico dutifully paid installments, raising the money through the desperate means of forced loans, until in 1844 the bankrupt nation was unable to borrow further cash for this purpose. The zeal with which the United States pursued collection of this dubious debt from an impoverished neighbor contributed further to the Mexican image of the grasping, aggressive Americans.

However, this financial dispute was of less concern than the overall question of American expansion which, after 1836, played an increasingly important role in the internal affairs of both countries. In the United States the Texas issue became closely linked to the sectional controversy over slavery and abolitionism. Because Texas had been colonized chiefly by southerners, because Americans from the southern and western slave states most actively supported the Texan revolutionaries, because Texas, if annexed to the Union, would enter as a slave state, and because President Jackson himself a southerner, sympathetic to slavery had recognized Texas independence, many northerners believed that the events in Texas resulted from a southern conspiracy to expand slavery. Party politics was also involved, for Jackson was a Democrat, and the Democrats appeared most sympathetic toward the South and the cause of slavery. On the other hand, the Whig party included most of the northern opponents of slavery and of Texas annexation. Indeed, neither Jackson nor his successor in the White House, Martin Van Buren, dared to annex Texas because of the opposition of the northern, anti-slavery Whigs (joined by some northern Democrats) in Congress.

In the "Log Cabin" campaign of 1840 the Whig candidate, William Henry Harrison, gained the presidency and apparently ended any hope of Texas annexation for at least four years. However, Harrison died only one month into his term and was succeeded by John Tyler of Virginia who, though nominally a Whig, was a typical southerner of the states' rights, pro-slavery persuasion. Southerners dominated Tyler's administration, and by 1843 they had launched a national campaign of propaganda designed to enlist support for Texas annexation. For northern consumption the Tyler administration advanced the thesis that annexation of Texas would help end slavery by drawing slaves to the southwest from exhausted agricultural land in the older southern states. From Texas they would eventually disappear into Mexico and Central and South America. In the South, pro-annexation supporters suggested that England planned to intervene in Texas and promote emancipation there. Despite these efforts to make annexation appear an urgent necessity, in June 1844 the Senate failed to ratify a treaty that would have brought Texas into the Union.

The issue of western expansion, especially as it applied to Texas, dominated the presidential election campaign of 1844. The Democrats were inclined toward nominating Martin Van Buren, who had occupied the White House for one term prior to his defeat in 1840. But Van Buren, a New Yorker, announced his opposition to annexation on the grounds that it would probably cause a war with Mexico, and that such a war, against an unoffending neighbor, to advance the cause of slavery, would be immoral. The Democratic Party, responsive to the demands of its southern wing, thereupon rejected Van Buren in favor of James K. Polk of Tennessee. Polk ran on a platform pledging not only to annex Texas, but also, to acquire all of the Oregon Territory, a region that the United States had jointly occupied with England for more than two decades. The Whigs nominated Henry Clay of Kentucky who, despite being from a slave state, was known to oppose annexation and whose platform ignored the issue of expansion. Polk's victory, though narrow, seemed to prove that the nation at large favored expansion, thereby providing the outgoing President, John Tyler, with the opportunity to achieve annexation before the inauguration of Polk. At his urging, Congress passed a joint resolution annexing Texas. This method required the approval of a simple majority rather than the more difficult two-thirds majority of the Senate necessary for approval of a treaty. Thus, when Polk entered office in the spring of 1845 Texas annexation was an accomplished fact. How Mexico would react become an important question.

Conditions in Mexico had deteriorated rapidly after 1836. Governmental administrations rose and fell in quick succession, each failing to cope with the prevailing problems of political instability, economic failure, and social chaos. This turmoil, combined with continuous American pressure on Mexican territory, caused many Mexicans to become concerned about the very survival of their nation. The Texas revolution itself had been devastating to Mexico's confidence in her ability to repel the American advance. Following 1836, Mexicans insisted that the loss of Texas was not final, that, when conditions permitted, they would reconquer the province and restore Mexican control. However Mexico remained too weak to threaten seriously the independence of Texas, although a major effort to do so was attempted as late as 1842. By that time it was widely believed in Mexico that the permanent loss of Texas would lead to American acquisition of still more Mexican territory and perhaps to the eventual extinction of Mexico.

There was evidence to support these fears. In 1841 an armed expedition of Texans invaded the neighboring Mexican province of New Mexico, hoping to establish control over the region in order to gain access to the lucrative trading center of Santa Fe. Mexican authorities easily subdued the invaders but this episode heightened Mexican concern over the continuing threat to their territories. Then in

1842 an American naval force seized Monterey, the Mexican capital of upper California. The American commander justified his actions by claiming he had learned of the outbreak of war with Mexico; he soon withdrew his forces, but the incident was most alarming to Mexicans, signaling that California was now on the list of American territorial objectives.

Mexicans were by no means ignorant of affairs within the United States. From diplomatic representatives in Washington they learned much about the activities and attitudes of the American government. American newspapers received much attention in Mexico, and the Mexican press regularly printed remarks made by political leaders in the United States. The information that was obtained in these various ways lent support to Mexican fear of being consumed by the Americans. It was not merely a matter of American expansionists urging the acquisition of all Mexico; perhaps of even more vital concern was the attitude toward the Mexican people that accompanied the American desire for Mexican territory. That attitude increasingly resembled the one with which Americans viewed Indians and blacks, both of whom had suffered terribly because white Americans considered them inferior. If Indians in the United States had been despoiled of their land and had seen their civilization shattered in the process, and if the black man had been reduced to a brutal form of servitude, then what awaited Mexicans should they too fall under American control? And if the American failed to honor his agreements with Indians, why would he be more trustworthy with Mexicans? Perhaps this is what Mexicans had in mind when they insisted time and again that, should Texas fall to the Americans, other territory would follow.

At about the time of the Texas revolution Mexicans began to realize fully that they too were considered by many Americans to be inferior beings, possessing no rights that a "white" man need respect. As early as 1827 a Mexican newspaper had reported that Americans thought of Indians as savages because their customs differed from those of Anglo-Saxons, and the writer feared that Americans thought the same of Mexicans. During the Texas revolution Mexican newspapers frequently observed that Mexico simply could not afford to permit the Americans to enforce their will upon those they considered inferior, and a pamphlet of 1837 warned that when the United States acquired dominion in Mexico the Catholic Church would be destroyed and Mexicans, like Indians, would be "stripped of the last traces of their civilization." The Mexican press frequently informed the public that Americans justified their efforts to acquire Mexican territory by declaring that Mexicans were incapable of governing themselves. Some Mexicans even suggested that they would be enslaved and bought and sold like blacks in the United States should they fall under American control, simply because their skin color was not as white as that of the Americans.

Mexicans therefore were aware of the undercurrent of racism involved in the expansionist policy of the United States. While Mexicans may have exaggerated these racist tendencies, there was nonetheless enough truth to them to make them believable. In the United States the close relationship between slavery and expansionism was obvious. Although the southern states may not have organized a conspiracy to acquire Mexican territory in order to expand the institution of slavery, there is no doubt that southern leaders did feel that the rapid growth in the population of northern states and the activities of abolitionists threatened the position of influence and power held by the South in national affairs. It seemed essential to protect their vital interests by acquiring additional territory, and in the late eighteen thirties the only remaining areas suitable for supporting cotton and slavery were those belonging to Mexico. Nor was it coincidental that the United States seemed most aggressive in pursuit of Mexican territory when southerners occupied the White House. The Tennessean, Andrew Jackson, had encouraged the revolutionaries in Texas by ignoring the illegal activities of American citizens, and in the early eighteen forties Texas annexation had been most vigorously pursued by another southerner, President John Tyler of Virginia. Tyler's director of foreign policy, Secretary of State Abel P. Upshur, also was a Virginian and an extreme advocate of the southern, pro-slavery position. Upon Upshur's accidental death, none other than John C. Calhoun, the political and intellectual leader of the southern extremists became Secretary of State. During 1843 and 1844 these men made annexation their principal goal, and made no secret of their desire to acquire Texas in order to expand slavery. In the 1844 presidential election the issue of expansion dominated the campaign, and the victory of James K. Polk of Tennessee became a national mandate for annexation.

This clear connection between slavery and expansion prompted many Mexicans to denounce the hypocrisy of a nation proclaiming democratic principles, the equality of man and other lofty ideals while seeking to "expand the area of freedom" by eradicating Indians and trampling upon their rights of a neighboring nation in order to expand the institution of human slavery. Mexicans were fundamentally opposed to the institution of slavery and upon gaining independence had abolished the institution. For this reason alone many Mexicans opposed American expansion. But a more factor explaining this opposition was the Mexican sense of pride and honor, an acute sensitivity to insults real and imagined, an attitude which caused Mexicans to feel that yielding to the Americans in Texas and elsewhere would be a loss of not only territory but of self-respect. Having once expressed a determination to retain Texas at all costs, to do otherwise would be to surrender pride and honor, to disgrace Mexico in the eyes of the world by demonstrating her inability to preserve her territorial integrity.

It was only natural that the Mexican sense of honor was further offended by the arrogant, condescending attitude of Americans toward Mexicans, which in its more extreme form did approach the racist views of many Americans toward Indians and blacks. American officials gave the impression that Mexicans were undeserving of respect and that Mexican officials and diplomatic representatives were not entitled to the dignified, courteous treatment normally accorded other nations. During the Texas revolution, for instance, the Mexican minister to the United States was Manuel Eduardo de Gorostiza, an urbane, cultivated playwright and man of letters The Jackson administration rudely and contemptuously dismissed Gorostiza's legitimate complaints concerning American violations of neutrality agreements. The arrogant conduct of American officials so deeply offended and insulted Gorostiza that he never forgave the United States for subjecting him to such indignities. Upon returning to Mexico he became one of the more influential and outspoken opponents of the United States.

American diplomatic representatives in Mexico displayed similar attitudes. Poinsett had launched diplomatic relations on a note of discord, his chief offense having been his failure to recognize that American interference in the internal affairs of Mexico would offend the Mexican sense of national integrity and that Mexicans would he insulted by the assumption of American superiority which motivated his conduct. When the Mexican government requested Poinsett's recall, he was replaced by Anthony Butler, a crude, overbearing, obnoxious person who was bent on the acquisition of Texas and who climaxed his offensive tour by publicly threatening to cane the Mexican foreign minister should he encounter the Mexican official on the streets. At this point the Mexican government requested that Butler, like Poinsett before him, be removed. But the diplomatic successors to Poinsett and Butler continued to be offensive, arrogant, and insulting. In 1842, for instance, when American naval forces seized Monterey in Mexican California, the American minister to Mexico informed his superiors in the Tyler administration that on the premise that the best defense was an offense, he had avoided apologizing for the unwarranted seizure of Monterey and instead attacked the Mexican government for exaggerating the importance of the incident, if not for actually provoking it.

One effect of sending such people to Mexico to represent the United States was to convince Mexicans that they were held in low esteem by Americans. Chauvinism also affected the nature of the reports concerning conditions in Mexico that American diplomats sent to Washington. Upon such biased information American leaders based their knowledge of Mexico, her people, and their public affairs In other words, American officials in Mexico gave offense to Mexicans and at the same time reinforced the widely shared view of Americans that Mexicans were indeed inferior and helpless, undeserving of respect. The pro-southern, pro-slavery, and racist sentiment of most presidential administrations in the United States between 1821 and 1846 also were reflected in the persons appointed to represent the United States in Mexico during those years. A total of ten men received such appointments, of whom all but one came from southern slave states. In their reports to Washington these men continually (with the exception of Poinsett, who under stood Mexican conditions and was generally sympathetic in his attitude) represented Mexicans as childlike, irresponsible, mentally and physically inferior, incapable of managing their affairs, cowardly in their defense of their imagined national honor. It was generally concluded that such people were incompetent to govern themselves or to use their land and its resources to economic advantage. Mexicans therefore deserved their treatment at the hands of the United States and though they might complain loudly were neither willing nor able to resist American acquisition of Texas or any other territory the United States might feel it convenient to acquire.

Indeed, Mexico was at that time a backward, poor, misgoverned and chaotic country, circumstances that Americans attributed to the inferiority of the Mexican people which in turn justified depriving them of their territory for reasons similar to those used to justify the dispossession of Indians from their land: Americans would use it more productively.

And in Mexico a profound sense of national honor, a deep commitment to the preservation or territorial integrity, and the awareness that Mexicans, like Indians and blacks, were viewed as inferior beings by Americans, contributed to the creation of a climate of opinion that feared the complete destruction of Mexican civilization should the nation not withstand the westward advance of the United States. One newspaper summarized these feelings by declaring that to make territorial concessions to the United States would open the door to the triumph of the Anglo-Saxon race, to the enslavement of Mexicans, to the destruction of the Mexican Church, language and customs, and to the loss of "what was most precious and dear," Mexican nationality.

Hence the determination to prevent the loss of Texas. Indeed, except for the continual struggle between centralists and federalists, Texas had become by the early eighteen forties the paramount issue in the turbulent world of Mexican politics, for it represented the ground upon which the nation's ability to survive would be tested, and all national leaders were measured by the depth of their determination to preserve Texas. Any Mexican government which appeared willing to make compromises with or concessions to the United States would not be permitted by the public or by its political opponents to remain long in power.

In 1843 General Santa Anna, who once again headed the Mexican government, announced that the annexation of Texas would result in an immediate declaration of war against the United States. But Santa Anna failed to demonstrate sufficient opposition to the United States during 1844, and the issue was therefore turned against him by his political enemies, who now accused him of having abandoned Texas in 1836 and of repeating his crime by failing to respond more energetically to the renewed threat resulting from the outcome of the presidential election in the United States. In December, 1844, General Mariano Paredes y Arrillaga led a successful revolt against Santa Anna and installed General José Joaquin de Herrera in the presidency, who avowed that the new government would more vigorously oppose American expansion.

When James K. Polk entered the White House following his inauguration in the spring of 1845, the annexation of Texas was an accomplished fact, and because of Mexico's threats to declare war in such an event, Polk ordered an army commanded by General Zachary Taylor to assume a position on the gulf coast of Texas to guard against the threatened Mexican invasion. The Mexican minister to the United States registered his protest by returning to Mexico and ending formal diplomatic relations with the United States. However, President Herrera discovered soon after taking office that his nation was in no condition to support a war against the United States. His treasury was empty and the country lacked the resources to improve its ill-equipped and starving army. Mexico therefore did not declare war, and it appeared toward the end of 1845 that the United States had acquired Texas without having to fight for it.

But the crisis was not yet over, for the spirit of Manifest Destiny was abroad in the United States, and the Polk administration was determined to carry out a wide program of expansion that included acquiring even more territory from an already deeply offended Mexico. In addition to Texas annexation the Democrats had included on their expansionist platform of 1844 the acquisition of the entire Oregon territory which, if achieved, would mean ending a long-standing agreement of joint occupation with England. To succeed in his expansionist program Polk thus risked the possibility of war with both England and Mexico. But once again, the abiding sectional controversy had a direct influence upon the course of American expansion.

In the southern slave states there was little interest in acquiring all of Oregon because that region was clearly not suited to support cotton and slavery. It was primarily the middle west that coveted Oregon as a territory that would eventually produce a number of free states. Polk and the Democrats had sought votes in these states by including Oregon on their platform, but once in office, the new administration appeared to be devoted exclusively to serving the interests of the south. Among other things, its banking and tariff policies were designed to please southerners, who were already delighted by the successful conclusion of Texas annexation. Yet the new president was equally determined to acquire California from Mexico.

California had not been an issue in the 1844 campaign, but Mexicans nonetheless suspected that it would become the next of their territories to be threatened by the United States, and President Polk set out during 1845 to confirm these suspicions Polk recognized that Mexico, already deeply offended by the annexation of Texas, might go to war over California, and American insistence upon all of Oregon might also provoke a war with England. The president, therefore, decided to prevent such dangerous developments by compromising -- over Oregon. Despite his pledge to those northerners who were interested in the region, that he would acquire the entire territory of Oregon to the 54^0, 40' parallel, Polk now decided to accept far less. As it happened, England was at that time preoccupied with affairs at home, wished if possible to avoid a war with the United States, and was therefore willing to agree to a compromise. But it was not until mid-1846 that the two nations agreed that the boundary should be drawn at the forth-ninth parallel. By this time war had erupted between Mexico and the United States, and the Mexicans may have been encouraged by the possibility of a war between the United States and England over Oregon. In the United States many northerners were disappointed at the Oregon compromise, feeling that their interests had been abandoned by a president dedicated solely to serving the south.

In the meantime Polk had begun to seek the real object of his expansionist program, California. The American president hoped to do this peacefully through negotiation, but formal diplomatic relations did not exist in 1845 since Mexico had recalled her minister to the United States in displeasure over Texas annexation. But during the fall of 1845, the Polk administration was delighted to learn from the American consul in Mexico City that the Mexican government was willing to receive a "commissioner" from the United States to discuss the settlement of issues dividing the two countries. As far as Mexico was concerned, these issues were American claims and Texas, but decidedly not California. Here it seemed was the diplomatic opening that might lead to peaceful acquisition of California -- or so it appeared to Polk. In November 1845 he dispatched John Slidell of Louisiana to Mexico with instructions to offer up to twenty-five million dollars for California, if in return the Mexican government would recognize the Rio Grande River as the boundary between Texas and Mexico.

The Herrera administration's offer to renew relations with the United States reflected its realization that Mexico was too weak to wage war over Texas annexation, but it did not indicate willingness to surrender California. The Mexican government had attempted throughout 1845 to convince the public that it would not be a disgraceful blow to the national honor for Mexico to recognize the permanent loss of Texas and to receive for it a payment from the United States which would help to relieve the nation's financial problems. Nevertheless, when Slidell reached Mexico in December, 1845, he was not received by the Herrera administration, partly because the American envoy was authorized to discuss not only claims and Texas, but also California, and partly because the Herrera administration had failed to receive public support for its conciliatory policy. The Mexican public by this time was so rigidly hostile to the United States that it viewed as treasonous any attempt to compromise with the Americans. Herrera therefore sought to retain public support by refusing to negotiate with Slidell. The last-ditch effort was to no avail, for in December, 1845, Herrera was replaced by General Paredes, the leader of the earlier revolt through which Herrera had first come to power. Paredes announced that the government would be implacably opposed to the United States.

When the Polk administration learned of Slidell's rejection in January, 1846, it ordered General Taylor's army to depart Corpus Christi and to proceed to the Rio Grande. Mexico viewed this tactic as a highly aggressive measure, considering it an American invasion of Mexican territory. The traditional and generally recognized boundary between Texas and the Mexican states of Coahuila, Nuevo Leon, and Tamaulipas was the Nueces River, which entered the Gulf of Mexico some 150 miles north of the Rio Grande. The Polk administration supported the Texas claim to a Rio Grande boundary, a rather flimsy assertion based solely on a treaty signed by Santa Anna after his capture at the battle of San Jacinto in 1836. Mexican authorities and

Santa Anna himself, upon release by the Texans, repudiated this claim; nor was it taken seriously by anyone other than Texans and their expansionist allies in the United States. Consequently the Mexicans had reason to believe Taylor's advance across the disputed territory between the Nueces and the Rio Grande was the beginning of the long-feared American invasion.

The other point of controversy between the two nations was the long-standing issue of American claims against Mexico, upon which no installments had been paid since 1844. Despite the absence of formal diplomatic relations during the months of late 1845 and early 1846, the American consul in Mexico City and a "confidential agent," William Parrott, kept Polk informed of events in Mexico. Both observers repeatedly sent word that Mexico was in a state of utter economic collapse and was financially unable to continue installments on the American claims. It would seem, then, that Mexico defaulted more because of her bankrupt condition than out a bad faith.

The Polk administration also learned from its agents in the Mexican capital that Mexico offered no military threat to the United States. When General Paredes seized the presidency in December, 1845, he vowed to take a strong stance against the Americans, but he soon discovered that the nation was in no condition to wage war. Almost daily, the Mexican president received word from his generals on the frontier adjacent to Texas that the army was pitifully unprepared to curb an American advance; to launch offensive operations was out of the question. Communications reporting similar conditions also came to Paredes from garrisons throughout Mexico. All of this was known to the American consul and to William Parrott, who passed the information on to Washington. The American informants described in detail the dilemma that had led to Herrera's fall and which his successor, General Paredes, had inherited: the army was weak; the nation's resources were inadequate; chaos and confusion prevailed; yet the public, the press, and the political opposition clamored for war. But Polk's agents in Mexico gave repeated assurances that, even if the opposition should overthrow Paredes, war would not result. The agents believed that the criticism of the Mexican president for his failure to act was only a political device through which the opposition hoped to seize power, and that they too would then recognize the folly of fighting the United States.

Furthermore, the Mexican government had received word from its representatives in England and France that neither of those nations could be relied upon to assist Mexico in a war against the United States. This dismal news further increased Mexico's reluctance to become involved in such a war. However, the Polk administration was not aware of this development, nor did it know with absolute certainty during the early months of 1846 that England would indeed compromise over Oregon. Only here, then, in the possible intervention of England on the side of Mexico, could the Polk administration have seen a potential threat to the United States, for it was abundantly clear that Mexico, acting alone, offered none.

The most important history of the war between the United States and Mexico yet to appear is Justin H. Smith's *The War With Mexico*, published in 1919. So thorough was Smith in his research that his book has deeply influenced all subsequent accounts of the war. He believed that Mexico desired war with the United States and that her leaders were supremely confident of their nation's ability to win such a war. According to Smith, Mexicans remembered that the United States had performed poorly from a military standpoint in the War of 1812; they believed their army to be larger and stronger, and they assumed that in the event of war, the slaves would revolt and fight along-side Mexicans against their white masters. Smith suggested also that Mexicans were further encouraged by the promise of foreign assistance, especially from England. To Smith the United States was patient and forbearing toward Mexico, seeking in every way possible to avoid war. Until the appearance in 1973 of David M. Pletcher's work, *The Diplomacy of Annexation; Texas, Oregon and the Mexican War*, no American historian since Smith utilized Mexican documentation in analyzing the origins of the war. While Pletcher's excellent diplomatic study does not overtly attack Smith's work, it does include material that undermines Smith's interpretation of Mexican bellicosity. Other writers have criticized the United States for its aggressive pursuit of Mexican territory, but they have not challenged Smith's basic assertion that Mexico was herself warlike and confident of victory.

Smith's error lay in his use of the anti-Americanism of the public and of the press and of the demands for war from the political opponents of Presidents Herrera and Paredes as the genuine attitude of the Mexican government. Many Mexicans did demand war and did express confidence in their ability to win such a contest, but these Mexicans were not in power and were therefore not so painfully aware of the nation's weaknesses. In any event, if Mexico sought a war with the United States, why did she not use the occasion of Texas annexation as the reason for launching it? Mexicans had threatened for years that this would be her response to annexation. Yet more than a year passed between the annexation of Texas and the outbreak of war in April, 1846, during which the Mexican government, as duly reported to President Polk by Americans in Mexico, sought peace. Indeed the war came only after the entrance of General Taylor's army into territory Mexicans considered theirs, an event

251

accompanied by other American military measures that appeared most threatening to Mexico.

Thus, by the beginning of 1846 President Polk was frustrated in his efforts to acquire California peacefully. It probably seemed perfectly reasonable to the president and to his associates that Mexico should be willing to negotiate with their envoy, Slidell, for the sale of California to the United States. Mexico did not, after all, exercise very firm control of California. The distant territory received little attention from the government, its residents were not strongly attached to the Mexican nation and frequently revolted against Mexican authorities. Therefore, by selling California, Mexico could rid herself of the difficult task of trying to govern the troublesome province and receive in payment a handsome sum, which would help relieve the over-burdened Mexican treasury of its bankruptcy. Logical as such calculations may have seemed to the Polk administration, they did not take sufficiently into account that Mexicans considered their national honor and cultural survival to be at stake and that the public mood in Mexico was so hostile to the United States that the Mexican government simply could not negotiate the sale of additional territory. Consequently, President Paredes continued the inaction of his predecessor, Herrera, and refused to recognize the American envoy, Slidell.

Relations between the two nations were tense by March, 1846: Texas annexation had been achieved a year earlier and Mexico had not responded with the threatened declaration of war; the American claim to the Rio Grande boundary had been established by General Taylor's advance during the early months of that year, and once again Mexico had failed to respond by declaring war; and for two years Mexico had failed to pay installments on American claims against her. President Polk wanted California, but Mexico would not negotiate a peaceful transfer of that territory.

Mexican officials may have been playing a waiting game, hoping for a war between England and the United States over Oregon, but President Polk was not one to play waiting games. If Mexico would not peacefully cede California then sterner measures were required. Throughout March and into April, 1846, tensions intensified between the two nations. Attention was focused on the Rio Grande, where General Taylor was now encamped with his army, his artillery aimed at the town of Matamoros on the south bank of the river. Still the Mexican army on the Rio Grande waited, urgently, but vainly, requesting reinforcements and supplies. In early April General Taylor established a blockade at the mouth of the Rio Grande, a measure generally recognized as an act of war. It was expected that a Mexican attack would occur, launching the war by which California would be acquired. John C. Fremont, the "pathfinder," was already in California on an "exploratory" expedition, accompanied by armed troops. Fremont received word that in the event of war with Mexico he was to aid American settlers in California in a revolt against Mexican authority. But if the Mexicans, despite American provocations, would not attack, how then could the United States begin the war without appearing to be the obvious aggressor? At this point the unpaid claims provided Polk with what seemed to him just cause for declaring war. The president prepared a message requesting Congress to declare war against Mexico because she had refused to pay American claims. Congress would very likely have been reluctant to declare war on such grounds, but before delivering his war message, Polk learned that in late April a small unit of the Mexican army on the Rio Grande had crossed to the north bank and engaged a detachment of Taylor's army in a brief skirmish. Alert to the implications of this event, President Polk requested Congress to declare war as a defensive measure, for "American blood," said the president, had been shed on "American soil."

To this day historians remain divided over the causes of the war between the United States and Mexico. Those who believe that Mexico was to blame stress her failure to pay American claims as sufficient reason in itself for the United States to have gone to war, especially when Mexico refused the offer of peace presented by John Slidell mission to Mexico. They can also point to the insistent demands for war which emanated from a large body of the Mexican public and the confidence expressed by many Mexicans as evidence of Mexican belligerence that made war unavoidable despite American patience and forbearance. Moreover, there was Mexico's refusal to recognize Texas independence and the presence of a large Mexican army on the Rio Grande which seemed to be a threat that required American action. Finally, it is true that Mexicans fired the first shot.

To the contrary, defenders of Mexico can point to the flimsy grounds upon which American financial claims against Mexico were based, the relatively small sum of the claims (about two million dollars) as a poor excuse for war, and the fact that many states in the United States were themselves guilty of defaulting at this very time on large sums owed to European creditors. Besides, it was highly questionable whether Polk's justification for a declaration of war was legitimate, since the area between the Nueces and the Rio Grande, where "American blood" had been shed, was at best disputed territory rather than "American soil." Despite the widespread clamor for war in Mexico, American agents had repeatedly informed the Polk administration that the Mexican army was in no condition to wage war and that Mexican leaders, aware of their weakness, would not respond to the war-like demands of those who were out of power. As for the Slidell mission, President Paredes declared that it was impossible to negotiate when an American army was upon Mexican territory and the American navy in Mexican waters, for to negotiate implies a willingness to give and take, and under these circumstances Mexico could only surrender to American demands. President Polk had not seen fit to mention in his war message that when the initial clash took place American troops under John C. Fremont were already in California, that other American troops stood ready to take New Mexico, that American warships hovered near Veracruz and off Mexico's Pacific coast, or that the blockade of the Rio Grande was itself an act of war.

It seems unlikely that the United States would have resorted to war merely to collect its claims against Mexico, nor was the disputed boundary an issue in itself sufficient to touch off hostilities, for in both nations it was seldom mentioned prior to the war. The annexation of Texas had been accomplished well over a year before the war broke out, and was therefore at most only an indirect cause. Mexicans appeared willing, after all, to discuss with an American envoy a settlement of the claims issue and the Texas boundary. What they would not and could not entertain was the American offer to purchase California, a territory that President Polk was equally determined to acquire. Possession of California seems, then, to have been the central issue causing the war.

If Mexico was indeed aware that she was outmatched by the United States militarily, she suffered from an empty treasury, and California was a distant, troublesome province, barely recognizing allegiance to Mexico in any event, then why did the Mexican government not avoid war by recognizing Slidell and selling California, using the proceeds to help relieve her financial distress? Why, in short, was Mexico unalterably opposed to surrendering, through purchase or otherwise, additional territory to the United States?

Mexican honor, dignity, and pride were involved. For two decades Mexican opinion had been prepared to oppose American expansion at Mexico's expense, and relations between the two nations during these two decades had been marked by American insults and contempt toward Mexico. There was genuine fear that should Mexicans fall under American control the result would be national destruction and cultural extinction at the hands of a racist people who viewed Mexicans, like Indians and blacks, as inferior beings.

Once the war was under way, events quickly proved the superiority of American arms. General Taylor defeated Mexican forces at Matamoros and then advanced well into the interior to further successes at Monterrey and Saltillo. Both California and

New Mexico were conquered by the close of 1846. In early 1847 General Winfield Scott led an invasion of central Mexico, landing at Veracruz and advancing rapidly upon the capital, Mexico City, which he seized in September, 1847. With an utterly defeated Mexico under American domination, all that now remained was for the United States to determine how much Mexican territory it wished to keep.

The war had touched off rancorous debate in the United States. Both opponents and defenders of the war could be found in all sections and in both political parties but in general terms it was New England and the Whig party that harbored the most vocal and enthusiastic opposition; from the south and the west and from the Democratic Party came the staunchest support.

One critic was an obscure, first-term Illinois Congressman, Abraham Lincoln, who on a number of occasions introduced what became known as "spot resolutions," requesting President Polk to identify the precise spot on a map where American blood had been shed, implying that the President had misled the nation in his justification for declaring war. Lincoln, like many others, was aware that the initial clash had occurred on disputed territory, not American soil. Other critics frequently appealed to justice and morality, insisting that the United States had committed aggressions against an unoffending neighbor for the purpose of territorial conquest. More important, since it was impossible in the United States of the eighteen forties to isolate slavery and sectionalism from any other public issue, opponents often accused the Polk administration of waging an unjust war for the evil purpose of extending slavery. This point of view, after the outbreak of hostilities, led to the "Wilmot Proviso", an amendment to an appropriations bill in Congress that would exclude slavery from any territories which might be acquired from Mexico. Though defeated, the Wilmot Proviso was frequently reintroduced, thus kindling constant congressional debate and clearly linking the objectives of the war to the slavery controversy.

Support for the war was strong among those who believed it disloyal to oppose the war effort when the lives of American soldiers were at stake, and the Polk administration often accused its opponents of aiding the enemy by encouraging Mexico to continue resisting. The principal support came from those who desired to "expand the area of freedom" by acquiring territory from Mexico. The basic question was the extent of Mexican territory to be retained, and it is interesting that as the war progressed some who spoke loudest in favor of acquiring "all Mexico" were those who had originally opposed the war and who were most opposed to the expansion of slavery. Their new rationale was based on the belief that the Mexican people ignorant, impoverished, exploited, and apparently incapable of self government, would only profit from having the "blessings of liberty" bestowed upon them by being incorporated into the United States; moreover, since the new territory appeared unsuitable for cotton farming, it would not support slavery and would therefore expand the power and influence of the free states in the Union. On the other hand, many who originally favored the war reversed their position upon realizing that the Mexican territory was not suitable for the expansion of slavery. Furthermore, many Americans were deterred by the tear that the acquisition of all Mexico would perhaps mean the granting of citizenship and constitutional guarantees of equal rights to several million Mexicans, whom they believed incapable of assuming the responsibilities of American citizenship.

Thus, just as racist attitudes had affected American relations with Mexico for the entire period between Poinsett's mission and the outbreak of war, similar attitudes would help influence the American decision not to acquire all of the conquered nation. In 1848, the war was ended by the Treaty of Guadalupe Hidalgo whereby the United States retained only California and New Mexico (which included the territory comprising the present states of Arizona, Nevada, Utah, and parts of New Mexico, Colorado, and Wyoming), consisting of some one million, two hundred thousand square miles of land, approximately one half of the Mexican nation.

"Manifest Destiny" was itself a racist notion, connoting an American self-image of racial, cultural, and institutional superiority, justifying the contemptuous disregard for the rights of weaker peoples who had been left unprepared by their history and culture to cope with the greater physical force of the United States. Inevitable though it may have been that the United States would expand to the Pacific at Mexico's expense, it is to be regretted that she did so by invoking the will of God to justify the principal that "might makes right."

Suggestions for Reading

Eugene C. Barker, *Mexico and Texas, 1821-1835* (Dallas, 1928). Still the best account of the origins of the Texas issue. Gene M. Brack, "Mexican Opinion, American Racism, and the War of 1846." *Western Historical Quarterly*, 1 (April, 1970), 161-74. Documents many of the assertions in the foregoing essay. Bernard Devoto, *The Year of Decision, 1846* (Boston, 1942). A classic, of great literary distinction. Robert Selph Henry, *The Story of the Mexican War* (New York, 1950). The best and most complete modern account of military affairs. Frederick Merk, *Manifest Destiny and Mission in American History, A Reinterpretation* (New York,

1963). Brilliant analysis of motives and methods underlying American expansionism. The serious student should also consult Merk's other works on this topic. David M. Pletcher *The Diplomacy of Annexation; Texas, Oregon, and the Mexican War* (Columbia, Mo., 1978). The best account of the diplomatic background. Charles Grier Sellers, *James K Polk, Continentaltalist: 1843-1846* (Princeton, 1966). Excellent treatment of Polk's activities. Justin H. Smith, *The War With Mexico*, 2 vols. (New York, 1919).

extraordinary
exceptional
first-time

finished
terminated

give up
surrender
abandon

power
rule
control
dominion

The Treaty of Guadalupe Hidalgo ended the Mexican American War of 1846-1848 and defined the terms of peace. Article V culminated United States expansionistic schemes on Mexican territory dating back to the early 19th century. It forced Mexico to relinquish sovereignty over its northern frontier zones, todays American Southwest. Ultimately these regions would become the states of California, Arizona, New Mexico, Colorado and Nevada. In addition, portions of the states of Texas, Utah and Wyoming would be absorbed by the United States through Article V. For Mexico, the treaty represented an unprecedented national humiliation highlighted by the loss of approximately fifty percent of its national territory. For the United States, it culminated the successful conclusion of expansion on the North American continent. For the newly incorporated Mexicans who resided in these territories, estimated to be as many as 120,000, Articles VIII, IX and X promised unprecedented property, civil, constitutional, and religious protections. Richard Griswold del Castillo, in an article in this section, uncovers the United States governments failure to honor the letter and spirit of this international treaty.

The Treaty of Guadalupe Hidalgo, Selected Articles

authorize
approve
sanction
endorse
consent

Mexico: February 2, 1848

Treaty of Guadalupe Hidalgo. Treaty of Peace, Friendship, Limits, and Settlement (with additional and secret article which was not ratified), with Map of the United Mexican States and with Plan of the Port of San Diego, signed at Guadalupe Hidalgo February 2, 1848. Originals of the treaty and additional secret article in English and Spanish.

Treaty and additional and secret article submitted to the Senate February 23, 1848. Ratified by the United States March 16, 1848. Ratified by Mexico May 30, 1848. Ratifications exchanged at Querétaro May 30, 1848. Proclaimed July 4, 1848.

Article V.

The Boundary line between the two Republics shall commence in the Gulf of Mexico, three leagues from land, opposite the mouth of the Rio Grande, otherwise called Rio Bravo del Norte, or opposite the mouth of its deepest branch, if it should have more than one branch emptying directly into the sea; from thence, up the middle of that river, following the deepest channel, where it has more than one, to the point where it strikes the southern boundary of New Mexico; thence, westwardly, along the whole southern boundary of New Mexico (which runs north of the town called *Paso*) to its western termination; thence, northward, along the western line of New Mexico, until it intersects the first branch of the River Gila; (or if it should not intersect any branch of that river, then, to the point on the said line nearest to such branch, and thence in a direct line to the same) thence down the middle of the said branch and of the said river, until it empties into the Rio Colorado, following the division line between Upper and Lower California, to the Pacific Ocean.

The southern and western limits of New Mexico, mentioned in this Article, are those laid down in the Map, entitled *"Map of the United Mexican States, as organized and defined by various acts of the Congress of said Republic, and constructed according to the best authorities. Revised Edition. Published at New York in 1847 by J. Disturnell:"* of which Map a Copy is added to this Treaty, bearing the signatures and seals of the Undersigned Plenipotentiaries. And, in order to preclude all difficulty in tracing upon the ground the limit separating Upper from Lower California, it is agreed that the said limit shall consist of a straight line, drawn from the middle of the Rio Gila, where it unites with the Colorado, to a point on the coast of the Pacific Ocean, distant one marine league due south of the southernmost point of the Port of San Diego, according to the plan of said port, made in the 1782, by Don Juan Pantoja, second-sailing master of the Spanish fleet, and published at Madrid in the year 1802, in the Atlas to the voyage of the schooners *Sutil* and *Mexicana*: of which plan a copy is hereunto added, signed and sealed by the respective plenipotentiaries.

In order to designate the Boundary line with due precision, upon authoritative maps, and to establish upon the ground landmarks which shall show the limits of both Republics, as described in the present Article, the two Governments shall each appoint a Commissioner and a Surveyor, who, before the expiration of one year from the date of the exchange of ratifications of this treaty, shall meet at the Port of San Diego, and proceed to run and mark the said boundary in its whole course, to the mouth of the Rio Bravo del Norte. They shall keep journals and make out plans of their operations; and the result, agreed upon by them, shall be deemed a part of this Treaty, and shall have the same force as if it were inserted therein. The two Governments will amicably agree regarding what may be necessary to these persons, and also as to their respective escorts, should such be necessary.

The Boundary line established by this Article shall be religiously respected by each of the two Republics, and no change shall ever be made therein, except by the express and free content of both nations, lawfully given by the General Government of each, in conformity with its own constitution.

Article VIII.

Mexicans now established in territories previously belonging to Mexico, and which remain for the future within the limits of the United States, as defined by the present treaty, shall be free to continue where they now reside, or to remove at any time to the Mexican Republic, retaining the property which they possess in the said territories, or disposing thereof, and removing the proceeds wherever they please; without their being subjected, on this account, to any contribution, tax or charge whatever.

Those who shall prefer to remain in said territories, may either retain the title and rights of Mexican citizens, or acquire those of citizens of the United States. But they shall be under the obligation to make their election within one year from the date of the exchange of ratifications of this treaty: and those who shall remain in the said territories, after the expiration of that year, without having declared their intention to retain the character of Mexicans, shall be considered to have elected to become citizens of the United States.

In the said territories, property of every kind, now belonging to Mexicans, not established there, shall be inviolably respected. The present owners, the heirs of these, and all Mexicans who may hereafter acquire said property by contract, shall enjoy with respect to it, guaranties equally ample as if the same belonged to citizens of the United States.

Article IX.

The Mexicans who, in the territories aforesaid, shall not preserve the character of the citizens of the Mexican Republic, conformably with what is stipulated in the preceding article, shall be incorporated into the Union of the United States and be admitted, at the proper time (to be judged of by the Congress of the United States) to the enjoyment of all the rights of citizens of the United States according to the principles of the Constitution; and in the mean time shall be maintained and protected in the free enjoyment of their liberty and property, and secured in the free exercise of their religion without restriction.

Article X.
(*prior to its omission by the United States Senate*)

All grants of land made by the Mexican Government or by the competent authorities, in territories previously appertaining to Mexico, and remaining for the future within the limits of the United States, shall be respected as valid, to the same extent that the same grants would be valid, if the said territories had remained within the limits of Mexico. But the grantees of land in Texas, put in possession thereof, who, by the reason of circumstances of the country since the beginning of the troubles between Texas and the Mexican Government, may have been prevented from fulfilling all the conditions of their grants, shall be under the obligation to fulfill the said conditions within the periods limited in the same respectively; such periods to be now counted from the date of the exchange of ratifications of this treaty: in the default of which the said grants shall not be obligatory upon the State of Texas, in virtue of the stipulations contained in this Article.

The foregoing stipulation in regard to grantees of land in Texas, is extended to all grantees of land in the territories aforesaid, elsewhere than in Texas, put in possession under such grants; and, in default of the fulfillment of the conditions of any such grant, within the new period, which, as is above stipulated, begins with the day of the exchange of ratifications of this treaty, the same shall be null and void.

The Mexican Government declares that no grant whatever of lands in Texas has been made since the second day of March one thousand eight hundred and thirty six; and that no grant whatever of lands in any of the territories aforesaid has been made since the thirteenth day of May one thousand eight hundred and forty-six.

After United States Senate ratification of the Treaty of Guadalupe Hidalgo, Mexican and American commissioners met to discuss and explain changes and omissions to the treaty. Of particular interest to Mexican officials was the alteration of Article IX and the omission of Article X. The Protocol of Querétaro, originally an oral explanation, was subsequently placed into written form and submitted to Mexican commissioners. Mexican officials were apparently satisfied that the omission of Article 10 did not endanger the Mexican-held land grants and that language in the Protocol, the second paragraph in particular, would provide the legal framework for such protections. Satisfied that these changes would not result in subsequent denials of the intent of the articles, the Mexican commissioners accepted what came to be known as the Protocol of Querétaro.

The Protocol of Querétaro
May 26, 1848

Protocol

In the city of Querétaro on the twenty sixth of the month of May eighteen hundred and forty-eight at a conference between Their Excellencies Nathan Clifford and Ambrose H. Sevier Commissioners of the United States of America, with full powers from their Government to make to the Mexican Republic suitable explanations in regard to the amendments which the Senate and the Government of the said United States have made in the treaty of peace, friendship, limits and definitive settlement between the two Republics, signed in Guadalupe Hidalgo, on the second day of February of the present year, and His Excellency Don Luis de la Rosa, Minister of Foreign Affairs of the Republic of Mexico, it was agreed, after adequate conversation respecting the changes alluded to, to record in the present protocol the following explanations which Their aforesaid Excellencies the Commissioners gave in the name of their Government and in fulfillment of the Commission conferred upon them near the Mexican Republic.

First.

The American Government by suppressing the IXth article of the Treaty of Guadalupe and substituting the III. article of the Treaty of Louisiana did not intend to diminish in any way what was agreed upon by the aforesaid article IXth in favor of the inhabitants of the territories ceded by Mexico. Its understanding that all of that agreement is contained in the IIId article of the Treaty of Louisiana. In consequence, all the privileges and guarantees, civil, political, and religious, which would have been possessed by the inhabitants of the ceded territories, if the IXth article of the Treaty had been retained, will be enjoyed by them without any difference under the article which had been substituted.

Second.

The American Government by suppressing the Xth article of the Treaty of Guadalupe did not in any way intend to annul the grants of lands made by Mexico in the ceded territories. These grants. notwithstanding the suppression of the article of the Treaty, preserve the legal value which they may possess; and the grantees may cause their legitimate titles to be acknowledged before the American tribunals.

Conformably to the law of the United States, legitimate titles to every description of the property personal and real, existing in the ceded territories, are those which were legitimate titles under the Mexican law in California and New Mexico up to the 13th of May 1.846, and in Texas up to the 2d March 1.836.

Third.

The Government of the United States by suppressing the concluding paragraph of the article XIIth of the Treaty, did not intend to deprive the Mexican Republic of the free and unrestrained faculty of ceding, conveying or transferring at any time (as it may judge best) the sum of twelve millions of dollars which the same Government of the United States is to deliver in the places designated by the amended article.

And these explanations having been accepted by the minister of Foreign Affairs of the Mexican Republic, he declared in name of his Government that with the understanding conveyed by them, the same Government would proceed to ratify the Treaty of Guadalupe as modified by the Senate and Government of the United States. In testimony of which their Excellencies the aforesaid Commissioners and the Minister have signed and sealed in quintuplicate the present protocol.

Richard Griswold del Castillo offers a fascinating study of the American courts and the Treaty of Guadalupe Hidalgo. The vast majority of Mexicans in the newly acquired United States territories chose to become American citizens, in part due to protections guaranteed by the treaty. But these former Mexican citizens faced political, civil, property and citizenship challenges on an unprecedented scale. They saw a systematic erosion of their rights as guaranteed by the treaty. Within a generation they "became a disenfranchised, poverty-stricken minority."

Citizenship and Property Rights: U.S. Interpretations of the Treaty

Richard Griswold del Castillo

We have come here under this treaty; gentlemen sit in this convention under this treaty; it is in virtue of this treaty alone that we are possessed of this territory. . . . If we violate the stipulations of this treaty, we violate the constitution.

Mr. Hastings
Debates in the Convention of California

Articles VIII and IX of the Treaty of Guadalupe Hidalgo set forth the terms by which the former Mexican citizens and their property would be incorporated politically into the United States. These articles in the treaty affected some 100,000 Mexicans in the newly acquired territories, including a large number of Hispanicized as well as nomadic Indians in New Mexico and California.[1] As provided by Article VIII, a person had one year to "elect" his or her preference for Mexican citizenship. If this were not done, it was stipulated that they had elected to become United States citizens and that they would be granted citizenship by Congress at some future time. The two articles also treated the property rights of the conquered people. Absentee Mexican landholders would have their property "inviolably respected," and others would "be maintained and protected in the free enjoyment of their liberty and property." In the six decades following the ratification of the treaty, its provisions regarding citizenship and property were complicated by legislative and judicial interpretations. In the end the U.S. application of the treaty to the realities of life in the Southwest violated its spirit.

[handwritten: to return a person) back to the country of birth.]

MEXICAN CITIZENSHIP AND REPATRIATION

[handwritten: abonded, let go, yield]

A number of persons living in the territories ceded to the United States chose to remain Mexican citizens, either by announcing their intent before judicial officials or by returning to Mexico. No one knows their exact number, but they were probably few in comparison to the total population in the Southwestern states and territories. The Mexican government was anxious to encourage its nationals to return to Mexico in order to populate the sparsely settled northern frontier regions. Since colonial times, Mexican governmental officials had looked toward their far northern frontier with apprehension and had tried to populate it with hardy settlers. The idea of the northern frontier as a buffer zone protecting the more civilized and wealthy settlements to the south emerged time and again in imperial planning. During the negotiation of the Treaty of Guadalupe Hidalgo, General Santa Anna proposed the creation of a buffer zone to separate the two republics. The year 1848 presented the Mexican administration with an opportunity to reorganize frontier defenses. The Mexican government hoped that new colonists migrating from the American Southwest would defend their frontier from Indian attacks as well as from U.S. incursions. ~ raid, attack, invasion

In the governmental decrees of July and of August 1848, Herreras administration drew up detailed plans to establish eighteen military colonies along the newly defined U.S.-Mexico border, which were to be populated with repatriated Mexican citizens.[2] The resettlement zone was to be divided into three sectors of colonization. Families from New Mexico would have lands reserved for them in Chihuahua; those from Texas would settle in Tamaulipas and Nuevo Leon; and those from California, in Baja California or Sonora. As an incentive, each settler over the age of fourteen would be given twenty-five pesos and his children twelve pesos each. Land, transportation, and initial living expenses were to be paid from a fund of $200,000, to come from U.S. payments provided for under the treaty.[3]

To implement this ambitious plan, beginning in 1849, the Mexican government sent three commissioners who would receive, in addition to expense money, a bounty of one peso for each settler they encouraged to move. In California several repatriation expeditions were organized but the numbers who actually left were few.[4] The Californios were unwilling to give up their mild climate for the barren deserts of Baja California or Sonora. Besides, the gold rush was a powerful reason to remain. The two commissioners to the more populous province of New Mexico, Padre Ramon Ortiz and Manuel Armendarias, met with somewhat more success. After a few months of activity, between fifteen hundred and two thousand New Mexicans reportedly left the territory, taking with them their slaves and property. According to Ortizs report, there was a great interest in repatriation; he estimated that up to eighty thousand might be induced to leave. Without doubt this number was exaggerated, but it indicated that there was widespread dissatisfaction with the U.S.

administration of the territory. The military governor of New Mexico, fearful that the Mexican commissioners might instigate a rebellion, refused to allow them to visit other New Mexico counties.[5] Repatriation efforts from New Mexico continued sporadically into the next decade, with the Mexican government making occasional protests regarding the American governments lack of cooperation in the project. Nevertheless a number of frontier towns were founded in Chihuahua by the New Mexicans who returned to Mexico: Guadalupe, La Mesilla, Santo Tomas, and Refugio.[6]

In Texas the repatriation program was a qualified success. At least 150 families left that state before ratification of the treaty, settling on lands set aside by the government. On June 22, 1850, Commissioner Antonio Menchaca brought 618 people and more than 100 families from Nacogdoches to Coahuila and requested 20,602 pesos in expenses. Other groups from Texas moved to establish new border towns or settled in existing ones on the south bank of the Rio Grande. In this way the Mexican border towns of Guerrero, Mier, Camargo, Reynosa, and Matamoros grew in size, and new towns of Nuevo Laredo, Guadalupe, and Ascension were founded.[7]

Under the provisions of the treaty, the conquered peoples of the new territories could elect to remain Mexican citizens and continue to reside in the U.S. territories. In New Mexico "a large number" chose to appear before the local county official as provided for by the governor to announce their continued Mexican citizenship. This was despite the very short interval allowed for them to declare their intention of remaining Mexican citizens (between April 21, 1849 and May 30, 1849). Their names were published and circulated among the county officials to prevent future voter frauds. There were, however, a number of problems that arose when those who declared their Mexican citizenship changed their mind later on and petitioned to become U.S. citizens without success. Approximately two thousand New Mexicans declared to retain their Mexican citizenship. There is no record that Mexicans in California or Texas chose to remain Mexican citizens.[8]

UNITED STATES CITIZENSHIP

Article IX provided that those who did not choose to remain Mexican citizens would be considered "to have elected" to become U.S. citizens. As early as 1849 the nature of the citizenship rights of these Mexicans became the subject of controversy. In California the delegates to the state constitutional convention wrestled with the problems of race, rights of citizenship, and the Treaty of Guadalupe Hidalgo. Six of the delegates were native Californios (former Mexican citizens) who were aware that Mexicans who looked like Indians faced the prospect of racial discrimination. Ultimately they argued for the protection of their class even if it meant endorsing the racist views of their Anglo colleagues towards Indians and Blacks. Mexico had granted citizenship to "civilized" Indians and to Blacks, and the Treaty of Guadalupe Hidalgo clearly stated that former Mexican citizens would be given the opportunity to become citizens of the United States. Following the biases of their age, the framers of the state constitution sought wording that would exclude Blacks and Indians while including Mexicans. A Mr. Edward Gilbert introduced a proposal that eventually became the first section of the state constitution defining suffrage. It extended the vote to "every white, male citizen of Mexico who shall have elected to become a citizen of the United States." The convention agreed that Indians and Blacks might at some future date be given the franchise but that because voting was not an absolute right of citizenship, they could be excluded. There was some concern over whether in fact the Mexicans remaining were citizens of the United States. Ultimately the delegates that agreed that "it would seem that they are not in fact American citizens, but require some further action of congress to make them citizens of the United States."[9] Californias admission as a state presumably would be that conferring act. (Later court cases challenge this assumption.) The ambiguous citizenship of the Californios meant that they could not expect the full protection of the laws during a stressful and violent period in Californias history.

The discovery of gold in 1848 created a situation in which thousands of Yankee immigrants were competing with native-born Californio miners in the gold fields. One estimate is that about thirteen hundred native Californios were in the gold regions in 1848 and that probably an equal number returned in 1849.[10] Xenophobia, nativism, residuals of war-time patriotism, and racism resulted in violent confrontations between English speaking immigrants and other residents. Eventually, most of the latter were driven from the most profitable gold fields. As a consequence of vigilantism and its attendant lynchings, harassment, and abuse of "foreigners," several countries lodged diplomatic protests and financial claims against the U.S. government. The Mexican government was active in lodging formal complaints in Washington, D.C., even though many of them lacked specificity. As late as 1853 the Mexican ambassador to Washington, Larráinzar, protested the treatment of Mexican miners in California, invoking the protections of the Treaty of Guadalupe Hidalgo. The American secretary of state responded that it was not clear that the treaty was being violated since there was a legal distinction between the Mexicans who had migrated to California after 1848 and those who were there before the gold rush.[11] Generally the Mexican government failed to present clear evidence that native Californios were being deprived of their property and civil rights in violation of the treaty.

There was evidence to substantiate the charges. In 1849 the military governor of California, General Percifor Smith, responding to nativist fears that foreigners were taking all the gold out of the mining regions, announced his "trespass" orders prohibiting non-citizens from mining gold on public property. He appealed to Americans to help him enforce his policy and under the protection of the military, Anglo-American miners robbed and harassed foreigners. In his reminiscences, Antonio Coronel, a native Californio from Los Angeles, vividly described stabbings, extortions, and lynchings as commonplace American reactions to native Californios, whom they regarded as interlopers. Some Spanish-speaking natives were issued passes, supposed proof of their new status as citizens of the United States, but this had little effect on the hordes of people crowding into the mining district from the eastern United States. Because neither the mass of Americans nor the Mexican government considered the Californio citizens, they were without the juridical protection of either nation.

The violations of their rights under the Treaty of Guadalupe Hidalgo were finally tested in the U.S. courts. In the California Supreme Court case of *People v. Naglee* (1851), the issue was whether or not a newly enacted Foreign Miners Tax Law violated the U.S. Constitution, the Treaty of Guadalupe Hidalgo, or the California State Constitution.[12] The defense argued, "It does not appear that this act [the Foreign Miners Tax Law] has ever been enforced against any person entitled to the benefit of this treaty or even against any citizen of Mexico." The Foreign Miners Tax Law specifically exempted Mexicans who had become U.S. citizens under the treaty. In the Naglee case the defense did not introduce evidence of the violation of treaty rights.[13] The prosecution, on the other hand, argued that the law should apply to Mexican Americans because they were not yet officially U.S. citizens. This view was rejected by the court but it reemerged twenty years later in the case of *People v. de la Guerra* (1870).

In *People v. de la Guerra,* the status of the former Mexican citizens finally was resolved. Pablo de la Guerra, a venerable Californio landholder who signed the California Constitution, ran for district judge in 1869. His political opponents in that election challenged his right to office based on the argument that he, along with thousands of other Californios, had only elected to become citizens of the United States under the provisions in the treaty. In fact, none of these people were yet citizens because Congress had not yet formally given them citizenship. The California Supreme Court ruled against this view in de la Guerra's favor, stating that the admission of California as a state constituted the positive act that conferred citizenship on former Mexican nationals.[14]

The fate of the California Indians is further evidence of the violation of the spirit of the treaty. Under the Mexican Constitution of 1824, Indians were considered full Mexican citizens. Upon the transfer of territory to the U.S. government, however, the Indians received neither U.S. citizenship nor the protections of the treaty as specified in Article VIII. The California state constitutional convention recoiled from the idea of granting Indians full citizenship. In violation of the treaty, the California Indian tribes were deprived of the protections specified in the treaty. Consequently they became the victims of murder, slavery, land theft, and starvation. The Indian population within the state declined by more than 100,000 in two decades. Whites overran tribal lands and people were exterminated. Genocide is not too strong a word to use in describing what happened to the California Indians during that period.[15]

In New Mexico, where the largest Hispanicized Indian population lived, there was little debate about the citizenship rights of these people. In the territorial framework the franchise was limited to whites only. On September 24, 1849, a convention met to draw up an organic act to govern the territory during its wait for statehood. A majority of the delegates were from old line Hispano families. They declared that the rights of citizenship would be restricted to "free white male inhabitants residing within the limits of the United States, but who [were residents] on the 2nd day of February, 1848."[16] They specified that former Mexican citizens would have to take an oath of affirmation before a territorial or federal court renouncing allegiance to the Mexican Republic before they would be considered citizens of the territory. This stipulation was approved with no debate and approved by the U.S. Congress the next year.[17]

Because New Mexico became a territory rather than a state, the civil rights of its inhabitants were less than those in California. Following the pattern established under the Northwest Ordinances of 1787 and the Wisconsin Organic Act of 1836, the people resident in the territories were conceived of as a dependant people who were not entitled to full participation in the national body politic. The laws and administration of the territory were subject to controls of Congress. The citizens of the New Mexico territory (which, until 1863, included Arizona) did not have full civil rights: they were not allowed to vote for their governor or for the president of the United States; the decisions of their elected representatives were subject to federal approval; and they did not have an independent judiciary. It was not until the period from 1901 to 1922, when the Supreme Court heard the Insular Cases, that the rights of the residents in the territories of the United States were articulated. The high court determined that the Constitution did not necessarily apply with full force to the residents in the U.S. territories. As Secretary of War Elihu Root put it, "The Constitution follows the flag--but doesnt quite catch up with it."[18]

The Hispanos of New Mexico did not obtain all the rights of U.S. citizens under the terms of the Treaty of Guadalupe Hidalgo until statehood in 1912. For them the key phrase in the treaty was contained in Article IX: "and in the meantime [they shall] be maintained and protected in the free enjoyment of their liberty and property, and secured in the free exercise of their religion." Essentially these "citizens-in-waiting" had their rights guaranteed by the treaty until they gained full citizenship status.

As in California, the most obvious victims of the transfer of sovereignty in New Mexico were the Indians. Approximately eight thousand Pueblo Indians who had been Mexican citizens in 1848 were disenfranchised. In 1849 several pueblo villagers had participated in local elections under the assumption that they were citizens. U.S. officials believed, however, that the Indian vote was too easy manipulated by various factions and moved to convince the residents of the nineteen pueblo villages that it would be in their interest to reject full citizenship and accept a ward status under the 1834 Indian Intercourse Act. Accordingly, in 1849 the presidentially appointed Indian Agent at Santa Fe, James S. Calhoun, traveled to visit all the Pueblos to convince them to accept federal protection under the Intercourse Act. In 1851, as a result of Calhouns labors, representatives of several tribes met and voted not to participate in New Mexican politics, apparently rejecting their rights under the Treaty of Guadalupe Hidalgo. In 1854 the legislature passed a law prohibiting the Pueblo tribes from voting except in the election of local water officials.

Despite this early history of disenfranchisement, some of it voluntary on the part of the Indians, the New Mexico Territorial Courts later decided cases that confirmed the citizenship of the Pueblo Indians. The *Lucero* case in 1869, the *Santistevan* case in 1874, the *Joseph* case in 1876, the *Delinquent Taxpayers* case in 1904, and the *Mares* case in 1907 were all decisions of the Territorial Supreme Court that confirmed the citizenship rights of the Pueblos. This judicial tradition, however, had little effect on the ward-like status of the Pueblos. A U.S. Supreme Court decision in 1913, *United States v. Sandoval* 231 U.S. 28 (1913), found that the Pueblos were entitled to federal protection and their citizenship status was not clear. When New Mexico was admitted as a state in 1912, its constitution contained a provision denying voting rights to "Indians not taxed," which include the Pueblo tribes. It was not until 1948 that this provision was declared unconstitutional and not until 1953 that the New Mexican Constitution was changed to allow Pueblo Indians to vote.[19]

There was little argument about the citizenship status of the other Indian groups in New Mexico. The Apaches and Navajos, who had fought so long to escape Hispanicization, remained the traditional enemies of the whites well into the 1870s and 1880s. They were eventually defeated in battle, placed on reservations, and treated as conquered nations with separate peace treaties. They were given citizenship at the same time as the Pueblo tribes.

LAND

Admittedly the rights and benefits of U.S. citizenship were somewhat abstract blessings for Mexican Americans, considering that for a long time the Anglo Americans treated them all as foreigners. A more tangible promise offered by the treaty, included in Articles VIII an IX and the Protocol of Querétaro, was promise of protection for private property. It was in the realm of property rights that the greatest controversies erupted.

In California thousands of gold-rush migrants encroached on the Californio land grants and demanded that something be done to "liberate" the lands. The result was the passage in Congress of the Land Act of 1851. This law set up a Board of Land commissioners whose job would be to adjudicate the validity of Mexican land grants in California. Every grantee was required to present evidence supporting title within two years, or their property would pass into the public domain. The land commissioners were instructed by law to govern their decisions according to the Treaty of Guadalupe Hidalgo, the law of nations, Spanish and Mexican laws, and previous decisions of the U.S. Supreme Court.

A basic principle underlying the establishment of the Land Commission and the land-confirmation processes in New Mexico and Texas was that the vast majority of Mexican land grants in the ceded territory were "imperfect," meaning that the claimants had not fulfilled Mexican regulations for legal land ownership. In years subsequent to the treaty, American courts ruled that the U.S. government had inherited the Mexican governments sovereignty and thereby the right to complete the processes of land confirmation.[20]

Under this assumption the Land Commission in California examined 813 claims and eventually confirmed 604 of them involving approximately nine million acres.

This, however, did not mean that the majority of Mexican land-holders were ultimately protected by the courts. On the contrary, most Californio landholders lost their lands because of the tremendous expense of litigation and legal fees. To pay for the legal defense of their lands, the Californios were forced to mortgage their ranchos. Falling cattle prices and usurous rates of interest conspired to wipe them out as a landholding class. Pablo de la Guerra summarized the dilemma for the California legislature: "Sir, if he gained his suit--if his title was confirmed, the expenses of the suit would confiscate his property, and millions have already been spent in carrying up cases that have been confirmed by the (Land Commission), and land owners in California have been obligated to dispose of their property at half its value, in order to pay for the expenses of the suit."[21]

Even if some landholders were able to fulfill the terms of the 1851 land law, they soon encountered tremendous pressure from Anglo-American squatters to vacate their rights. Perhaps one of the most celebrated and controversial cases was that of Joseph Yves Limantour. Limantour was a Frenchman whose son later became a famous secretary of treasury under President Porfirio Diaz. In 1843 the governor of California, Manuel Micheltorrena, gave Limantour a grant of four square leagues comprising about half of the unpopulated area known as Yerba Buena, land that later became part of the city of San Francisco. When gold was discovered in northern California in 1848, thousands of immigrants flooded San Francisco, settling on lots carved from Limantours grant. To protect his rights Limantour presented his case before the Land Commission, and in 1856 that body confirmed his title. Limantour was an absentee landholder whose rights were ostensibly protected under Article VIII of the treaty, as well as under Mexican law. Because he did not intend to reside in California, Limantour offered to sell his land rights to settlers at 10 percent of their true market value. A number of squatters settled along these lines but a majority formed an Anti-Limantour party to challenge his ownership. The political pressure of the squatters, many of them wealthy and influential San Franciscans, resulted in accusations of fraud. Following an indictment by a grand jury, Limantour was jailed on charges of fraud and perjury in 1857. Released on bond after a few months, he returned to Mexico to gather evidence to substantiate his case. He returned in 1858 for the trial with new documents and witnesses. Nevertheless the court decided against him and he lost his land.[22]

Other individuals who held perfect titles to their land under the Mexican government and who were able to survive economically lost their holdings because they had not fulfilled the terms of the 1851 land law. A number of court cases in this regard involving Mexican and Spanish grants emerged, but the most famous one pertaining to the Treaty of Guadalupe Hidalgo was *Botiller et al. v. Dominguez* (1883).[23]

In 1848, Dominga Dominguez, owner of Rancho Los Virgenes, just east of Mission San Fernando in California, had a perfect title to her land, a grant from the government of Mexico dated August 28, 1835. Her ancestors had taken all the steps required to legalize this claim. For some reason she and her relatives neglected to bring their papers before the Land Commission within the specified time provided for in the 1851 law. For the next thirty years a number of Mexican-American and European immigrant families settled on the Rancho assuming that the land was part of the public domain and that it had been opened for homesteading. Finally, in 1883, Brigido Botiller, a French-born Mexican citizen headed a group of squatters to oust Dominguez from her land, claiming that by the 1851 law she had no legal title to it.[24] Dominga then sued Botiller and the other squatters for reclamation of her land and back rents. In the 1880s both the district court and the California Supreme Court ruled in her favor. Both courts were convinced that her title was legitimate because the provisions in the Treaty of Guadalupe Hidalgo meant that the Dominguez family was "not compelled to submit the same for confirmation...nor did the grantee Nemecio Dominguez forfeit the land described."[25]

Botiller and the squatters appealed their case to the U.S. Supreme Court, where, in a decision issued on April 1, 1889, the Court reversed the California Supreme Court decision ruling that, despite the Treaty of Guadalupe Hidalgo guarantees, Dominguez did not have legal title. The Court reasoned that by admitting the legality of this title under this treaty, the government would not open the floodgates to others who had perfect titles but had not presented them to the Land Commission. The result would be to wreak havoc on California land ownership. Further, the justices argued that the Supreme Court had no power to enforce the Treaty of Guadalupe Hidalgo and that matters of treaty violation were subject to international negotiation and more treaties. Specifically, they stated, "This court has no power to set itself up as the instrumentality for enforcing provisions of a treaty with a foreign nation." They held that the Land Law of 1851 did not violate the due process provision of the Constitution because property holders were "at all times liable to be called into court of justice to contest [their] title to it." Congress, the court ruled, had the power to require land-holders to verify their claims and to fix penalties for failing to follow the law.[26]

In *Botiller et al. v. Dominguez* the Supreme Court held that the sovereign laws of the United States took precedence over international treaties. This appeared to contradict the Constitution, which (in Article VI, Section 2, and Article III, Section 2, Clause I) gave treaties the same status as the Constitution. The ruling thus sparked learned debate. John Currey, a San Francisco attorney, published a booklet challenging the courts logic.[27] The Supreme Courts decision, he argued, sanctioned the confiscation of property and violated the due process provision of the Constitution: "The fact of the existence of a title in fee simple to land cannot be destroyed by a sweep of the pen, nor by the *obiter dictum* of a learned judge."[28] *Botiller et al. v. Dominguez* was an important precedent, guiding the court in its future interpretation of conflicts between treaty obligations and domestic laws. In this case the protection of private property ostensibly guaranteed by the Treaty of Guadalupe Hidalgo was essentially invalidated.

The compromise of 1850 made New Mexico a territory while California entered the Union as a state. This difference in political status produced different resolutions of land-tenure problems. In California a state judiciary functioned to render relatively swift interpretations of the Treaty of Guadalupe Hidalgo; in New Mexico federally appointed officials had to have their decisions approved by Congress, a lengthy and often politicized process. Ironically, New Mexicos more direct link to the national government meant that the property-rights guarantees under the Treaty of Guadalupe Hidalgo would be even less important than in California.

In 1848 private and communal land grants in New Mexico covered about 15 million square miles. To determine the federal domain, Congress established the Office of Surveyor General, who was given broad powers to "issue notices, summon witnesses, administer oaths, etc.," and to report to the secretary of the interior and, ultimately, to Congress regarding the status of New Mexico land grants. Until Congress acted to confirm the findings of the surveyor general, all lands were to be withheld from sale.[29]

In August 1854, congress appointed William Pelham to the office of surveyor general. Once in New Mexico, Pelham had considerable trouble getting the Hispano land-grant owners to file their claims with his office; as a result, by 1863, only twenty-five town and private claims and seventeen Pueblo Indian grants had been confirmed by Congress. By 1880, 1,000 claims had been filed by the surveyor general but only 150 had been acted upon by the federal government. As the number of unconfirmed grants in litigation before the surveyor general and the Congress lengthened, so too did the legal expenses incurred by the Hispano pueblos and ranchers. Such lawyers and politicians as Stephen Benson Elkins and Thomas Benton Catron formed the nucleus of the Santa Fe Ring, a confederation of opportunists who used the long legal battles over land grants to acquire empires extending over millions of acres. The most famous example of the land-grabbing activities of the ring was the creation of the Maxwell Land Grant, a Spanish claim of 97,000 acres that became inflated through the actions of the ring to a final patent of 1,714,074 acres.[30]

In addition to losing their lands to rapacious lawyers and politicians, the Hispanos suffered the changing whims of national politics. In 1885 the newly elected Democratic president, Grover Cleveland, removed the Republican surveyor general of New Mexico and replaced him with his own man, William Andrew Sparks, an individual described by historian Ralph Emerson Twitchell as "steeped in prejudice against New Mexico, its people and their property rights."[31] The new surveyor general decided that his predecessor had been corrupt and had given away far too much federal land and that his decisions and those of the Congress regarding land should be reviewed. In the name of reform, the new surveyor general revoked the approval of twenty-three grants. The process of reviewing the New Mexico claims gave no assurance that the Treaty of Guadalupe Hidalgo, or indeed the rule of law, outweighs the political influence of those behind the scenes.

When Benjamin Harrison became president in 1889, the federal land policies in New Mexico changed again. Under pressure from developers and New Mexico Hispanos, Congress in 1890 began to consider legislation that would settle the outstanding land claims. Railroad interests wanted to have the public domain established, so that they could get federal grants. Hispano landholders in New Mexico sought to speed up the land-confirmation process or to reverse previously adverse rulings. Writing to Manias Romero, the Mexican minister plenipotentiary to the United States in 1890, the predominantly Hispano Commercial Club of Las Vegas, New Mexico, laid out their complaints. They urged Minister Romero to use his influence to secure passage of a new land law.

> The American government has thus far, though over 40 years have elapsed, neglected a competent court to pass on the validity of the claims of those who were once Mexican citizens... We, with great respect petition you to champion the cause of our people and again represent to the State Department at Washington evil inflicted on us by the failure of the U.S. government to fulfill in this respect its obligations incurred by the Treaty of Guadalupe Hidalgo.[32]

For its part, the Mexican government followed the proposed legislation with interest but was unable, for diplomatic reasons, to advocate the Hispanos cause in Congress. The Mexican government did instruct Romero to react to court cases when it appeared that there was prejudice against former Mexican citizens in the application of the law once it passed Congress. Romero, for his part, suggested that his government publicize its concern for its former citizens so that they would be better able to oppose unjust action taken against them in violation of the Treaty of Guadalupe Hidalgo.[33]

On March 3, 1891, the president signed into law a bill to establish a Court of Private Land Claims. The Treaty of Guadalupe Hidalgo was specifically invoked as a guiding document for this court, although wording in the act provided that it would apply only to "persons who became citizens by reason of the Treaty of Guadalupe Hidalgo and who have been in the actual adverse possession on tracts not to exceed 160 acres."[34] The court was made up of five judges plus an attorney representing the interests of the U.S. government. Unlike the California Land Commission, the New Mexico Court of Private Land Claims did not require those holding perfect titles to apply the court for confirmation--only those who had not fulfilled all the regulations of the Spanish and Mexican laws. Those not presenting their claims within two years would be considered to have abandoned their grant. The law also restricted to eleven square leagues (about thirty-six square miles) the amount of land that would be allowed for a communal or town grant and stipulated that errors in previous decisions by Congress would be indemnified at not more than $1.25 per acre.

Meeting in Denver, Colorado and in Santa Fe, New Mexico, between 1891 and 1904, the New Mexico Court operated by the strict rule that confirmation of a land grant required proof that the Spanish or Mexican granting official had legal authority. There had been a good deal of confusion in Mexicos political history; therefore, many New Mexican grants were held not to be legitimate because of the "illegitimacy" of the Mexican governing bodies.[35] The court was also very strict regarding what it considered a proper survey, documentation, and full compliance with every Mexican law regarding land tenure. As a result of this less-than-liberal interpretation of Spanish and Mexican laws, the New Mexico court rejected two-thirds of the claims presented before it. Ultimately only eighty-two grants received congressional confirmation. This represented only 6 percent of the total area sought by land claimants. Thus, using the Court of Private Land Claims, the U.S. government enlarged the national domain at the expense of hundreds of Hispano villages, leaving a bitter legacy that continued to fester.[36]

In 1856 the U.S. Supreme Court ruled that the Treaty of Guadalupe Hidalgo did not apply to Texas. In *McKinney v. Saviego* the justices ruled that Articles VIII and IX of the treaty referring to property rights and citizenship, "did not refer to any portion of the acknowledged limits of Texas. The territories alluded to (in Articles VIII and IX of the treaty) are those which previous to the treaty had belonged to Mexico...The Republic of Texas had been many years before acknowledged by the United States as existing separately and independently of Mexico."[37]

This decision seemed to invalidate the meaning of the Protocol of Querétaro, which specifically identified Texas land grants as being protected. Under this agreement grants made before March 2, 1836--the date of Texas self-proclaimed independence from Mexico--would remain as legal land grants.[38] Thus, according to the Supreme Court, Texas was not to be considered part of the Mexican Cession. Congress had admitted Texas into the Union in 1845, and that states constitution ran counter to the Treaty of Guadalupe Hidalgo (Article VIII) in forbidding aliens from holding property. (The Texas government had already declared as aliens those Tejanos who had left the Republic during the Texas Rebellion.)

The Mexican government took exception to this interpretation. In 1895, R.S. Sanchez, a legal consultant to the Secretaría de Relaciones Exteriores published his views, arguing that U.S. courts were in violation of the Treaty of Guadalupe Hidalgo because Mexico had never recognized the independence of Texas and the treaty specifically and formally recognized Texas as part of the United States by the delineation of the boundary (in Article IV).[39]

The issue of Texas and the treaty remained a point of contention well into the twentieth century. U.S. courts discounted arguments that cited the treaty when arguing for Texas land claims. In 1911, in *State v. Gallardo et al.*, a Texas Civil Appeals Court reaffirmed the Supreme Court view that "the validity of the title under consideration should be determined without reference to any provision of the treaty," but, at the same time, recognized that prior decisions of the local courts in Texas had upheld grants of land based, in part, on interpretations of the Treaty of Guadalupe Hidalgo and the Protocol.[40]

During the Bucareli Conferences held in 1923 between the United States and Mexico, the issue of the status of the Texas land grants and the applicability of the Treaty of Guadalupe Hidalgo resurfaced. This conference was convened to settle the outstanding claims of both countries and to pave the way for U.S. diplomatic recognition of Mexicos revolutionary government. To counter U.S. claims for damages suffered by Americans during the revolution of 1910, the Mexican government decided to present the claims of its former citizens in the Southwest. Initially they presented 836 claims amounting to 245 million dollars. Almost 193 million of this amount was for Texas land claims invalidated in violation of the Treaty of Guadalupe Hidalgo.[41] The Mexican government, through its consulate in Texas, actively solicited land claims from heirs of the original land-grant owners who had been dispossessed of their lands after 1848. Increased Anglo-American migration into South Texas after 1848 was the origin of a large number of these claims. This was the area of Texas in which the first battles of the Mexican War had occurred and over which there had been much diplomatic disagreement prior to the signing of the Treaty of Guadalupe Hidalgo. Many Tejano grants in this region were perfected Spanish claims that had been recognized by the Mexican government.[42]

Unlike New Mexico or California, Texas had been admitted to the Union with full control over its public lands. Instead of federal laws guiding the settlement of land disputes, state laws and courts played a dominant role. It is difficult to generalize about the Texas claims because of the decades of litigation surrounding them. Two Texas historians, Arnoldo De Leon and Kenneth Stewart, concluded that most Tejanos lost portions of their patrimony or all of it through "a combination of methods including, litigation, chicanery, robbery, fraud, and threat."[43] As early as 1847 the citizens of Laredo, Texas, fearing how they would fare under the Texas administration, requested assurances form the state government that their property rights would be protected. Receiving no reply, they petitioned to be allowed to remain part of Mexico.[44] Many violent episodes marked the struggle between Tejanos and Anglo-Texans for control of the land. The Cortina Rebellion, in the Brownsville-Matamoros area in the 1850s and 1860s and the El Paso Salt War in the 1870s pitted entire communities against the Texas rangers in a struggle for the land. Hundreds of lesser struggles that resulted in lynchings, beatings, and riots also had their origin in conflicts over the land.[45] Tejanos had good reason to distrust the Texas government in its implementation of laws.

Tejano families found their lands in jeopardy because they had been forced to flee Texas during the Mexican war. The Las Mestenas grant near Reynosa is one example. The original heirs vacated their lands between 1846 and 1848. Their decision to reoccupy the grant in 1848 was an expensive one, for it meant selling their lands to pay back taxes and paying the expense of rounding up stolen or stray cattle. The large families and the Hispanic tradition of equal inheritance worked against continuing land ownership. There were numerous heirs, some of whom had never seen the grant. American speculators bought up interests from these absentee owners, made high-interest loans, assumed mortgages on portions of the ranch, and purchased sections at tax sales. Tejano sued Tejano and Anglo-Texan sued Tejano over conflicting claims against until 1915, when a million-dollar lawsuit finally cleared title with few of the original claimants retaining an interest.[46]

Other Tejano grantees lost their lands because they had left Texas during the Texas Rebellion in 1836. The Republic declared their lands vacant and issued certificates of land ownership to individuals who had fought in the Texan army. Litigation between these certificate holders and recipients of older Mexican and Spanish grants resulted in further violations of the Treaty of Guadalupe Hidalgo. Andrew A. Tijerina, who studied the process up to 1850, concluded, "Across the state, Tejano emigres lost their lands to fictitious law suits, sheriffs auctions, and dubious transfer of titles."[47]

David Montejano, who had also studied the loss of Tejano lands, concluded that the process was a complex one involving fraud, confiscation, and the operation of the mechanisms of market competition. In the late nineteenth century the Tejanos did not have access to capital to develop their lands so that they could remain solvent during the changes in the ranching industry. They also inherited the traditional noncapitalist view of the use of their lands. The death of a patriarch often meant the dismemberment of the ranch as it was sold for back taxes and old debts. A large portion of the famous King ranch in south Texas was pieced together during the forced sale of Tejano ranches during unfavorable market conditions in the period 1886-1889.[48]

The conflicts between Spanish and Mexican claims and those granted by the Republic and State of Texas resulted in various legislative attempts to clear titles. In 1850, Governor P. H. Bell appointed a commission to investigate land claims arising from the Treaty of Guadalupe Hidalgo in South Texas.[49] The Bourland-Miller Commission, created by the legislature, gathered abstracts of titles and made recommendations to the Texas legislature. More than 135 claims were reviewed and presented to the legislature for confirmation. In 1854, 1861, 1866, 1870, 1881, and 1901, the Texas legislature passed laws providing mechanisms for the examination and confirmation of Spanish and Mexican grants. A number of claims rejected by the Texas legislature became issues for further litigation.

In the nineteenth century, Texas courts regularly considered the Treaty of Guadalupe Hidalgo as it applied to Spanish and Mexican grants made before March 2, 1836. In *Texas v Gallardo et al.* (1911), the Texas Supreme Court ruled that the validation acts passed in earlier decades should not apply to titles that were valid under the Treaty of Guadalupe Hidalgo--meaning those that were legitimate prior to March 3, 1836. The court ruled that "a title to lands within the original Mexican states of Tamaulipas and the present boundaries of Texas...is within the protection of the Treaty and entitled to recognition in the Supreme Courts." Subsequent court decisions affirmed the point of view that the treaty took precedence over state legislation, but many Tejanos became landless because they could not afford lengthy legal appeals.[50]

Whether by laws, force, foreclosure, or litigation, many Tejanos lost title to their ancestral lands in the period from 1848 to 1923. Many had their cases presented on their behalf by the Mexican government during the Bucareli negotiations. On September 8, 1923, the United States and Mexico agreed to establish a commission to review the Texas land grants. Eventually 433 cases, valued at 121 million dollars, were presented on behalf of the heirs. In 1941, after much delay, the Texas land claims were settled on the international level with the Mexican government assuming the obligation of compensating the Texas heirs. The issue was not resolved, however, for although both the United States and Mexico recognized the legitimacy of the Texas claims under the Treaty of Guadalupe Hidalgo, the Mexican government refused to carry out its financial obligations--this despite constant pressure from the Tejano land-grant heirs.[51]

In the first half century after ratification of the Treaty of Guadalupe Hidalgo, hundreds of state, territorial, and federal legal bodies produced a complex tapestry on conflicting opinions and decisions. The citizenship rights seemingly guaranteed in Articles VIII and IX were not all they seemed. The property rights for former Mexican citizens in California, New Mexico, and Texas proved to be fragile. Within a generation the Mexican Americans who had been under the ostensible protection of the treaty became a disenfranchised, poverty-stricken minority.

NOTES

1. Oscar Martinez, "On the Size of the Chicano Population" *Aztlán*, 4, no. 1 (Spring 1975):43-67.
2. Francisco F. de la Maza, ed., *Codigo de Colonización y Terrenos Baldios de la Republica Mexicana* (Mexico, D.F.: Secretaría de Fomento, 1873), pp. 402-427.
3. Hubert Howe Bancroft, *History of Arizona and New Mexico* (San Francisco: The History Book Co., 1889), p. 473. The Mexican government made only 25,000 dollars

available for the recruitment drive; the funds were to be drawn from those paid by the United States under the terms of the Treaty of Guadalupe Hidalgo. By 1851 eighteen frontier outposts were established, with 1,093 Mexican soldiers including people from the northern provinces and repatriated Mexicans from the United States. The Mexican government also recruited Seminole and Muskogee Indians to establish settlements. See Angela Moyano Pahissa, *México y Estados Unidos: Orígenes de una relación*, 1819-1861 (Mexico, D. F.: Secretaría de Educación Pública, 1985), pp. 206-207.

4. Richard Griswold del Castillo, *The Los Angeles Barrio: 1850-1890: A Social History* (Los Angeles: University of California Press, 1980), pp. 123-124.

5. Bancroft, p. 472; Ralph Emerson Twitchell, *The Leading Facts of New Mexican History*, vol. 1, (1911-1912; Reprint, Albuquerque: Horn and Wallace, 1963), p. 102.

6. The most detailed account of the activities of the commissioners in New Mexico is Mary Childers Mangusso, "A Study of the Citizenship Provisions of the Treaty of Guadalupe Hidalgo," (Masters thesis, University of New Mexico, 1966). For later protests see Manuel Marrimar to the Minister of Relaciones Exteriores, June 2, 1852, Archivo de la Secretaría de Relaciones Exteriores (ASRE), Mexico City, no. 2-12-2904. See Also Angela Moyano Pahissa, *México y Estados Unidos: Orígenes de una relación, 1819-1861* (Mexico, D.F.: Secretaría de Educación Pública, 1985), pp. 182-184.

7. Official correspondence, ASRE, nos. 2-13-2976 and 2-13-2975.

8. Twitchell, p. 241. Later problems with non-citizens serving on juries in New Mexico led the territorial legislature to pass a law to allow persons who had declared their intention of becoming naturalized citizens to serve; see Mangusso, pp. 67-68.

9. J. Ross Browne, ed., *Report of the Debates on the Convention of California on the Formation of the State Constitution in September and October 1849* (Washington, D.C.: John Towers, 1850), p. 62.

10. Leonard Pitt, *Decline of the Californios: A Social History of the Spanish-Speaking Californians, 1846-1890* (Berkeley: University of California Press, 1970), p. 50.

11. The history of the Mexican governments protests regarding the treatment of Mexicans in the United States in the period immediately after the Mexican war can be found in a number of published works: William R. Manning, ed., *Diplomatic Correspondence of the United States, Interamerican Affairs*, vol. 9 (Washington, D.C., 1937), pp. 129-130, 133-134, 568-570; Maria de Los Angeles, " La anexación de Texas a los Estados Unidos," (Thésis, U.N.A.M, 1959), pp. 192-195; and Torbijo

Esquivel Obregon, *Apuntes para la historia del derecho en Mexico,* 4 vols. (Mexico, D.F.: Porrua e hijos, 1948), 3:426-427.

12. I Cal 232; Cal Stats 1850, Ch. 97; Pitt, pp. 66-67. The legal history of the Foreign Miners Tax Law is given in Carl I. Wheat, ed., "Californias Bantam Cock: The Journals of Charles E. De Long, 1854-1863," *California Historical Quarterly* 8 (1929):353-355.

13. Pitt, pp. 48-57.

14. The argument against de la Guerras full citizenship is a revealing comment on the status of Mexican Americans after 1848. "In conclusion we insist that the respondent was an alien enemy up to the ratification of the Treaty of Guadalupe Hidalgo; that between that time and the date of the admission of California into the Union, he joined, by virtue of his silence, that class of Mexicans who are deemed to have elected to become citizens of the United States, but he is not and never was a citizen." *People v. de la Guerra 40 Cal 311 (1870).*

15. Van Hastings Garner, "The Treaty of Guadalupe Hidalgo and the California Indians," *The Indian Historian 9,* no. I (Winter, 1976):10-13.

16. Robert W. Larson, *New Mexicos Quest for Statehood*, 1846-1912 (Albuquerque: University of New Mexico Press, 1968), p. 19.

17. See U.S. Congress, House of Representatives, *New Mexico-Convention of Delegates: Journal and Proceedings*, 31st Cong. 1st sess., 1850, House Misc. Doc. 39, pp. 1-13.

18. Quoted in Walter La Feber, "The Constitutions and United States Foreign Policy: An Interpretation," *Journal of American History*, vol. 74, no. 3 (December 1987):705. See *Downs v. Bidwell*, 182 US 244 and *Balzac v. Puerto Rico* 258 US 309; Also Whitney Perkins, *Denial of Empire: the United States and Its Dependencies* (The Netherlands: A. W. Sythoff-Lyden, 1962), pp. 13, 28. The question of citizenship for residents of the territories was a thorny one for jurists. The net effect of the Spanish-American War was to restrict the rights of citizenship to those residing within the borders of continental United States. By 1901 the people of Puerto Rico and the Philippines were made citizens of those places, not of the United States.

19. U.S. v. Lucero, 1 NM 422 (1869); *U. S. v Santistevan* 1 N. M. 583 (1874).

20. For a complete discussion of Pueblo Indian citizenship after 1848 see Mary Childers Mangusso, "A Study of the Citizenship Provisions of the Treaty of Guadalupe Hidalgo." (Masters thesis, University of New Mexico, 1966), pp. 77-99.

Ralph Rowley, "The Acquisition of the Spanish Borderlands: Problems and Legacy" (Ph.D. diss., University of New Mexico, 1975), p. 168.

21. See Teschmacher v. Thompson 8 Cal 23.

22. See Griswold del Castillo, pp. 41-49; "Speech of Hon. Pablo de la Guerra of Santa Barbara," April 17, 1855 (Sacramento: State Tribune Office, 1855), p. 7.

23. Jan Bazant, "Joseph Yves Limantour (1812-1885) y su aventura californiana-I," *Historia Mexicana,* 28, no. I (julio-septiembre, 1978): I-23; "Joseph Yves Limantour (1812-1885) y su aventura californiana-II," *Historia Mexicana,* 29, no. 3 (enero-marzo, 1980): 353-374. Bazant uncovered new evidence at the University of Texas archives that seems to support Limantours case.

24. 130 U.S. 238 (1889); for a citation of cases that challenged the 1851 land law citing the Treaty of Guadalupe Hidalgo see *Mintern v. Brower* 24 Cal 644 (1864). An excellent discussion of the court cases affecting Mexican land grants is Richard Powell, *Compromises of Conflicting Claims: A Century of California Law, 1760 to 1860* (Dobbs Ferry, New York: Oceana Publications, 1977), pp. 170-171.

25. U.S. Supreme Court, *Brigido Botiller et al. v. Dominga Dominguez,* File copies of the Briefs, October Term, 1888, vol. 15, pp. 1-23; others who opposed Domingas claim were Pedro Sepulveda, Manuel Felix, Manuel Sanchez, Pablo Bojorquez, Gregorio Tapia, and Ramon Tapia.

26. Willard B. Cowels, *Treaties and Constitutional Law: Property Interferences and Due Process of Law* (Washington, D.C.: American Council of Public Affairs, 1941), p. 240.74 Cal 457 (1887).

27. 130 US 238; 9 S. Ct. 525, 527.

28. John Currey, *The Treaty of Guadalupe Hidalgo and Private Land Claims and Titles Existing in California at the Date of the Treaty* (San Francisco: Bancroft Whitney, 1891), p. 22.

29. Ralph Emerson Twitchell, *The Leading Facts of New Mexicos History* (Albuquerque: Horn and Wallace, 1963), 2:458. New Mexican land-grant litigation, a complex subject, can be treated only superficially in a survey such as this. For a more detailed analysis of the legal and historical aspects involved, see: Victor Westphall, *The Public Domain in New Mexico: 1854-1891* (Albuquerque: University of New Mexico Press, 1965); and J. J. Bowden, *Spanish and Mexican Land Grants in the Chihuahuan Acquisition* (El Paso: Texas Westernlore Press, 1971).

30. Howard Robert Lamar, *The Far Southwest, 1846-1912: A Territorial History* (New York: W.W. Norton, 1966), pp. 141-146.

31. Twitchell, 2:462.

32. Commercial Club of Las Vegas, New Mexico, to Matias Romero, Minister Plenipotentiary, December 27, 1890, ASRE, no. 11-5-1.

33. Matias Romero to Secretaría de Relaciones Exteriores, April 20, 1891, ASRE, no. 11-5-1.

34. *Analysis of the Act to Establish a Court of Private Land Claims,* ASRE, no. 11-5-1, p. 309.

35. Rowley, p. 210.

36. Ibid., pp. 213-214.

37. *Mckinney v. Saviego,* S.C. 18 Howard 235.

38. Miller, Doc. 129, p. 381.

39. R.S. Sanchez to the Secretaría de Relaciones Exteriores, June 10, 1895, *Boletin oficial,* tomo I, num. 1 (1895), p. 135. This volume also contains correspondence regarding the applicability of the treaty to Texas.

40. *State v. Gallardo et al,* 135 S.W. 664; "Juridical Decisions Involving Questions of International Law," *American Journal of International Law,* vol. 6 (1912), p. 227.

41. Rudolfo O. de la Garza, and Karl Schmitt, "Texas Land Grants and Chicano-Mexican Relations: A Case Study," *Latin American Research Review* 21, No. 1 (1986): 123-138.

42. Florence Johnson Scott, *Royal Land Grants North of the Rio Grande,* 1771-1821 (Rio Grande City: La Retama Press, 1969). This book studies the histories of the grants in the area of Reynosa, Texas: Llano Grande, La Feria, Las Mestenas, San Salvador de Tule, Santa Anita, and Padre Island.

43. Arnoldo De Leon and Kenneth L. Stewart, "Lost Dreams and Found Fortunes: Mexican and Anglo Immigrants into South Texas, 1850-1900," *Western Historical Quarterly,* vol. 14, no. 3 (July 1983):296.

44. Gilberto Miguel Hinojosa, *A Borderlands Town in Transition: Laredo,* 1775-1850 (College Station: Texas A & M University Press, 1983), pp. 58-59.

45. Arnoldo de Leon, *They Called Them Greasers* (Austin: University of Texas Press, 1983).

46. Scott, p. 38.

47. Andrew A. Tijerina, "Tejanos and Texans: The Native Mexicans of Texas, 1820-1850" (Ph.D. diss., University of Texas Austin, 1977), pp. 319-320.

48. David Montejano, *Anglos and Mexicans in the Making of Texas, 1836-1986* (Austin: University of Texas Press, 1987), pp. 63-70. This discussion of the Tejano lands is the best summary of a complex process.

49. *Message of the Governor Transmitting the Report of the Commissioners to Investigate Land Titles West of the Nueces* (Austin: Cushney and Hampton, 1851). The commissioners reported on Webb, Kinney, and Cameron counties, recommending the vast majority of the land grants; See Scott, pp. 105-106.
50. *State of Texas v. Gallardo et al.,* 135 SW 664 (1911); *State of Texas v. Bali, 173 SW 2nd 522.*
51. Robert Salazar, "Texas Land Grant Heirs Seek Compensation," *Ajenda: A Journal of Hispanic Issues,* vol. 9, no. 2 (March/April, 1979): pp. 14-16. *Asociación de reclamantes et al. v. The United Mexican States,* no. 81-2299, U.S. Court of Appeals for the District of Columbia Circuit, 561 F. 2d. 1190 (June 20, 1983); *Asociación de reclamantes et al. v. The United Mexican States,* no. 83-1596, U.S. Court of Appeals for the District of Columbia Circuit, 735 F. 2d. 1517 (June 5, 1984).

Key Terms
&
Discussion Questions

Aztlán, Cíbola, and Frontier New Spain
John R. Chávez

Key Terms

Aztlán/Nayarit

Aztatlán

Cabeza de Vaca

Esteban

Francisco Vázquez de Coronado

"Uto-Aztecan"

Chicomoztoc

Cíbola

Quivira

Juan de Oñate

Discussion Questions

1. Discuss the significance of the American Southwest to modern Chicanos.

2. What is the relevance of the "Uto-Aztecan" language for the Aztec tie to Aztlán?

3. Discuss two examples of the Spanish image of the fantastic projected to the northern frontier.

4. How did the Juan de Oñate expedition to the northern frontier represent an important shift in Spanish thinking with regard to the function of the region?

5. What is meant by the perception of the northern frontier as a "buffer zone?"

6. Discuss, in general, what Chávez means by the terms Aztlán, Cíbola and Frontier New Spain.

Settlement Patterns and Village Plans
in Colonial New Mexico
Marc Simmons

Key Terms

tierras realengas y baldías

plaza mayor

Juan de Oñate

genizaros

reducciones

Ordinances of 1573

poblaciones

plazas

rancho

Discussion Questions

1. How did spanish settlement regulations dictate the laying out of towns?

2. What was the significance of the Ordinances of 1573?

3. How did the original municipal tradition erode in the New Mexico regions?

4. Describe the most important change in settlement patterns during the 18th century.

5. Why did the change occur?

6. What was the *reduccion*?

Arrival of the Europeans
Thomas E. Sheridan

Key Terms

Akimel O'odham
The Columbian Exchange
Francisco Vásquez de Coronado
Querechos
Juan de Oñate
Eusebio Kino
José Romo de Vivar
Tucsonenses

Alvar Nuñez Cabeza de Vaca
Estevan
Fray Marcos de Niza
Cíbola
Antonio de Espejo
reducción
Juan Bautista de Anza

Discussion Questions

1. What were some of the "quiet" events that revolutionized human society in Arizona?

2. What were the devastating consequences of European contact at the microbial level?

3. How did Coronado's party make the first systematic exploration of the Southwest?

4. What was the primary importance of the Oñate expedition?

5. Who were the Athapaskans?

6. What were the various purposes of the *reducción*?

7. Tubac eventually became an ethnic melting pot. Explain.

8. What special circumstances did the Apache present to the Spanish colonists?

Colonizers of the Frontier
Andrew Rolle

Key Terms

Eusebio Francesco Kino
Juan Maria de Salvatierra
Juan de Ugarte
José de Gálvez
palos colorados
palo alto
La Punta de los Muertos

Junípero Serra
Gaspar de Portolá
San Carlos
San Antonio
Fernando Rivera y Moncada
Juan Crespi
Pedro Fages

Discussion Questions

1. How did the Seven Years' War impact Spanish colonial policy and its settlement plans?

2. What was the four-pronged expedition into Alta California?

3. What problems did the settlers encounter en route to Alta California?

4. Name some of the points visited by the overland settlers.

Sexual Violence in the Politics and Policies of Conquest:
Amerindian Women and the Spanish Conquest of Alta California
Antonia I. Castañeda

Key Terms

Junipero Serra

Pedro Font

Pedro Fages

Fermín Francisco de Lasuén

Echeveste Regulations

Toypurina

Felipe de Neve

Discussion Questions

1. According to Serra, how did the sexual assaults of some Spanish soldiers retard the conquest of California?

2. How did the sexual attacks violate significant principles of Catholic moral theology?

3. What was contained in Serra's "Report on the General Conditions . . .?"

4. What was the "plague of immorality"?

5. What was the significance of the *Echeveste Regulations*?

6. Who was Toypurina?

7. In what ways has revisionist scholarship altered our modern view of colonial California?

8. According to some scholars, what are some of the symbolic meanings of rape?

9. In what ways were Amerindian women devalued in colonial thought?

10. Why was violence against Amerindians permissable, yet punishable?

The Origins of Anti-Mexican Sentiment
in the United States
Raymund A. Paredes

Key Terms

hispanophobia   *The Spanish Colonie*
Bartolome de las Casas   *Book of Martyrs*
New England Primer   *Principall Navigations*
López de Gómara   Samuel Sewall
History of America   *Natural and Moral History of the Indies*

Discussion Questions

1. In what ways was anti-Catholicism evident in the 16th century?

2. How were American colonists influenced by anti-Catholicism?

3. In what ways did some European writers express admiration for Mexican aborigines?

Between the Conquests

4. In what ways was the preponderance of European opinion heavily against the Mexican?

5. How were American colonists influenced by these writings?

6. What was the impact of Robertson's "History?"

Texas, "This Most Precious...Territory"

Gene M. Brack

Key Terms

Lorenzo de Zavla

José María Tornel

Viage a los Estados Unidos

1819 Treaty

General Manuel Mier y Terán

Freedonian rebellion

Nicolás Bravo

1830 Colonization law

Lucas Alamán

Discussion Questions

1. How did the Mexican attitude toward the United States change after 1830?

2. How does Zavala's *Viage a los Estados Unidos* reflect his complex attitude towards the United States? Slavery?

3. How would you characterize Mexican attitudes toward American Slavery?

4. According to the Mexican press and government, how was the United States involved in the Texas rebellion?

5. What were the various Mexican strategies employed to prevent the loss of Texas?

6. According to José María Tornel, why was Texas "This Most Precious Part" of the Mexican republic?

Initial Contacts:
Redeeming Texas from Mexicans,1821-1836
Arnoldo De León

Key Terms

Xenophobia
Samuel M. Lowrie
Stephen F. Austin
David G. Burnet

Bexareños
Tlascalan Indians
criollos

Discussion Questions

1. What did the "Americanization of Texas" mean to Stephen F. Austin?

2. In what ways did Americans in Texas regard the region as primitive?

3. Discuss aspects of European-rooted rivalry which led to anti-Spanish and Mexican sentiment in the Texas region.

4. How does De León demonstrate cultural clashes between Americans in Texas and the native Mexican population?

5. Discuss how distinctions were drawn between Mexican men and women in the Texas region.

6. According to the article, how important was racism as a factor in the Texas Revolution?

The 'Texas Game' Again?
Peopling California and New Mexico
David J. Weber

Key Terms

Colonization Law of 1824

José Maria Híjar

Tadeo Ortiz

Manuel Armijo

Bidwell-Bartelson party

Juan Almonte

1843 decree

Santiago Abreu

countercolonization

Miguel Ramos Arizpe

Antonio José Martínez

Thomas Catesby Jones

Híjar-Padrés colony

April 6, 1830 law

Discussion Questions

1. Why was Mexico reluctant to permit foreign immigration into California and New Mexico after the 1830s?

2. What were the particular problems for settlers in Arizona during the early 19th century?

3. What was the primary significance of the failure of the Híjar-Padrés colonization project?

4. What factors discouraged Mexicans from migrating to the north?

5. Describe the Armijo approach to land grants to foreigners in New Mexico during the early 19th century.

6. What were the various long term consequences of the Mexican inability to attract settlers to New Mexico and California?

The Diplomacy of Racism:
Manifest Destiny and Mexico, 1821-1848
Gene Brack

Key Terms

Manifest Destiny

Joel R. Poinsett

General Zachary Taylor

Rio Grande

Abraham Lincoln

General Winfield Scott

Treaty of Guadalupe Hidalgo

Antonio López de Santa Anna

James K. Polk

John Slidell

Rio Nueces

"spot resolutions"

John C. Fremont

Discussion Questions

1. In what ways was nineteenth century Mexico burdened by its colonial past?

2. How did Poinsett contribute to Mexican mistrust of the United States in the 1820s?

3. Why did Mexico believe the United States was involved in the Texas revolt?

Between the Conquests

4. Discuss the undercurrent of racism toward Mexicans involved in United States expansionism.

5. Why did Mexico believe the Polk declaration of war was illegitimate?

6. How was Mexican pride and honor a factor in the events leading to war with the United States?

7. Which interests in the United States supported the war?

8. Why did some supporters reverse their position and oppose the war?

The Treaty of Guadalupe Hidalgo

Discussion Questions

1. Discuss the significance of Article V. Which American states would eventually result from this territorial acquisition?

2. What does Article VIII assert with regard to the citizenship of Mexicans who remained within the acquired territories?

3. Could the Mexicans in the acquired territories keep Mexican citizenship? Why or why not?

4. Identify and explain how Article IX is distinct from Article VIII. What does it guarantee in terms of the rights of United States citizenship for those remaining in the newly acquired territories?

5. What did the negotiators of the treaty mean by "shall be incorporated into the Union of the United States and be admitted, at the proper time (to be judged of by the Congress of the United States)...?"

6. What does Article X (prior to its omission) assert in terms of ownership of Spanish and Mexican land grants?

Discussion Questions

1. Why was the Statement of Protocol necessary?

2. What does the Protocol assert with regard to the legal ownership of Spanish and Mexican land grants?

3. What did the negotiators mean by ". . . the grantees may cause their legitimate titles to be acknowledged before the American tribunals?"

Citizenship and Property Rights:
U. S. Interpretations of the Treaty
Richard Griswold del Castillo

Key Terms

Article VIII
Repatriation
People v. Naglee
Land Act of 1851
Court of Private Land Claims
Bucareli Conference, 1923

Article IX
Antonio Coronel
People v. de la Guerra
Botiller et al. v. Dominguez
McKinney v. Saviego

Discussion Questions

1. What were the various motives behind the Mexican repatriation campaign of the middle nineteenth century?

2. How effective was the repatriation campaign in the various regions of the Southwest?

3. What historical factors account for the strong anti-Mexican hostilities in California during the gold rush?

4. What was the historical significance of *People v. de la Guerra?*

5. What historical factors account for the delay in the extension of all the rights of citizens of the United States to the people of New Mexico?

6. How did the Land Act of 1851 work to the disadvantage of Californio land grantees?

7. What was the historical significance of *McKinney v. Saviego?*

8. What special circumstances played a role in the loss of lands in Texas?

Index

Texian and Emigrant's Guide, 180, 188
Texians, 147-150, 180, 184, 186-188
Tijerina, Andrew A., 280, 286
Tlacaelel, 6
Tovar, Pedro de, 61
Toypurina, 90, 91, 102
Travis, William Barrett, 184, 188
Treaty of Guadalupe Hidalgo, 149-151, 153, 154, 156, 157, 235, 256, 259, 263, 265, 266, 268, 269, 271, 272, 274-284
    Article V, 150, 154, 155, 259-260
    Article VIII, 155, 156, 261, 265, 270, 273, 278
    Article IX, 156, 261, 263, 268, 271
    Article X, 157, 262, 263
Treaty of Limits, 144, 164
Treaty of Velasco, 145, 148, 149, 195
Trist, Nicholas, 150, 154
Tubac, 66-68, 70, 72-74, 86, 203, 204, 225
tucsonenses, 70, 203
Tula, 6
Tyler, John, 241, 242, 244

U
United States v. Sandoval, 272
Upshur, Abel P., 244
Urrea, José de, 73
Ute, 19, 47
Uto-Aztecan, 19, 64
Utopia, 10

V
Vaca, Manuel, 214, 231
Vacaville, 214

Vallejo, Mariano Guadalupe, 216
Van Buren, Martin, 172, 173, 241, 242
Viage a los Estados Unidos, 162, 172
Virmond, Heinrich, 209, 224, 228
Vivar, José Romo de, 66
Voyages, 115, 120, 121

W
Ward, Henry, 163, 237
Wilmington Emigrating Society, 181
Wilmot Proviso, 255
Wisconsin Organic Act of 1836, 270
Woodman, David, 181, 188

X
xenophobia, 178, 268

Y
Yorkinos, 238

Z
Zaragoza, Ignacio, 150
Zavala, Lorenzo de, 159, 161, 172
Zuni, 61, 62, 68

Instructions

Click here to view the
Table of Contents

Click here to view
information about
the author

Click here to exit
the program

| Table of Contents | About the Author | EXIT |

Table of Contents

Significant Events in Early Chicano History

| Previous Chapter | Next Chapter | Search |

While viewing a chapter,
click here to view
the chapter before it

While viewing a chapter,
click here to view
the next chapter

Click here to use
the Search Engine

In the Table of Contents,
click a chapter's name to view it's contents

Search Engine Instructions

1. Enter the word or words you would like to search for here

2. Click here to initiate the search

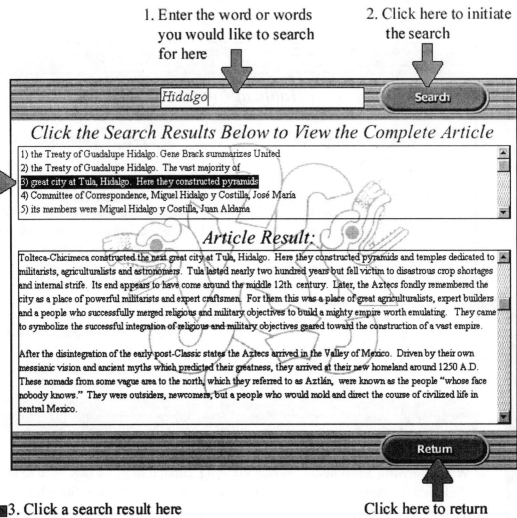

Hidalgo

Search

Click the Search Results Below to View the Complete Article

1) the Treaty of Guadalupe Hidalgo. Gene Brack summarizes United
2) the Treaty of Guadalupe Hidalgo. The vast majority of
3) great city at Tula, Hidalgo. Here they constructed pyramids
4) Committee of Correspondence, Miguel Hidalgo y Costilla, José María
5) its members were Miguel Hidalgo y Costilla, Juan Aldama

Article Result:

Tolteca-Chicimeca constructed the next great city at Tula, Hidalgo. Here they constructed pyramids and temples dedicated to militarists, agriculturalists and astronomers. Tula lasted nearly two hundred years but fell victim to disastrous crop shortages and internal strife. Its end appears to have come around the middle 12th century. Later, the Aztecs fondly remembered the city as a place of powerful militarists and expert craftsmen. For them this was a place of great agriculturalists, expert builders and a people who successfully merged religious and military objectives to build a mighty empire worth emulating. They came to symbolize the successful integration of religious and military objectives geared toward the construction of a vast empire.

After the disintegration of the early post-Classic states the Aztecs arrived in the Valley of Mexico. Driven by their own messianic vision and ancient myths which predicted their greatness, they arrived at their new homeland around 1250 A.D. These nomads from some vague area to the north, which they referred to as Aztlán, were known as the people "whose face nobody knows." They were outsiders, newcomers, but a people who would mold and direct the course of civilized life in central Mexico.

Return

3. Click a search result here to view the complete article in the window below

Click here to return to the Table of Contents